NARRATIVE
DESIGN

**A WRITER'S
GUIDE TO
STRUCTURE**

ALSO BY MADISON SMARTT BELL

Ten Indians

All Souls' Rising

Save Me, Joe Louis

Dr. Sleep

Barking Man and Other Stories

Soldiers' Joy

The Year of Silence

Zero db and Other Stories

Straight Cut

Waiting for the End of the World

The Washington Square Ensemble

W.W. NORTON

& COMPANY

NEW YORK

LONDON

NARRATIVE

DESIGN

A WRITER'S

GUIDE TO

STRUCTURE

MADISON SMARTT BELL

Copyright © 1997 by Madison Smartt Bell

The text of this book is composed in Electra
with the display set in Fenice
Composition by White River Publishing Services
Manufacturing by Maple-Vail Book Group
Book design by JAM Design
Cover Illustration: "Wall Street" Collage © David McGlynn

Library of Congress Cataloging-in-Publication Data
Bell, Madison Smartt
    Narrative design : a writer's guide to structure / Madison Smartt Bell.
        p.   cm.
    Includes bibliographical references (p.).

    ISBN 0-393-97123-6 (pbk.)

    1. College readers. 2. English language—Rhetoric.   3. Short stories, American. 4. Narration
(Rhetoric) 5. Fiction—Authorship. 6. Creative writing. 7. Short story.   I. Title.
PE1417.B397 1997
808.3'93—dc21   96-53226
                                                                                                  CIP

W.W. Norton & Company, Inc., 500 Fifth Avenue, New York, N.Y. 10110
http://www.wwnorton.com

W.W. Norton & Company Ltd., 10 Coptic Street, London WC1A 1PU

 2 3 4 5 6 7 8 9 0

Contents

PREFACE

THIS TEXTBOOK IS DESIGNED to approach the teaching of fiction writing with a special emphasis not found in other books on the market. The particular thesis of this book is that form or structure (hereinafter designated as "narrative design") is of first *and* final importance to any work of fiction. Without by any means ignoring the other elements of fiction (plot, characterization, voice, imagery, etc.) my approach takes them to be secondary to structural design; these elements of fiction are always discussed in relation to the places they take in the design of a finished piece of work.

This book is primarily driven by example rather than precept; it is explicitly *not* an exercise-driven text. The main body of the text consists of short stories by contemporary writers, each followed by a general discussion of the roles the various elements of fiction play in supporting the final design of each story. Each of these short stories is also closely annotated page by page in an endnote format; this annotation will help the instructor and students analyse the stories in extremely close detail. The object of the analyses is to teach the students to read *as writers* and to guide students through the conscious or unconscious decisions the authors of the sample stories have made in arriving at the finished form of their works.

The categorical division of the discussion following each story under the subheads "Plot," "Character," and so on cross-references the text in a way which allows the student or instructor to pursue certain topics all the way through—for example, a student particularly interested in tone can study twelve different variations here. However, the discussions are also written holistically with regard to the stories they follow: the categories are ordered according to their importance for each story (and if a category is completely irrelevant it is simply omitted).

About half of the sample stories are the work of well-known contemporary authors; the rest were composed by students in graduate and undergraduate workshops who may or may not have continued on to significant publication. Inclusion of these latter stories allows me to talk more knowledgeably about processes of composition which I have been able to observe directly, as a teacher; these stories should also appeal particularly to students in workshops since they were written by their peers.

Labeling the "students" represented here is a little dubious since several of them are now published professional authors and I have high hopes for the rest. For the record, I can say that I first saw the stories by Craig Bernardini, Miriam Kuznets, Holden Brooks, Marcia Golub, and Gilmore Tamny as works-in-progress in various teaching situations. I've also had the honor of working with Carolyn Chute on some of her early fiction, though not on the particular story reprinted here.

Although this book is primarily "craft-centered" rather than "process-centered," the opening part does identify both of these pedagogical approaches and discusses the differences between them. The purpose of this discussion is to foster autonomy on the part of the students who use the book by encouraging them to protect the privacy of their creative intuition—which I strongly believe can be jeopardized by many repeated sessions of typically craft-centered workshops.

PART
I

UNCONSCIOUS

MIND

To TEACH CREATIVE WRITING, or to be taught it, is a paradox. "Creativity," whatever it is, must be innate. Our intuition tells us that much. But creativity is now taught constantly, in reasonably formal settings all across the country; this teaching has become a totally common classroom activity. The creativity which is thus professed takes many forms: the plastic arts, dance, theater, and music are commonly taught, as *crafts*, along with the writing of poetry and fiction.

To be the target of creative writing instruction, a student whether novice or advanced, is quite a different experience than to be apprenticed in any other art. You have no paint or clay, no instrument, no concrete material to work with. Nor can you use your body as material to be shaped, as an actor or a dancer would. The substance of creative writing is (relatively) abstract.

On the other hand, creative writing is qualitatively different from other abstract fields of study. You will not encounter universal axioms and theorems, as in mathematics, or a fixed corpus of information to be learned, as in history, or even a generally agreed-upon set of rules for procedure, as in expository writing. More likely, you will find yourself adrift in a cloud of conflicting opinions: your teacher's, your classmates', your own. Out of this perhaps salubrious confusion you are asked to make something—a structure of words—which this audience will *for some reason* find to be aesthetically satisfying.

The lack of fixity, the flux of most creative writing classes, permits at least some kind of freedom—but freedom can be a spooky thing to handle. Precisely because the methods of instruction tend to be in a process of constant metamorphosis, it's important for the student to understand what that process is and where it may lead. Let the student beware, or at least, be aware.

ONE OF THE DIFFICULTIES of creative writing as an academic discipline is that it is so new. The teaching of music and visual art as crafts in some systematic fashion is centuries old; it goes back as far as Renaissance ateliers, even to the medieval guilds. There is no long-standing tradition of guilds or ateliers for fiction writers. The form itself, as we now understand it, is quite new. The novel itself did not completely find its feet until the nineteenth century. As for the modernist short story (still and likely long to remain the fundamental writing workshop text), it is mainly a twentieth-century phenomenon.

Imaginative writing has always been a solitary and indeed a somewhat antisocial activity. Apprenticeship existed, no doubt, but it was an apprenticeship to books and not to living masters of the craft. Fifty years ago, there was no such thing as a creative writing workshop; forty years ago, such workshops were novelties. Now there are hundreds of them all around the United States, both in and out of colleges and universities. The rate of change has been so very rapid that the big surprise would be if there were not a huge welter of confusion surrounding the whole enterprise.

But creative writing education is also judged (hostilely in a great many cases) by the result, that is to say, by the published and often popular work of that interesting *minority* of creative writing students who do go on to become "professional writers" and who are indeed charged with the burden of creating the literature of the future. To say that a book smacks of the creative writing workshop has become a sort of reviewer's cliché, a shorthand expression for the idea that the work in question is trite, hackneyed, stale, spiritlessly mechanical, mediocre, myopically self-involved, and so on and so on.*

This hostile description of work by writers who have served their apprenticeships in creative writing workshops is by no means universally true. However, it is sometimes true, and perhaps turns out to be true a little too often. Therefore, it has to be taken quite seriously.

Several years ago, I spent two semesters teaching at the Iowa Writers' Workshop. It is the oldest "studio" writing program in the country, and by many standards it is still probably the best. The Iowa workshop not only attracts the best applicants to graduate writing programs in the nation, it also *turns away* more than half of them. It was there that the workshop method, now common to about 95 percent of all creative writing programs across the academic landscape, first evolved. The Iowa workshop, in short, is the ur-creative writing program.

It has also been, for a very long time, a bugaboo for critics hostile to the workshop method. In the mid-seventies, the Iowa workshop already had a reputation not only for attracting talented writers and launching successful literary careers, but also for turning out mechanized, soulless, homogenized fiction. There was, supposedly, an official Iowa academy style, as tyrannical in its own way as, for instance, the editorial policy of a magazine such as the *New Yorker* of those days. As a student, I was sufficiently put off by this latter reputation that I did not even consider applying to the Iowa graduate program. Later on, I went there to teach with a certain amount of trepidation.

What I found was not quite what I'd expected. If Iowa-generated fiction did have a distinctive academy style, I'd have looked for it to be handed down from the masters. That was not at all the case. No one teacher or teaching

---

* For an exhaustive discussion along these lines, see *Talents and Technicians: Literary Chic and the New Assembly-Line Fiction*, by John Aldridge (New York: Scribner's, 1992). The extreme bias against the workshop system suggested by Aldridge's title is more than fulfilled in the body of the book—but although Aldridge's discussion is very one-sided, his description of the disadvantages of creative writing education as it's practiced today is accurate enough to be informative reading for anyone involved in writing workshops either as student or as instructor.

approach was dominant; the very size of the program, and the way it was organized, made it virtually impossible for any one teaching method, or the influence of any one teacher, to gain the kind of ascendancy that was rumored without the walls.

In the fiction half of the Iowa workshop, there were then about fifty graduate students in either their first or their second year, enough to make it far and away the largest program in the country, I believe. These students were divided in roughly equal numbers among the four fiction workshops which ran concurrently each semester. Of the workshop leaders, only two were permanent members of the faculty. The other two were visiting writers like myself, likely to be on the scene for no longer than a semester or two. Furthermore, none of these workshop leaders had any oversight of what the others were doing in their classrooms. No particular approach to the task was endorsed or promoted by anyone. Within the limits of law and propriety, we were free to do whatever we damn well pleased.

Under these conditions, it was virtually impossible for any one teacher to accumulate much influence over the writing style of even *one* student (although that might have happened, occasionally, if one particular student sought out the workshops of one of the permanent faculty again and again, thus in effect choosing a specialized apprenticeship). And it was completely impossible for any one teacher to dominate the group at large. The students just weren't in the hands of any particular workshop leader for long enough for a singular influence to harden. The students rotated among workshops, and the teachers themselves rotated in and out regularly. There was a lot more variety and diversity in the whole situation than I would have supposed before I arrived there.

However, there *were* enormous, crushing pressures to conform in those Iowa fiction workshops. The pressure came not from any teacher but from the students themselves. It was a largely unconscious exercise in groupthink, and in many aspects it really was quite frightening.

The basic strategy of a fiction workshop is probably well known to anyone who's read this far—or if not, it soon will be. The mold for it was originally cast at Iowa. The student writes a piece of fiction, most likely a short story, in solitude, with some degree (quite large, we hope) of psychological privacy. He brings it in and distributes it to twelve or fourteen classmates and the teacher, who take it home, read it, make their notes, and bring it back the following week for perhaps an hour-long discussion of its merits and defects. The task of the teacher is to guide this discussion, with a hand gloved in either velvet or iron, depending, and to produce a synthesis of the result: a prescription for revision—if revision is required.

What's wrong with this picture? It sounds almost idyllic: a happy community of cooperating artists. But there are snakes in the garden.

I was aware of the first pitfall before I ever came to Iowa. Fiction workshops are inherently almost incapable of recognizing *success*. The fiction workshop is designed to be a fault-finding mechanism; its purpose is to diagnose and prescribe. The inert force of this proposition works on all the members, and the teacher too. Whenever I pick up a student manuscript and read a few pages without defect, I start to get very nervous. Because my *job* is to find those flaws. If I *don't* find flaws, I will have *failed*. It takes a wrenching sort of effort to perform the inner *volte-face* that lets me change from a hostile to an enthusiastic critic and start rooting for the story to succeed. (Though in fact there's nothing more exciting than that moment, and probably it's the main thing that makes me want to teach.)

As for the other students, they are just as influenced by the factors above as the teacher, and on top of that, there's the probability that in confronting a successfully realized piece of fiction, the classmate has to cope with a certain amount of conscious or unconscious envy. (Indeed, envy may sometimes arise for the teacher too, but with a little effort it can be transformed into an enjoyable experience.) Well, once the group is back in the classroom, these forces militate against any *consensus* that a given story has succeeded, is finished, and requires no further work. Take that to its logical extreme and you see that the student as writer has been assigned the task of Sisyphus. There is no way to ever finish anything. . .

A smart teacher, though, will learn to beat this demon. There are certain signs, in classroom discussion, that a work has in fact succeeded in whatever its intended mission was. When the talk begins to shift from flaws in realizing the story's apparent intention to the idea that the intention itself ought to have been different—i.e., that the writer should have written some different *kind* of story—that's a signal to the teacher that the story may have been successfully completed. It's a good thing for students whose work is under discussion to learn to listen for that signal, too.

And when a teacher identifies a piece of finished work in preparing class, it calls for a different kind of classroom presentation. Instead of performing the customary autopsy, the teacher must present the story as literature. (Well, it *is* literature now. Isn't it?) The teacher has to show how and why the story has succeeded (and thus, how it is exemplary for the others). The fault-finding force of inertia inherent in all workshops means that it will be hard for the teacher to convince all the other students that the work has succeeded, but if he argues skilfully he will probably manage to convince the author, which is the main thing that matters at the end.

At Iowa, I began to recognize some other hazards of the workshop method of which I'd been previously unaware. At Iowa, the students were very diligent about annotating each manuscript and writing an overarching commentary at the end—each student producing a separate version of the instructor's work (and some of them were already teaching undergraduate workshops). When the classroom discussion was finished, these fourteen annotated copies would be handed over to the unfortunate author, along with mine. My heart misgave me every time I watched the student (victim) gather them up, and an inner voice whispered, *Please, when you get home, just burn those things.*

But of course they didn't do that. It would be idiotic if they had. After all, this was the criticism they'd come to receive—they'd paid for it, worked for it, striven for it. I found out through private conversations that many of these students, if not all, would indeed spread out the fifteen different annotated copies and try somehow to incorporate *all* the commentary into a revision of the work.

The results of this kind of revision were often very disheartening. I'd get second drafts that very likely had less obvious flaws than the first, but also a whole lot less interest. These revisions tended to live up to commonly heard, contemptuous descriptions of workshop work, being well-tooled, inoffensive, unexceptional, and rather dull.

Bear in mind that I myself, the teacher, was particularly trying *not* to exert any undue influence at this stage of the game. I let the group have its head and do much as it would. It was all very democratic. Those depressing revisions were the outcome of the individual student trying to please the group mind—trying to please everyone at once—trying to satisfy fifteen different line editors. The inevitable result was to pull the work toward the middle. The middle, of course, is where mediocrity flourishes.

Well, I was beginning to understand how a specific "Iowa style" could develop, how any workshop anywhere could develop its own academy style over time, and how there were a lot of things about this process that really weren't so great. There are inherent tendencies in all workshops to enforce conformity, *no matter who is leading them.*

At Iowa the situation was actually exacerbated by the fact that the students were so good. The uniformly high level of talent meant that the students were more deferential to each other's opinions than they might have been in a more average program with a wider spectrum of ability among its writers—allowing the leaders to separate more quickly from the pack. And so the group mind's pressure to conform was magnified.

What was going to happen to all that talent? Fifty students in fiction at the Iowa workshop . . . Admission to the program was so competitive that all of them must have written at least one story that was publishable or the next thing to it simply in order to get in. But I knew it was statistically impossible for all of them to succeed in becoming "professional writers." Most would probably not publish even one book. They all wanted to. Desire was not an issue. But there had to be some trait that separated the ones who would "make it" from the ones who would not.

I remembered writing two-thirds of my own first novel under the scrutiny of a graduate workshop. Every few weeks I'd have my hour of attention. I'd listen to the discussion and the summation, infrequently make a few notes. At the end I would smile and say thank you and go my way. By the time I got home, most likely I'd forgotten most of what had been said. I'd sit down and write the next five chapters . . .

Now this was a kind and nurturing workshop where the group mind did not withhold its fundamental approval of what I was doing. But still, my classmates liked to editorialize as much as any workshoppers. If I had set out to satisfy everyone in matters of *detail*, I might still be fiddling with the first chapter even today.

I opened my second-semester workshop at Iowa with remarks along these lines: Assume that when your work is being discussed, about 90 percent of what you hear will be useless to you and irrelevant to what you have done. Learn to listen carefully and to discriminate what's useful to you from what's not. Remember the relevant part and ignore the rest. If even *one* person understands what you intended to be understood, then you can say you have succeeded. Past that, the only issue is just how widely accessible you want your work to be. Don't try to please the group. Don't even try to please *me*. The person you have to please is yourself. Your job is to become the best judge of your own work. If you *do* become a professional writer at some point, you'll need that skill more than ever before.

Well, okay, this is pretty weird. It is tantamount to declaring at the outset that everything that you're about to do is pointless. I can't think of any other form of pedagogy that would require such an opening disclaimer. It is a large paradox to swallow, though no larger than the paradox of claiming that creativity can be *taught*, when we all know, intuitively, that it can't be.

I have been opening classes that way ever since. Thereafter, things went on very much as before. It wouldn't have been completely impossible to alter the nature of the process radically, but I felt that the risks and costs would well outweigh the gain. Let the process remain as it was and try to change the attitude of the students—show them where the pitfalls are laid in the forest and teach them to be wary and suspicious.

WORKSHOPS ON THE IOWA MODEL (95 percent of all workshops in academia) are nothing if not craft-driven. Their general mission is to teach a repertory of techniques. Probably these techniques will not be taught in any specific programmatic order, but instead are more likely to be brought up apropos of a particular student's needs for a particular story. Thus a student who is ambitious to write many different *kinds* of stories will acquire a larger bag of technical skills than one who is not.

But the talk is always technical. It is all about the mechanics of plot, of characterization, setting, description, point of view, voice, tone, and so on. The attitude of the group toward the work is surgical. A process of dissection is going on. The text is handled as a machine in need of repair. Or at best, the successful functioning of the machine is analysed and admired.

All this is much as it should be: You cannot really learn anatomy without dissection. But the risk is that the process will lead the student to forget that the story is supposed to be a living organism. Tilted too far in the direction of mechanics, the process will turn out monsters of mere technique.

The procedure for passing on that craft tends to ignore that no stories are *originally* written on craft intelligence alone. There's something else operating at the inception, something which needs to operate all the way through the period of composition, something which is much, much harder to talk about than craft. The overworkshopped student is at risk of losing this indescribable thing. You go home from class with your head crammed with specific techniques. When you pick up your pencil to write, you no longer think, This or that is *happening* in my story, but, I am implementing this or that technique. Even worse, you are no longer alone. Your teacher and classmates have burrowed through your earholes into your skull and are now taking up a whole lot of space in your brain. Without your psychological privacy, it's very hard for you to function. With a tremendous amount of stress and strain, you may achieve an anatomically correct sort of Frankenstein monster, but it's not very likely to get up and walk on its own.

Even worse, this whole paradigm is a recipe for writer's block. Once you have internalized the voices of your whole workshop, you're not just second-guessing yourself, you've multiplied it by a factor of fifteen. How to go forward in that situation? In situations where craft-training becomes overwhelmingly dominant, writer's block spreads faster than bad news or viruses.

There is another way. The great defect of craft-driven programs is that they ignore the writer's inner process. Creativity, the inner process of imagination, is not discussed. So far as the craft-driven workshop is concerned, creativity is sealed in a black box; you're supposed to remember that the box is there, but there is a tacit agreement not to open it in public.

Some teachers, though, take the opposite tack. They try to attack inner process head-on. A teacher of this stripe wants to pry or coax open the black box and come up with hands dripping with that mysterious ectoplasmic creativity stuff.

The tactics of such teachers may be either gentle or violent, but the ultimate strategy is the same in either case: to open to the teacher and to the group that private area of primary process where the imagination does its work. They may employ meditation, or soporific music, or various mental and writing exercises intended to bypass the left brain hemisphere and activate the right. By putting inner process in the center of the whole enterprise, these approaches seek to remedy the great defect of craft-driven workshops, which is to be so polite about not discussing inner process that students are at risk of forgetting that it ever existed.

On the more violent end of the spectrum is found a more jolting technique which a hostile observer might define as brainwashing. More neutrally, one might call it hypnosis by confusion. In fact these two are one and the same. The strategy is to assume tremendous authority, elicit enormous trust, and then abuse both, deliberately and to the maximum. Psychological shock tactics. Similar methods are used by hypnotists when they're in a hurry, and by cult leaders everywhere. The purpose is to reach areas of the target personality that are otherwise inaccessible. For the religious, it's the soul; for the Freudian, it might be the id. The cult leader wants to get into this place to awaken his disciple to the glory of God. Your more bloody-minded writing teacher, meanwhile, wants to get into this place to awaken his disciple to the glory of art. He is in one hell of a hurry and he is willing to use dynamite to open the black box.

The inner-process teaching strategy can indeed get interesting results. But to my mind the risks it presents to the individual student writer are too great. One's inner process should in fact remain private. If you admit into it the writing teacher, and/or the writing group, you risk forming a quasi-pathological dependency. What happens if the group dissolves or the teacher withdraws (or withdraws approval)? All inadvertantly, they may take the irreplaceable contents of your black box with them.

To put it in metaphysical terms, while you may with good reason choose to offer up your soul to God, or to a lover, it probably is not a smart idea to hand it over to a creative writing instructor. The writing teacher probably didn't want your soul all *that* much in the first place, is unlikely to be equal to the responsibility of caring for it, and will probably be incapable of returning it to you in a useable condition.

WHERE DO WE GO FROM HERE? Consider the two halves of the brain. Research in psychology has assigned specific faculties to one hemisphere or the other with a reasonable degree of certainty. The right brain is generally supposed to be the locus of creativity, among other things. Dancing, music, intuition, imagination, and falling in love are all the provenance of the right hemisphere. The left brain, meanwhile, is in charge of math, logic, chess-playing ability, income tax, and . . . language.

What this means for creative writers is that the two hemispheres must somehow be trained to cooperate in the process of realizing imaginative work in a concrete form. Presumably the two faculties should cooperate on a roughly equal basis, without one gaining great ascendancy over the other. They must work in concert and in harmony.

The left brain is the home of craft consciousness. Here is the warehouse for however many specific technical abilities you are able to acquire. Somewhere in the right brain, meanwhile, the black box full of creativity is stored. Craft-driven workshops have a natural tendency to exercise the left brain at the expense of the right, with craft consciousness becoming so dominant that creativity is squelched. Inner-process approaches, on the other hand, may concentrate so exclusively on releasing creative energy by whatever means available that the necessary craft controls are overwhelmed and anarchy ensues.

Good teachers have always known, intuitively, how to guide students between these two extremes. Wise and discerning students may often find the right path on their own. But the fact remains that both the student writer and the teaching writer really do have to have two heads and considerable facility in shifting their consciousness from one to the other. You cannot do without critical intelligence. Much, most of the time in workshops is spent on developing the critical faculty. It is indispensable for talking about texts, for finding their flaws and also their merits, for both appreciation and troubleshooting. But critical intelligence *originates* nothing.

Critical analysis is a perfectly safe and acceptable group activity. Creative process, on the other hand, is by nature private and solitary. The writer must maintain psychological privacy in order to remain capable of imagining the work. The strange paradox of all imaginative writing is that it is an isolated and secretive project that one undertakes in order to communicate (in most cases, for the desire of your private writer for public recognition is usually quite insatiable) with the greatest possible number of other people.

The purpose of this book is to outline a method for writing fiction that will allow the craft and creative faculties to remain in balance. Of necessity, it will spend more words on craft, for craft is what can safely be talked about; creative process is the secret that no writer can afford to give up to another. But one must never forget that the inner process is not only where all ideas begin but also where final recognitions are made. Everything of *primary* importance happens inside the black box. Difficult and dangerous as it is to talk about it, it is the most important thing of all.

A FEW YEARS AGO, I began to visit a hypnotist because I had noticed with some consternation that the force of circumstances seemed to be quite rapidly changing my personality from Type B to Type A. Alas, hypnosis was not able to retard this transformation very much. Still, it was not wasted time.

I went into the first session with the false expectations common to most people who never have been hypnotized. I thought I would be swiftly and

more or less against my will plunged into a black trance, that while unconscious I would be made to impersonate a chicken, and that afterward I would
(mercifully) be unable to remember anything that had transpired.

The actual experience was quite different from that. I was first of all
advised that my conscious consent to the whole procedure was crucial—if I
withheld it, the hypnosis would fail. All hypnosis is essentially *self*-hypnosis, I
was told.

All right, I was good to go with that. He dimmed the lights. There was even
one of those Op-Art spirals on the wall, quite similar to those HypnoDiscs you
used to be able to order out of the back of comic books, and I regarded this
for a couple of minutes. I was told that upon completion of a countdown
from ten, my eyes would involuntarily close. They did so. I descended into a
state resembling twilight sleep, that condition between deep slumber and
waking where, for instance, you may be aware that you are dreaming at the
same time that you dream, know that you have a choice whether to awaken
completely or dream on . . .

The hypnotist began to direct my dream by reciting to me a sort of story, a
narrative in the present tense, starring myself as the ostensible protagonist.
Many hypnotists use these routines as part of the "deepening" stages of hypnotic induction, to intensify the level of hypnotic trance. It went more or less
like this.

*You are walking on a warm grassy hillside, spangled with yellow sunlight . . .
Tall grass is stroking at your ankles, it makes a whisking sound as you walk
through it . . . The sun is very warm on your back, you begin to sweat a little,
though you are still quite comfortable, feel a warm trickle of sweat down your
back . . . The field is full of red and yellow flowers, and all the flowers are
swarming with bees, and as you pass you hear the buzzing of the bees, a growing, rising hum . . . You smell the flowers as you pass, sweet dusty aroma of
pollen . . .*

*At the foot of the hill there is a lake, clear blue water and dark at the center
. . . You are very warm, you are quite hot, you take off your clothes and go in to
swim. The water is cool on your face as you break the surface, cool in the cups
of your hands while you are swimming . . . Your strokes are strong but completely relaxed. You are swimming alongside a granite wall, in the shadow of the
rock, and near you a shaft of sunlight strikes a lily pad where dragonflies are
hovering . . .*

*At the center of the lake you dive. The water changes color as you go down,
dark blue, purple blending into black . . . You hear only water rushing past your
ears, then silence, and you are going deeper now . . .*

*. . . Now you are climbing out onto the flat rocks by the shore. Dip your
cupped hand in for a drink of water . . . It is cold and fresh to your taste . . .
You let what's left run out between your fingers, back into the lake. You stretch
out on the warm flat rock and let the sun's warmth dry you slowly . . . When*

you close your eyes, your eyelids are stained a deep warm red with the sunlight and the heat, you drift, you dream, you are going deeper now . . .

And so on. I made this one up, but that's the way they go.

While listening to all this (it went on for quite a lot longer), I felt that my awareness was dividing. The sensation was not like being split with an ax, but a slow, gradual, willing process, like the division of a cell. The actor in the induction narrative was not my whole self, but I did occupy his sensibility, so that I could experience, sensorily, everything he felt, as you *feel* the experience of characters in your dreams.

At the same time as a part of me was actually responding to the experience it was suggested I was having, another part was watching the whole business and taking account of what was going on. Some sort of a little left-brain homunculus with a stopwatch, which was by no means my whole self but another partial *I* that saw, among other things, that the whole deal was *working*, that indeed I was entering an altered state. Soon after, the hypnotist, satisfied with the induction's progress, was able to open direct discourse with my autonomic nervous system, while my left-brain consciousness (which had not been put to sleep) was able to watch everything that happened, with wonder and a pleasurable level of fright, as if through the porthole of a diving bell . . .

Afterward, the whole experience seemed to have important ramifications beyond the therapeutic. The first thing I noticed was how well that induction narrative succeeded in the task that you try and try to get beginning writing students to achieve: that is, to make a convincing address to all five senses. Literally speaking, the induction narrative didn't do much of anything else (it wasn't supposed to), but it did this one thing extremely well. It created what writer George Garrett calls a *sensuously affective texture*, a sculptural surface that, so far as the mind's experience of it was concerned, was virtually indistinguishable from reality. And the purpose for hypnosis was much the same as it would be for writing: to convince the subject/reader of the visual/auditory/tactile *reality* of what was being described. For the hypnotist it was very important to win this conviction at some location below the level of ordinary workaday left-brain awareness. It occurred to me then that the process of imagining a work to be written (as well, perhaps, as the process of reading it) might also require a similar kind of "deepening."

Because after all, that sense of bifurcation, slow division of the consciousness, was really quite familiar. *All hypnosis is self-hypnosis.* Yes, I had been there before. Often. At my desk, for three or four hours every day.

Then I remembered something the novelist Andrew Lytle had told me about the process of composition. The first step and for him I believe the most important: "You put yourself apart from yourself, and you enter the imaginary world."

You put yourself apart from yourself. If he had set out to describe the initial stages of hypnosis, he couldn't have done a better job. That state of being slightly out of yourself . . . detachment . . . obliviousness, as the people who are trying to get your attention may irritably describe it . . . isn't it familiar?

I remembered a photograph I had once seen of a friend of mine, a writer, caught behind her typewriter and clearly in the midst of deep concentration. She was a beautiful woman, but not in this picture. In a fundamental way she had ceased to be physically present at that moment. She had withdrawn so profoundly into the recesses of her imagination that her features had actually lost their form.

I remembered all the time I had spent in my childhood, daydreaming— out to lunch, as they say. When it got good, I would often talk to myself quite audibly (to the dismay of my classmates). I have since partially broken myself of this habit—I still talk to myself (plenty) but I have quit moving my lips. And as for daydreaming . . . when you get right down to it, daydreaming is my vocation. *You put yourself apart from yourself, and you enter the imaginary world.*

Then I recognized that the process of imagination that underlies creative writing, what happens as or just before you are putting the words down on the page, must inevitably involve a process of autohypnosis. Not that the practitioner would be likely to call it that. You could be doing it without knowing that you were. Most likely you would never have heard of hypnosis, certainly not in such an application. You might call it meditation. You might not call it anything. But you would sure enough be doing it, any time you worked successfully, happily, and well.

Here's the explanation for all those strange little tics and ceremonies you hear about writers having, the ones that interviewers always try to ferret out and put on display, as if they were themselves the magic secret. Sharpening a dozen pencils, caressing some lucky charm such as a rabbit's foot or a netsuke . . . At an extreme is Graham Greene's going down into the street and waiting to see a certain combination of characters on the license plate of a passing car before he began work for the day (which must have produced considerable delays, I fancy). Here's why so many writers prefer to break off in the middle of some passage, fearing that if they stop work at the end of something it will be too difficult to begin again—as when, upon your next stretching out to sleep, some tendril of your last night's dream may once again appear to you . . . Here's why you'll frequently start your work by rereading the last few pages of what you've done, futzing around with unimportant corrections, simply as a way of *getting into it* again . . . All these rituals belong to a process of autohypnotic induction, though you may call it what you will.

Now the implications for students and teachers of writing become quite interesting. You will recognize that if the inner process of imagination involves a process of autohypnosis, then teachers who concentrate on inner process are, knowingly or not, actually functioning as hypnotists. The sorts of exercises beloved of this kind of teacher are all tools of hypnosis, really.

Soothe yourself with relaxing music. Lay your head down on your desk and try real hard to *picture* something. Use cutups and arbitrary combinations of images, words, or situations to try to jump-start your right brain.

Hypnotic approaches can work in the classroom—sometimes rather impressively—but the drawbacks should by now be fairly obvious. Even assuming the best will in the world, if you are a teacher who relies, knowingly or not, on hypnotic strategies, you risk drifting over the line from pedagogy into psychotherapy, and since you are unlikely to be qualified as a *therapist*, all sorts of inadvertant abuses are likely to occur. And if the teacher's good will is less than perfect, well . . . what a nasty thought.

It's not that a student's inner process can't be influenced from without. It's that it shouldn't be. Inner process is the student's business and not the teacher's. An ethical teacher may *recommend* devices to stimulate the process of imagination, but that is a different matter from *participating* in them. It's probably true that, for the individual, the practice of art is not entirely distinct from the practice of working out one's private psychological problems, but as a teacher, you don't want to go fooling around in the area where these two overlap. As a student, you really probably don't want anyone else messing around with the *inside* of your head.

As a matter of fact, most students and teachers do understand all these things, consciously or unconsciously, and for this reason inner-process-focused workshops are much in the minority, and have never really caught on in academic contexts. We are left with the Iowa-model workshop: craft-driven. Here the participants leave the black box shut, they don't get their hands all sticky with that creativity goop, there are no projects of group hypnosis by any description, nothing on the order of a Vulcan mind-meld. All they want to do is teach you technique.

So you go home from class with your pumped-up craft consciousness sitting on your shoulder. Your left-brain homunculus has been elevated to a position of absolute power (when it should be operating in concert and harmony with your right-brain homunculus). When you sit down to write, you are stuck in yourself, paralyzed by self-consciousness, unable to separate yourself, unable to relax your mind, unable to pass through the autohypnotic gate into the realm where the narrative you are working with becomes true and alive for you. Whatever you write falls over dead on the page. Anyone with any experience of writer's block will know exactly what that feels like.

The composition of fiction can, at least theoretically, be broken into two stages. First, and most important, comes imagination. Next is rendering. Imagination is no more or less than a highly structured form of daydreaming. Daydreaming is fun, a form of play. Once the people, the places, the events you are imagining become fully present to your senses, then it's time for rendering. The left-brain homunculus must go to work to express your vision in language. But the problem has been made much easier because it is no longer a task of creating a separate reality constructed of words, but only of describing what your inner eye has *seen*. For an experienced writer on a good day, the synapse between imagination and reading fires so rapidly as to be imperceptible; conception and realization are one.

Ultimately, you have to believe. If it is not real for you, you cannot talk about it persuasively. Because the writing of fiction is all about producing an illusion, it's all-important that *you* believe in the illusion absolutely. You will never fool anyone else if you can't fool yourself.

All the rest is craftsmanship.

There is not a whole lot of difference between teaching writers and student writers in the end. As Norman Mailer once put it, the main difference between an experienced and an inexperienced writer is the ability to work on a bad day. That's not inconsiderable, but you wouldn't call it essential either. The worst, most paralyzing periods of my own career have come when I thought I finally knew it all.

THIS PAST YEAR, finding (sweetly and surprisingly) a little extra time on my hands, I started learning how to play lead guitar. I should admit at the outset that I am a crummy musician and that my most strenuous efforts would never make me even a fifth-rate guitarist. My musical apotheosis is being able to play along with a Bonnie Raitt record. Wheeee!

Anyway, I already knew how to bang on chords and do a little folky-style flat-picking—a holdover from my high school days in Nashville. The project was to add in some kind of melody line. When I started with this (and still to this day), my knowledge of musical *theory* was absolutely zero. I don't even know how to read music. However, someone had once shown me (in high school) how the five notes of a blues scale were laid out on one position of the guitar neck. The basic box scale is what they call it. With some vague memory of this, I started trying to dope out notes that would fit over chord progressions I had previously taped. Bonehead stuff we're talking now, three-chord music (though as a matter of fact, most *pop* music doesn't get a whole lot more complicated than this). My ear was just barely good enough to recognize which notes were dissonant, which were sweet . . .

After a while I figured out that the blues scale ran the whole length of the guitar in a varied snakelike pattern, which would begin repeating itself at an interval of twelve frets, and that all the notes on the scale would fit a given chord progression—if I could find the right scale. Somewhat later I discovered that I could change the key of the scale by shifting the starting position and thus, through trial and error, a certain amount of fumbling around, play in tune with any chord progression.

This was all very exciting. (If only I had figured it out while *still* in high school—I coulda been in Guns 'n' Roses. Well, maybe not . . .) After another while, a longer time than it would have taken someone with more talent, I found that I had attained sufficient fluency to actually improvise around these chord progressions with a reasonable degree of tunefulness. I didn't any longer have to play by rote, as I had always done before, but was able to play whatever came into my head. True enough, the patterns of notes which came into my head were not all that interesting or challenging, but still, there had been a qualitative change. It allowed me to entertain myself in quite an engaging way and gave me more insight than I'd ever had before into what the experience of *real* musicians might be like.

Now since all this guitar playing was a physical and intuitive activity, it left vast blank spaces of my brain free for other use. I was free to daydream, to free-associate . . . As a matter of fact, a quick session with some instrument, not practicing exactly but just playing something that's easy for you, can serve very nicely as an autohypnotic induction, relaxing your unconscious mind into the mood to make up stories . . . as some of you doubtless already know. Or it could be something, almost anything else. The vacancy of long cross-country driving puts some people in the story-imagining mode. For a student, it might be classes that *don't* interest you; the sonorous drone of a tiresome sociology or math instructor may induce in you a creatively receptive trance . . .

One of the advantages of being a writer, instead of some other kind of artist, is that the overhead is low. You don't require a lot of specialized equipment to do what you have to do. Computers may have changed that a little, but still, the writing supplies you have to replenish are simple and cheap. You don't have to be constantly running out to the store for more clay or more paint. But with this advantage comes a drawback: you don't have anything to *play* with . . . except your mind. Other arts have built-in components of physical activity that automatically help relax the inhibitory strictures of your left brain and allow your unconscious mind to limber up and come forward to help you with the project. The quest for something of this sort explains why some writers resort to arbitrary physical behaviors like maniacal pacing or beating their heads against the wall.

At the same time as I was teaching myself the blues scale, and often enough in the same room too, my infant daughter was teaching herself to talk. There was a big chunk of my awareness free to observe her and to talk back to her sometimes. I knew among other things that she had been able to understand all sorts of complex sentences (and complicated ideas) long before she had been able to *say* more than a few isolated words. (By analogy: the ability to listen to music is one stage of development; to play music requires another step.) I knew that she could imagine more complicated strings of communication than she was able to actually put into words—a situation that made her mad as hell sometimes. Now the barrier was breaking down. She was increasingly able to speak in sentences, in periods of English of one kind or another, and it was apparent that the whole process was exciting and delightful for her and that it was itself a form of play.

Of course, there's tragedy here too. Once you have crossed the river into language, there is virtually no way to ever get back. For a writer, this is a peculiarly frustrating state of affairs, because language, as a left-brain project, is *ipso facto* an inhibitor of the imagination and of the unconscious mind. Language is the material with which you must make the work, and yet (because language inhibits the freest forms of creativity) this material works against you. You know that there is still a vast prelinguistic or nonlinguistic region of your being, where sound is clearer and color is brighter, where all experience is primary, but it is very very difficult to reach that place again. *There* is the realm of essences; new meanings are being formed there all the time, but as a writer, you *can't* express those meanings wordlessly. You run your head against that paradox every day.

I don't believe that anyone fully understands the process of infant language acquisition, but it was evident enough to me from watching my daughter (as it would be to anyone who's spent much time around a two-year-old) that she wasn't doing it by rote. Nor yet by any explicit pattern of rules, I wouldn't think. She wasn't imitating grammar, she was generating grammar. The words themselves were being learned. The structure of words was being discovered. It was all improvisation. She was improvising on a scale of words over various repeating patterns of arrangement she had just begun to find out about . . . to understand and grasp, in principle.

For quite a while before this period, I had been in the habit of using visual, musical, and architectural analogies when I tried to talk about a certain kind of formal issue in fiction. The issue was the shapeliness of a text (or lack thereof) as it was made by the writer and apprehended by the reader. There seemed to be no way to talk about this point except through analogy, because after all there are not the kinds of strictly defined formal patterns in fiction that there are in poetry. You don't get to talk about rhyme schemes, you haven't got sonnets or villanelles.

But there is still form in fiction. There has to be. Ultimately, form is where it's at.

At this point (guitar on my right hand, chattering infant on my left), I recalled a remarkable performance I'd seen a while before, delivered by the editor, teacher, and writer Gordon Lish. The stage was a summer writers' conference on Long Island. When Lish arrived at the podium, he announced that he would do something unprecedented. He would improvise a long short story for this audience, on the spot. He had no draft of the story, not even any notes. Only this: four business cards. On the back of each he'd written a word or a phrase. One was "the watch." Another was "the oil." I have forgotten the other two, but I believe they were only slightly more abstract.

Whereupon Lish proceeded to deliver on this extraordinary promise with a surprising degree of success. He talked for close to two hours with scarcely a bobble or tremor of hesitation. The elements of fiction (plot, characterization, description, and so on) were all present in at least adequate strength. It did not, as I might have expected, sound like two hours' worth of disjointed rambling; on the contrary, the structure of the whole presentation was remarkably coherent and the end product revealed considerable integrity. This improvisation was recorded, transcribed, and ultimately published (with no more than modest revision, if any) as a Gordon Lish novel entitled *My Romance.* For my money it may be his best book; I like it as well as or better than others he's composed in a more orthodox fashion.

How did he do it? Well, first of all he has an ability which hardly anyone else can rival nowadays, a talent for speaking extemporaneously at great length in prose of some considerable complexity, evocative language which presents that sensuous affective texture we demand of fiction (usually), and all this without any stumbles, missteps, stuttering or clearing of the throat. This is not a freak ability, by any means; on the contrary, it is well within the reach of ordinary human achievement. The Roman rhetoricians made an explicit craft of it; it was something one could be trained in, long ago. But since Gutenberg, since the spread of print, it has atrophied and become vestigial. Maybe Lish acquired the skill through secret midnight application, or maybe it emerged in him spontaneously as an atavistic trait. But by itself it would not have been enough to carry him through the improvisation of this story.

Lish's great fluency alone would have produced no more than two hours' worth of disjointed rambling, however glib. There had to be some underlying structure. Here's where the cards came in. Suppose that those cards (and the words on them) were arranged, visually, like four points of a compass. Lish's discourse kept describing a circle around those points. The points constituted an underlying pattern he could rely on for navigation. Often, as he approached a point, he would pick up one of the cards and flash it, to show us where he was (and more importantly, I suspect, to show himself where he was).

The points were not, so to speak, pointile. They were three-dimensional. Each word or phrase represented a constellation of images, information, and ideas, for Lish from the beginning, and for the audience in the end, when the progress of the story had taught us more about them. All this information was arranged to form the point on the card, much as, shall we say, notes are arranged to form a chord.

The musical analogy should be apparent now. The four cards functioned for Lish as a chord progression would function for an improvising musician. (Even his fluency, so unusual for a writer/speaker, would not be at all remarkable for a jazz musician—to play jazz at all, you *have* to know how to do that stuff.) Over that progression, that repetitive cycle of images, ideas, themes, motifs, he could improvise on scales of language long familiar to him.

Aside from its impressiveness as a parlor trick, I think this demonstration shows Lish's writing method at its very best. In a sense it was a process of spontaneous or "automatic" composition, regulated by a handful of simple organizational markers. Those four cards provided him with just enough organization to prevent his losing his way, but the story was not by any means overplanned or overdetermined. This very lack of determination would have been liberating; it would have released the unconscious mind to come to the fore and do its work, operating under the quite mild restraints of the four points and of the craft consciousness represented by Lish's fluency in extemporaneous speaking. The whole point is that he didn't precisely know what he was going to do when he came to the podium. He knew *how* he was going to do it, but not just *what* he was going to do. In that limited sense, he was free.

That's one way to maintain your own sense of novelty, of discovery, in the work you are trying accomplish in fiction. Not the only way, perhaps not the best way, but a way that would, within its limitations, succeed. And if you do lose your sense of discovery in your work, you are in some real trouble. An imbalance toward craft training does risk choking it out.

MUSICAL IMPROVISATION (saving a few geniuses, people with perfect pitch, etc.) is not, strictly speaking, a conscious process. Real musicians measure improvisational facility as being able to play what they hear. Meaning that they play what they imagine, not what they intellectually project. In an improvisational situation where you don't already know the tune, you haven't got time to plan out anything really. You have to just play it . . . the synapse between imagination and action is so tightly compressed that they come to be simultaneous. Not likely that you'll be naming the notes as you play them. Instead, you are simply following the current of the tune as you intuitively perceive it.

Or take the example of martial arts (another discipline in which, through long and arduous study, I have attained a laughable degree of incompetence). For the purpose of this discussion, this is an architectural analogy. The study of martial arts involves spatial relationships to an almost chesslike degree. We know that the object is to reach your opponent's face with your foot before she can reach your face with hers. A contest between two opponents of equivalent physical ability (i.e., of equivalent craftsmanship) will be decided by other factors. You have to use your opportunity at the instant you perceive it, almost, it seems, *before* you perceive it, but certainly not a half-second later. If you are talking to yourself—"Oho, I see an opening, why certainly I should kick in that direction"—then the opening will surely be gone by the time you arrive.

On those quite rare occasions when I successfully score a really good point, I don't have much idea how I did it. It's the same old story: Consciousness is a great inhibitor. A great deal of martial arts training is directed toward purging the awareness, emptying it out, erasing its barrier, so that your physical responses and reactions take place at a reflexive level.

Anyway, the same sorts of processes occur in most other athletic endeavors, or so I've been told, be it tennis, football, ice hockey, baseball, or anything else that requires something more than brute strength or brute endurance for success. Skills that have been *learned* consciously, through practice and rote repetition, are *deployed* unconsciously, intuitively, instinctively, without the stuttering delay required by a conscious decision.

In writing, of course, you are not under the same kind of pressure to react instantaneously as you would be in a jam session or a fight. You can take all the time you want . . . more or less. Still, it is a good idea to remember how to react intuitively. The quality of the behavior remains the same even when its speed has ceased to be especially relevant.

Musicians improvise over chord progressions, using an infinite number of combinations of notes. Writers improvise over narrative patterns (i.e., formal arrangements of events and/or images) using an infinite number of particular details. Most writers don't put themselves under the pressure of doing this improvisation in front of a live audience. Under more usual conditions, you are free to screw up and go back to start over when you have to. But it is improvisation, just the same.

Consider too analogies from the plastic arts. Whether a sculptor will build on an actual armature depends on the material being used and the size and scale of the piece. But in all cases the underlying structure of sculpture will have been consciously or intuitively perceived. The sculptor always has to know the disposition of the bones before he can convincingly model the flesh. Likewise, not every painter finds it necessary to do underpainting on the canvas or to sketch the composition in advance. But the compositional substructure of the painting must have been somehow realized in the artist's mind before the painting's surfaces can be successfully achieved.

An analogous method for writers must provide just enough underlying organization but not too much. Enough is just enough to hold you back from the brink of chaos. The right dose of organization will shape the working of the unconscious mind so that it does not become incoherent, without disciplining it to the point that it feels fettered. Harmony, balance are the goals. The right brain pulls in harness with the left; intuition and inspiration cooperate with craftsmanship.

The outward form of a work of art is determined by this internal substructure, and the form of the finished work is of both first and final importance. The teleology of a work is expressed by its form; form is what reveals the intended total effect. In apprehending the form you also comprehend the meaning. The two processes are one.

In speaking of structure, I am not necessarily talking about plot structure, though the form of a work will often be most obviously expressed by its arrangement of events. Still, it may be something else that defines the form of a narrative. An arrangement of images, of motifs, or even (less frequently) of abstractions.

But form is primary, whatever defines it. In the beginning, through the middle and all the way to the end, form is what orients both writer and reader within the text. All other elements are melodic, not structural. You must learn to play melodies too. But the form of a work is its skeleton, if not its heart. There is the articulating armature, and if it is absent, or if too much is wrong with it, no quantity of fine writing will bring the work to life—the story will not stand or walk or live.

We are all continually in the process of learning to apprehend narrative structures, in their integrity and in their best possible wholeness. That apprehension is both the value and the pleasure of reading; it's also the process whereby we try to make sense of the events and images of our own lives. The reader who wants to write as well has got to go beyond the intuitive grasp of form to the deliberate construction of form. That is the process of narrative design.

PART II

LINEAR

DESIGN

SUPPOSE THAT THE ELEMENTAL INGREDIENTS of fiction may be grouped in one or another of four major categories: plot, character, tone, and form. To define these terms quickly and simply: plot is what happens in a narrative; character is who it happens to (or who makes it happen); and tone is what it sounds like. Form is the pattern of its assembly, its arrangement, structure, and design.

Form is the aspect of a story that can be abstracted from everything else and expressed in some other medium, for instance, a graph, or some other geometrical figure. Not that a recreational reader would be likely to need or want to undertake this procedure—no more than you'd want to get to know your pet cat by dissecting it. But for writers it is sometimes (not always) necessary to perform such a maneuver of abstraction so that form can be rendered in ways that yield to analysis.

Form is of primary importance, always. Ingredients of fiction from the other three groupings (regardless of appearances, which may often be to the contrary) are always subordinate to form, to design. Indeed, any or all of these ingredients can and do function as elements of design. We are accustomed to thinking of plot as what defines structure in a story. But elements from other categories—point of view, imagery, shifts and alterations of tone—may also be used structurally and often are.* In reading and writing, you must consider (consciously or unconsciously) all of these aspects of fiction in terms of their relationship to the overall design. Even the overall meaning or theme of the narrative cannot be separated from this relationship. In a properly realized work, form and function are one and inseparable.

For the writer, some sense of the final formal design of the work really ought to precede the first stages of composition. The level of prior refinement of this sense of design will vary wildly from one writer to another. It may be quite specific and detailed (though it is risky for it to become *too* specific and detailed in the early stages—lest you create a paint-by-the-numbers design whose execution will suck the life from your conception). Or it may be no more than a vague and cloudy sense of where the story is headed—where *you* are headed, across the terrain of the story.

The length of the narrative being contemplated has a good deal to do with how evolved the writer's idea of its form needs to become before it is written. Most writers can navigate their way through a short story on sheer intuition at

---

*For the structural use of imagery, see the discussions of "Depth Charge," p. 49, "Daisy's Valentine," p. 120, and "O Man Alive," p. 157. For the structural use of characterization, see the discussion of "The Sky Is Gray," p. 189. For the structural use of tone, see the discussion of "Red Hands," p. 284.

least some of the time: write a story successfully clean through without a deliberate, conscious plan—flying blind, as it were, and without frequent reference to the instruments either. In this situation, the writer discovers the form of the story in the process of writing it, just as the reader discovers the story's form in the process of reading it. This sense of discovery has much to do with the pleasure of reading, and for the writer who can work in the analogous way, it can truly be an ecstatic pleasure, akin to Hopkins's inscape or Joyce's epiphany. There's no better thrill, in this business, than to realize your intention at the very moment you write the last line. What makes it all possible, however, is the *unconscious* apprehension of an underlying structure. Without that, you'll become confused and lose your way.

Anyone who's ever grappled with a longer narrative, something approaching the length of a novel, say, will have discovered (quite painfully, perhaps) that sheer intuition won't carry the project all the way through. At least not successfully on the first attempt. To end up with a first draft of a novel that is structurally sound, you must do *some* structural planning in advance. Without it, you end up with an anarchic mass of material that must be arduously rewritten toward some sort of formal coherence. At the opposite extreme is the risk that excessive structural planning, prior to the actual writing, will overdetermine the work before it is realized and leach the life out of it.

To steer a safe course between these two shoals is a demanding undertaking. In practice, most writers actually zigzag back and forth between them. Some writers can tolerate a very high level of detailed advance planning for a long work without losing their own interest and sense of discovery in actually writing it. Others are so differently constituted that they cannot tolerate any abstract advance planning at all and must proceed through novels as intuitively as they would through short stories (with the result that they suffer more and have to write a lot more drafts).

But for structural purposes, there's really no *essential* difference between a novel and a short story. The only difference is size, which means that while a short story potentially can be written in a single inspired sitting, a novel absolutely can't be. One's intuitive idea of a novel's design must be propped up with some sort of scaffolding, in order to last out a longer period of composition. But the fundamental principles of a narrative's design are apt to be much the same, regardless of scale.

THERE ARE MANY POSSIBLE STRUCTURES for a narrative, but the most common, familiar, and conventional of these is linear design. Linear stories start at the beginning, traverse some sort of middle, and stop at the end. Furthermore, all linear designs bear some relationship to what is known as the Freitag triangle.

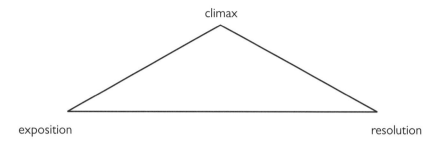

This diagram will be familiar to many students and teachers as an instrument, like a protractor, for stripping the life and interest from Shakespeare's plays. The triangle can be divided to correspond to the five acts of Elizabethan drama. According to this reading, Act I is responsible for the "exposition" (the establishment of principal characters and the situation that obtains at the opening of the narrative); Act II constitutes "rising action" (a series of complications which leads to the climax); Act III presents the "climax" itself (the moment where whatever forces have been released in the opening stages of the narrative have their definitive confrontation—i.e., the point where the conflicts of the story are ex- or imploded); Act IV contains "falling action" (a decline of the plot's movement down from the climax—thus *away* from the highest peak of interest and excitement); and Act V presents the "denouement" or "resolution," where the final outcomes are disposed of, weddings, funerals, and the like. The picture looks like this:

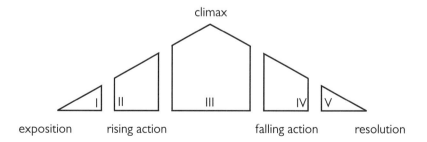

This pattern is so rigid and programmatic that even Elizabethan plays don't conform to it very strictly. Much less do fictional narratives of our own period. In modern narratives, the climax— the moment of the most important insight—will frequently be placed nearer to the end of the whole story, creating a different diagram, something like this:

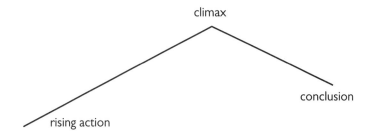

As frequently, there may occur a pattern of many smaller peaks and valleys. These represent smaller subclimaxes and resolutions to subplots and subordinate conflicts over the course of a story and may be diagrammed in a figure that resembles a dragon's back:

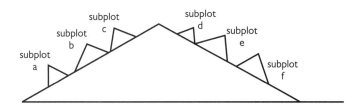

It's easy to get silly with these pictures. And indeed, most writers can get by very handily without them (or at any rate, without actually chalking them on the board) during the process of writing. The diagrams are no more than crude representations of the shape which the writer's intuition should be giving to the material as the process of composition goes forward. The Freitag triangle is a left-brain superimposition over what is for the most part a right-brain activity. But if intuition fails or goes astray, the triangle and its variants can be quite useful as diagnostic tools, perhaps even as problem-solving devices.

It is a familiar truism that all stories must always present some problem to be solved, some conflict in need of resolution— be it ever so humble, so apparently trivial. Conflict, the question which requires the story to answer it, is what generates the energy to ascend the rising slope of the triangle, toward the peak where the conflict will be, for better or worse, resolved; on the descending slope, the byproducts of the climactic fission or fusion settle back

toward a (temporarily) steady state. This, by some standards, is the very definition of what a story is; all narratives must share these qualities. There are
probably just enough exceptions to this rule around to prove it.

Still, it would be difficult to think of (or write) a story in which no problem
or conflict whatsoever arose at any point. At this moment, I can think of no
example. The point is that all stories do bear some relationship to the structure of rising and falling action that the triangle is intended to graph. Suffice
it to say that we do still expect some pattern of conflict and resolution from
our narratives. To write a story with no vestige of these would be virtually
impossible.

According to the Freitag triangle, the structure of a narrative is a function
of plot and time.

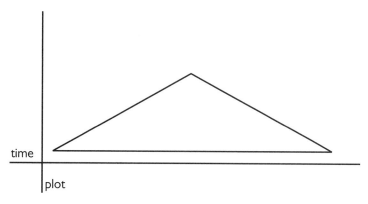

The vertical axis represents plot; the horizontal axis represents time. The sup-
position here is that events will be told in chronological order, which does
tend to be true in Elizabethan drama, but is not at all a fixed rule in more
modern narratives. A second presumption is that plot is the primary structural
element in the pattern. That presumption does not always hold for linear
designs, but it is true often enough to be significant.

Because the figure represents the progress of events over time, you must
consider that it is a process of motion as much as it is a fixed geometric form.
That is to say, it is neither, or both. The difficulty of this distinction is reminiscent of the difficulty quantum physics encounters in distinguishing between a
wave and a particle. But to the writer, this ambiguity is an advantage, because
it offers two different ways of furnishing shapeliness to the work.

AS A PROCESS OF MOVEMENT, the linear narrative is timebound and sequential. The rule, proved by dazzling exceptions such as Martin Amis's *Time's
Arrow* and Charles Baxter's *First Light*, is that movement in time will be for-

ward. The temporal vector runs out of the past toward the future, and the linear narrative follows it in a sequence of causes and effects, like a string of dominoes falling. Suspense, which controls the reader's desire to keep reading, is generated by the manipulation of the cause-and-effect cycle as it rolls toward the future, each effect becoming the cause of the next one. What effect will this cause produce? That's only a hifalutin version of the reader's fundamental question—*what's gonna happen?* Suspense (no narrative will hold a reader's interest without offering at least some *mild* form of suspense) comes out of a dextrous withholding of the answer to this question. With skill, you can string this withholding out almost forever—but as soon as you answer one question, you immediately have to think of another. Your task is to make the movement toward outcome, from first cause to final effect, seem inexorable. (In backward-running works such as *First Light* or *Time's Arrow,* the question is reversed: what first cause produced this final effect?)

The reader is interested in the outcome of a narrative as a scientist is interested in the outcome of an experiment. The writer of course may have other fish to fry—other aspects of the narrative may be infinitely more important to the writer. But plot and suspense are the instruments with which the reader is led (by the nose, if you like) across the passage of time that the narrative requires to take place.

Plot, suspense, causality, and time are inextricably intertwined, in linear narratives especially. But *real time,* the time in which our lives are lived second by second and hour by hour, remains a problem, sometimes an intractable problem, for the linear narrative. No story is long enough to actually express real time completely, absolutely, moment by moment. (Nicolson Baker's *Mezzanine,* a shortish novel which adheres with excruciating fidelity to the real time it takes the protagonist to traverse the mezzanine level of a department store, is the exception which proves *this* rule.) All narratives end up having to compress real time in some way or other—sometimes by summary and sometimes by skipping.

Before the twentieth century, the method for compressing real time in fiction was summary. Certain events and scenes of the plot would be given full dramatic rendering, as in theater, while the passages in between them would be summarized—most typically by the voice of an omniscient author. This voice would simply tell the reader—winningly, persuasively, and beautifully one might hope, but, failing that, at least economically—what happened between one fully dramatized scene and the next one. Exposition, the recounting of what led up to the scenes to be dramatically rendered, was the provenance of summary. In those days, successful and/or popular writers became very skilled in the writing of appealing and engaging summary, because they had to be.

All that was changed for our times by two new features of twentieth-century life: the movies and Ernest Hemingway. Perhaps Hemingway's most influential demonstration was that expository recitations of the past experiences of the characters could be eliminated entirely from stories, and that these lean-er, meaner stories (his own if not those of his hosts of imitators) could be as interesting and even more energetic than their meatier, wordier predecessors. During approximately the same period, the movies were gradually teaching the audience to unconsciously accept transitions from one scene to another, across widely varying lengths of real time, with no explanation whatsoever. Look at an old silent movie, and you'll often see long title screens that sum-marize what happened between one scene and the next. Watch *Ordinary People* or *Jaws III* and you won't even get a voice-over to explain how one scene relates to another—and yet, somehow, you'll know.

For film editors, the term for these forward leaps across time is *jump cut*. This device—the unstated, unsummarized, unmentioned forward transi-tion—has become increasingly popular for fiction writers also. In fiction, the jump cut is usually signaled, typographically, by the space break.

Time, however it is managed, determines the movement of the linear nar-rative. Plot, the all-important structural element according to the Freitag tri-angle, can only exist as a function of time. But other elements of fiction may at least aspire to a condition of timelessness, and these elements may also be used structurally, thus becoming design elements. Their structural use affects the triangle in its aspect not as a process of movement but as a stable geomet-ric figure.

The classic Freitag triangle is an isosceles triangle, meaning that two of its three sides are of equal length. It is a bisymmetrical figure:

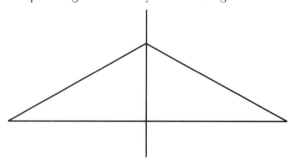

in which a line dropped to bisect the figure produces two equal halves which are mirror images of each other. The two halves are symmetrically in balance across that dividing line, as two weights might hang in balance across the ver-tex of a scale.

So far as the movement of a narrative goes, this symmetrical quality isn't so important. But if you think of a story more holistically, less as a temporal process and more as an integrated, unified artifact, then the issue of symmetry becomes much more significant. In linear design, this final symmetry need not be exact—no more than the two halves of your face are precisely symmetrical with each other, perhaps not even so much. But most narrative designs will bear some relationship to this principle of symmetry, in the same way that most plot structures will bear some relationship to the movement aspect of the Freitag triangle.

For this reason, the placement and timing of other elements of fiction — patterns of imagery, shifts of point of view or back and forth between first- and third-person narration, arrivals and departures of characters (the possibilities are very broad) — become, in fact, elements of design and are just as important to the overall design as is the plot, and sometimes more so. All these elements are to be arranged, to be used to create a sense of shapeliness, orderliness, balance, and integrity. Each must contribute to the reader's sense of the narrative as an integrated whole, for the moment when the narrative is apprehended as a whole is the moment when it is fully understood.

Narratives based on linear design do operate, on at least one level, like vectors; they are arrows fired into the future. In the final analysis, they should also be intelligible sculpturally, architecturally, as expressions of a static form. Abstracted, the triangular shape of a linear design is quite nondescript. But it is only an armature, a substructure around which you, the writer, deploy all your ingenuity, all your improvisational ability, to make the work your own. There are as many different *variations* on linear design as there are stories to be told.

DEPTH CHARGE

C R A I G   B E R N A R D I N I

It had been the hottest summer since three years before he was born. He hadn't thought he could get enough breath, the air so thick and moist, like the world was a giant's greenhouse cellar. He had learned not to swallow his breath, not to tighten up his chest. On an August day he started four times. Three false starts, but on the fourth he was sure. Fifty meters isn't that far, anyway, and the water is warm and clear.[1]

"It didn't settle with me," Alexis said: "it didn't sound right." He slid his elbows unhindered and leaned against the bar. "Last Thursday, I think it was: an Indian incense vendor told me Cyrano de Bergerac was a black man. Do you know who Cyrano de Bergerac is?"

Gavin nodded, but he didn't know.

"It was like he told me to beware the Ides of March, you know?"[2]

Gavin nodded again, but he didn't know.

"I mean, if I was Julius Caesar—are you going to light that?"[3]

Gavin was what Alexis called thick; heavy-set, yes, but something more. Lines had begun to weave into his smooth black skin, marks of sun and time, like the finest furrows from a clay knife; and the first silver hairs had settled, subtly, into the half-dome of black wire. He owned the bar, the Satellite Lounge, and had been its sole proprietor and tender for five years last week.[4] "I'll light it when you shut up."

"All right," and Alexis held out his hands. "All right." He watched the match dip and crown the shot glass, how the liquor lapped the flame.[5] "I thought afterwards, what if he's right? I thought of Shakespeare again, damn it! and it didn't settle with me, like the thought went bad and gave me the runs in my brain."

Gavin nodded, cornered into a smile and lost in the shuffle of a soliloquy. He was thinking about the drink.[6]

"Now I'm not saying that lessens my faith in or fear of the white or black man, respectively—"

"You're losing it," said Gavin, "you're losing it. Drink up, Alex."

"Son of a bitch . . . drop it."[7]

Gavin held the flaming shot like a candlestick over a half-filled glass of beer.

"I mean the shot," Alexis said, and he rested one hand loose around his glass.

Gavin let go: the flame extinguished in a kind of bloated beer lava lamp, the smaller glass bobbed inside the larger as he drew his hand away, and the drinks mixed and foamed into a piss-colored whitewater sea.[8] Alexis hunched, drank until the foam had settled on the bottoms of the glasses. These were tasting better, like Gavin was coming closer to the perfect balance of beer, liquor and showmanship with each try. In his mouth the drink was Heaven, but he was starting to feel bloated and sick.

He heard applause, but the bar was empty, except for two girls at a window seat that had been here the night through, and a bum passed out on the toilet, or so Gavin said. Gavin was holding a couple of quarters over the jukebox. He was putting on an old live tune, something mellow, maybe Frampton. Alexis wiped his sleeve across his face and turned in his stool.[9]

"Why don't you open it up?" he said, and motioned to the record coming down on the arm.

"Too much trouble. 'Sides, I'm trying to get rid of some change."

Alexis looked through his glasses. "Son-of-a-bitch, Gavin. I didn't get to finish what I was saying."[10]

"Finish it now."

"The moment, Gavin. The moment is gone."

"The soul," said Gavin, and he walked up to Alexis, and leaned close to him on the bar. "The soul was going quicker than you could talk. 'Sides, you forgot by now, anyway." Because that was Gavin's firmest conviction as a bartender and bar owner; that liquor, at least most liquor, had a soul, and once the tumbler was lit the blue crest of the flame meant it was on its way out, and up, to wherever the hell liquor heaven was. You don't want to lose the soul of your drink, he'd say, that's bad, very bad. But seeing as some liquor had none, it was best to know if it took flame first. If it didn't take flame he'd let it go.[11]

"I didn't forget," Alexis said. "What about a molotov cocktail?"

"A molotov cocktail," Gavin repeated. He was wiping the counter with a stiff towel. Then: "It's gonna break out if you stuff towels down the throat." He pointed with his towel in his hand: "You see what I'm saying? If it's in there it's gonna come out, once you give it the chance. When it goes out it's gone. That"—he pointed at the glass with a glass—"was almost gone. I saved your ass, again."

"All right," said Alexis. "What about beer?"

"Beer's not liquor, Alex. It's a working man's drink."

"Working men have no soul?"

"You're getting confused."

"Yeah, I am."

Gavin poured a beer.

"You a working man, Gavin?"

"If talking is work," he answered, "then yeah. I'm a working man."

One of the girls at the window seat had staggered over.[12] "What's the occasion?" He looked at her. "It's Monday night, there's got to be some occasion . . . "but he couldn't make out the rest, it was too slurred.[13]

"The occasion is, I'm twenty-one."

"Twenty-one today?"

"Yes."

"Congratulationszz . . ." She held up one hand, and one finger, and swayed. "Haven't I seen you here before?"

He tipped his head, and measured her with his eyes. "Yes?"

She looked at Gavin, but he was wiping the bar, holding his head down. "You're twenty-one," she said. "I want a kiss, with tongue."

Did she make that up? he thought. She was swaying and smiling, her hair was dark, her eyes nearly black, she was pretty, very European. He obliged, and met her mouth with his, a little open. When Gavin laughed he held up his middle finger in any direction. His tongue was numb, more numb than his skin, but he thought the feeling, a warm wet together, was there, and he shut his eyes.

The kiss went on for longer than either of them expected, so long, it seemed they would move up the sexual ladder. But he pulled away, finally, and opened up his eyes to see her stagger back a step. She pulled up a strap of her dress that was loose by her arm, brushed herself off, and combed her hair with her fingers, self-conscious, childlike. "I'm going to throw up," she announced.[14]

Gavin didn't laugh until after she was gone, and if holding it in had made him think of sexual stress, then letting it out was as rewarding as it was painful. He laughed away the smell of her perfume, pungent like skunk cabbage to him. The bar, he often thought, had the rich and stale smell of the pages of a damp old paperback.[15]

"I was that good," Alexis said, and he laughed too, a little flustered, listening for sounds in the bathroom and trying to convince himself he wasn't.

"Poor boy," said Gavin. "Lemme make you a drink. Make you feel better. What can I getcha, son?"

"Sir the usual sir." Which meant the usual for tonight, because the usual usual was a Lawngiland ice tea ("nostalgia," Alexis would say, and stir vehemently), and depth charges were for the occasion.

Gavin lined up another glass of beer, and another ounce of Amaretto teased with half an ounce of 151. "Now you gotta promise me," he said, "that your words of wisdom ain't gonna go longer than this Bacardi can burn."[16]

Alexis considered. "How long is that?"

"Never let it run its course, Alex."

"Then how do you know if it ever goes out?"

"All fires go out."

"If you're worried about how long it burns," Alexis said, "why don't you use more Bacardi?" but he was smiling and laughing already, and he did a half a spin in his stool.

Gavin bit off his smile. "That time again. Talk to me."

"Light it. I've got nothing to say."

"Isn't that a nice surprise," said Gavin, "Alex has nothing to say. I think that means something, I do." He struck a match and waved it over the liquor, let the fire climb to his fingers before shaking it out. He tried a second match, but the shot stayed cold.

"Hell, it does mean something." Alexis smiled a drunken smile, the kind that sculpts his face in wet clay.[17]

The girls had left without coming over again; Gavin shuffled the bum out the door, holding his pants up for him. It was one-thirty, last call, and Alexis was the only one left, a typical Monday night.[18]

Gavin turned up the jukebox like he always did, the Monday night one-thirty ritual. He started to shuffle his feet to an upbeat reggae tune this time, but Alexis preferred the Frampton.

"You dance like an old man."

"You ain't got the right no more, to call me old. Not at twenty-one, you ain't." He doubled his step.

"Twenty-one and a day. My birthday's come and gone."

"A-lex," Gavin sang, "three years in my bar, and he ain't learned to shut up and drink, drink, drink like e'ryone e-helse."

"Three years and still talking! I thought all black, I said, I thought all black people could da-hance . . ."[19]

Gavin stopped. He mocked a wounded look. "You come out and try-hy," he teased, "before you get, I said, you get hemorrhoids on stoo-hool."

"I'm too drunk, I'll fall da-hown, I said da-hown."

"Ain't nothing wrong with falling down in my bar, friend," Gavin said, but he picked up the rhythm again. "You fallen down in here plenny o' times befohore, yes befo-ho-hore."

Alexis came to him, unsure if he was trying to prove something. He moved like a novice skater, trying to walk on the blades, to his parents on the ice. Holding his head, too: his vision as skewed as his balance, spinning before trying to spin.

With a fourth and final try he clasped Gavin's hands, and they danced through this song, and then three more. Gavin had force-fed that tacky horse-shoe jukebox, pumped in a half hour's worth of music. They never noticed the cop who peered in the window and watched until his coffee was cold.[20]

They collapsed into bar stools, Gavin with a glass of water. He practiced a conditional abstinence on Mondays, and Mondays always lasted until 2:30 a.m.[21] Alexis panted quietly and hung his head low, but when Gavin nudged him he looked over and snorted.

"Silly fuckin day. Silly head."

Gavin didn't smile, but nudged again and said, "Gringo," to Alexis. "Up. Last chance to dance."

"Lemme sleep . . ."

"Last chance ever."

"Says who?"

"Says you." Then he hesitated, changed his tone, and dropped his voice. "You did."[22]

"When?"

Gavin finished the water and spoke. "Nights I had to call cabs for you. And drag you into 'em, and give the cabby money and directions 'sides."

"Slander," Alexis said.

Gavin stared through the glasses, the Bacardi and Amaretto bottles and near-empty beers. He held out his hands like they were evidence. "I don't know Shakespeare. But I know Alex. I got a headache three years old from hearing you talk."[23]

Alexis worked up to a shrug. "Two years of which I don't remember."[24]

"You forget about the numbers?" Alexis woke up and fixed on him, a dead-man's stare. "I didn't forget about the numbers. I quizzed you on those dumb fuckin numbers. Last time last week. Checker cab, and I don't know why. Am I ringing bells?"[25]

Alexis said, "The numbers. I take it I don't slur." He was running a finger on the edge of a glass, like he was trying to make it sing. "I don't lie, not when I'm drunk, not even guilt-lying."

"You said you were scared."

Alexis smiled. "I told you. I don't lie."

"You're scared, Alex. You said so yourself."[26]

"So, don't tell me about it."

"One night you grabbed me, Alex," and he reached out his hands and pulled Alexis by the collar, "just like this, only you were hanging off me. You said, 'I'm scared, Gavin. O Jesus,' you said, 'I'm scared.' You started crying, Alex—"

"I told you," and he struck Gavin's hand away, "I don't want to know—"

"But you should know, goddamnit!" Gavin shut his eyes and opened them, expecting to see a different face, maybe.[27] "Which Alex was that talking, huh? And which one is it now?"

"One and the same," said Alexis. He hit his fingers against the wet of the bar. In memory of a cigarette. Sighed heavy. "Quiz me."

The black man shook his head. "Won't do it."

"Last week, Checker cab. You just said so."

Gavin put his head down, like he had when the girl came to the bar, like he always did when he didn't want to speak. He kneaded the stiff towel with one hand.

"C'mon, Gavin. Take me through the numbers. Tonight, tonight, or did you forget?"

"I didn't forget about the numbers," said Gavin, and he leaned close to Alexis, who shrugged back, expecting his collar to be grabbed again. "I figured you forgot, because I never said anything about it. I figured it was drunk talk." He leaned back. "It's like dying, Alex, you try not to think about it, even if you know you gotta deal with it someday."

"You don't just have to deal with it. You have to do it."[28]

"That's because God says so!" Gavin snapped, and he pointed at the ceiling, to the single slow turning fan. "God doesn't say you have to pull a bullshit stunt to prove anything."[29]

"Quiz me!" Alexis screamed, and smiled thickly when Gavin held fast to his promise:

"I won't do it!"

"One," said Alexis; and quickly and quietly, as a bedtime prayer: "bolt the doors. Two, brace for collision. Three, quick breaths—three quick breaths. Four, the seatbelt comes off. Five, crack the windows. Six pop my ears, seven wait—eight big breath, nine windows down, ten—"[30]

"There's not gonna be a ten," said Gavin. "Don't you see that?"

But Alexis was tapping the bar. He liked the way his ears had plugged, the way his skin felt thick, like he was wearing a wetsuit.[31] "C'mon," he said. "Depth charge." He pounded the bar, for service this time, instead of effect. "One for the road."[32] He went through the motions of the drink, striking his finger on the wood of the bar, and touching it to an invisible glass of invisible liquor.

"It's called a depth charge, Gavin."

Gavin gave a long exhale, something he thought he could see. "It's called a Dr. Pepper here in Baltimore," and Alexis said, "I know." He put the pieces one by one back on the bar. Maybe he'll get too drunk to drive, he thought, if

I keep him here, keep him drinking, until he can't even stand.[33]

"Regular Monday crowd," said Gavin, "me and you. Whaddya say we go head to head?"

Alexis smiled, and wondered if he'd seen through Gavin, just like Gavin wondered if Alexis had seen through him. "No can do," he said. "Maybe tomorrow."

Gavin shook his head.

"I know," said Alexis, and growled, "there's no tomorrow." It was a song, but he couldn't remember the name.[34]

The Coors clock chimed twice: the first gave Gavin a start, and the second coincided with the toilet's flush. He heard the bathroom door kicked behind him; one, two, he thought, and stopped there. He was staring at the glasses, empty or half-empty, and at the bottles of Bacardi and Amaretto. Random, they looked like the glass pieces of a game that had been interrupted.[35]

"I've been thinking about tonight," Alexis said. Gavin spun in his stool. "I tend to think clearly when I shit."

"Shitting sobers you up?"

"I said it helps me think clearly."

"You changed your mind," Gavin said. "You're gonna sit here and sober up. Then, you're gonna drive home and go to bed." But Alexis was soured. Try again, Gavin thought. "You're gonna drink with me this fine Tuesday morning. See the sun up. I'll keep open for that."

"I've been thinking about tonight since before I came to Baltimore."[36]

"You're gonna disappoint me, Alex."

"I changed my mind so many times," Alexis said, and scratched his Adam's apple in denial. Gavin felt he was getting towed Alexis' way, into a place stuck somewhere between a confession and a story. And then he heard Alexis say, "Did you ever hear of Russian roulette?" and he knew something was coming. He nodded, top-heavy.

"That's where it started." Alexis waited for Gavin to say something, and when he didn't Alexis said, "I'm not shitting you."

"I didn't say you were."

"Please, say I'm not."

"You're not shitting me."

"I had a friend who worked in the stockroom of a surplus store. He used to steal shit for us all the time. Knives, mostly: bayonets. We paid him for everything, so he kept taking. He had a machine gun in his closet, unassembled, in a little white box. So a handgun wasn't so tough, except that they don't come in pieces, I don't think.

"Cost me fifty dollars. It was like I bought myself a present for my eighteenth birthday, but it was something I needed, not something I wanted. Like getting socks.[37]

"Anyway, I didn't use it when I turned eighteen. I said I'd use it next year, or the year after. But nineteen is a prime number, right? And twenty is one less than twenty-one. So here I am, on a three year excuse." He held out his arms.

"Blackjack," said Gavin. "It's gambling."[38]

"Right!" Alexis palmed the bar, elbows up and lizardlike. "Russian roulette is luck: Luck is for pussies. It doesn't take guts to put a gun to your head just because you have a one in six chance of killing yourself. I want to do something that takes skill. Skill proves shit."[39] He whistled, and smiled to himself, at his passion. "But the trick is, I've still got the gun. So if I don't do this tonight—if I put it off again—I go home, put one, maybe two bullets in the chamber, spin it, and play until I lose." He made a gun with his hand.[40]

"Same Alex," said Gavin. "Still talking."

"Mm. But never talking shit."

"Hey, hey, I grew up in this city. I know what you're talking about ten times over. I used to do wild shit with my friends when I was young. We got knives and guns. Because almost all our fathers were veterans, Alex, and there ain't much difference between thirty years ago and today, except I'm looking back." He smiled, and his hand found the bar towel. "We even robbed a gas station one time. I ever tell you that?" Alexis shook his head. "My friend Jay worked the register, he dreamed it up. Inside job, cops never caught on. Nobody talked.

"We thought we were so old; you're not old, Alex."[41]

"How much did you get?"

Gavin walked behind the bar. He poured a beer and slid it. "Remember: God's way." Alexis sighed. "Things come natural. When you try'n force 'em— that's when they go wrong.[42]

"None of my friends from school are still living." And, nodding: "Things catch up to you." He poured a new shot of Amaretto and 151. "Drink up, Alex. It's been a half an hour, you must've thought of something to say." Twenty-eight dollars, Gavin thought.[43] Wouldn't cover a busted stool today.

"You know I had oatmeal for breakfast this morning?" Alexis said, brightly. "The last time I had oatmeal I must've been ten. Coming in from playing in the snow." He frowned. "It's good for you, too. Go ahead and light that."

Gavin struck a match, tipped it, and the soul appeared, phantom blue, dancing into and out of visible. It reminded him of the girls who danced with feathers: huge blue exotic plumes. Something he hadn't seen in a long time, or maybe only on TV.[44]

In Gavin's hand, the match smoldered and bled black. Alexis took the shot away, stopping Gavin with one hand.

"I'm doing this one."

"Hurry up," said Gavin. "Damn, that's a bright one."

"Is that better, that it's brighter?"

"Dunno," said Gavin. "Drop the shot."

"Does that mean it burns longer?"

"Drink it." Gavin reached out to take the glass away but Alexis stepped back, even in his stupor, and cupped his free hand around it, secreting it.[45] His stool fell back and cracked through the middle, a cold fleshy line down the darkstained wood.[46]

The flame rolled sideways and regained its balance: it had disappeared on parts of the surface, and Gavin had said, "Drink it" again, threateningly. But Alexis was backed almost against the Coors clock. Neither was looking at the other's face: they were staring at the shot, and over the shot at the flame, where it was dying. The glass had cracked.[47] It had done that before, from the heat, from the waiting. Then the flame went out.

Gavin spoke to the shot. "You broke the rules," he said, "and if that ain't enough . . ." He put his head down.[48] "Twenty-one years old, Alex. They call you a boy one day and a man the next. Something's not right with that. Because you're still a kid, thinks he's got to prove shit."

Kid? Alexis thought. "Kid?" He looked at Gavin with eyes so unlike a doll's, so full of life. A photograph of intensity; through silver, he burns. He drank the spent shot and rifled the empty glass against the bar, where it shattered.

Like someone had thrown a switch, he backed up one more step, stuttered the clock's free hands, turned his head on a cogwheel and marched out the door. Gavin picked up the phone and put it back down.[49]

Alexis fell lengthwise across the front seats and peeled himself up by the steering wheel, legless. The light in the car cast a reflection on the windshield, his face rising from a dark quarry.[50]

"So, I'm drunk," he said, and smiled, then frowned. His lips curled thick on the windshield, like clown's lips. Disembodied mouth beyond, floating in the city.[51] He puckered his lips, stretched his face, yanked his cheeks, clamped his mouth shut, teeth first. Then he shut his eyes.

"One, lock the doors," he whispered,[52] and shut and locked each, front and back. "Wait," he said. He swallowed air, and his head spun violently. He knew he was going to throw up, felt his throat constrict and open as he clawed for the latch to unlock the door.[53] And for the most part he made it out of the car. Even when he was puking the numbers ran through his head, backwards and forwards, as if he could reverse the process. "Ten," he said when his stomach was empty. "Out and up." He giggled and spit.

He looked to the sky, a clear night except for thin clouds scribbled across the moon. He saw Gavin, too, clean-up forsaken and bar closed, standing by the puke puddle at the open door.

They stared at one another like when the liquor had been between them.

But it was all around them now; they waded in an ocean of it.[54]

"Aren't you going to wish me luck?" Alexis said.

"Luck?" said Gavin. "Luck is for pussies, remember?"[55]

"Red light, stop." His buzz wasn't warm anymore. Maybe it wasn't a buzz at all. He had to piss. It was the only thing that reminded him of his birthday night, but he wondered where the urge had come from.[56]

"Forty feet," Gavin had said. "Forty feet and cold, it's cold in March. Remember the sea is cold in March." Alexis remembered Sunday night, the way he had spoken with an air of finality to his parents. He'd called a girl he'd met that summer and dated for a week, a girl he knew more by her phone number than by her name. Tonight wasn't the same, not at all, because he didn't hear the voices of his parents, or his ex- and double-ex-girlfriends, most of whom were weeklong party favors, anyway. Instead, he heard the voice of a fifty-year-old black man, native of the city; someone he saw two, sometimes three times a week like he'd visit a hooker. And while one or two of the two or three days were toss-ups between schoolwork and parties and dates, there was always Monday. It was never crowded on Mondays, and there was never an occasion, none except talking. Wasn't it fate that his twenty-first birthday had come on a Monday? or had he planned it that way from the start? He wondered what it was that kept him going back, if it was what Gavin said about the soul.[57]

There were five square blocks between himself and the inner harbor. The scene stood in dark grey and glass against the scribble-cloud sky, five blocks and a walkway away. The walkway was fronted by a thin iron railguard, a dip for the tracks of a streetcar, and a high curb. The curb set off a stage of brick that sloped once and dropped into ocean, ocean deep enough to hold a stranded clipper and a "Flying Tigers" painted U-boat, tourist attractions. There were lights woven on wires, strewn up and down buildings and on ship's masts, around the port to the other bank. The far bank was hazier, maybe a quarter of a mile further, but there was grand neon and smokestacks where the city rolled over.[58]

Behind him the city climbed up and away from the water, dipping at Monument Street, then rising again. He studied his eyes, reflected in the diver's mask of the mirror.

"Don't walk" flashed on the crosswalk, then froze when the cross-light turned yellow. Potty trained, he thought; just run the fucking thing.[59] He waited for the first light to turn, then ran three reds, and a fourth, but the crosswalk "don't walk" had frozen already, and he counted it as anticipation. The engine shifted; a stick, he thought, a stick, my kingdom for a stick.

The car bit the railguard in two, it was a six-cylinder American car, he thought hurrah for American engineering. Through the rail, and over the curb, knocking the car into a clumsy pushup, coming down on worn shocks to push up the rear and burn off half the oil pan. When the needle had finished dancing it was down in the twenties. Traction on the brick was strong, though, and the slope meant another ten miles an hour.

There was the second when Alexis realized he had reached the point of no return, and that no matter what he did, nothing in the physical universe could stop this car from going over the edge. Instead of his life he saw colors, and faces without names; he smelled pipe and disinfectant.[60] The car's bones rattled, and under the racket he heard:

One, lock the door. Two, brace yourself. Three, etc.[61]

Before the front tires had left the last strip of brick, he had pounded the door latch to "locked" and molded himself to the seat. The car sailed into the night, a mechanical Flying Dutchman.[62] It hung there, the rattle disappeared, and the silence that followed was golden, my God, he thought, my first grade teacher would have had an orgasm in this kind of quiet, in this kind of still.[63] If the wheels were spinning he couldn't hear them, and if there was traffic in the city or people on the walkway he'd never known it. The car hitting the ocean felt a lot, he suspected, like the car hitting hard ground, except that the ocean swallowed the first five feet instead of grinding them into pulp. The car bobbed once so the ocean could froth, but he didn't see the part that stuck out, only what was underneath.

Four, goddamnit—what was four? He was sinking now, and fast. Three, he'd forgotten three, and he remembered that he'd forgotten three, but he also remembered that he'd forgotten four, and he remembered three and took three quick breaths, or gasps, and then three more gasps, as they did less take in air than they did make him dizzy.[64] He pressed his hands out against the windshield when the snake's-mouth tide swallowed the body of the car, and his screams were sealed, fossilized, in the pocket of air. The water was coming in, through imperfections in the engine and holes behind the trunk. The water was around his knees, and it was cold, because the sea is cold in March. It was dark, too. "Fucking nigger didn't tell me it was dark at night," he whispered, and giggled, and took it back all at once.

The car went completely under before all the air was gone, the weight pushing the pocket under the tide like a cook stuffing a turkey. He wondered how long it would take to sink, how long before the air would be gone. The first ten feet, the water at his chest, he watched the sinking, because the lights stayed on. He saw dark ripples in his beams of light, shapes moving back and forth. Then the lights flickered and shut off.

How far? he wondered. How deep? Four, four . . . he hammered the windows.[65] How many feet had he sunk? Crack the windows, he thought, but not like this. Wasn't it already too late for five? Forty feet, how much was that? Ocean bottoms aren't flat, they dip and split into valleys and trenches. And the harbor is studded with stone pylons, and not all of them come all the way to the top.

There were rocks on the bottom, too. He could get wedged between two rocks without even enough room to squeeze out through an open window. Or he could go down so deep the windows would implode and kill him with glass.

Oh Jesus, he said, over and over again, like the Don't Walk sign at the dry corner of Charles and Lombard, oh Jesus.[66] Five, crack the windows, but it was too late for that, because he was doing a chin-up to breathe and opening the windows would drown him. He felt himself piss through his coldhard prick and shit his pants when the water came in the corners of his mouth.

Still falling? He wondered if he needed four, or six, or any even numbers. Maybe it was only the odds. But ten is even. But that's double digits, and that doesn't count.

Eight came before nine, deep breaths, but the breaths were full of salt and brine. It was too cold for a last deep breath, his chest was so tight in the freezing water. This is a false start, he screamed in his soaking brain, I want to start again.[67]

He rolled the window down as the water settled over his head, and his eyes adjusted to the dark, the cold, and the sting, and his being adjusted to the fear of the dark, and then to the ocean bottom, because he had finished falling, he thought. The numbers came back, but they were empty, they didn't mean anything. His hands had lost feeling. He saw into the dark, almost past the hood, to the steady rise and fall of the bottom.

The fear came back when he felt the pains in his chest, when the buoyancy pushed his waist against the locked seatbelt, when the cold started to feel less comfortable and more draining. It came back in questions, some the same as before (how deep), some new, because his brain had spent the twenty numb seconds looking for what scared him, what could wake him up. The sensation came back into his hands, he felt his muscles spasm and his heart kick in with a mouthful of air, and the thought that he was still alive and twenty-one.[68]

He panicked first, swallowing his air and fumbling for the seatbelt release. It took both thumbs to unlock and his whole body to shuffle off. This was something beyond panic, because he was sure he'd done all the screaming and shitting and pissing he could do for a week, and there was nothing left to be scared of, not now. He was in a world between, a slow motion world, mixed fear and euphoria, hypnotized by the slow, smooth motions of his arms, primitive, the stroke of a manta ray.

He pushed off the ceiling of the car, into the hole of the window, and on his way out his knee hit the dashboard. For all the car's imperfections there was something perfect in the wiring, something immaculate, because he jarred something there, and the light inside the car flickered and came on. Hallucinating, he thought, I'm dead and dreaming or tripping or just fucking crazy. Against the windshield he made out something dark and familiar. First he turned to swim, but before he was halfway out he turned back to the ghost reflection. His hair was sewn in white weeds over his head, his skin was pale and purple, livid, lavender. He had started a beard three days ago, but it had grown full in the shadows of the reflection.[69] He reached out to touch the glass, but pulled his hand away before the fingers met, and turned to swim, frightened, and breathless.

In the ascent he didn't feel the things that brushed against him, because he couldn't see, and his skin couldn't feel, and the only knowledge of feeling was that of his own ribs being driven through his chest.[70] It was getting lighter out, like day was breaking. Now he did see his life, in a film instead of a flash. The faces had names, the smells were candy and corn. It was comfortable; it numbed the pain, one kind of pain, the way the buzz had before.[71]

Day did break: day for night, anyway, because the dark sky was almost blinding white when he exploded from the ocean twenty feet further than the car had entered. He turned a full breath into a scream.[72] The numb in his body turned to hot, the scream was so full of emotion as to be emotionless, like the colors mixing into white, or nulling to black.[73]

HE WAS WATCHING a piece of crumpled paper on the tide when they surrounded him with towels and forced him into an ambulance.[74] Confined at the one time in his life when he most felt like running and singing. He thought of Gavin on the way to the hospital. He saw other faces, too, but the one he remembered best was his own, in the windshield, for all he knew ten fathoms down and fifty years away.[75]

ANALYSIS

Plot

At the surface level, the plot of this story is straightforward and uncomplicated—at least when you look back on it. And the suspense of the present action is strong enough that it distracts your attention from subtext or backstory. There is, however, a tissue of background events that may be of some importance to a final understanding of the story.

Backstory
What's Alexis's motive for undertaking what Gavin describes quite reasonably as (at best) "a bullshit stunt"? You can hardly say that he is doing it just for kicks—the tone is too grim and serious for that, and he is much too afraid for such a reading to be possible. The little we learn of Alexis's history and background doesn't reveal anything in the way of a *specific* trauma that might explain his quasi-suicidal impulses:

Alexis remembered Sunday night, the way he had spoken with an air of finality to his parents. He'd called a girl he'd met that summer and dated for a week, a girl he knew more by her phone number than by her name. Tonight wasn't the same, not at all, because he didn't hear the voices of his parents, or his ex- and double-ex girlfriends, most of whom were weeklong party favors anyway. Instead, he heard the voice of a fifty-year-old black man, native of the city; someone he saw two, sometimes three times a week like he'd visit a hooker. And while one or two of the two or three days were toss-ups between schoolwork and parties and dates, there was always Monday. It was never crowded on Mondays, and there was never an occasion, none except talking. Wasn't it fate that his twenty-first birthday had come on a Monday? or had he planned it that way from the start? He wondered what it was that kept him going back, if it was what Gavin said about the soul.

What the passage conveys is a generalized sense of Alexis's failure to connect, a failure to live his life wholeheartedly—a sense of what an existentialist would call inauthenticity. We can't claim that the semi-suicide attempt is some kind of response to his catastrophic drinking pattern either, since I would say that the drinking itself is motivated by his general discontent, rather than being the motive for it. Certainly his motive remains very obscure, and I can well imagine a workshop situation in which complaints about that obscurity would be used to tear down the whole story and perhaps destroy it completely. The counterargument is that a bit of mystery here makes the story all the more intriguing. On the other hand, an explanation is possible:

In the first volume of his autobiography, *A Sort of Life*, Graham Greene talks a good deal about how severely, as a young man, he suffered from ennui. On one occasion, he went to the dentist and faked symptoms of an abscessed tooth, simply in order to get anesthetized; the loss of a perfectly sound tooth was not too high a price to pay for an hour's release from the tedium of his own consciousness. During another period, when a pistol somehow fell into his possession, he went to a deserted place and played Russian roulette—one time, with one bullet. The click of the hammer on an empty chamber restored the health of his sensibility most marvelously. The colors were brighter, the birds sang sweeter, and his interest in living was completely renewed . . . for about six weeks. Then it was necessary to repeat the treatment. Greene played six times at six-week intervals, then abandoned the practice. Maybe Alexis is applying a similar remedy to a similar sort of ennui. One must hope that he won't require booster doses . . .

We also learn a scrap of Gavin's history—he did something stupid and reckless when he was Alexis's age: sticking up a gas station. His friends from that time are mostly dead, but Gavin is a survivor. It's implied that he'd like to guide Alexis in the direction of survival if he can.

Present Action

Simple. Alexis has a plan to celebrate his twenty-first birthday by crashing his car into a body of deep water and seeing if he can scramble out before he drowns. To brace himself for this episode, he drinks colossally in a bar. His friend, the much older bartender Gavin, tries to talk him out of his scheme, but Gavin won't resort to force if persuasion fails. Persuasion does fail, so Alexis goes through with his stunt, and (quite surprisingly) survives it.

Character

Alexis must certainly be considered as the *main* character of what is essentially a two-person story, so it's odd that we almost know less about him than we do about Gavin, and see him a bit less clearly too. The tactics the writer uses to characterize these two are different in each case.

In general, Alexis's characterization is much more weakly specified than the characterization of Gavin (which among other things shows that the writer is competent to do it both ways). Gavin is a very particular individual. We know his status in life, his background, the pattern of his thoughts. We get rather more specific anecdotal detail about his past than we do about Alexis's. Even the physical descriptions of Gavin are more concrete and thorough than any given of Alexis.

By contrast, Alexis is almost a generic middle-class college student (or perhaps a recent alumnus). The only way we even know he has white skin is by some of the ways he relates to Gavin. No particular events of his past are recounted (apart from the first Russian roulette endeavor). All the information on his background is generalized, almost hazy. Except for his odd obsession (which does make quite a difference), Alexis could be almost anyone.

Weak specification of character is a risky thing to fool with, since it tends to lead toward flat, unlifelike characterization. It's important to remember that Alexis isn't exactly depersonalized—his personality comes through very powerfully in his dialogue, and his voice controls the tone of most of the story—but rather dehistoricized. Because he isn't furnished with a detailed personal history exclusively his own, the reader can identify with him more easily. Identification gives the action of the story a stronger, more visceral effect, and also brings the reader toward a closer engagement with the themes.

Tone

There are two slightly different tones operating in the story, though both are the property of Alexis. The first is defined by the sound of Alexis's inner voice—the voice which generates the story's weirdly dislocated opening paragraph. Here the pace is slow and the tone is quiet, contemplative, somewhat wistful and sad.

The second tone is established by the dialogue in the first dramatized scene of the story and is defined by the sound of Alexis's speaking voice: his glib but increasingly urgent, almost desperate monologues. This latter tone, dominant for most of the story's length but superseded by the other at certain key moments (like the period Alexis spends underwater), is louder and faster and (as we come to understand just what it is Alexis is talking about) increasingly grim. The grim urgency of this prevailing tone is one of several factors in the story that enhance its suspense. Occasional returns to the more contemplative tone, meanwhile, also contribute to suspense because they interrupt and delay the progress of the action. The general effect of the tonal contrast is of vivid, rapid movement against a dark and cloudy background.

Time Management

This story runs fairly close to real time—a few hours in a bar followed by a few minutes on the road—so it doesn't have long, intractable time blocks to cope with. Nevertheless, the writer has chosen to move through the hours-long bar scene in a series of jump cuts. The jump cut tactic is efficient for making certain minor plot points; for instance, it enables us to see Alexis getting progressively drunker without our having to follow him through every single drink. And as the story progresses, the jump cuts come more rapidly, speeding up the pace of the story and helping to build suspense toward the major climax.

Dialogue

The heart of this story is the conversation between Alexis and Gavin; here's where all the important thematic points are enunciated. Great pains have been taken to make the dialogue sound genuine, sometimes at the risk of making it hard to follow. Alexis and Gavin both have the tendency to skip back to a topic mentioned several exchanges previously, so that they are often talking about several different subjects at once. Indeed, there is a jazzlike improvisational quality to their talk, as they both riff off the several motifs that float through their conversation, trading lines. That quality is much more typical of real-life conversations than of scripted dialogues in stories, and it can be confusing. But it's to the writer's advantage that the Alexis-Gavin dialogue be somewhat hard to follow. The conversation is deliberately picked up in the middle; thus Alexis and Gavin know just what it is they're talking about all along, but at first we don't. Our problem is to figure out their subject by eavesdropping on their talk—a puzzle which is another means of building up suspense.

Suspense

Along with the tactics mentioned above, the great suspense of this story is sustained by developing layers of obscurity around the structure of the present action plot (see summary above). The fundamental plot hook, Alexis's plan, is a very nifty idea, but in order to sustain suspense, that idea must be handled very tactfully. Suppose the story opened this way:

> *Alexis:* Well, tonight's the night. I'm gonna drive my car into the harbor and see if I can crawl out before I drown.
> *Gavin:* Man, I don't think you really oughta do that . . .

Boring. Well, maybe it's not exactly boring, but at least half the suspense is blown. Skillful, agile withholding of this piece of essential information is what makes suspense work here. It's a tease. The writer dances around this plot point for a long long time, forcing us to wonder what it is and to try to figure out what it is by listening carefully to Alexis's and Gavin's cryptic allusions and by studying the imagery very closely indeed. Slowly, the plot point comes into focus as the context is filled out, and when we finally see it completely it has a larger shock effect than it otherwise would.

Point of View

Most of the story is told from Alexis's point of view, and if asked to locate the point of view at a glance, you'd probably say the camera is positioned behind Alexis's eyes. But it isn't always there. Sometimes it shifts to Gavin, as a close examination of the first few pages will show.

Shifting point of view is a tricky thing to do correctly, and if it's done wrong it will make the story seem awkwardly lopsided. There should be a reason to take such risk. What's the reason for it here? The tone of the story is mostly sourced in Alexis's voice, his language, and he's all alone for the climactic scene. However, Gavin's reactions to Alexis's speech and behavior are important too, and (for important plot reasons) Gavin can't say everything he thinks out loud. So we need to have some access to Gavin's head as well.

The shift of point of view is introduced gradually. In the opening scene, point of view swings back and forth with the dialogue lines. When it's Gavin's turn to speak, we often get a flash of his thought instead. Gradually these incursions into Gavin's thought become a little longer, a little more sustained, so that when what he's thinking begins to matter to the story (for instance, when he's plotting to detain Alexis by getting him hopelessly drunk) we've already become subliminally accustomed to the point of view shift and we accept it without really noticing it. It's a smooth transition instead of a jerk.

Imagery

Although the plot of this story is more than powerful enough to provide its main driving force, its imagery is almost equally important. The story is extremely rich with all sorts of minor, almost ornamental image patterns (like the nice matching of the cracking of the bar-stool with the cracking of the shot glass on page 41), but the most critical, of course, is the one suggested by the title. A great deal of the pleasure of reading the story comes from the reader's gradual understanding of how the image of the shot glass sinking in the beer mug reflects the image of the car sinking into the water. The sequences of imagery which build up to this identification also reinforce suspense.

The greatest complexity of the story, and perhaps its most admirable feature, is the intricate interplay of imagery, pun, and metaphor. Of course the use of double reference has been a common factor in narrative art for a long long time. Here, however, the pun on "depth charge" that becomes the controlling metaphor for the whole story has been worked out with an unusual, almost scholastic thoroughness. Through the metaphor, the identification of images becomes an identification of meanings, so that every element of the story drives toward defining what a "depth charge" *is*.

What it is to Gavin and Alexis, anyway. From the outside (the perspective of that cop peering in the bar window) those two may look like crazy people. But once we are inside their world, it turns out to be such a perfectly self-contained closed system that we cannot quarrel with their definitions. Thus the story persuades us, most powerfully, of its truth.

Design

Structurally, this story has a classic simplicity (if you look through the density of the writing itself to see the armature on which it has been layered). The amount of real time to be dealt with is conveniently brief, no more than three or four hours. The design of the narrative organizes this period around three questions:

> What is Alexis planning to do?
> Will he really do it?
> Can he survive it?

The questions themselves create suspense, tension, our sense of rising action. Their answers become climaxes.

If we graph this story on the Freitag triangle, we see that the first climax or subclimax—the moment when Alexis lets us infer what he is going to do by enunciating the title phrase *depth charge*—is actually a spike in the forward flow of the rising action, a peak on the ascending slope of the pyramid. The point of no return, when both we and Alexis realize that he really is going through with it, is the main climax and so must be positioned at the apex of the whole triangle. It follows that the third climax, which answers the question of Alexis's survival, is a spike in the flow of falling action, the descending slant of the triangle.

This arrangement is as easy as one-two-three: a near-perfect example of a linear design. This pattern is as solid and simple as a I-IV-V chord progression in the blues. Likewise, the very simplicity of the arrangement allows the writer to improvise over the stable structure in free and complicated ways.

His handling of exposition is an example of this sort of complication. Instead of delivering the exposition *a priori*, up front, he presents it almost *ex post facto*, stirred into the current of the rising action. To begin with action and shift to exposition at some later point has become a quite conventional device of contemporary fiction, but this writer withholds more essential information for longer than is usual, so that the reader must strain a little to grasp the situation. That carefully calculated strain contributes to the general sense of tension and suspense and so becomes part of the pleasure of reading the story.

And one more thing. That oddly dislocated paragraph at the start of the story? At the end of the workshop discussion, which included a certain amount of puzzling over this problem, Craig disclosed that it didn't exactly belong in this position. He meant to put it somewhere down in the body of his story, but he couldn't quite figure out where, so he just left it hanging at the top of his text file . . .

I tried cutting the paragraph clean out of the story—beginning the story with paragraph 2 instead—but I just didn't like it as well. It struck me that there were several reasons to leave it right where it was. For one thing, it is symmetrical in its brevity with the one-paragraph subsection at the end of the story. Also, the content and imagery (water, temperature, time, and distance) reflect and foreshadow the story's conclusion, albeit in a quite opaque fashion. Finally, since the overall management of the exposition is somewhat bemusing, it seemed appropriate to me that the story should open with something altogether bewildering. I recommended he leave that paragraph unmoved. There *is* virtue in accident sometimes . . .

Theme

Most stories don't require a discussion of theme separate from plot, character, and above all design. Insight into a story's theme is usually a simultaneous event with comprehension of its design. In fact it's extremely counterproductive for a writer to start thinking of theme as a separate ingredient—an abstraction to be inserted into a story like a ghost into a machine. But because of the problem of motivation, understanding the ideas of "Depth Charge" seems to require us to go a little beyond apprehending the formal principles of its structure.

Is there anything that makes this story fall short of being completely satisfactory? My own feeling is that there is not. The story is most elegantly structured, as we have seen, and you can't say it doesn't hold your interest. The one question a reader might claim has gone unanswered is *why?*

In *The Myth of Sisyphus,* Albert Camus presents an argument that life cannot really be lived without confronting the potential choice of suicide. Following the path Camus defined, the Christian existentialist Walker Percy divides all people into "exsuicides" and "nonsuicides." The nonsuicide passively drifts through an unexamined life; one cannot say that he's exactly *living.* The exsuicide, having contemplated and rejected self-assassination, has chosen his life, deliberately, and so freed himself to live life fully. He has authenticated himself through this process.

I think Alexis has done something similar by the end of this story (although I seriously doubt that Craig Bernardini was consciously burdened with all this existentialist philosophy in the writing of the story or that he had set out to illustrate it; it may be that some of it was kicking around in the back of his head all along, but that's another matter). He devises a very dangerous recipe for revivifying himself, and as a matter of fact, it works. In *his own terms,* he is right, unassailably so, much as Gavin is unassailably right within the closed set of terms which provides his reasoning about the soul of liquor. Indeed, here is the main point of contact between Alexis and Gavin, even when they disagree. They each have systems of belief which, however bizarre, are very meticulously articulated, and even when they disagree, each still respects the integrity of the other's system. Ultimately, that's why Gavin doesn't physically prevent Alexis from going through with his plan, or call anyone else in to restrain him. Ultimately, this quality makes "Depth Charge" a story about faith, though it's a faith unsupervised by any religious orthodoxy.

Is Alexis crazy? I'm not sure. For sure, he is not the only twenty-one-year-old in our society to enjoy a pathological relationship with risk. He has taken it an eccentric step further than most do, certainly. But I'm not sure that makes him crazy.

This kind of reading makes Alexis's motive less obscure than abstract, impersonal. It is a little less an evolution of his private experience, a little more of a philosophical construct.

NOTES

1.   The design of this story *is* linear, although I wouldn't quite say that makes it simple—on the contrary. This opening passage is a bit hard to relate to

what immediately follows—perhaps it's hard to relate it to the story as a whole. What's the project here? and who's undertaking it? For the time being you can't answer either question, but the mystery itself provokes suspense, and the image of a "giant's greenhouse cellar" is attractive. A single paragraph isn't long enough to get you really perplexed, because you're through it very quickly, onward and upward along the single narrative vector that defines the plot of this particular story.

2.   This second beginning is even more sudden than the first—a plunge into the center of events. Whirling, the reader lands *in medias res*. Aside from the questions of who these people are, what they're doing, and what they're talking about, we have to figure out what to do with all these literary allusions—or do we?

    Whether or not we can map Cyrano, Caesar, and Shakespeare onto the situations of Gavin and Alexis at this point (or ever), the conversation does inform us that they know each other well in some respect, so that their dialogue is ongoing and growing in complexity. The effect is much as if we have just walked into the bar and begun eavesdropping on them, and that effect carries its own sense of conviction and adds to the sense of realism. Although we've landed in the story without any exposition (without any that makes any sense, at least), the voices of these characters make them believable, even when the voices are disembodied.

3.   Light what? Instead of answering this question, the writer gives us a different piece of information than what we'd like to have . . .

4.   . . . the embodiment of one of the characters. This description is elegantly done: the "clay knife" simile is a deft touch, and the "half-dome of black wire" is a fine way of conveying the partial baldness of this black bartender, Gavin. The expository fillip at the end of the paragraph helps orient us further.

    We'll wait a long time before we see such a detailed description of Alexis, because the story is mostly (not entirely) in Alexis's point of view, and it would be awkward to have him reflecting on his own appearance for purposes of description—in this stage at least.

5.   Okay, now we can recognize the activity: Gavin is lighting liquor on fire. Notice how the action is introduced by a cryptic allusion in the dialogue. In a movie, we'd probably see the shot glass at the same time that we heard Alexis's first reference to it, but in fiction, the author can skew the timing, thus creating some small friction of suspense. This pattern repeats itself (like the ignition of shots) throughout the story as the tensions escalate.

    Some effective alliterations here: "liquor lapped," "shuffle of a soliloquy." And the sentences have a seductively pleasant metrical balance. They have been listened to—by reading aloud or simply by the writer's inner ear. Watch for similar balances in the arrangement of events.

6.   Notice the movement of point of view—at places in the conversation

where Gavin might speak, he nods and we get a brief glimpse of his thought—then back to Alexis's perceptions. Is there any reason for this shifting? If not, it's a mistake, and could be confusing.

7. Here another repeating motif is introduced: the double entendre. Alexis means for him to drop the shot, not the subject . . . or is it both? These are puns—not the sort to make you groan, but functional puns that vertically deepen the images, and hence the meanings of the story. The title itself is just such a pun, as we're due to learn.

8. There's the depth charge. Our first depth charge, though now it's evident that Alexis has already had more than a few.

9. Alexis's ingurgitation creates a pause in the conversation and a natural opportunity for the writer to expand the scene—till now almost claustrophobically focused on the two principal characters. The lens of the story tracks Gavin as he moves toward the jukebox, and for the first time we have a long, complete view of the whole bar.

   At this point, a lot of scene-setting exposition has in fact been accomplished . . . obliquely. There's been no passage explicitly devoted to describing the bar, but apropos of the characters' movements, we now have a fairly clear sense of the place.

10. Unlike real-life conversations, most fictional dialogue works like Ping-Pong, with each line replying to the one immediately before. But here Alexis is referring several exchanges back to where Gavin interrupted him by urging him to drink. This tactic reinforces the reader's awareness of a complex pattern of cross-reference in the story.

11. And here the cryptic ritual these two are performing gets at least a partial explanation. Gavin's mystical sense of the meaning of igniting the depth charge not only deepens our sense of his character, but begins to prepare us for what is to come. His idea may be a little nutty, but it also commands a certain respect. Alcohol has often been intertwined with religious observance, and maybe it is again here. The stakes have been raised, somehow. This isn't just a drunken binge—souls are being weighed and refined.

    Alexis and Gavin make a number of mysterious allusions to the enactment of the depth charge before the writer lets us see the action and before Gavin explains what it means to him. This simple act of withholding on the part of the writer creates a small, suspenseful, forward momentum, and defines a pattern which will repeat in the story as a whole.

    For strong phraseology, note "hell liquor heaven," a curious seesaw of opposites.

12. Jump cut. The use of the pluperfect "had staggered" lets us know that some time has elapsed during the space break. At this stage of the story, there's no obvious reason to skip forward here, but maybe a pattern will emerge later on.

13. Well, the writer doesn't have to tell us that this girl is drunk—not in so

many words. Even through Alexis's extremely blurry vision, we can see that for ourselves.

14. An odd little scene—providing comic relief, for one thing, from the tension raised by Gavin's discussion of the depth charge and its meaning. The scene also does a bit of expository work, letting us know that the occasion for this binge is Alexis's twenty-first birthday.

   Alexis seems quite comfortable here, so the reader may not immediately ask this question, but isn't this an odd way to celebrate a major birthday? The girl is a stranger. Does Alexis have any friends? besides Gavin?

15. Here's another, more sustained incursion into Gavin's point of view. In this story, point of view is subtly managed. Alexis is really both the main character and our window on the story; *most* of the time we're located in his head. But later on it will become important to know something of Gavin's unspoken thoughts, and the writer is preparing us for this by switching to Gavin's point of view at reasonably regular intervals and for passages of increasing length.

16. We're prepared (subliminally) by earlier phases in their conversation to realize that the meanings here may be doubled. Is there a greater risk here than the flame dying out before the shot's consumed? What fires are we talking about exactly? Is some other soul involved than the soul Gavin sees in liquor?

   We still don't quite know what they're talking about but we can feel the edge of it—thematically, the tension is rising, climbing the near side of the triangle of a linear design.

17. The convergence of Gavin's line with the unsuccessful effort to light the shot makes a strong association between the liquor's soul and Alexis's. The liquor is cold; glib Alexis is mute. Yes, this probably does mean something.

18. Jump cut number 2. The usefulness of this technique becomes a little more apparent. For one thing, there's simple efficiency. Skipping forward allows the writer to elide vast desert spaces of real time, reaching different stages of the evening and of Alexis's drunkenness without being required to report every instant, every drink consumed.

   Also, the very jerkiness of the jump-cutting seems appropriate to character and story here. It helps reinforce our impression of Alexis's increasing drunkenness—as if perhaps he were blacked out for the spaces of time that aren't reported. Indeed, that may be the case.

19. How important are racial issues to this story—this passage, the earlier proposition that Cyrano was a black man, and so on? What they mainly seem to do is establish the level of intimacy that Gavin and Alexis enjoy—Alexis is enough of an insider in Gavin's eyes that he can say the things he's saying without offending Gavin—they appreciate the same gags on

the same level.

That said, this isn't a story about race relations, particularly. It's nice to think that the story can include a cross-racial friendship without the race issue eating the whole story up.

20. Here's another way of getting over awkward lengths of real time: summary. The introduction of the policeman lengthens the perspective—as if the camera had dollied back from the scene. To be so close to Alexis and Gavin all the time might be suffocating, so the author is giving us a little break.

21. A third jump cut. Of course summarizing can always be combined with jump-cutting, as here.

22. Now things are getting serious all of a sudden. There may seem to be no real advance in the action—just a couple of guys shuffling around in a bar, but this is definitely an escalation of the conversation. It's this conversational intensification that for the time being plays the structural part of *rising action* in this linear design.

23. Whatever it is they're talking about, they've been talking about it for three years now.

24. And maybe Alexis really is a blackout drunk.

25. They're sneaking up on this subject the same way they snuck up on the subject of lighting that first drink. Both of them know what they're talking about, but the reader, so far, does not.

26. But whatever it is they're talking about, it has to be pretty severe, because Alexis is afraid of it—very afraid.

The mild suspense we felt while waiting to learn exactly how Gavin was preparing that drink in the first pages of the story becomes very intense here, now that the stakes, by implication, have grown much larger. But the technique for generating this suspense is very much the same in both cases—same pattern of presentation.

27. Gavin's inner responses become more important in this scene; thus we understand why it was necessary to establish his point of view earlier in the story. If the writer cut into his point of view for the first time here, it would be awkward, jarring, distracting.

28. Whatever it is they're talking about is coming a little more clearly into focus. Interesting how Gavin seems to be using the idea of death metaphorically, while Alexis ("You have to do it") seems to be taking it quite literally.

29. The lines here reinforce the idea that Gavin has a religious sensibility which extends beyond liquor. Maybe the real contest here is over Alexis's soul.

30. The reader's sense of tension is rapidly building toward a climax. By this time it's a lot easier to infer what Alexis is referring to than it was to infer Gavin's ignition of the original cocktail . . .

31. ... and this suggestive imagery clarifies Alexis's intention still further.

32. The tension is released in another pun. This moment qualifies as a sub-climax—one of those dragon-back ridges in the triangle of a linear design. We know the "depth charge" Alexis is talking about now will happen on the road, not in the bar. At the same time, he seems to be ordering another drink. The functional pun on the title, "Depth Charge," has evolved, organically over the course of the story, into a metaphor which controls the action and ideas.

33. From this subclimax, there comes a sort of falling action. There's a sort of weariness in the scheme Gavin thinks of now; they both see through it, both know it's not going to work ...

34. ... and Alexis's last line here has the downbeat of finality—in the sub-structure of this subclimax, it is a miniaturized denouement.

35. Jump cut—and start again. A new ascent, new tension rising. The clock's chime helps ring in another movement of the story. The game those "glass pieces" allude to is going to be resumed.

36. In this section of the story, the exposition is played straight: Alexis tells what he has to tell in logical order, instead of suggesting it via mysterious and obscure allusions, as both he and Gavin have done earlier. On the literal level, the more straightforward presentation makes sense because this next packet of information is new to Gavin, while earlier in the story they were both retracing conversations they'd had previously. So far as we readers are concerned, this new directness is the writer's way of making sure we haven't missed the point.

37. It's a strange conception of *need* Alexis has. We've got the idea of what he's planning to do, but *why* he thinks he has to do it is still very much a mystery.

38. Gavin's "blackjack" is another pun—on twenty-one, gambling, and roulette. These more minor double references lack the overarching metaphorical significance of the "depth charge" pun, but they reinforce the story's impression of integrity and depth—its intricate interconnected-ness.

39. Is Alexis trying to commit suicide or instead *win* a game with death? There's some fine distinction in his thinking; he's trying to convert a gamble with mortality into a game of skill.

40. Now this *is* suicide. It's clear that even if Alexis fails the task he's set himself, he does mean to go through with it.

41. There is a reason, after all, that Alexis's one friend should be black and so much older. Heretofore, Gavin has been trying to argue with Alexis on Alexis's level. Now he changes the terms. What does this anecdote prove? The gas station robbery is more clearly motivated by a kind of necessity than what Alexis is planning, or is it?

42. Gavin doesn't seem to think so. In his mind, it may be that the robbery

and Alexis's plan stand for the same kind of youthful foolhardiness and daredeviltry, which is why he won't answer Alexis's question about the take . . .

43. . . . out loud.

44. How beautiful this image has become. It's intensified by the development of the context as much as by the enhancement of the descriptive writing here. Now the reader can hardly help but see it exactly the way Gavin does.

45. Alexis really wants to do his own depth charge—but somehow he can't bring himself to drop it. By this time, we are so accustomed to the double reference that we feel the significance without consciously thinking of it.

46. Notice how this first crack . . .

47. . . . is echoed by the second crack. No big deal here—nothing you could call symbolic, just a well-integrated weave of image and sound that, in this case, enhances our sense that things are going awry.

48. We know that by letting the flame expire, Alexis has violated the ritualized parameters of his friendship with Gavin. But in his response, Gavin is blundering onto Alexis's wavelength. In Gavin's terms, *not* to drop the shot is the wrong thing to do . . .

49. . . . which may be why Alexis is all the more determined to go through with the literal action after his metaphorical failure—and why Gavin doesn't go through with the phone call which could stop him.

50. Jump cut, and start again.

51. This bit of description foreshadows a more important image still to come.

52. The reader should feel a certain *frisson,* to think that the countdown has started for real this time . . .

53. . . . but in fact, it's just another false start.

54. This image may be the weirdest of them all. Who'd have thought of making a "puke puddle" take on such a comprehensive resonance? On the literal level, it's repulsive. Metaphorically, it is almost beautiful, out of its sheer appropriateness.

55. It could be said that Gavin falls short of the "friends don't let their friends drive drunk" model of suitable concern, but could it be that your real best friend is the one who holds you up to your *own* standards?

56. Jump cut, and start again. The accelerating pattern of jump cuts (between the increasingly briefer last few blocks of text) has now built a considerable momentum. From here on, momentum is where it's at; we're accelerating along the vector toward the major climax of the story—the apex of the triangle.

57. This passage gives us a bit more of an inkling of what Alexis's motive for his strange act may be. Somehow his life is not real to him. His connections to other people lack authenticity (as one might put it in existential

terms); his ambitions are without real flavor. It's true, his only friend is Gavin, and I'd say that's almost undoubtedly because of what Gavin said about the soul. It's as if Alexis's project is to verify his own existence somehow, or to verify that he really does have a soul.

58. The expansive movement of the description in these two paragraphs repeats the first expansive movement of the description of the bar—but much more broadly. Till now, we've been claustrophobically contained in the tight space of the bar and in Alexis's drunken consciousness (which tend to reflect one another). Now for the first time we have a panoramic view of the city where all this is taking place, quite as if Alexis's world does become more vivid to him as he approaches the point of leaving it.

59. A nice irony here, and doubtless a true one.

60. The writer is playing with the old conceit of "your life flashes before your eyes" (and, I would say, "making it new" like nobody's business). But somehow it doesn't seem to be working out for Alexis quite the way he planned.

61. The mere suggested repetition of this litany is now enough to send chills down our spines—we don't even need to read through the whole thing.

62. This is it, the climax of the story's whole structure, the moment where we find out what a depth charge really means. Everything up to now simply teased our expectations. *Now* we know he really *is* going to do it . . . really *has* done it. The writer shows a lot of skill, as well, in sustaining the climax slowly over these delicately composed paragraphs, so that it seems to take almost forever for the car to hit the water.

63. This silence is really an inspired touch, since we are more accustomed (by the movies) to think of big automotive action scenes as being very noisy.

64. Just how useful does that whole litany of steps turn out to be in practice? Not very. Alexis is too paralyzed with fear to accomplish much of it.
From here on out, in terms of the overall structure of the story, everything is (pardon the pun) *falling action,* declining away from the main climax, which is the moment when the car launched off the waterfront. At that point, our central question (will he *really* do it?) is answered.

At the same time, the action is rising toward another subclimax, another spike on the dragon's back, on the descending side of the triangle now. We still want to know (quite urgently, no doubt) if it's possible for Alexis to survive.

65. Alexis's feeble efforts to reorient himself to his list of numbers might be comic if the situation weren't so deadly serious.

66. Note this minor but agreeable payoff on the pulsating rhythm of the Don't Walk sign described earlier. Small unities of this kind increase the story's overall integrity.

67. All through this phase of the story the reader will be too involved in the urgency of the situation—that adrenal rush of primary process—to even

pay much attention to the felicities of the writing. Alexis's experience is doubtless much the same . . .

. . . but recall this earlier description: "Gavin let go: the flame extinguished in a kind of bloated beer lava lamp, the smaller glass bobbed inside the larger as he drew his hand away, and the drinks mixed and foamed into a piss-colored whitewater sea." Well, this is what's happening to Alexis, more or less. The contents of the car are mixing and foaming into the contents of the ocean.

68. And, now, somewhat to our surprise, when it seems it must already be too late (in terms of the numbers, it's definitely too late), he shakes off his paralysis enough to recognize that he's alive, and that perhaps ("still . . . twenty-one") there is some point to his living.

69. Here's the follow-up on the reflection that Alexis saw when he first got into the car. Its ghostliness is no coincidence. Alexis is seeing the image of his own dead self.

70. Formally, Alexis's ascension is parallel to the "soul" of the liquor ascending.

71. Now it seems that Alex really is getting what he was after. In this review, his life becomes real to him, vividly present to his senses.

72. His breaking of the water's surface completes this subclimax in a satisfactorily dramatic fashion.

73. In returning to the world of the living, Alexis finds his emotional life restored—the emotion is correctly connected to the event.

74. Thenceforward, there's nothing to be done but a brief denouement, following the subclimax of Alexis's rise from the harbor bottom, and concluding the story as a whole.

75. Reality is restored to Alexis. Somehow this deliberate brush with death has served its purpose, renewing his sense of connection with other people, with himself. What the last line lets us know is that now he's able to leave his obsession with death—his own dead self—where it belongs (as Gavin might have put it), somewhere indefinitely far off in the future.

A WIFE OF NASHVILLE

PETER TAYLOR

The Lovells' old cook Sarah had quit to get married in the spring, and they did-n't have anybody else for a long time—not for several months. It was during the Depression, and when a servant quit, people in Nashville (and even people out at Thornton, where the Lovells came from) tried to see how long they could go before they got another. All through the summer, there would be knocks on the Lovells' front door or on the wooden porch floor, by the steps. And when one of the children or their mother went to the door, some Negro man or woman would be standing there, smiling and holding out a piece of paper. A recom-mendation it was supposed to be, but the illegible note scribbled with a blunt lead pencil was something no white person could have written if he had tried. If Helen Ruth, the children's mother, went to the door, she always talked a while to whoever it was, but she hardly ever even looked at the note held out to her. She would give a piece of advice or say to meet her around at the back door for a handout. If one of the boys—there were three Lovell boys, and no girls—went to the door, he always brought the note in to Helen Ruth, unless John R., their father, was at home, sick with his back ailment. Helen Ruth would shake her head and say to tell whoever it was to go away! "Tell him to go back home," she said once to the oldest boy, who was standing in the sun-par-lor doorway with a smudged scrap of paper in his hand. "Tell him if he had any sense, he never would have left the country.[1]

"He's probably not from the country, Mother."

"They're all from the country," Helen Ruth said. "When they knock on the porch floor like that, they're bound to be from the country, and they're bet-

ter off at home, where somebody cares something about them. I don't care anything about them any more than you do." [2]

But one morning Helen Ruth hired a cheerful-looking and rather plump,
light-complexioned young Negro girl named Jess McGehee, who had come
knocking on the front-porch floor just as the others had. Helen Ruth talked to
her at the front door for a while; then she told her to come around to the
kitchen, and they talked there for nearly an hour. Jess stayed to fix lunch and
supper, and after she had been there a few days, the family didn't know how
they had ever got along without her. [3]

In fact, Jess got on so well with the Lovells that Helen Ruth even decided
to let her come and live on the place, a privilege she had never before allowed
a servant of hers. Together, she and Jess moved all of John R.'s junk—a grass
duck-hunting outfit, two mounted stags' heads, an outboard motor, and so
on—from the little room above the garage into the attic of the house. John R.
lent Jess the money for the down payment on a "suit" of furniture, and Jess
moved in. "You would never know she was out there," Helen Ruth told her
friends. "There is never any rumpus. And her room! It's as clean as yours or
mine."[4]

Jess worked for them for eight years. John R. got so one of his favorite
remarks was "The honeymoon is over, but this is the real thing this time." Then
he would go on about what he called Helen Ruth's "earlier affairs."[5] The last
one before Jess was Sarah, who quit to get married and go to Chicago at the age
of sixty-eight. She had been with them for six years and was famous for her pies
and her banana dishes.[6]

Before Sarah, there was Carrie. Carrie had been with them when the two
younger boys were born, and it was she who had once tried to persuade Helen
Ruth not to go to the hospital but to let her act as midwife. She had quit them
after five years, to become an undertaker. And before Carrie there was Jane
Blakemore, the very first of them all, whom John R. and Helen Ruth had
brought with them from Thornton to Nashville when they married. She lasted
less than three years; she quit soon after John R., Jr., was born, because, she
said, the baby made her nervous.[7]

"It's an honorable record," John R. would say. "Each of them was better
than the one before, and each one stayed with us longer. It proves that experience is the best teacher."[8]

Jess's eight years were the years when the boys were growing up; the boys
were children when she came, and when she left them, the youngest, little
Robbie, had learned to drive the car. In a sense, it was Jess who taught all three
boys to drive.[9] She didn't give them their first lessons, of course, because, like
Helen Ruth, she had never sat at the wheel of an automobile in her life. She
had not ridden in a car more than half a dozen times when she came to the
Lovells, but just by chance, one day, she was in the car when John R. let John

R., Jr., take the wheel. The car would jerk and lunge forward every time the boy shifted gears, and his father said, "Keep your mind on what you're doing."[10]

"I am," John R., Jr., said, "but it just does that. What makes it do it?"

"Think!" John R. said. "Think! . . . *Think!*"

"I *am* thinking, but what makes it do it?"[11]

Suddenly, Jess leaned forward from the back seat and said, "You letting the clutch out too fast, honey."[12]

Both father and son were so surprised they could not help laughing. They laughed harder, of course, because what Jess said was true. And Jess laughed with them. When they had driven another block, they reached a boulevard stop, and in the process of putting on the brake John R., Jr., killed the engine and then flooded the motor. His father shouted, "Well, let it rest! We're just stuck here for about twenty minutes!"[13]

Jess, who was seated with one arm around a big bag of groceries, began to laugh again. "Turn off the key," she said. "Press down on the starter a spell. Then torectly you turn on the key and she'll start."[14]

John R. looked over his shoulder at her, not smiling, but not frowning, either. Presently, he gave the order, "Try it."

"Try what *Jess said?*" John R., Jr., asked.

"Try what Jess said."

The boy tried it, and in a moment he was racing the motor and grinning at his father. When they had got safely across the boulevard, John R. turned around to Jess again. He asked in a quiet, almost humble manner—the same manner he used when describing the pains in his back to Helen Ruth—where she had learned these things about an automobile.[15] "Law," she said, "I learnt them listening to my brother-in-law that drives a truck talk. I don't reckon I really know'm, but I can say them."

John R. was so impressed by the incident that he did not make it one of his stories. He told Helen Ruth about it, of course, and he mentioned it sometimes to his close friends when they were discussing "the good things" about Negroes. With his sons, he used it as an example of how much you can learn by listening to other people talk, and after that day he would permit John R., Jr., to go for drives in the car without him provided Jess went along in his place.[16] Later on, when the other boys got old enough to drive, there were periods when he turned their instruction over to Jess. Helen Ruth even talked of learning to drive, herself, with the aid of Jess.[17]

But it never came to more than talk with Helen Ruth, though John R. encouraged her, saying he thought driving was perhaps a serious strain on his back. She talked about it for several months, but in the end she said that the time had passed when she could learn new skills. When John R. tried to encourage her in the idea, she would sometimes look out one of the sun-parlor windows toward the street and think of how much she had once wanted to learn to drive.[18] But that had been long ago, right after they were married, in the days when John R. had owned a little Ford coupé. John R. was on the road for the Standard Candy company then, and during most of the week she was alone in their apartment at the old Vaux Hall. While he was away John R. kept the coupé stored in a garage only two blocks east, on Broad Street; in those days traveling men still used the railroads, because Governor Peay hadn't yet paved Tennessee's highways. At that time, John R. had not believed in women driving automobiles, and Helen Ruth had felt that he must be right about it; she had even made fun of women who went *whizzing* about town, blowing horns at every intersection. Yet in her heart she had longed to drive that coupé![19] Jane Blakemore was working for them then, and one day Jane had put Helen Ruth's longings into words. "Wouldn't it be dandy," she said, "if me and you clomb in that car one of these weekdays and toured out to Thornton to see all the folks — white and black?"[20]

Without a moment's hesitation, however, Helen Ruth gave the answer that she knew John R. would have given. "Now, think what you're saying, Jane!" she said. "Wouldn't we be a fool-looking pair pulling into the square at Thornton? Think about it. What if we should have a flat tire when we got out about as far as Nine Mile Hill? Who would change it? *You* certainly couldn't! Jane Blakemore, I don't think you use your head about anything!"[21]

That was the way Helen Ruth had talked to Jane on more occasions than one. She was a plain-spoken woman, and she never spoke plainer to anyone than she did to Jane Blakemore during the days when they were shut up together in that apartment at the Vaux Hall. Since Jane was from Thornton and knew how plain-spoken all Helen Ruth's family were, she paid little attention to the way Helen Ruth talked to her.[22] She would smile, or else sneer, and go on with her work of cooking and cleaning. Sometimes she would rebel and speak just as plainly as Helen Ruth did. When Helen Ruth decided to introduce butter plates to their table, Jane said, "I ain't never heard tell of no butter dishes."

Helen Ruth raised her eyebrow. "That's because you are an ignoramus from Thornton, Tennessee," she said.

"I'm ignoramus enough to know ain't no need in nastying up all them dishes for me to wash."[23]

Helen Ruth had, however, made Jane Blakemore learn to use butter plates and had made her keep the kitchen scrubbed and the other rooms of the apartment dusted and polished and in such perfect order that even John R. had noticed it when he came on weekends. Sometimes he had said, "You drive yourself too hard, Helen Ruth."[24]

Jess McGehee was as eager and quick to learn new things as Jane Blakemore had been unwilling and slow. She would even put finger bowls on the breakfast table when there was grapefruit. And how she did spoil the three boys about their food! There were mornings when she cooked the breakfast eggs differently for each one of them while John R. sat and shook his head in disgust at the way she was pampering his sons. John R.'s "condition" in his back kept him home a lot of the time during the eight years Jess was with them.[25] He had long since left off traveling for the candy company; soon after the first baby came, he had opened an insurance agency of his own.

When Jane Blakemore left them and Helen Ruth hired Carrie (after fifteen or twenty interviews with other applicants), she had had to warn Carrie that John R.'s hours might be very irregular, because he was in business for himself and wasn't able merely to punch a time clock and quit when the day ended. "He's an onsurance man, ain't he?" Carrie had asked and had showed by the light in her eyes how favorably impressed she was. "I know about him," she had said. "He's a life-onsurance man, and that's the best kind to have."[26]

At that moment, Helen Ruth thought perhaps she had made a mistake in Carrie. "I don't like my servant to discuss my husband's business," she said.[27]

"No'm!" Carrie said with enthusiasm. "No, *ma'am!*" Helen Ruth was satisfied, but afterward she had often to tell herself that her first suspicion had been right. Carrie was nosy and prying and morbid—and she gossiped with other people's servants. Her curiosity and her gossiping were especially trying for Helen Ruth during her and John R.'s brief separation.[28] They actually had separated for nearly two months right after Kenneth, the middle boy, was born. Helen Ruth had gone to her father's house at Thornton, taking the two babies and Carrie with her. The boys never knew about the trouble between their parents, of course, until Kenneth pried it out of his mother after they were all grown, and, at the time, people in Nashville and Thornton were not perfectly sure that it was a real separation. Helen Ruth had tried to tell herself that possibly Carrie didn't know it was a real separation. But she was never able to deny completely the significance of Carrie's behavior while they were at Thornton. Carrie's whole disposition had seemed to change the afternoon they left Nashville. Up until then, she had been a moody, shifty, rather loud-mouthed brown woman, full of darky compliments for white folks and of gratuitous promises of extra services she seldom rendered. But at Thornton she had put the old family servants to shame with her industriousness and her respectful, unassuming manner. "You don't find them like Carrie in Thornton any more," Helen Ruth's mother said. "The good ones all go to Nashville or Memphis."[29] But Helen Ruth, sitting by an upstairs window one afternoon, saw her mother's cook and Carrie sauntering toward the back gate to meet a caller. She saw Carrie being introduced and then she recognized the caller as Jane Blakemore. Presently the cook returned to the kitchen and Helen Ruth saw Carrie and Jane enter the servants' house in the corner of the yard. During the hour they visited there, Helen Ruth sat quietly by the window in the room with her two babies. It seemed to her the most terrible hour of her separation from John R.[30] When Carrie and Jane reappeared on the stoop of their servants' house and

Carrie was walking Jane to the gate, there was no longer any doubt in Helen Ruth's mind but that she would return to her husband, and return without any complaints or stipulations. During that hour she had tried to imagine exactly what things the black Jane and the brown Carrie were talking about, or, rather, *how* and in what terms they were talking about the things they must be talking about. In her mind, she reviewed the sort of difficulties she had had with Jane and the sort she had with Carrie and tried to imagine what defense they would make for themselves—Jane for her laziness and contrariness, Carrie for her usual shiftiness and negligence. Would they blame her for these failings of theirs? Or would they blandly pass over their own failings and find fault with her for things that she was not even aware of, or that she could not help and could not begin to set straight? Had she really misused these women, either the black one or the brown one?[31] It seemed to her then that she had so little in life that she was entitled to the satisfaction of keeping an orderly house and to the luxury of efficient help. There was too much else she had not had—an "else" nameless to her, yet sorely missed—for her to be denied these small satisfactions. As she sat alone with her two babies in the old nursery and thought of the two servants gossiping about her, she became an object of pity to herself. And presently John R., wherever he might be at that moment—in his office or at the club or, more likely, on a hunting or fishing trip somewhere—became an object of pity, too. And her two babies, one in his crib and the other playing on the carpet with a string of spools, were objects of pity. Even Carrie, standing alone by the gate after Jane had gone, seemed a lone and pitiful figure.[32]

A few days later, Helen Ruth and Carrie and the two baby boys returned to Nashville.

In Nashville, Carrie was herself again; everything was done in her old slipshod fashion. Except during that interval at Thornton, Carrie was never known to perform any task to Helen Ruth's complete satisfaction. Hardly a meal came to the table without the soup or the dessert or some important sauce having been forgotten; almost every week something important was left out of the laundry; during a general cleaning the upper sashes of two or three windows were invariably left unwashed. Yet never in her entire five years did Carrie answer back or admit an unwillingness to do the most menial or the most nonessential piece of work.[33] In fact, one of her most exasperating pronouncements was, "You are exactly right," which was often followed by a lengthy description of how she would do the thing from then on, or an explanation of how it happened that she had forgotten to do it. Not only that, she would often undertake to explain to Helen Ruth Helen Ruth's reason for wanting it done. "You are exactly right and I know how you mean. You want them drapes shut at night so it can seem like we're living in a house out in the Belle Meade instead of this here Vox Hall flat, and some fool might be able to look in from the yard."[34]

"Never mind the reasons, Carrie" was Helen Ruth's usual reply. But her answers were not always so gentle—not when Carrie suggested that she have the second baby at home with Carrie acting as midwife, not when Carrie spoke to her about having the third baby circumcised. And the day that Helen Ruth began packing her things to go to Thornton, she was certain that Carrie would speak out of turn with some personal advice. That would have been more than she could bear, and she was prepared to dismiss Carrie from her service and make the trip alone. But neither then nor afterward did Carrie give any real evidence of understanding the reasons for the trip to Thornton.

In fact, it was not until long afterward, when Carrie had quit them to become an undertaker, that Helen Ruth felt that Carrie's gossip with other Nashville servants had, by accident, played a part in her separation from John R. She and John R. had talked of separation and divorce more than once during the first two years they were married, in the era of Jane Blakemore.[35] It was not that any quarreling led to this talk but that each accused the other of being dissatisfied with their marriage. When John R. came in from traveling, on a weekend or in the middle of the week—he was sometimes gone only two or three days at a time—he would find Helen Ruth sitting alone in the living room, without a book or even a deck of cards to amuse herself with, dressed perhaps in something new her mother had sent her, waiting for him. She would rise from her chair to greet him, and he would smile in frank admiration of the tall, graceful figure and of the countenance whose features seemed always composed, and softened by her hair, which was beginning to be gray even at the time of their marriage. But he had not come home many times before Helen Ruth was greeting him with tears instead of smiles. At first, he had been touched, but soon he began to complain that she was unhappy. He asked her why she did not see something of other people while he was away—the wives of his business or hunting friends, or some of the other Thornton girls who were married and living in Nashville. She replied that she did see them occasionally but that she was not the sort of woman who enjoyed having a lot of women friends. Besides, she was perfectly happy with her present life; it was only that she believed that he must be unhappy and that he no longer enjoyed her company. She understood that he had to be away most of the week, but even when he was in town, she saw very little of him. When he was not at his office, he was fishing out on Duck River or was off to a hunt up at Gallatin. And at night he either took her to parties with those hunting people, with whom she had little or nothing in common, or piled up on the bed after supper and slept. All of this indicated that he was not happy being married to her, she said, and so they talked a good deal about separating.

After the first baby came, there was no such talk for a long time—not until after the second baby. After the first baby came, Helen Ruth felt that their marriage must be made to last, regardless of hers or John R.'s happiness. Besides, it was at that time that one of John R.'s hunting friends—a rich man named Rufus Brantley—had secured the insurance agency for him; and almost before John

R. opened his office, he had sold policies to other rich hunting friends that he had. For a while, he was at home more than he had ever been before. But soon, when his business was established, he began to attend more and more meets and trials, all over Tennessee and Alabama and Kentucky. He even acquired a few dogs and a horse of his own. With his friends he began to go on trips to distant parts of the country. It seemed that when he was not deer hunting in the State of Maine, he was deep-sea fishing in the Gulf.[36] Helen Ruth did sometimes go with him to the local horse shows, but one night, at the Spring Horse Show, she had told Mrs. Brantley that she had a new machine, and Mrs. Brantley had thought she meant an automobile instead of a sewing machine. That, somehow, had been the last straw. She would never go out with "people like the Brantleys" after that. She was pregnant again before the first baby was a year old, and this soon became her excuse for going nowhere in the evening. The women she did visit with very occasionally in the daytime were those she had known as girls in Thornton, women whose husbands were bank tellers and office managers and were barely acquainted with John R. Lovell.

After the second baby came, Helen Ruth saw these women more frequently. She began to feel a restlessness that she could not explain to herself. There were days when she could not stay at home. With Carrie and the two babies, she would traipse about town, on foot or by streetcar, to points she had not visited since she was a little girl and was in Nashville with her parents to attend the State Fair or the Centennial. She went to the Capitol, to Centennial Park and the Parthenon, even out to the Glendale Zoo. Once, with Nancy Tolliver and Lucy Parkes, two of her old Thornton friends, she made an excursion to Cousin Mamie Lovell's farm, which was several miles beyond the town of Franklin. They went by the electric interurban to Franklin, and from there they took a taxi to the farm. Cousin Mamie's husband had been a second cousin of John R.'s father, and it was a connection the Thornton Lovells had once been very proud to claim. But for a generation this branch of the family had been in decline. Major Lovell had been a prominent lawyer in Franklin and had been in politics, but when he died, he left his family "almost penniless." His boys had not gone to college; since the farm was supposed to have been exhausted, they did not try to farm it but clerked in stores in Franklin. There was said to be a prosperous son-in-law in St. Louis, but the daughter was dead and Cousin Mamie was reported to have once called her son-in-law a parvenu to his face. Helen Ruth and her friends made the excursion because they wanted to see the house, which was one of the finest old places in the country and full of antiques.[37]

But Cousin Mamie didn't even let them inside the house. It was a hot summer day, and she had all the blinds closed and the whole L-shaped house shut up tight, so that it would be bearable at night. She received them on the long ell porch. Later, they moved their chairs out under a tree in the yard, where Cousin Mamie's cook brought them a pitcher of iced tea. While they were chatting under the tree that afternoon, they covered all the usual topics that are dealt with when talking to an old lady one doesn't know very well—the old times and the new times, mutual friends and family connections, country living and city living, and always, of course, the lot of woman as it relates to each topic.

"Where are you and John R. living?" Cousin Mamie asked Helen Ruth.

"We're still at the Vaux Hall, Cousin Mamie."

"I'd suppose the trains would be pretty bad for noise there, that close to the depot."

"They're pretty bad in the summer."

"I'd suppose you had a place out from town, seeing how often John R.'s name's in the paper with the hound and hunt set."

"That's John R.'s life," Helen Ruth said, "not mine."[38]

"He runs with a fine pack, I must say," said Cousin Mamie.

Nancy Tolliver and Lucy Parkes nodded and smiled. Lucy said, "The swells of Nashville, Miss Mamie."

But Cousin Mamie said, "There was a day when they weren't the swells. Forty years ago, people like Major Lovell didn't know people like the Brantleys. I think the Brantleys quarried limestone, to begin with. I guess it don't matter, though, for when I was a girl in upper East Tennessee, people said the Lovells started as land speculators hereabouts and at Memphis. But I don't blame you for not wanting to fool with Brantleys, Helen Ruth."[39]

"John R. and I each live our own life, Cousin Mamie."

"Helen Ruth is a woman with a mind of her own, Miss Mamie," Nancy Tolliver said. "It's too bad more marriages can't be like theirs, each living their own life. Everyone admires it as a real achievement."

And Lucy Parkes said, "Because a woman's husband hunts is no reason for her to hunt, any more than because a man's wife sews is any reason for him to sew."[40]

"Indeed not," Cousin Mamie said, actually paying little attention to what Lucy and Nancy were saying. Presently, she continued her own train of thought. "Names like Brantley and Partee and Hines didn't mean a thing in this state even thirty years ago."

What Lucy and Nancy said about her marriage that day left Helen Ruth in a sort of daze and at the same time made her see her situation more clearly. She had never discussed her marriage with anybody, and hearing it described so matter-of-factly by these two women made her understand for the first time what a special sort of marriage it was and how unhappy she was in it.[41] At the time, John R. was away on a fishing trip to Tellico Plains. She did not see him again before she took the babies and Carrie to Thornton. She sent a note to his office saying that she would return when he decided to devote his time to his wife and children instead of to his hounds and horses. While she was at Thornton her letters from John R. made no mention of her note. He wrote about his business, about his hounds and horses, about the weather, and he always urged her to hurry home as soon as she had seen everybody and had a good visit. Meanwhile, he had a room at the Hermitage Club.[42]

When Helen Ruth returned to Nashville, their life went on as before.[43] A year later, the third boy, Robbie, was born, and John R. bought a large bungalow on Sixteenth Avenue, not too far from the Tarbox School, where they planned to send the boys. Carrie was with them for three years after the separation, and though her work did not improve, Helen Ruth found herself making excuses for her. She began to attribute Carrie's garrulity to "a certain sort of bashfulness, or the Negro equivalent to bashfulness." And with the three small boys, and the yard to keep, too, there was so much more for Carrie to do than there had been before! Despite the excuses she made for her, Helen Ruth could see that Carrie was plainly getting worse about everything and that she now seemed to take pleasure in lying about the smallest, most unimportant things. But Helen Ruth found it harder to confront Carrie with her lies or to reprimand her in any way.

During the last months before Carrie quit, she would talk sometimes about the night work she did for a Negro undertaker. To make Helen Ruth smile, she would report things she had heard about the mourners. Her job, Carrie always said, was to sweep the parlors after the funeral and to fold up the chairs. It was only when she finally gave notice to Helen Ruth that she told her what she professed was the truth. She explained that during all those months she had been learning to embalm. "Before you can get a certificate," she said, "you has to handle a bad accident, a sickness, a case of old age, a drowning, a burning, and a half-grown child or less. I been waiting on the child till last night, but now I'll be getting my certificate."[44]

Helen Ruth would not even let Carrie go to the basement to get her hat and coat. "You send somebody for them," she said. "But *you*, you get off these premises, Carrie!" She was sincerely outraged by what Carrie had told her, and when she looked at Carrie's hands she was filled with new horror. Yet something kept her from saying all the things that one normally said to a worthless, lying servant who had been guilty of one final outrage. "*Leave*, Carrie!" she said, consciously restraining herself. "*Leave* this place!" Carrie went out the kitchen door and down the driveway to the street, bareheaded, coatless, and wearing her kitchen slippers.[45]

After Carrie, there was old Sarah, who stayed with them for six years and then quit them to get married and go to Chicago.[46] Sarah was too old to do heavy work even when she first came, and before she had been there a week, John R. had been asked to help move the sideboard and to bring the ladder up from the basement. He said it seemed that every minute he was in the house, he was lifting or moving something that was too much for Sarah. Helen Ruth replied that perhaps she should hire a Negro man to help in the house and look after the yard. But John R. said no, he was only joking, he thought Sarah far and away the best cook they had ever had, and besides business conditions didn't look too good and it was no time to be taking on more help. But he would always add he did not understand why Helen Ruth babied Sarah so. "From the first moment Sarah set foot in this house, Helen Ruth has babied her," he would say to people in Helen Ruth's presence.[47]

Sarah could neither read nor write. Even so, it took her only a short while to learn all Helen Ruth's special recipes and how to cook everything the way the Lovells liked it. For two weeks, Helen Ruth stayed in the kitchen with Sarah, reading to her from *How We Cook in Tennessee* and giving detailed instructions for every meal. It was during that time that her great sympathy for Sarah developed. Sarah was completely unashamed of her illiteracy, and it was this that first impressed Helen Ruth. She admired Sarah for having no false pride and for showing no resentment of her mistress's impatience. She observed Sarah's kindness with the children. And she learned from Sarah about Sarah's religious convictions and about her long, unhappy marriage to a Negro named Morse Wilkins, who had finally left her and gone up North.[48]

While Sarah was working for them, John R. and Helen Ruth lived the life that Helen Ruth had heard her friends describe to John R.'s Cousin Mamie. It was not until after Sarah had come that Helen Ruth, recalling the afternoon at Cousin Mamie's, identified Lucy Parkes's words about a wife's sewing and a husband's hunting as the very answer she had once given to some of Carrie's impertinent prying. That afternoon, the remark had certainly sounded familiar, but she had been too concerned with her own decision to leave her husband to concentrate upon anything so trivial.[49] And after their reconciliation, she tried not to dwell on things that had led her to leave John R. Their reconciliation, whatever it meant to John R., meant to her the acceptance of certain mysteries—the mystery of his love of hunting, of his choice of friends, of his desire to maintain a family and home of which he saw so little, of his attachment to her, and of her own devotion to him. Her babies were now growing into little boys. She felt that there was much to be thankful for, not the least of which was a servant as fond of her and of her children as Sarah was. Sarah's affection for the three little boys often reminded Helen Ruth how lonely Sarah's life must be.[50]

One day, when she had watched Sarah carefully wrapping up little Robbie in his winter play clothes before he went out to play in the snow, she said, "You love children so much, Sarah, didn't you ever have any of your own?"

Sarah, who was a yellow-skinned woman with face and arms covered with brown freckles, turned her gray eyes and fixed them solemnly on Helen Ruth. "Why, I had the cutest little baby you ever did see," she said, "and Morse went and killed it."[51]

"Morse *killed* your baby?"

"He rolled over on it in his drunk sleep and smothered it in the bed."

After that, Helen Ruth would never even listen to Sarah when she talked about Morse, and she began to feel a hatred toward any and all of the men who came to take Sarah home at night. Generally, these men were the one subject Sarah did not discuss with Helen Ruth, and their presence in Sarah's life was the only serious complaint Helen Ruth made against her. They would come sometimes as early as four in the afternoon and wait on the back porch for Sarah to get through. She knew that Sarah was usually feeding one of them out of her kitchen, and she knew that Sarah was living with first one and then another of them, but when she told John R. she was going to put her foot down on it, he forbade her to do so. And so through nearly six years she tolerated this weakness of Sarah's. But one morning in the late spring Sarah told her that Morse Wilkins had returned from up North and that she had taken him back as her husband. Helen Ruth could not find anything to say for a moment, but after studying the large diamond on her engagement ring for awhile she said, "My servant's private life is her own affair, but I give you fair warning now, Sarah, I want to see no more of your men friends — Morse or any *other* — on this place again."

From that time, she saw no more men on the place until Morse himself came, in a drunken rage, in the middle of a summer's day. Helen Ruth had been expecting something of the sort to happen. Sarah had been late to work several times during the preceding three weeks. She had come one morning with a dark bruise on her cheek and said she had fallen getting off the streetcar. Twice, Helen Ruth heard the racket at the back-porch door, she knew at once that it was Morse. She got up from her sewing machine and went directly to the kitchen. Sarah was on the back porch, and Morse was outside the screen door of the porch, which was hooked on the inside. He was a little man, shriveled up, bald-headed, not more than five feet tall, and of a complexion very much like Sarah's. Over his white shirt he wore a dark sleeveless sweater. "You come on home," he was saying as he shook the screen door.

Helen Ruth stepped to the kitchen door. "Is that her?" Morse asked Sarah, motioning his head toward Helen Ruth.

When Sarah turned her face around, her complexion seemed several shades lighter than Morse's. "I got to go," she said to Helen Ruth.

"No, Sarah, *he's* got to go. But *you* don't."

"He's gonna leave me again."

"That's the best thing that could happen to you, Sarah."

Sarah said nothing, and Morse began shaking the door again.

"Is he drunk, Sarah?" Helen Ruth asked.

"He's so drunk I don't know how he find his way here."

Helen Ruth went out onto the porch. "Now, you get off this place, and be quick about it," she said to Morse.

He shook the screen door again. "You didn't make me come here, Mrs.

Lovellel, and you can't make me leave, Mrs. Lovellel."

"I can't make you leave," Helen Ruth said at once, "but there's a bluecoat down on the corner who can."[52]

Suddenly Sarah dropped to her knees and began praying. Her lips moved silently, and gradually she let her forehead come to rest on the top of the rickety vegetable bin. Morse looked at her through the screen, putting his face right against the wire. "Sarah," he said, "you come on home. You better come on now if you think I be there."

Sarah got up off her knees.

"I'm going to phone the police," Helen Ruth said, pretending to move toward the kitchen.

Morse left the door and staggered backward toward the driveway. "Come on, Sarah," he shouted.

"I got to go," Sarah said.

"I won't let you go, Sarah!"

"She can't make you stay!" Morse shouted. "You better come on if you coming!"

"It will be the worst thing you ever did in your life, Sarah," said Helen Ruth. "And if you go with him, you can't ever come back here. He'll kill you someday, too—the way he did your baby."[53]

Sarah was on her knees again, and Morse was out of sight but still shouting as he went down the driveway. Suddenly, Sarah was on her feet. She ran into the kitchen and on through the house to the front porch.

Helen Ruth followed, calling her back. She found Sarah on the front porch waving to Morse, who was halfway down the block, running in a zigzag down the middle of the street, still shouting at the top of his voice. Sarah cried out to him, "Morse! Morse!"

"Sarah!" Helen Ruth said.

"Morse!" Sarah cried again, and then she began mumbling words that Helen Ruth could not quite understand at the time. Afterward, going over it in her mind, Helen Ruth realized that what Sarah had been mumbling was, "If I don't see you no more on this earth, Morse, I'll see you in Glory."

Sarah was with the Lovells for four more months, and then one night she called up on the telephone and asked John R., Jr., to tell his mother that she was going to get married to a man named Racecar and they were leaving for Chicago in the morning.[54]

Jess McGehee came to them during the Depression.[55] Even before Sarah left the Lovells, John R. had had to give up all of his "activities" and devote his entire time to selling insurance. Rufus Brantley had shot himself through the head while cleaning a gun at his hunting lodge, and most of John R.'s other hunting friends had suffered the same financial reverses that John R. had. The changes in the Lovells' life had come so swiftly that Helen Ruth did not realize for a while what the changes meant in her relationship with John R. It seemed as though she woke up one day and discovered that she was not married to the same man. She found herself spending all her evening playing Russian bank with a man who had no interest in anything but his home, his wife, and his three boys. Every night, he would give a brief summary of the things that had happened at his office or on his calls, and then he would ask her and the boys for an account of everything they had done that day. He took an interest in the house and the yard, and he and the boys made a lily pool in the back yard, and singlehandedly he screened in the entire front porch. Sometimes he took the whole family to Thornton for a weekend, and he and Helen Ruth never missed the family reunions there in September.

In a sense, these were the happiest years of their married life. John R.'s business got worse and worse, of course, but since part of their savings was in the bank at Thornton that did not fail, they never had any serious money worries. Regardless of their savings, however, John R.'s loss of income and his having to give up his friends and his hunting wrought very real, if only temporary, changes in him. There were occasions when he would sit quietly and listen to his family's talk without correcting them or pointing out how foolish they were. He gave up saying "Think!" to the boys, and instead would say, "Now, let's see if we can't reason this thing out." He could never bring himself to ask for any sympathy from Helen Ruth for his various losses, but as it was during this time that he suffered so from the ailment in his back (he and Helen Ruth slept with boards under their mattress for ten years), the sympathy he got for his physical pain was more than sufficient.[56] All in all, it was a happy period in their life, and in addition to their general family happiness they had Jess.[57]

Jess not only cooked and cleaned, she planned the meals, did the marketing, and washed everything, from handerkerchiefs and socks to heavy woolen blankets. When the boys began to go to dances, she even learned to launder their dress shirts. There was nothing she would not do for the boys or for John R. or for Helen Ruth. The way she idealized the family became the basis for most of the "Negro jokes" told by the Lovells during those years. In her room she had a picture of the family, in a group beside the lily pool, taken with her own box Brownie; she had tacked it and also a picture of each of them on the wall above her washstand. In her scrapbook she had pasted every old snapshot and photograph that Helen Ruth would part with, as well as old newspaper pictures of John R. on horseback or with a record-breaking fish he had caught. She had even begged from Helen Ruth an extra copy of the newspaper notice of their wedding.[58]

Jess talked to the family a good deal at mealtime, but only when they had addressed her first and had shown that they wanted her to talk. Her remarks were mostly about things that related to the Lovells. She told a sad story about a "very loving white couple" from Brownsville, her home town, who had been drowned in each other's arms when their car rolled off the end of a river ferry.

The point of the story was that those two people were the same, fine, loving sort of couple that John R. and Helen Ruth were. All three of the boys made good grades in her scrapbook, which she periodically passed around for the family to appreciate. When Kenneth began to write stories and articles for his high-school paper, she would always borrow the paper overnight; soon it came out that she was copying everything he wrote onto the big yellow pages of her scrapbook.[59]

After three or four years, John R. began to say that he thought Jess would be with them always and that they would see the day when the boys' children would call her "Mammy." Helen Ruth said that she would like to agree with him about that, but actually she worried, because Jess seemed to have no life of her own, which wasn't at all natural.[60] John R. agreed that they should make her take a holiday now and then. Every summer, they would pack Jess off to Brownsville for a week's visit with her kinfolks, but she was always back in her room over the garage within two or three days; she said that her people fought and quarreled so much that she didn't care for them. Outside her life with the Lovells, she had only one friend. Her interest was the movies, and her friend was "the Mary who works for Mrs. Dunbar." Jess and Mary went to the movies together as often as three or four times a week, and on Sunday afternoons Mary came to see Jess or Jess went to see Mary, who lived over the Dunbar's garage. Jess always took along her scrapbook and her most recent movie magazines. She and Mary swapped movie magazines, and it was apparent from Jess's talk on Monday mornings that they also swapped eulogies of their white families.[61]

Sometimes Helen Ruth would see Mrs. Dunbar downtown or at a P.T.A. meeting; they would discuss their cooks and smile over the reports that each had received of the other's family. "I understand that your boys are all growing into very handsome men," Mrs. Dunbar said once, and she told Helen Ruth that Jess was currently comparing one of the boys—Mrs. Dunbar didn't know which one—to Neil Hamilton, and that she was comparing Helen Ruth to Irene Rich, and John R. to Edmund Lowe. As the boys got older, they began to resent the amount of authority over them—though it was small—that Jess had been allowed by their parents and were embarrassed if anyone said Jess had taught them to drive the car. When John R., Jr., began at the university, he made his mother promise not to let Jess know what grades he received, and none of the boys would let Jess take snapshots of them anymore. Their mother tried to comfort Jess by saying that the boys were only going through a phase and that it would pass in time. One day, she even said this in the presence of Robbie, who promptly reported it to the older boys, and it ended with John R., Jr.'s complaining to his father that their mother ought not to make fun of them to Jess. His father laughed at him but later told Helen Ruth that he thought she was making a mistake, that the boys were getting big enough to think about their manly dignity, and that she would have to take that into consideration.[62]

She didn't make the same mistake again, but although Jess never gave any real sign of her feelings being hurt, Helen Ruth was always conscious of how the boys were growing away from their good-natured servant.[63] By the time Robbie was sixteen, they had long since ceased to have any personal conversation with Jess, and nothing would have induced Robbie to submit to taking drives with her but the knowledge that his father would not allow him to use the car on dates until he had had months of driving practice. Once, when Robbie and Jess returned from a drive, Jess reported, with a grin, that not a word had passed between them during the entire hour and a half. Helen Ruth only shook her head sadly. The next day she bought Jess a new bedside radio.

The radio was the subject of much banter among the boys and their father. John R. said Helen Ruth had chosen the period of hard times and the Depression to become more generous with her servant than she had ever been before in her life. They recalled other presents she had given Jess recently, and from that time on they teased her regularly about how she spoiled Jess. John R. said that if Jess had had his back trouble, Helen Ruth would have retired her at double pay and nursed her with twice the care that he received. The boys teased her by saying that at Christmas time she reversed the custom of shopping for the servant at the ten-cent stores and for the family at department stores.[64]

Yet as long as Jess was with them, they all agreed that she was the best help they had ever had. In fact, even afterward, during the war years, when John R.'s business prospered again and his back trouble left him entirely and the boys were lucky enough to be stationed near home and, later, continue their education at government expense, even then John R. and the boys would say that the years when Jess was with them were the happiest time of their life and that Jess was the best servant Helen Ruth had ever had. They said that, and then there would be a silence, during which they were probably thinking about the summer morning just before the war when Jess received a telephone call.[65]

When the telephone rang that morning, Helen Ruth and John R. and the boys had just sat down to breakfast. As was usual in the summertime, they were eating at the big drop-leaf table in the sun parlor. Jess had set the coffee urn by Helen Ruth's place and was starting from the room when the telephone rang. Helen Ruth, supposing the call was for a member of the family, and seeing that Jess lingered in the doorway, said for her to answer it there in the sun parlor instead of running to the telephone in the back hall.

Jess answered it, announcing whose residence it was in a voice so like Helen Ruth's that it made the boys grin. For a moment, everyone at the table kept silent. They waited for Jess's eyes to single out one of them. John R., Jr., and Kenneth even put down their grapefruit spoons. But the moment Jess picked up the instrument, she fixed her eyes on the potted fern on the window seat across the room. At once her nostrils began to twitch, her lower lip fell down, and it seemed only an act of will that she was twice able to say, "Yes, ma'am," in answer to the small, unreal, metallic voice.

When she had replaced the telephone on its cradle, she turned quickly away and started into the dining room. But Helen Ruth stopped her. "Jess," she asked, her voice full of courtesy, "was the call for you?"

Jess stopped, and they all watched her hands go up to her face. Without turning around, she leaned against the door jamb and began sobbing aloud. Helen Ruth sprang up from the table, saying, "Jess, honey, what *is* the matter?" John R. and the boys stood up, too.

"It was a telegram for me—from Brownsville."

Helen Ruth took her in her arms. "Is someone dead?"

Between sobs, Jess answered, "My little brother—our baby brother—the only one of 'em I cared for." Then her sobs became more violent.

Helen Ruth motioned for John R. to move the morning paper from the big wicker chair, and she led Jess in that direction. But Jess would not sit down, and she could not be pulled away from Helen Ruth. She held fast to her, and Helen Ruth continued to pat her gently on the back and to try to console her with gentle words. Finally, she said, "Jess, you must go to Brownsville. Maybe there's been some mistake. Maybe he's not dead. But you must go, anyway."

Presently, Jess did sit in the chair, and dried her eyes on Helen Ruth's napkin. The boys shook their heads sympathetically and John R. said she certainly must go to Brownsville. She agreed, and said she believed there was a bus at ten that she would try to catch. Helen Ruth patted her hand, telling her to go along to her room when she felt like it, and said that *she* would finish getting breakfast.[66]

"I want to go by to see Mary first," Jess said, "so I better make haste." She stood up, forcing a grateful smile. Then she burst into tears again and threw her arms about Helen Ruth, mumbling, "Oh, God! Oh, God!" The three boys and their father saw tears come into Helen Ruth's eyes, and through her tears Helen Ruth saw a change come over their faces. It was not exactly a change of expression. It couldn't be that, she felt, because it was exactly the same on each of the four faces. It hardly seemed possible that so similar a change could reflect four men's individual feelings. She concluded that her own emotion, and probably the actual tears in her eyes, had made her imagine the change, and when Jess now pulled away and hurried off to her room, Helen Ruth's tears had dried and she could see no evidence of the change she had imagined in her husband's and her sons' faces.[67]

While Jess was in her room preparing to leave, they finished breakfast. Then Helen Ruth began clearing the table, putting the dishes on the teacart. She had said little while they were eating, but in her mind she was all the while going over something that she knew she must tell her family. As she absentmindedly stacked the dishes, her lips moved silently over the simple words she would use in telling them.[68] She knew that they were watching her, and when Robbie offered to take Jess to the bus station, she knew that the change she had seen in all their faces had been an expression of sympathy for *her* as well as of an eagerness to put this whole episode behind them. "I'll take Jess to her bus," he said.

But Helen Ruth answered, in the casual tone she had been preparing to use, that she thought it probably wouldn't be the thing to do.

"Why, what do you mean, Helen Ruth?" John R. asked her.

"It was very touching, Mother," Kenneth said in his new, manly voice, "the way she clung to you." He, too, wanted to express sympathy, but he also seemed to want to distract his mother from answering his father's question.

At that moment, Jess passed under the sun-parlor windows, walking down the driveway, carrying two large suitcases. Helen Ruth watched her until she reached the sidewalk. Then, very quietly, she told her family that Jess McGehee had no baby brother and had never had one. "Jess and Mary are leaving for California. They think they're going to find themselves jobs out there."

"You knew that right along?" John R. asked.

"I knew it right along."

"Did she know you did, Helen Ruth?" he asked. His voice had in it the sternness he used when questioning his boys about something.

"No, John R., she did not. I didn't learn it from her."

"Well, I don't believe it's so," he said. "Why, I don't believe that for a minute. Her carrying on was too real."

"They're going to California. They've already got their two tickets. Mrs. Dunbar got wind of it somehow, by accident, from Mrs. Lon Thompson's cook, and she called me on Monday. They've saved their money and they're going."[69]

"And you let Jess get away with all that crying stuff just now?" John R. said.[70]

Helen Ruth put her hands on the handlebar of the teacart. She pushed the cart a little way over the tile floor but stopped when he repeated his question. It wasn't to answer his question that she stopped, however. "Oh, my dears!" she said, addressing her whole family. Then it was a long time before she said anything more. John R. and the three boys remained seated at the table, and while Helen Ruth gazed past them and toward the front window of the sun parlor, they sat silent and still, as though they were in a picture. What could she say to them, she kept asking herself. And each time she asked the question, she received for answer some different memory of seemingly unrelated things out of the past twenty years of her life. These things presented themselves as answers to her question, and each of them seemed satisfactory to her. But how little sense it would make to her husband and her grown sons, she reflected, if she should suddenly begin telling them about the long hours she had spent waiting in that apartment at Vaux Hall while John R. was on the road for the Standard Candy Company, and in the same breath should tell them about how plainly she used to talk to Jane Blakemore and how Jane pretended that the baby made her nervous and went back to Thornton. Or suppose she should abruptly remind John R. of how ill at ease the wives of his hunting friends used to make her feel and how she had later driven Sarah's worthless husband out of the yard, threatening to call a bluecoat. What if she should suddenly say that because a woman's husband hunts, there is no reason for *her* to hunt, any more than because a man's wife sews, there is reason for him to sew.[71] She felt that she would be willing to say anything at all, no matter how cruel or absurd it was, if it would make them understand that everything that happened in life only demonstrated in some way the lonesomeness that people felt. She was ready to tell them about sitting in the old nursery at Thornton and waiting for Carrie and Jane Blakemore to come out of the cabin in the yard. If it would make them see what she had been so long in learning to see, she would even talk at last about the "so much else" that had been missing from her life and that she had not been able to name, and about the foolish mysteries she had so nobly accepted upon her reconciliation with John R. To her, these things were all one now; they were her loneliness, the loneliness from which everybody, knowingly or unknowingly, suffered. But she knew that her husband and her sons did not recognize her loneliness or Jess McGehee's or their own. She turned her eyes from the table, and it was strange to see that they were still thinking in the most personal and particular terms of how they had been deceived by a servant, the ignorant granddaughter of an ignorant slave, a Negro woman from Brownsville who was crazy about the movies and who would soon be riding a bus, mile after mile, on her way to Hollywood, where she might find the friendly faces of the real Neil Hamilton and the real Irene Rich. It was with effort that Helen Ruth thought again of Jess McGehee's departure and the problem of offering an explanation to her family. At last, she said patiently, "My dears, don't you see how it was for Jess? How else can they tell us anything when there is such a gulf?" After a moment she said, "How can I make you understand this?"

Her husband and her three sons sat staring at her, their big hands, all so alike, resting on the breakfast table, their faces stamped with identical expressions, not of wonder but of incredulity. Helen Ruth was still holding firmly to the handle of the teacart. She pushed it slowly and carefully over the doorsill and into the dining room, dark and cool as an underground cavern, and spotlessly clean, the way Jess McGehee had left it.[72]

ANALYSIS

Plot

What's more prominent in this story, the background or the foreground? From the strictly technical point of view, this story is ninety percent subtext. It is a great mass of expository information, delivered in a couple of different ways, through summary spiced with half-scenes (see below), or through full scenes presented as flashbacks.

Backstory

Helen Ruth marries John R. Lovell, a man from her hometown of Thornton, and the couple moves to Nashville, bringing along a black servant from Thornton, Jane Blakemore. As he begins to succeed in business, John R. neglects his wife, and Helen Ruth is unhappy enough about that to discuss divorce (a very radical notion indeed in the pre-Depression South). Helen Ruth also takes out some of her unhappiness, though very obliquely, on the maid Jane Blakemore.

When a child comes, divorce is out of the question in Helen Ruth's eyes, but she's still very unhappy. She tries to mask her unhappiness with lines like "Just because a man hunts is no reason for his wife to hunt," etc., but she has no one to practice these platitudes on but her new servant, Carrie. Carrie gossips to Helen Ruth's friends' servants, and when Helen Ruth hears her own evasive statements reflected from the mouths of her friends, she's shocked into a recognition of their inadequacy, and she actually leaves her husband to go back to Thornton with her two children and Carrie. But John R. disarms her by refusing to acknowledge the significance of her action, and when Helen Ruth realizes how pathetic she must appear—even in the eyes of Carrie and Jane Blakemore—she decides that the lesser evil is to return to the marriage.

Nothing in Helen Ruth's circumstances has really changed, but she herself begins to change. She is deepening and maturing—as evidenced by her sympathy for the new maid Sarah (who shares several of the faults of her two predecessors) and by her ability to handle the crisis of Sarah's drunk husband's intrusion calmly and correctly. Helen Ruth's relationship with Sarah helps her put her disappointment with her own husband in a larger perspective, and she learns to derive some happiness from what is good in her own life.

Then the Depression and a fourth maid, Jess McGehee, arrive simultaneously. Somewhat ironically, the failure of John R.'s business in the downslide of the general economy actually improves the Lovells' marriage, by giving him good reason to stay home. Also, Jess is a real jewel, the sort of servant who not only enacts her role perfectly but also transcends it to become a member of the family. During the eight years she stays with them, the Lovells really *are* a happy family for the first time, partly though not entirely owing to her presence.

Present Action

The telephone rings . . . for Jess. After elaborate histrionics, Jess hangs up and reveals that her little brother has died and she must hasten away to her home-town, Brownsville. After a very emotional parting scene, she leaves. Following her departure, Helen Ruth lets her family know that Jess has not been telling them the truth. There hasn't been a death in the family; instead, Jess plans to move to California with a friend, to be closer to the movie stars that fascinate her. Helen Ruth's husband and sons are astonished that she would allow such an involved deception to pass over without reacting to it angrily. As a matter of fact, Helen Ruth does have some very good reasons for the attitude she takes to Jess's behavior, but, although she *feels* these reasons very vividly at the end of the story, she is not able to put them into words.

Now, it really should not be possible to make a good short story out of this mass of raw material. On the basis of this summary, it looks like there's way too much exposition—the story is so top-heavy with exposition it's almost certain to cap-size. Really, there's enough information here to fill a novel. How could it be possible to cram all this information into the length of a *short story* without hav-ing the text degenerate into a dense and tedious summary of all these events?

Character

There's very little physical description of any of the characters in this story. Even for Helen Ruth, there's only this: "the tall, graceful figure," and "the countenance whose features always seemed composed, and softened by her hair, which was beginning to be gray even at the time of their marriage." That's not much to go on, but in the context of other information, it's suggestive; Helen Ruth is characterized by constant effort to maintain an outward compo-sure which often belies her inner turmoil.

For the most part, Helen Ruth is characterized by her reactions to things. She's seldom an initiator of events, but must deal with them as they arise from other sources. Her responses are usually based on an effort to maintain deco-rum (in the deepest sense of that word). At the beginning of the story, her com-posure is often artificial and ineffective; by the end, it has deepened and become quite real.

John R. is never described at all so far as his appearance is concerned; the one salient physical detail reported about him is his back pain. He first materi-alizes in the story through his speech, which tends to be pompous and arrogant and (vis-à-vis Helen Ruth and the black servants) patronizing. The effect of his pontifical lines early in the story is to show us a man full of a smug, unexam-ined confidence in himself and his place in the world—an interesting contrast to Helen Ruth's much more considerable insecurity, and at times the cause of that insecurity.

But we are also shown, first in the driving scene with Jess, that John R. is capable of more depth than first appears in him. He's sometimes able to stop his stream of bluster to listen and learn from what's going on around him. And when the Depression wipes out his business, we see that his somewhat obnoxious sense of self-worth can be a virtue; when times are good, he's overbearing, but when times are bad he can be tough enough to withstand them.

The maids are characterized with ascending degrees of detail from the first to the last to work for the Lovell family. We know least about Jane Blakemore—no more than that she comes from Thornton like the Lovells themselves and that one of her "country" qualities is a stubborn resistance to newfangled innovations like butter plates.

We learn considerably more about Carrie's personality than about Jane Blakemore's, partly because the interaction between Carrie's character and Helen Ruth's predicament is more complex and more important. The scenes in which Carrie appears (e.g., when she talks to Jane at the Thornton garden gate or when she announces to Helen Ruth just how she's completed her qualifications as a mortician) are more fully rendered and detailed than the scenes involving Jane. Those scenes characterize Carrie through action, but we also learn a lot about her personality through summary and direct discourse: that she is superficially devious, promising a great many things that she fails to deliver. She also forces a kind of intimacy on Helen Ruth by offering unwanted comments on Helen Ruth's personal life. And yet both of these qualities, in a way, are reflected in Helen Ruth, or perhaps reflected *from* Helen Ruth, whose own statements tend to misrepresent what's really happening in her marriage, and who uses Carrie as a captive audience for those remarks in something of the same way that Carrie uses her.

Of Carrie and Jane we know almost nothing that isn't relevant to their performance in the Lovell household. But Sarah's private life has some relevance to the story, and so some crucial parts of it are revealed to us. Some of this information comes through summary (as with *all* the characterizations), some through dialogue with Helen Ruth, and some through full scenes, like the scene in which the drunken Morse appears at the Lovells' door.

Of the appearance of Jess McGehee, we know no more than that she is "a cheerful-looking and rather plump, light-complexioned Negro girl," though of all the maids she is the most vivid and most constant presence in the story. Her family background is given with more thoroughness than that of any of the others, and we have the opportunity of learning how she spends *all* of her time (though of course she spends most of it in the Lovell household). A single scene—the driving lesson episode—is enough to characterize her as capable and knowledgeable, yet not too aggressively so. A line of her speech: "I don't reckon I really know'm, but I can say'm," sets the tone of her personality with wit and a kind of wisdom too.

Consider too the characterization of a cameo character, Cousin Mamie:

Cousin Mamie's husband had been a second cousin of John R.'s father, and it was a connection the Thornton Lovells had once been very proud to claim. But for a generation this branch of the family had been in decline. Major Lovell had been a prominent lawyer in Franklin and had been in politics, but when he died, he left his family "almost penniless." His boys had not gone to college; since the farm was supposed to have been exhausted, they did not try to farm it but clerked in stores in Franklin. There was said to be a prosperous son-in-law in St. Louis, but the daughter was dead and Cousin Mamie was reported to have once called her son-in-law a parvenu to his face.

Given that the part Cousin Mamie plays in the story is of very minor importance, the depth of this characterization recalls the novelist Ford Madox Ford's famous remark that if you're going to have a character appear in a story long enough to sell a newspaper, he'd better be real enough that you can smell his breath. And the method for this characterization is also used for the other people whose roles in the story are more significant. The writer places all the characters very accurately and thoroughly in their social/historical context, so that we come to know them not only through their speech and their actions but through knowing generations' worth of their past. These historicized summary presentations of character don't *replace* action and dialogue—the story would still be viable on the basis of the scenes and half-scenes recorded—but add an extra dimension.

Then again, none of the characters (with the possible exception of the three Lovell sons) appears to be nothing more than the predictable result of the social and historical forces operating in his or her background. Even Cousin Mamie, as we can hear in that "parvenu" remark, has a cranky personality all her own which in some ways frets against her family background. Our foretaste of that tension in her summary introduction makes the brief scene in which she appears all the more effective.

Characters are seen through a number of different lenses in this story (and finally through all those lenses together). The writer's summary descriptions of the characters give us one way of understanding them. These summaries are not usually given all in one lump as in the case of Cousin Mamie. Regarding the more important characters, summary information is dispersed through the story, gradually accruing toward its intended total effect at the conclusion.

Somewhat atypically for a modern short story, this writer doesn't depend much on the sense of sight in establishing the characters. We have very little visual information about any of these people, and in many cases we begin to hear them before we see them at all. The major characters are made known to us more through the sorts of things they typically say, and by the tone of what they say, than by any other aspect of their behavior. And yet the characters are vividly present, and the reader's sense of their reality is such that they seem to be as "visible" as characters in any other narrative, if not more so.

Tone

The tone of this story is noticeably *something*—in contrast to the glassine transparency of tone in a great many contemporary short stories. The density of tone creates a kind of filter between the reader and the events of the story. The linguistic gestures all suggest the mannerisms of a raconteur—a polished and capable storyteller who has politely but firmly grasped your attention. It's a story you listen to rather than watch; its most immediate appeal is not to the eye but to the ear. Still, I find it hard to read this story without forming some sort of visual image of the person who's telling it, a courtly and mellifluous master of anecdote who makes a total claim to my trust but who may not always be altogether trustworthy. But who is that person? After all, there *isn't* any first-person narrator present in the story.

Point of View

If we apply the standards we've used previously, we'll decide that the story is in Helen Ruth's point of view. We can only observe the exterior behavior of the other characters, but we have access to her thoughts and feelings. On that evidence, the "camera" must definitely be situated behind Helen Ruth's eyes. Right?

But somehow the situation feels a little different here. We sense that other ghostly presence, the source of the story's tone, hovering beside Helen Ruth's intelligence, and that presence seems to have a point of view of its own. Helen Ruth is sometimes the observer through whom we apprehend the events of the story, but also sometimes the object of the observation of this other presence. The long, powerful closing paragraph is an example of the first case; we are fully located *within* Helen Ruth's sensibility there. Here's an example of the latter case:

> In fact, it was not until long afterward, when Carrie had quit them to become an undertaker, that Helen Ruth felt that Carrie's gossip with other Nashville servants had, by accident, played a part in her separation from John R. She and John R. had talked of separation and divorce more than once during the first two years they were married, in the era of Jane Blakemore. It was not that any quarreling led to this talk but that each accused the other of being dissatisfied with their marriage. When John R. came in from traveling, on a weekend or in the middle of the week—he was sometimes gone only two or three days at a time—he would find Helen Ruth sitting alone in the living room, without a book or even a

deck of cards to amuse herself with, dressed perhaps in something new her mother had sent her, waiting for him. She would rise from her chair to greet him, and he would smile in frank admiration of the tall, graceful figure and of the countenance whose features seemed always composed, and softened by her hair, which was beginning to be gray even at the time of their marriage. But he had not come home many times before Helen Ruth was greeting him with tears instead of smiles. At first, he had been touched, but soon he began to complain that she was unhappy. He asked her why she did not see something of other people while he was away. . . .

For the most part the narration of the story is *externally omniscient* concerning all the characters; only for Helen Ruth is it *internally omniscient*. That's to say that the narration can report the speech and behavior of all the characters (regardless of Helen Ruth's presence as observer), but it reports on the thought and emotions of only Helen Ruth—usually.

In the passage quoted above, however, there is a subtle movement of point of view from the mind of one character toward the mind of another. The paragraph begins in Helen Ruth's head—reporting on her inner response to a plot point. Then it moves to a stance of external omniscience—summarizing the arguments between husband and wife without reporting the private thoughts of either. By the middle of the passage, we are seeing Helen Ruth from without— as John R. would see her. And toward the end we even get a hint of John R.'s private reaction to the scene ("he had been touched . . ."). It's not a major excursion into his mind, just a quick peek, and so not noticeably distinguishable from the style of summary in which so much of the story is composed. From this position, the narration quickly returns to the middle ground between the internal viewpoints of the two characters: a paraphrase of dialogue, which is a mode of external action.

"Central intelligence" is the term coined by Henry James to define this sort of roving point of view. James himself is a crucial transitional figure between the conventions of nineteenth-century fiction and the evolving techniques of twentieth-century modernist fiction (and, not incidentally, a writer from whom Peter Taylor learned a great deal). In most nineteenth-century English or American novels, the stance of authorial omniscience is a given. It is explicitly understood by the reader that the voice telling the story belongs to the author. This authorial presence stands over the story like an all-knowing God presiding over his creation, and may even step between the reader and the action from time to time, to explain things or make predictions. Unlike today's "postmodern" authors, however, the nineteenth-century author does not usually assume the power to tamper with the clockwork of the plot he's previously created; thus, he is omniscient but not precisely omnipotent.

In the typical twentieth-century realist story, authorial presence has been expunged. If the author were suddenly to appear on the stage of Bernardini's "Depth Charge" and start talking to us directly, we would be shocked and offended, for such behavior violates the major conventions of stories of this kind. Such manifestations are nowadays defined as "authorial intrusions" and almost always handled as flaws (except when they occur within the clear context of "postmodern surrealism"—see Gilmore Tamny's "Little Red"). In the modern realist short story, shifts of point of view occur directly from character to character (quite similarly to shifts of points of view in film), without any mediation through the authorial voice. The point of view shifts between Alexis and Gavin in "Depth Charge" are a typical example of that technique.

Central intelligence moves along the spectrum between these two extremes. Central intelligence may also be defined as a ghostly remnant of the old nineteenth-century authorial presence, which has ceased to be visible or tangible but continues to be audible. (Hence our odd sense in "A Wife of Nashville" that someone is *there*, telling us the story.) A skillful manager of central intelligence can use it to move point of view smoothly and seamlessly between characters. The point of view may hover very near a character (as it usually seems to hover near Helen Ruth in this story) or move entirely within the character's mind. Central intelligence can be used to move point of view almost imperceptibly among numerous characters in a story, but the transitions must be smoothly mediated, as in the passage quoted above; they must not be jerky or abrupt.

In this story, the writer has not pushed central intelligence anywhere near its limits. Point of view is usually located within Helen Ruth or very near to her. But our sense of the palpable presence of a central intelligence in the story keeps us aware that other points of view are potential. It's instructive to consider what attitudes other characters—Jess McGehee, for example—might take to the events of this story.

Time Management

One of the great difficulties in writing this story (see "Plot," above) is presented by the large amount of real time that has to be covered somehow. At least twenty years of the Lovells' marriage are under observation here. If the writer had set out to dramatize all the events of their married life alluded to in the story in *full scenes*, the tale would most certainly have ballooned to novel length—and not an especially short novel either.

The writer gets around this problem by summarizing a great deal of the action—a tactic seldom seen in contemporary short stories. Why is it so rare nowadays? For one thing, good engaging summary is harder to write than action and dialogue. Long passages of uninspiredly written summary make a story plod and drag, and therefore writers trained in the schools are usually directed to excise large lumps of exposition and move directly into action and dialogue—"cut to the chase," in the popular phrase.

But this story contains more summary than scene, and yet somehow the summary isn't dull or plodding—it's every bit as interesting as the fully rendered scenes. What's the trick to it?

To begin with, the personality of the invisible narrative voice does a great deal to spark and hold the reader's interest, so that the reader can enjoy the pleasure of hearing the story from an accomplished tale-teller. The story's tone is always lively and engaging—though not associated with any particular character. This effect of immediacy is one of the advantages of central intelligence.

Let's look closely at an average summary passage:

> After Carrie, there was old Sarah, who stayed with them for six years and then quit them to get married and go to Chicago. Sarah was too old to do heavy work even when she first came, and before she had been there a week, John R. had been asked to help move the sideboard and to bring the ladder up from the basement. He said it seemed that every minute he was in the house, he was lifting or moving something that was too much for Sarah. Helen Ruth replied that perhaps she should hire a Negro man to help in the house and look after the yard. But John R. said no, he was only joking, he thought Sarah far and away the best cook they had ever had, and besides business conditions didn't look too good and it was no time to be taking on more help. But he would always add that he did not understand why Helen Ruth babied Sarah so. "From the first moment Sarah set foot in this house, Helen Ruth has babied her," he would say to people in Helen Ruth's presence.
>
> Sarah could neither read nor write. Even so . . .

First of all, this passage does move through time very rapidly and efficiently, arching over the whole period of Sarah's tenure with the Lovells. But it also has several different kinds of particularity to it, which makes us feel as we read less like we are absorbing an impersonal list of information and more like we are sharing an experience. The presence of specific objects—the sideboard and the ladder—helps us picture a full scene even though that scene is not fully rendered. The paraphrased dialogue has a similar effect, and with the interjection of that conversational "no, he was only joking," from John R., we're moved closer to hearing an actual conversation. Finally, just one line of dialogue surfaces into quotation marks, and even though it's a typical, generic statement, made many times and not just on one occasion, it seems to bring us closer to some particular event.

All these sorts of particularity are used to create *half-scenes*, which interrupt the flow of summary only briefly, but do a great deal to make us feel that we are witnessing events instead of merely being told about them. A half-scene doesn't give us exhaustive information about an event, but it gives just enough detail to convince us (in our *senses*) that the event occurred.

Even with the advantage of tone and half-scene, all this summary would probably begin to drag if it were given in strict and linear chronological order. But the central intelligence which is the source of the narrative voice has the power to release itself from the constraints of chronology, moving in a free and easy spiral pattern around the time line. Because the central intelligence has a "personality" independent from any of the characters, it is free to move through the story according to its own interest. Therefore the order of presentation in the story is defined by the motifs which the central intelligence chooses to bring to our attention.

Design

Central intelligence is in charge of the formal organization of this story, and because the tone of the narration is so pleasantly casual, it may seem that there is no organization beyond the apparently free associations the narrative voice makes. However, the casualness of the story's surface is deceptive, and the substructure beneath it is very carefully designed.

One of the writer's time management strategies is to present the Lovells' marriage as it is affected by their relationship to the series of different maids. This approach is very effective for compressing real time in the story, and it also creates a kind of shell pattern for the overall design: a spiraling pattern which loops continually backward to the time periods defined by the maids who came before Jess, and returns as constantly to Jess's own epoch. However freely the narration skips around in the chronology, the maids always serve as reference points to let us know what period we're in.

The substructural armature of the history of the maids functions like the chord progression in a jazz tune, or like those four one-word points that Lish used to keep his bearings when improvising *My Romance* on stage. With those substructural underpinnings firmly in place, the writer can use the amiable garrulity of the narrative voice to "blow free." That sense of freedom in the story's surface movement becomes part of the pleasure of reading and no doubt was part of the fun of writing it as well.

Meanwhile, of course, the story isn't *just* about those maids. The history of the maids provides pretexts for telling all about the Lovells and their marriage and especially about how Helen Ruth becomes the person she is seen to be in the story's final scene. At the most stupidly superficial level, one might say that the subject of this story is how Helen Ruth becomes more proficient at training and managing her servants, and indeed this reading is true enough, though very shallow. As the story progresses, the trainer/trainee relationship is set on its head, and we come to understand that the maids are providing Helen Ruth with her moral education.

The change in perspective necessary to give the reader this latter insight is accomplished by the repetitions built into the narrative design. As in a musical composition, once again, the story keeps returning to certain moments pinpointed in its chronology, as a piece of music will repeatedly restate certain phrases which become motifs. With each of these returns, the moment returned to gathers a deeper context, and the depth at which we can understand the crucial events of the story is increased.

The most important of these moments, of course, is the one that concludes the story. Here we see the purpose of the recursive, spiraling design. It resembles a complicated cat's-cradle sort of noose designed to tighten finally on this one conclusive instant. The intention here realized is to bring twenty years' worth of the Lovells' history forward to focus on this tiny area of time. It's a commonly understood physical principle that force is increased proportionally as the area to which it is applied is reduced (which is why it hurts more, pound for pound, to be stomped by a spike heel than by a combat boot). The psychological effect of this story's conclusion is very similar. The concentration of so many forces of the past onto this present moment allows us a revelatory insight into everything that makes Helen Ruth the person she is, the powers which furnish her with a kind of transcendent grace, in no more than the time it takes for her to roll the teacart into the cool interior of her house.

Part of the potency of this moment is that it is untranslatable. The reader is given a brilliant flash of insight which is beyond paraphrase or abstraction. The only way to retrieve it is to tell the story all over again—just the same way and without leaving anything out.

It's true that the story as a whole should furnish the reader with sufficient context to answer the two questions the Lovell men can't answer: why did Jess pull such a complicated stunt? and why did Helen Ruth respond to the deception as she did?

The answer requires the reader to do something that Helen Ruth has learned to do at this point: enter into Jess's point of view. The Lovell family has outgrown her, the children are embarrassed by her status as a member of the family, she's no longer getting much return on her investment in the family, so she's virtually forced to move on. But because of the "gulf" to which Helen Ruth alludes, none of these truths can be stated overtly. Therefore Jess has to concoct this dramatic parting scene in order to show what she really does feel about leaving the Lovell family. The scene is utterly false in its facts and absolutely true in its emotions. Helen Ruth understands all this and meets Jess halfway. Both women tacitly agree to a stratagem which allows them to show what they really feel for each other in ways that would otherwise be impossible, thus winning a momentary respite from "the loneliness from which everybody, knowingly or unknowingly, suffered."

And yet that bit of interpretation only goes to show that dissection usually kills the subject. It's true enough but it's also dead. To apprehend the story fully, we have to return within that final moment to feel all its complex resonances instantaneously, as Helen Ruth feels them, without subjecting them to the torture of analysis.

NOTES

1. There's no first-person narrator here—the story is told from the perspective of third-person omniscience—but the voice telling the story is so personable that it almost seems as if there is a first-person narrator on the stage. The presence of the personality telling the story is palpable. The speaker buttonholes you, talks to you directly. The pleasant conversational tone and the little asides—for instance, the enumeration of the children—enhance this effect.

2. The preceding paragraph of description is couched in the imperfect tense. Habitual action is being described; there were many such knockers on the door, not just one. Therefore whoever's "standing there, smiling and holding out a piece of paper," is not a particular individual but a generic presence, and yet the particularity of the detail ("the illegible note scribbled with a blunt lead pencil") forces us to picture some individual.

   In this context, the dialogue between Helen Ruth and her son is not something they said to each other on one particular occasion but an example of the sorts of things they said on many typical occasions. The whole passage is not really a particular scene, but general summary—but the specificity of the description and the brief flash of actual quoted dialogue make this an excellent example of a "half-scene." The use of scenic details and dialogue help keep the story's many long summary passages from seeming dry and dull.

3. Out of the generic type of knockers on the Lovell door emerges this specific individual, Jess McGehee, who's somehow different from all the others. We don't know exactly what distinguishes her from the undifferentiated cluster of others who came, but our curiosity is piqued because Helen Ruth does recognize some difference, perhaps without knowing herself just what it is she's responding to. Jess's arrival is a specific scene which happened one time only . . .

4. . . . but after this one paragraph the story cuts back into general summa-

ry, punched up by half-scene details (the particular objects which are moved from the maid's room) and by Helen Ruth's dialogue lines (which once again represent what she typically *would say* instead of what she *said* on some single occasion).

5. John R.'s first appearance is analogous to the shadowy appearance of the cluster of knockers on the door. His image begins to form out of the welter of summary information, and somehow we are hearing examples of his typical speech (whose somewhat irritatingly patronizing tone already begins to characterize him) before he's actually appeared on stage. Notice how the narrative voice doesn't need to state that John R. is Helen Ruth's husband, but simply proceeds as if we already knew that. One of the ways the narrative voice ingratiates itself with the reader is by assuming that the reader is a member of the fictional community and knows something about the Lovells already.

6. At the end of this paragraph, the story circles back, almost imperceptibly, to the chronological point where it began: the particular moment when Sarah left the Lovells to get married. As it proceeds, the story will describe further expanding circles in time, going deeper into the past and further into the future with each expansion. These looping movements seem desultory, unplanned; they partake of the casual manner of someone telling an anecdote (an effect which is strengthened by the personality of the narrative voice). However, the story's circularity is not at all random, and with each loop the narrative voice makes more connections with the story's substructural armature, as we will see.

7. This paragraph announces the shape the story is going to take. Eventually we will trace the history of the Lovells' relations with all their servants, up through Jess McGehee and beyond.

8. The story circles back to the present as John R. congratulates himself and the family on Jess. We haven't really *seen* John R. at all—there's not one line of physical description—but through these lines of his typical speech we get a quite vivid impression of his character: pontifical and more than a little smug.

9. The cut back to summary continues to lay out the chronological frame of the story—what generally happened during Jess's eight years with the family.

10. At the paragraph's end, there's a shift into half-scene.

11. And across this passage of dialogue we imperceptibly move into the full scene . . .

12. . . . which climaxes with Jess's punchline here.

13. Another full scene. The movement from summary through half-scene to full scene is so smooth a casual reader would not notice it at all.

14. Notice the rendering of dialect speech. Jess's lines aren't a forest of vari-

ant spellings and punctuation. One idiom, "a spell," and one word of Southern Black English, "torectly," are sufficient to let us hear just how she sounds.

15. Attention shifts from Jess's action to John R.'s reaction, and his character deepens for us, when we learn that he can, sometimes, listen as well as lecture and that he is capable of humility.

16. This little episode strikes John R. as significant enough that he won't turn it into an anecdote for entertainment purposes, although he does distort it in a couple of different ways, making it an exemplary story in one context and an instructional story in another.

17. A touch of free association in the last sentence of the paragraph . . .

18. . . . allows a transition into the subject of Helen Ruth's frustrated desire to drive. Note that it's the personalized quality of the narrative voice that makes these transitions possible; in a more neutrally toned text, these shifts of subject would seem very weird and distracting, like the obnoxious skipping of a scratched record.

19. This summary paragraph tells us a great deal about the society of the time and these three particular people who live in it, Helen Ruth, John R. . . . .

20. . . . and Jane Blakemore. Through dialogue we shift from summary directly to full scene this time.

21. The story has circled back to its chronological beginning: Jane Blakemore is the first servant the Lovells have in their married life.

22. Here that amiable narrative voice begins to evince a sort of Jamesian unreliability. Helen Ruth's speech in the preceding paragraph may sound "plain," but it certainly isn't telling the truth about what she thinks and feels. And the narrative voice participates in her evasion.

23. This "plain-spoken" conversation goes beyond butter plates. Mistress and maid are each trying to assert themselves and define their relationship with each other via this tiny power struggle.

24. Helen Ruth wins . . . sort of. It would be a little silly to read this story from a strict racialist or feminist perspective—there's no *major* suffering or oppression here. Still, the deployment of social forces is very plain indeed, and there's a certain perfectly ordinary awfulness to the situation. Of course John R.'s remark is a bit ridiculous—Helen Ruth is driving Jane Blakemore, not herself, and yet she is somehow being driven in her turn by some ill-defined and arbitrary social standard. From this situation real unhappiness will eventually result.

25. The story circles forward to its generalized present: Jess McGehee's tenure. The comparison between the two maids is the mechanism for this shift in time. And in general all the talk about the maids serves as a pretext for importing more exposition into the story.

26. And now the story loops backward in its chronology. We begin to sense

that the Lovells' marriage is divided (like Chinese dynasties) into periods named for maids:

Jane Blakemore
Carrie
Sarah
Jess McGehee

So now we're entering phase 2—the Carrie period. The maids are used (among other things) as chronological markers, defining the schedule of the story.

27. Helen Ruth defines herself in relation to her maids, by contrast or by commonality. They function as a kind of backboard off which she can bounce statements about herself. As previously: is it possible that Helen Ruth worries that she herself is as much "an ignoramus from Thornton, Tennessee" as Jane Blakemore?

28. Again, the narrative voice introduces the topic of the Lovells' separation in a tone that assumes we already know something about it.

29. This passage characterizes Carrie very efficiently as a good foul-weather friend; when all is well she's undependable and somewhat dishonest, but if there's a *real* crisis, she's someone Helen Ruth can really count on. Although that's a positive quality in Carrie, it's acutely uncomfortable for Helen Ruth, because it forces her to admit that the crisis *is* real, something she'd much prefer to deny. We begin to feel that there's something tortured in her relationships with her servants—regarding which the most important elements are seldom named or spoken of.

30. As this long passage segues from summary to full scene—the iconic tableau where Helen Ruth watches Carrie and Jane watch her—the mistress-servant power relationship is inverted. Helen Ruth is living in a fishbowl, helpless object of the scrutiny of her maids. What goes around comes around, you might say.

31. We don't yet know *why* Helen Ruth is so miserable, and in all likelihood neither does she. We simply know that she *is* miserable. The root causes will be discovered through hindsight.
    Has she really "misused these women?" Why ask herself that question now?

32. It's unbearable for Helen Ruth to be an "object of pity" in the eyes of her maids. Better that she should go back to her husband and at least keep up appearances. And yet there is a reciprocity in this pity. The maids are not just catalysts for changes in the marriage; they approach the status of members of the marriage.

33. The story continues to move forward along the line of its chronology, toward the end of the Carrie period.

34. And here's another problem with Carrie, perhaps the major problem: she

understands Helen Ruth's motives *too* well, and will give voice to things
Helen Ruth doesn't want said at all. That characteristic is most threatening at the time of the separation, but though Carrie is certainly smart
enough to understand the reasons for the trip, she's also loyal enough
(when the crisis is real) not to say anything about it.

35. The story loops backward, to the Jane Blakemore period again. Each
repeated movement across the same chronological terrain tells us more
about the Lovells and their marriage.

36. We begin to understand that, at least in the first phases of the marriage,
Helen Ruth sees more of her maids than she does of her husband.
Perhaps she feels, in this period of discontent, that she even has more in
common with her maids than with the social-climbing John R., since
Carrie and Jane Blakemore both come from Thornton, like Helen Ruth's
childhood friends.

37. Cousin Mamie only has a cameo role in this story, but look how thoroughly she's introduced. This chunk of novelistic exposition tells us more
about John R.'s family, and by implication about John R. and his current
social-climbing tendencies. We are also prepared for the notion that
Cousin Mamie may be much more genuinely "plainspoken" than Helen
Ruth.

38. Like Helen Ruth's earlier remark to Jane Blakemore about the butter
plates, these platitudes about her marriage sound forthright, but actually
are evasions of her real unhappiness.

39. Now here's some real plain speaking.

40. Now Nancy and Lucy are somehow picking up the platitudes that Helen
Ruth uses to justify the situation in her marriage. Where in the world did
they get them from?

41. Helen Ruth doesn't immediately have an answer to that question, but she
does know that the platitudes are a lot less comforting when they come
from mouths other than her own. It's a goldfish bowl effect similar to what
happens in Thornton (see note 30, above); Helen Ruth feels herself the
object of her friends' observation and (because she knows at heart that
her platitudes are evasions) perhaps of their pity. That sensation sends
her away from the marriage, while a similar sensation during the Thornton
episode sends her back.

   Note how the Cousin Mamie episode is prior in the chronology of
events but later in the order of presentation. The fluidity of the narrative
voice allows the writer a great deal of freedom to deviate from the linear
schedule of the plot.

42. On this pass through the separation episode, we pick up what may be the
most important detail of it: Helen Ruth left John R. an unmistakeable challenge (true plain speaking from her at last!), but he never, ever, acknow-

ledged it. How awful it must have been for her to return under those conditions . . .

43. . . . and this throwaway line underscores that awfulness. Helen Ruth is
     powerless to change her life.

44. Carrie's "confession" is certainly gruesome, but also irrelevant to Helen
     Ruth's serious problems.

45. The scene harks back to Helen Ruth's question from the Thornton
     episode: "had she really misused these women?" Here she has the oppor-
     tunity to make a grand symbolic statement: *Your behavior is intolerable—out
     of this house immediately*! She has power enough to get that message
     through to Carrie, but not to John R. There is an element of misuse in
     using the maids as accomplices and/or whipping persons in the difficulties
     of her marriage. Helen Ruth's unconscious sense of that injustice makes
     her restrain herself from "saying all the things that one normally said . . ."
     etc.

46. We're back to Sarah, the penultimate maid, so we're making progress
     through the chronology of the story.

47. Annoyingly patronizing though he seldom fails to be, John R. has raised an
     interesting point here.

48. On the bare face of it, Sarah seems to share many of the faults of Jane
     Blakemore and Carrie, but somehow Helen Ruth has become less sensi-
     tive to her defects and more sensitive to her virtues.

49. And this afterthought reveals one of the hazards of using your maid as a
     backboard for self-defensive statements: they spread all over town. In one
     sense, the society Helen Ruth inhabits is almost excessively concerned
     with maintaining decorum; in another sense, there's no privacy for anyone,
     mistress or maid.

50. During the Sarah period, Helen Ruth enters a kind of wisdom of resigna-
     tion, accepting things that can't be changed, and recognizing that John R.'s
     "attachment" is as real as his neglect. There are other compensations for
     her now . . .

51. . . . and also, the example of Sarah shows her that some wives have it a
     whole lot worse than she does.

52. Somehow Helen Ruth has evolved into a much stronger person than the
     insecure young woman who could barely manage to outface her own ser-
     vant over butter dishes . . .

53. . . . and maybe a wiser person too. Because she's right about this. It really
     is a boon to Sarah to make the final break with Morse . . .

54. . . . though it turns into a final break with the Lovells too.

55. At last we return to the story's general present: the Jess McGehee peri-
     od. In its most general outline, the story's structure has gone through
     some very conventional moves:

> 1. set the present scene
> 2. backtrack to cover exposition
> 3. return to present scene

Move 2 is a lot longer than we're accustomed to find in modern short stories—it constitutes the bulk of this story, in fact—and its subdivisions are much more complicated than usual. But the overall pattern is very familiar.

56. Real adversity brings out the best in John R. (as it did in Carrie). It turns him into the kind of husband Helen Ruth originally wanted. And the reader can respect him for not whining over his financial reverses (even if he does whimper a little about his back).

57. Are they delighted with Jess because Jess is so good or because the marriage has generally become happier? Probably a little of both.

58. But what about Jess herself?

59. Her whole being is enmeshed in the Lovells' life, so that nothing is hers that isn't theirs first.

60. And Helen Ruth (whose character has deepened over the years) can foresee that this may become a problem.

61. The one thing that engages Jess apart from "her white family" is movies and movie stars.

62. The boys are the most weakly characterized people in the story, indistinguishable from each other, less vividly rendered than Cousin Mamie even. Their fuzziness isn't a mistake; it's intended to make the boys vague and distant from Helen Ruth just as they are vague and distant from the reader. And John R.'s remark suggests that they are growing into replicas of their father.

63. It may be that as the boys grow away from Jess they also grow away from Helen Ruth.

64. Is it possible that Helen Ruth really is closer to her maids than to the other members of her family? Certainly there are circumstantial reasons that might be so.

65. Here the story shifts out of its generalized summary of the Jess McGehee period and into its culminating present scene.

66. Almost every piece of plot information given in this story's long expository middle is revised substantially by hindsight; the circular movement of the narration is the device that allows hindsight to operate. This bit of high melodrama between Jess, the telephone, and Helen Ruth will also be quite drastically affected by hindsight. But for the moment it is simply an excellent payoff on the suspense generated by the first allusion to the telephone call, during the shift out of general summary.

67. What is the nature of this mysterious change? The effect is one of separation—two women over here and four men way over there.

68. Now suspense starts building toward some other mystery. The other

parts of the story, its long phases of brilliantly rendered summary, don't have much requirement for suspense, but now when it's needed it comes on very strong.

69.   And the suspense is resolved by this 180-degree reversal.

70.   Only it isn't quite resolved after all. The last question has to do with Helen Ruth's attitude. Why isn't she furious? After all, when she found Carrie had been deceiving her (with much less fanfare than Jess has just displayed), she slung her out of the house without even letting her get her coat and hat.

71.   And here's where all that lengthy exposition, and the exceedingly complex time-management strategy required to deliver it, really pays off. At the end, everything is concentrated on this present moment, which is very brief— the few seconds Helen Ruth pauses before pushing the teacart back into the house and considers what she can say. But the density of this moment shows the immanence of the past in the present, and shows how Helen Ruth's every slightest word or gesture is informed by all her history.

72.   After all she can't really say what needs to be said. Her husband and children haven't really shared the experience of her life (though they have been physically present for it)—they don't have the context that Helen Ruth and the reader do. But although the focus of this conclusion is on a universal loneliness that can't be bridged, you couldn't really call it an unhappy ending. It's a Joycean epiphany, a moment in which Helen Ruth is able to witness all the elemental truths of her life, even if she can't share the moment with her family. She can share the moment with the reader ... and maybe she has already shared it with Jess McGehee.

DAISY'S VALENTINE

M A R Y   G A I T S K I L L

Joey felt that his romance with Daisy might ruin his life, but that didn't stop him. He liked the idea in fact. It had been a long time since he'd felt his life was in danger of further ruin, and it was fun to think it was still possible.[1]

He worked with Daisy in the clerical department of a filthy secondhand bookstore on the Lower East Side of Manhattan. The department was a square-tiled space between morose gray metal stacks of books and a dirty wall with thin white pipes running along the bottom of it.[2] There were brown boxes of books everywhere, scatterings of paper, ashtrays, Styrofoam cups, broken chairs, the occasional flashing mouse. Customers roamed the boundaries of the area, searching for the exit. Daisy, who sat nearest the bordering aisle, was always leaving her desk to sweetly assist some baffled old man with a sweating face and cockeyed glasses.[3]

Joey's desk was a bare diagonal yard from Daisy's, and he would pace from there to the watercooler staring at her, rattling the epilepsy identification plates he wore around his neck and sighing. Then he would sit at his desk and shoot rubber bands at her.[4] She usually wouldn't notice what he was doing until he'd surrounded her typewriter with red rubber squiggles. She'd look up and smile in her soft, dopey way, and continue shuffling papers with slow, long-fingered movements.[5]

He had watched Daisy for almost a year before making a pass at her. He had been living with Diane for eight years and was reluctant to change anything that stable. Besides, he loved Diane. They'd had such a good eight years that by now it was almost a system.[6]

He had met Diane at Bennington. He'd been impressed by her reputation in the art department, by the quality of the LSD she sold and by her rudeness. She was a tall, handsome thirty-three-year-old woman with taut, knit-together shoulders, and was so tense that her muscles were held scrunched together all the time. As a result, she was very muscular, even though she didn't do anything but lie around the loft and take drugs. He supported her by working in the bookstore as an accountant and by selling drugs. She helped out with the government checks she received as a certified mentally ill person.[7]

They got high on Dexedrine for three and a half days out of the week. They'd been doing it religiously the whole time they'd been together. On Thursday morning, Joey's first working day, they would start. Joey would work at the store all day, and then come home and work on projects. He would take apart his computer and spread it all over the floor in small gray lumps. He would squat and play with the piles for hours before he'd put it back together. He'd do other things too. He once took a series of blue-and-white photos of the cow skeleton they had in the living room. He'd make tapes of noises that he thought sounded nice together. He'd program the computer. Sometimes he would just take his wind-up toys out of the toy chest and run them around while he listened to records. In the past, Diane would work on her big blobby paintings. By Sunday the loft floor would be scattered with wax papers covered with splotches of acrylic paint, sprayed with water and running together in dull purple streams. She used to work on a painting for months and then destroy it. Now she didn't paint at all. Instead she used her staying-up time to watch TV, walk the dogs or work out biorhythm charts on the computer.[8]

On Sunday Joey would come home from work with bags under his eyes and his tendons standing out in funny ways. Diane would have two small salads ready in matching red bowls that her grandmother had given her. There would always be a moist radish neatly sliced and split apart on the top. They would eat the salad and go to sleep until Monday night. Then Diane would order sushi from the Japanese take-out place on the corner and arrange it on a long wooden chopping block when it came. They would cover it with salt and lemon and eat it with their fingers. Sometimes people would come over to buy drugs and they would play them records and chat. Then they would sleep. By Thursday morning they would be refreshed and ready to stay awake again until Sunday.[9]

They made love about once a month. It didn't last long because they both thought it was monotonous and because Diane was disgusted by most of the things people do to stretch it out longer. However, when Joey started to think about Daisy he stopped making romantic advances to Diane at all, and she resented it.[10]

She resented other things too. She was annoyed by his wind-up toys. If he left them out on the floor, she'd kick them. She didn't like the frozen pecan rolls he ate on Wednesday morning. She would complain about how revolting they looked, and then eat half of them.[11]

Daisy was living with somebody too, but she ran around the bookstore babbling about her unfaithfulness as if it were the only thing she had to talk about. He liked to watch her pattering from desk to desk in her white sneakers, her jeans rasping softly between her small thighs with each narrow stride. She had to know what Evelyn and Ariel and everyone else around her thought about so-and-so not calling when he said he would. Then she wanted to know what they thought of her calling him and swearing at him. Or something like that. Her supervisor, Tommy, tolerated her because he was the kind of gay man who liked to hear about girls' romantic problems. He disapproved of her running around behind her boyfriend's back, but he enjoyed having the chance to moralize each time some new man dragged her through the dirt, as she put it. Daisy would say, "Tommy, I'm trying to make him leave. He won't go. I can't do anything about it."[12]

Joey had once heard Tommy admit to another supervisor that Daisy was a terrible worker. "But she's a very special case," said Tommy. "I'd never fire her. What else could she do?"[13]

Joey felt a pang of incredulous affection. Could she actually be less competent than the other bums in the typing pool? Everyone in it was a bad worker, except Evelyn. Evelyn was the only other girl there. She was an energetic, square-jawed woman who could type eighty words a minute. She wore tight jeans and cowboy shirts and thick black eyeliner that gathered in blobs in the corners of her eyes. Her streaked blond hair hung in her face and made her look masked and brutal. She had a collection of books about various mass murderers on her desk, and she could tell you all their personal histories.[14]

The other three typists were fat, morose homosexuals who sat at their desks and ate from bags of cookies and complained. They had worked in the bookstore for years and they all talked desperately of "getting out." Ariel had been around the longest. He was six feet three inches tall and had round, demure shoulders, big hips and square fleshy breasts that embarrassed him. He had a small head, a long, bumpy nose and large brown eyes that were by turns sweetly candid or forlorn, but otherwise had a disturbing blank quality. He had enjoyed a brief notoriety in punk rock circles for his electric piano music. He talked about his past success in a meek, wistful voice, and showed people old pictures of himself dressed in black, wearing black wing-tipped sunglasses. He was terribly sensitive, and Tommy took advantage of his sensitivity to make fun of him. "Ariel is the spirit of the typing pool," Tommy would chatter as he ran from clerk to clerk with stacks of papers. "Whenever any of you are craving inspiration, just gaze on Ariel."[15]

"Please, Tom, I'm on the verge of tears," Ariel would answer funereally.

"That's exactly what I'm talking about!" Tommy would scream.

When Joey first noticed Daisy, he wondered why this pretty young woman had chosen to work in a filthy, broken-down store amid unhappy homosexuals. As time went on, it seemed less and less inappropriate.[16] She was comfortable in the typing pool. She was happy to listen to the boys talk about their adventures in leather bars, where men got blow jobs in open wooden booths or pissed on other men. She told jokes about Helen Keller and sex. She talked about her boyfriends and her painting. She was always crouching at Evelyn's desk, whispering and laughing about something, or looking at Evelyn's back issues of *True Detective* magazine. She wore T-shirts with pictures of cartoon characters on them, and bright-colored pants. Her brown hair was bobbed in a soft curve that ended on either side of her high cheekbones. When she walked, her shoulders and long neck were erect in a busy, almost ducklike way, but her hips and waist were fluid and gently mobile.[17]

The heterosexual men were always coming to stand by her desk and talk to her about their poetry or political ideas while she looked at them and nodded. Even the gay men developed a certain bravado in her presence.[18] Tommy kept on reassuring her that her prince was just around the corner. "I can feel it, Daisy," he would say exultantly. "You're on a collision course with Mr. Right!"

"Do you really think so, Tom?"

"It's obvious! Aren't you excited?"

Then Ariel would get up from his desk and lumber over to her and, bending from the waist, would put his large fleshy arms around her shoulders. Joey could see her small white hand emerge on Ariel's broad flank as she patiently patted him.[19]

And, as if it weren't enough to be the heartthrob of the basement crowd, she was kind to helpless, repulsive people. There was a grotesque old woman who would come into the store from time to time to seek out her kindness. The woman was at least sixty years old, and covered her face with heavy orange makeup. She bought horrible best-sellers and self-help books with lurid red covers. She'd stand by Daisy's desk for half an hour and talk to her about how depressed she was. Daisy would turn off her typewriter and turn toward the woman with her chin in her hand. She'd listen gravely, agreeing sometimes, letting the woman give her small bags of hard candy and kiss her on the cheek. Everyone made rude comments about Daisy and "that crazy old dyke." But Daisy remained courteous and attentive to the distressed creature, even though she often made fun of her after she left.[20]

Joey didn't think of having sex with Daisy, at least not in detail. It was more the idea of being near her, protecting her.[21] She was obviously so confused. She looked everywhere for answers, for someone to tell her what to think. "I just want your perspective," she'd say.

There was a customer she called the "answer man" because he claimed that he could predict the future through "automatic handwriting." He was a handsome elderly man who wore expensive suits and looked as though he'd had at least one face lift. He had been coming into the store for years. Every time he came in, Daisy would walk him off into a corner and ask him questions. He would scrawl down answers in thin red ink and hand them to her with an imperious, terribly personal look. She would become either stricken or joyous. Later she would run around talking about what he'd said, examining the red-scrawled pieces of store stationery. "He says my painting is going to start being successful in a year and a half." "He says there are no worthwhile men around me and that there won't be for months." "He says David will move out next month."

"You don't take that stuff seriously, do you?" asked Joey.

"Oh, not really," she said. "But it's interesting." She went back to her desk and stuck the papers in her drawer and began typing, her face still glowing and upturned because someone who was possibly crazy had told her that she would eventually be a success.[22]

He began thinking about her at home. He thought of her body resting against his, of his arm around her. He thought of her dressed in a white kimono, peeking from behind a fan, her eye makeup crinkling when she smiled. Diane became suspicious.[23]

"You're a thousand miles away," she said over the Sunday salad.[24] "What is it?"

"I'm preoccupied." His tone made it clear that her plaintiveness was futile, and she became frightened and angry. She didn't say anything, which was what he wanted.[25]

He did not lie down with her that evening, although he was exhausted. He walked around the loft, striking the furniture with Diane's riding crop, annoying the cats, making them skitter across the floor, their eyes unnerved, their tails ruffled. His eyes dried in their sockets. His back was sore and balled into knots from staying up for three days.[26]

He began doing things to attract Daisy's attention. He told jokes. He slapped his face with eau de toilette. He wore red pants and a sheathed knife in his belt. He did full splits and handstands. He talked about his active role in the theater department at Bennington and his classes with André Gregory. He mentioned the karate class he'd taken once, and punched a hole in a box of books. She said, "Joey has done everything!" There was a thrilling note of triumph in her voice.[27]

For a long time he just looked at her. That alone made him so happy, he was afraid to try anything else. Maybe it would be better to hold her winglike shadow safe in the lock of his memory than to touch the breathing girl and lose her.[28]

He decided to give her a card on Valentine's Day.[29]

He spent days searching for the valentine material. He found what he

wanted in an old illustrated children's book. It was a faded watercolor drawing
of three red poppies sharing a field with pink clover and some blameless little
weeds. A honey-colored bee with dreamily closed eyes was climbing a stalk. An
aqua-green grasshopper was flying through a fuzzy, failing blue sky, its eyes
blissfully shut, its hairy front legs dangling foolishly, its hind legs kicking, exul-
tant, through the air. It was a distorted, feverish little drawing. The colors were
all wrong. It made him think of paradise.[30]

He tore it from the book and covered it with a piece of fragile paper so that
the scene, veiled by the yellowing tissue haze, became remote and mysterious.
He drew five hearts in misshapen lines and senselessly alternating sizes on the
bottom of it. He colored them red. He wrote *"Voici le temps des assassins"*
under them.[31]

He carried it to work with him for several days before and after Valentine's
Day. He decided dozens of times to give it to her, and changed his mind every
time. He examined it daily, wondering if it was good enough. When he decided it was perfect, he thought perhaps it would be better to keep it in his drawer, where he alone knew it existed for her.[32]

Finally, he said, "I have a valentine for you."

She pattered around his desk, smiling greedily. "Where is it?"

"In my drawer. I don't want to give it to you yet."

"Why not? Valentine's Day was a week ago. Can't I have it now?" She put
her fingers on his shoulders like soft claws.[33] "Give it to me now."

When he handed it to her, she hugged him and pressed against him. He
giggled and put his arm around her. He sadly let go of his shadow captive.[34]

That night he couldn't eat his spinach salad. The radish, gaily flowering red
and white, was futile enticement.[35] Diane sat across from him, stonily working
her jaws. She sat rigidly straight-backed, her throat drawn so taut it looked as if
it would be hard for her to swallow. He picked at the salad, turning the clean
leaves this way and that. He stared past her, sighing, his dry eyes hot in their
sockets.

"You look like an idiot," she said.

"I am."[36]

The next day he took Daisy out to lunch, although he couldn't eat. He
ordered a salad, which appeared in a beige plastic bowl. It was littered with pale
carrot curls and flats of radish that accused him.[37] He ignored it. He watched
her eat from her dish of green and white cold noodles. They were curly and
glistened with oil, and were garnished with bright pieces of slippery meat and
vegetables. Daisy speared them serenely, three curls at a time.

"You can't imagine how wonderful this is for me," he said. "I've watched
you for so long."

She smiled, he thought, uncertainly.

"You're so soft and gentle. You're like a delicate white flower."

"No I'm not."

"I know you're probably not. But you seem like it, and that's good enough for me."[38]

"What about Diane?"

"I'll leave Diane."

She put down her fork and stared at him. The chewing movement of her jaws was earnest and sweet. He smiled at her.

She swallowed, a neat, thorough swallow. "Don't leave Diane," she said.[39]

"Why not? I love you."

"Oh dear," she said. "This is getting out of hand. Why don't you eat your salad?"

"I can't. I'm medicated."[40]

"You're what?"

He forced himself to eat the pale leaves and shreds of carrot.

They left the restaurant and walked around the block. Daisy butted her head against the harsh wind; her short gray coat floated in back of her like a sail. He held her mittened hand. "I love you," he said. "I don't care about anything else. I want to cast my mantle of protection over you."[41]

"Let's sit here," she said. She sat down on an even rise of yellow brick in front of an apartment building that was an impression of yellow brick and shadowy gray glass shielding the sad blur of a doorman.[42] He sat very near her and held her hand.

"I have to tell you some things about myself," she said. "I don't take admiration very well."

"I don't care if you take it well or not. It's there."

"But won't it make you unhappy if I don't return it?"[43]

"I'd be disappointed, I guess. But I'd still have the pleasure of feeling it for you. It doesn't have to be returned."[44] He wanted to put his hands on either side of her head and squeeze.[45]

She looked at him intently. "I said that to someone recently," she said. "Do you suppose it's a trend of some kind?"

The wind blew away her bangs, baring her white forehead. He kissed the sudden openness. She dropped her head against his shoulder.

An old woman in a pink coat bearing a sequined flower with a disturbing burst of petals on her lapel looked at them and smiled. Her white face was heavy with wrinkles and pink makeup, and her smile seemed difficult under the weight. She sat on the short brick wall about two feet away from them.[46]

"I'm not making myself clear," said Daisy. She lifted her head and looked at him with wide, troubled eyes. "If you're nice to me, I'll probably make you unhappy. I've done that to people."

"You couldn't make me unhappy."

"I'm only nice to people who are mostly mean to me. Once somebody told me to stay away from so-and-so because he beat up girls. They said he broke his girlfriend's jaw."

She paused, for emphasis, he supposed. The old lady was beginning to look depressed.

"So I began flirting with him like wild. Isn't that sick?"

"What happened?" asked Joey with interest.

"Nothing. He went to Bellevue before anything could. But isn't it awful? I actually wanted this nut to hit me." She paused again. "Aren't you disgusted?"[47]

"Oh, I don't know."

The old lady rose slowly, head down, and walked away with stiff, painful steps. Her coat blew open; her blue-veined legs were oddly pretty.

Daisy turned to watch her. "See," she said. "She's disgusted even if you aren't. We've ruined her day."[48]

Every day after work, he walked Daisy to a corner two blocks away from her apartment so he wouldn't meet her boyfriend, David. There was a drugstore on the corner with colored perfume bottles nesting in fistfuls of crepe paper in the window. The druggist, a middle-aged man with a big stomach and a disappointed face, stood at the door and watched them say good-bye. It was a busy corner; traffic ran savagely in the street, and people stamped by, staring in different directions, clutching their packages, briefcases and huge, screaming radios, their faces concentrated but empty. Daisy was silent and frail as a cattail, her fuzzy black mitten in Joey's hand, her eyes anxiously scanning the street for David. She would say good-bye to him several times, but he would pull her back by her lapel as she turned to cross the street.[49] After the second time he stopped her, she would sigh and look down, then begin to go through her pockets for scraps of unwanted paper, which she tore into snowflake pieces and scattered like useless messages in the garbage-jammed metal wastebasket under the street lamp, as if, trapped on the corner, she might as well do something useful, like clean her pockets.[50]

That day, when he finally let her go, he stood for a moment and watched her pat across the street, through the awful march of people. He walked half a block to a candy store with an orange neon sign, and bought several white bags of jelly beans. Then he caught a cab and rode home like a sultan. He ignored Diane's bitter stare as he walked through the living room and shut himself up in the bedroom with his jelly beans.[51]

He thought of rescuing Daisy. She would be walking across the street, with that airy, unaware look on her face. A car would roar around a garbage-choked corner, she would freeze in its path, her pale face helpless as a crouching rabbit. From out of nowhere he would leap, sweeping her aside with one arm, knocking them both to the sidewalk, to safety, her head cushioned on his arm.

Or she would be accosted by a hostile teenager who would grab her coat and push her against a wall. Suddenly he would attack. The punk's legs would fly crazily as Joey slammed him against a crumbling brick wall. "If you hurt her, I'll . . ."[52]

He sighed happily and got another pill and a handful of jelly beans.[53]

"My mother couldn't understand me or do anything for me," he said. "She thought she was doing the right thing."

"She sounds like a bitch," said Daisy.

"Oh, no. She did what she could, given the circumstances. She at least recognized that I far surpassed her in intelligence."

"Then why did she let her boyfriend beat you up?"

"He didn't beat me up. He was just a fat slob who got a thrill out of putting a twelve-year-old in a half nelson and then asking how it felt."[54]

"He beat you up."

They were in a small, dark bar. It had floors and tables made of old creaking wood, and a half-moon window of heavy stained glass in one wall. The tables were clawed with knife marks, the french fries were large and damp. The waitresses carried themselves like dinosaurs with ungainly little hands and had purple veins on their legs, even though they were young. They were friendly though, and they looked right at you.[55]

Daisy and Joey came here for lunch and sat in the deep, high-backed booths. Joey didn't eat, and by now Daisy knew why. He drank and watched her eat her hamburger with measured bites.

"I still can't understand why she married that repulsive pig. I ask her and she says 'because he makes me feel stable and secure.'"

"He doesn't sound stable to me."

"I guess he was, compared to my father. But then Dad was usually too drunk to make it down the stairs without falling, let alone hold a job. I mean, you're talking about a guy who died in the nut ward singing 'Joey, Foey, Bo-Poey, Bananarama Oh-Boey.' Any asshole is stable compared to that. But Tom? At least my father had style. He wouldn't have been caught dead in those ugly Dacron things Tom wears."

Daisy leaned into the corner of the booth and looked at him solemnly.

"When she first told me over the phone that she was getting married to Uncle Tom, I was happy. At least I'd get to come home instead of staying with my Christian Scientist relatives who made me wear those retarded plaid pants to school."

"She never should have sent you away like that," said Daisy. She sat up and pulled her drink closer, latching on to the straw with a jerking motion of her lip.

"She thought it was the right thing to do after my father died. Only she never knew how much my relatives hated me."

"I don't know how she could've thought it was the right thing to let him throw you out of the house when you were sixteen."

"He didn't throw me out. I just knew the constant fighting over whether or not I was a faggot was hurting my mother. I realized that I was more of an adult than they were and that it was up to me to change the situation."[56]

Daisy leaned back with both hands on her glass as she sucked the straw, her cheeks palpitating gently. There were dainty gurgle noises coming from the bottom of her glass as she slurped the last of her drink. He smiled and took her hand. She squeezed his fingers. He gulped his alcohol, his pulse beating wildly to and fro. He hadn't really been thrown out of the house when he was sixteen. He had been eighteen when Tom went berserk at the sight of his anti-Vietnam poster and broke his nose.[57]

Daisy put her glass on the table with a slurred movement. She leaned against him. He cradled her head and ordered more drinks.

"They couldn't believe it when I got that scholarship to Bennington. I didn't even tell them I applied. They already felt inferior to me."[58]

"Did you drop out of college to get back at your mother?" Her voice was blurry from his shoulder.

"I dropped out because I couldn't stand the people. I couldn't stand the idea of art. Art is only good at the moment it's done. After that it's dead. It's just so much dead shit. Artists are like people trying to hoard their shit."[59]

She sat away from him, reaching for her new glass. "I'm an artist. Diane is an artist. Why do you like us?"[60]

He kissed the blue vein on her neck and enjoyed the silly beat of his heart. "You're like a pretty shadow."[61]

Her eyes darted with worry. "You like me because I'm like you."

He smiled tolerantly and stroked her neck. "You're not like me. No one is like me. I'm a phenomenon."

She looked tired and turned away from him to her drink. "You're a misfit. So am I. We don't belong anywhere."[62]

"Aww." He reached under her shirt and touched her small breast. She put her forehead against his neck, she put her hand between his legs. Her voice fluttered against his skin. "David has a gig out of town next week. Will you come stay with me?"

"Maybe."[63]

Sometimes, though, he thought Daisy was sort of a stupid little thing. He thought it when he looked at Diane and noticed the stern, distinct line of her mouth, her strong nose, the muscles of her bared arms flexing as she furiously picked her nails. She didn't ask annoying questions about drugs. She never thought about being a misfit, or having a place in society. She loathed society.

She sat still as a stone, her heavy-lidded eyes impassively half-closed, the incli-
nation of her head in beautiful agreement with her lean, severe arm and the
cigarette resting in her intelligent fingers.[64]

But it was too late. Diane wouldn't talk to him anymore, except to insult
him. She changed her medication days so she wouldn't be on schedule with
him. Sometimes she didn't medicate at all. She said it made her cry.[65]

He found her crying one day when he came home from work. It was so
rare to see Diane cry that it was several minutes before he realized there were
tears on her face. She was sitting in the aging purple armchair by the window,
one leg drawn up and bent so that her knee shielded her face. Her shoulders
were in a tight curl, she held her long bare foot tightly in her hand. She
watched him walk past her. She let him reach the doorknob before she said,
"You're seeing someone."[66]

He stopped and faced her, thankful and relieved that she had said it first.
"I meant to tell you," he said. "I didn't know how."[67]

"You cowardly piece of shit."[68]

"It's nothing serious," he said. "It's just an obsession. "

"It's Daisy, isn't it?" She said the name like it was a disease.

"How did you know?"

"The way you mentioned her name. It was sickening."

"I didn't intend for it to happen."[69]

"What a slime-bag you are."[70]

It was then that he identified the glistening on her cheeks and chin. The
tears were wrenching and poignant on her still face. He dropped his bag of jelly
beans and moved toward her. He sat on the fat arm of the chair and put his
arms around her rigid shivering body.[71] "I'm sorry," he said.

"It's like before," she said. "With Rita. It's so repulsive."

"If you can stay with me through this, just wait it out . . ."[72]

"I want you out of here by the end of the month." The tears shimmered
through her voice, which quivered like sunlight in a puddle. He wanted to
make love to her.[73]

"You're the cruelest person I've ever known." Her voice almost broke into
panting. She yanked herself out of the chair and walked away, kicking the bag
of jelly beans as she passed, spraying them across the floor.[74] He waited until
she was out of the room and then went to scoop up a handful of the red, orange
and green ones.[75] He ate them as he looked out the picture window and down
into the street. There were two junkies in ugly jackets hunched beside the
jagged hole in a wire fence. I am a slime-bag, he thought.[76]

He went to his room to think about Daisy.[77]

The next morning he went to Daisy's desk and sat near her on a box of books
bearing an unflattering chalk drawing of the shipping department supervisor.

She held her Styrofoam cup of tea with both hands and drank from it, looking over its rim with dark-shadowed eyes.

"She said I was the cruelest person she'd ever known."

"Oh, you're not so bad. She just doesn't get out of the house much. She doesn't know what's out there."[78]

"You don't know me."

She put down her cup. "I talked to David last night. He cried too. He just lay there and stared at me with those big eyes. It was awful."

She picked up a piece of cardboard and began sweeping the mouse droppings on her desk into a neat pile. "So now they both know."[79]

"And we can go to the opera tonight. I have tickets to *Die Walküre*. You can medicate and we can stay out all night."

"I don't want to medicate."[80] She pulled the sticky, coffee-stained wastebasket out from under her desk and showered the mouse turds into it with a deft swish of cardboard.

Daisy had never been to an opera. "Will there be people in breastplates and headdresses with horns?" she asked. "Will there be a papier-mâché dragon and things flying through the air?" She looked hard at the curtained stage.

"Probably not," he said. "I think this production is coming from a German Impressionist influence, which means they'll eschew costumes and scenery as much as possible. They're coming from an emphasis on symbolism and minimal design. It was a reaction against the earlier period when—"

"I want to see a dragon flying through the air." She took a pink mint from the box of opera mints he'd bought, popped it into her mouth and audibly sucked it. She shifted it to her cheek and asked, "Why do you like the opera?"[81]

"I don't know, I like the music sometimes, I like to see how they put productions together. I like to watch the people."

"So do I."

"Sometimes I have this fantasy that the opera house is suddenly taken over by psychos or terrorists or something, and that I save everybody."

She stopped sucking her mint and turned to look at him. "How?"

"I jump from the balcony railing and scale down the curtain until I'm parallel with the cord. Then I jump for the cord, swing through the air—"

"That's impossible."

"Well, yes, I know. It's a fantasy."[82]

"Why would you have a fantasy like that?" She looked disturbed.

"I don't know. It's not important."

She continued to stare at him, almost stricken. "I think it's because you feel estranged from people. You want something extreme to happen so you can show that you love them, and that you deserve love from them."[83]

He pulled her head against his shoulder and kissed it. He said,

"Sometimes I just want to tear you apart."[84]

She put her box of mints in her lap and grabbed him tightly around the waist.

It was after midnight when they left the opera. They went to a neon-lit deli manned by aging waiters wearing red jackets, several of whom had violent tics in their jaws. Daisy persuaded him to order a salad and a milk shake; she was worried that he didn't eat enough. He sipped his shake uncomfortably and watched her eat her cream cheese and salmon.[85] She talked about her unhappy relationship with her father, pausing to bend her head so she could nip up the fallen croissant flakes with her tongue. Waiters ran around the table, some of them bearing three food-loaded plates in each hairy hand.

He tried to make her take some pills and stay out with him longer, but she said she felt too guilty about David. There was also some art work she wanted to do. She sighed and looked at the ground. She pulled away from him four times before he let her go.[86] He watched her walk away and thought, "Now it's too late to buy jelly beans."[87]

When he opened the door to his apartment, Diane hit him in the face. He was so startled, he stood there and let her hit him three more times before he grabbed her wrist.

"You filthy bastard!" she screamed. "You went to the opera with her! We always go to the opera together and you went with that cunt!"[88]

"I hardly thought you wanted to go."

"Well I did. I waited for you to come home from work." Her voice hobbled tearfully. "I never thought you would go with that cunt."

"She's not a cunt."

She swung with her free hand, catching his ear. She yanked at the lobe, tearing out his tiny blue earring. It pinged on the floor, sparkled and rolled away. "Shit!" he screamed. He dropped to his knees and felt the floor with his palms. "Don't you have any self-control?"

"I don't give a shit about self-control. Get the fuck out."

"Will you just wait until I find my earring?"[89]

"I don't care about your fucking earring. Get out before I kill you."

"God, you're so irrational."

He listened for sobbing from outside the slammed door. There was none. His ear was bleeding and his face burned, but he was oddly exhilarated. He was sorry Diane was so upset, but there was something stirring about a violent tantrum.[90] It was the sort of thing he liked to tell stories about.

The street was buzzing with junkies and kids with big radios. They stood in a jumbled line against buildings and crawled out of holes in the walls and fences. They mumbled at him as he walked past. "I got the blues, I got the reds, I got the greens and blacks, the ones from last week."[91]

He walked three blocks to Eliot's apartment; he didn't expect Eliot to answer the door, but he buzzed anyway. He was startled when Eliot's suspicious voice darted from the cluster of tiny holes that served as an intercom.

"It's the F.B.I.," said Joey.

There was a grudging silence before the buzzer squawked. When Joey reached the apartment door, Eliot poked his head out, one finger to his lips. His wispy brown hair stuck out in a ratty halo; his round, thin-lashed eyes were hysterically wide and moist.[92] "Whatever you do, don't mention drugs," he whispered. "If you have to refer to them at all, say 'gum' or something. Only don't be conspicuous."

"All right," said Joey.

"They've got the place wired," explained Eliot. "We tore the apartment apart and we still can't find the bug. Are you sure you weren't followed?"

Joey nodded. Eliot stretched his neck and stared into the empty hall, blinking his damp eyes hard. Satisfied, he let Joey in.[93]

Rita was lying on the couch in front of a partially dismantled TV screen with a soundless picture on it. Her large feet hung over the edge of the couch, her hands were limp at the ends of her thin, prominently veined wrists. Her head drooped sideways on her slender, listless neck, almost falling off the couch. When she saw Joey she lifted her head, and her dark eyes lighted.[94]

He flapped his hand at her and sat on a hard-backed chair. "Diane threw me out of the house," he said.

"Yeah?" said Eliot. He got on his knees and began looking through the records scattered on the floor.

"It doesn't matter. I wanted to move anyway. I'm in love. It's all over between Diane and me."

"You should've made that decision five years ago," said Rita.[95]

Eliot whirled around, waving a record. "You've got to hear this. It's the most incredible thing."

"Oh, Jesus Christ, that record came out ten years ago," said Rita. "Just because you've only heard it for the first time."

Eliot tore the record from its jacket, tossed the jacket across the room and knelt before the turntable. He lifted the needle and examined it, blowing delicately.

Rita threw her long legs up and sat with her small bony knees together, her feet toeing in. "Who are you in love with?"

"You know, she's still showing those stupid home movies of you in the bathtub," said Eliot. "She watches them and masturbates. It's hilarious. She shows them to everybody."[96]

"Who is it?" asked Rita.

"This girl at the store named Daisy."

"Oh. I guess it figures." She leaned forward to the cluttered table for a match. Her dark hair fell across her face with the graceful motion of a folding wing. She leaned back, exposing her face again. The lines under her eyes were deep and black with smeared makeup. "Got any pills, Joe?"[97]

Eliot jumped up. "Don't say that!" he screamed.

"Oh, you asshole," said Rita. "Got any . . . socks?"

"Sure." Joey poured a colorful tumble into her palm.[98]

"What are you trying to do to me?" said Eliot through his teeth. "Are you working for them or what?"

Joey looked around; they really had torn up the apartment. Dead plants were turned over in their broken pots, slashed pillows spilled yellow foam out onto the floor, cardboard boxes lay with their lids yanked open, their contents exposed and strewn. The filing cabinet was tipped over, its open drawers freeing a white dance of paper. At least the broken bottles had been swept safely into piles.

Eliot's rare book collection was preserved in a prim stack beside the couch. Joey could see the three Bartolovs he'd sold him. Eliot had been awed when he'd discovered that Joey's pill connection was Alexander Bartolov, the famous poet.[99]

"Oh, come on Rita, just a little blow job," said Eliot. "I won't come or anything."

"Forget it," said Rita. She lay back into the couch, her spidery white hand over her eyes. Her long limp legs recalled the flying grasshopper on Daisy's valentine.

"She's still hot for you, you know," said Eliot. "I still have to hear about the times you tied her up and spanked her."[100]

"Can't we change the subject?" said Joey.

"Okay," said Eliot cheerfully. "I'm going to the bathroom anyway. I'm nauseous."

"Don't relax," said Rita. "He'll be back in a minute."

"It's all right with me," said Joey. He took a magazine off the table. It was open to a picture of a masked woman dressed in a red rubber suit that a man was inflating with a pump. On the next page, a naked girl was tied with belts in a kneeling position on a bathroom floor. An ornery-looking young fellow approached her from behind with a rubber hose; she looked over her shoulder, her lips parted in a look of coy fear. He was surprised at how pretty she was. Her cheekbones and shoulders were like Daisy's.[101]

Daisy and Joey emerged from the movie theater holding hands. "We have no place to go," said Daisy. "It's been a month since we've been alone in a room. And David won't leave." They walked, still holding hands.[102]

"I feel so terrible about David," she said. "He's such a lovely, innocent person. He's the purest person I know."

"There are no pure people. "

"You haven't seen David. He has such naked eyes. When you touch him, it's like there's nothing between you and him." She looked at him quizzically. "You're not like that. When I touch you, I don't feel you at all."[103]

"There's nothing to feel."[104]

"Don't say that about yourself." She dropped his hand and rubbed his back with her mittened hand.

"Anyway, it's good you're not like David. Even as you are, I worry about you being too nice to me."

He put his hand around her neck. "I don't know what makes you think I have any intention of being nice to you."

She turned and kissed him. He took a handful of her hair in his fist and pulled her head tautly back while he kissed her.

They sat on the cold stone steps of an apartment building. They unbuttoned their jackets and huddled together, his hands on either side of her softly sweatered body.[105]

"You're so strange," she said. "It's hard to talk to you."[106]

"How so?"

"You're always talking at me. You don't listen to what I say."

"I seem strange because I'm special."

"I think it's because you take so many pills."[107]

"You should start taking them. Did you know the government gives them to soldiers who are about to go into combat? They sharpen the reflexes, senses, everything."

"I'm not going into combat."[108]

There was a sound from above. They turned and saw a handsome, well-dressed middle-aged couple at the head of the steps. Joey saw a flicker of admiration in Daisy's face as she looked at the tall blond lady in her evening dress.[109] The couple began to descend. Daisy and Joey stood and squeezed into a stony corner to let them pass. The man's shoulder scratched against Joey. The man coughed, quite unnecessarily.

"Excuse us," said the woman. "We only live here."

"You have plenty of room," said Daisy sharply.

"You have no business being here," said the man. The couple stood on the sidewalk and frowned, their shoulders indignant.

"Why do you care?" said Daisy. "We aren't in your way." Her voice quivered oddly.

"Sssh," said Joey. "Let them live their lives. "

"You are very rude," said the woman. "If you're here when we get back, we're going to call the police." She swept away, sweeping her husband with her. They were probably in a hurry.[110]

Joey watched the woman's dress fluttering along the pavement. "That was strange," he said. "I've sat on lots of steps before and that's never happened."

Daisy didn't answer.

"I guess it's different in the East Village."

Daisy sniffed wetly.

He reached into his pocket and got out his bag of jelly beans. He offered some to Daisy, but she ignored him. Her head was down, and slow, quiet tears ran singly down her nose. He put his arms around her. "Hey, come on," he said. He felt no response from her. She didn't move or look at him.[111]

He dropped his arm and looked away, confused. He ate his jelly beans and looked at the pool of lamplight in the black street.[112]

ANALYSIS

Plot

Much more so than "A Wife of Nashville," this story is concerned with a string of events along the present time line, though the line is more straggling, less compressed, than what we find in "Depth Charge." But there is a layer of antecedent action which can be pieced together, mostly to do with Joey's past.

Backstory

The reader may reconstruct a rough but reasonably complete version of Joey's history by combining what Joey tells Daisy from time to time (though it's important to realize that this information may not be entirely trustworthy) with what the authorial voice tells us about Joey. Thus we know that Joey probably had an unhappy childhood, with an alcoholic father who died insane and a somewhat unstable mother whose boyfriend/second husband was somewhat abusive to Joey. Estranged from this "dysfunctional" family in his late teens, Joey restores some sense of order to his life by making his way into an elite private college (Bennington). There he meets Diane and forms a relationship with her which, despite its florid eccentricities, has much of the stability of a marriage and which persists into the present action of the story.

It's interesting to note that while our information about Joey's past may be spotty and sometimes hard to verify, we end up knowing a good deal more about his history than we do about Daisy's, which is sometimes vaguely alluded to but usually passed over, as if it were of small importance . . . and maybe Daisy's past isn't very important to Joey.

Present Action

Joey begins to feel attracted to his coworker Daisy. He's aware from the start that following up on this attraction is likely to "ruin his life" (i.e., overturn the queer stability of his situation with Diane); nevertheless, he does follow it up. His attraction to Daisy is extremely similar to an adolescent or even prepubescent crush. Joey spends days and weeks staring sentimentally at Daisy; at home he indulges himself in silly fantasies about her. At work, he performs ridiculous stunts to attract her attention.

Finally Joey declares his feelings to Daisy by giving her a homemade Valentine. Daisy indeed agrees to "be his Valentine," and the couple begin "dating" (so to speak). Because both Daisy and Joey have live-in lovers, there are few opportunities for the two of them to be alone together in any private space, so there are few opportunities for their relationship to be consummated sexually. In any case, sex does not seem to be very important to their relationship—nowhere as important as it usually would be in an affair powerful enough to inspire infidelity to other mates. We never know for sure whether this sexual consummation ever occurs.

What does definitely happen is that Joey's live-in mate, Diane, finds out about his relationship with Daisy, and with a degree of violent drama, throws him out of the house. Daisy, meanwhile, seems to have also confessed her fling with Joey to her live-in lover, David, but these two continue living together just the same. Thus at the end of the story the "love" between Joey and Daisy has done nothing but disrupt the home lives of both (most drastically in Joey's case) and has caused a great deal of pain to all involved—for no return, or a very minor return.

Simple and sordid—a casebook account of pointlessly self-destructive behavior. Judged by such a bare-bones plot summary, the story is almost too depressing to read.

Character

From the start, however, our interest is displaced from what's happening in the story to whom it's happening to. Not that the cast members of this story are wonderfully likeable people really, but they are portrayed with such convincing detail that the reader cannot help but be interested in them. In a Gaitskill short story we are dealing (for better or worse) with specific individuals, rather than with types or stock characters. Thus, despite the drastic difference in their background and social milieu, Gaitskill's characters resemble those of Peter Taylor much more than (for instance) the comparatively indefinite Alexis in "Depth Charge." Both Joey and Daisy are very particularized portraits—we may be interested in learning about them, as we are interested in learning about people we meet in the real world, but we are unlikely to identify ourselves with them as we might more easily do with Bernardini's Alexis.

Several different techniques of characterization are used in this story. With Joey, we often have the sense that he is being *looked at* by the writer—that some external voice is telling us about him. The half-scenes of his and Diane's home life, which establish Joey's status quo at the outset of the present action, are controlled by this exterior presence.

By contrast, our impressions of Daisy are filtered through Joey's impression of her. Yet at the same time we also have the option of seeing Daisy through the comparatively cold eye that looks at Joey. Joey's vision of Daisy is soft-focused, warm and fuzzy—and not very accurate. When we look over Joey's shoulder instead of through his deluded eyes we see that Daisy is an irresponsible (albeit sweet-natured) airhead whose sense of purpose in life is defined by such idiocies as the predictions of the "answer man."

Diane is also seen through Joey's eyes, but in her case, his picture of her seems to agree pretty well with what we might see over his shoulder. The Diane that we eventually see in action is the same as Joey's idea of Diane—forceful, abrupt, powerful, angry, and definite about everything.

Everything about Diane is hard-edged and distinct—from her bizarre muscular tension to the bizarre inflexibility of her weekly routine with Joey, where everything is precisely worked out, down to the crisp organization of her Japanese salad. Everything about Daisy is vague and unclear—uncommitted. This essential difference of personality is reflected in the extremely detailed physical descriptions of both women. Diane is large and imposing, as cleanly outlined as a classical sculpture. Daisy is small, weak, and fuzzy around the edges. Where Diane's defined personality seems for better or worse adult, Daisy's watery, unclear character makes her childlike—many descriptions of her place her in some sort of childish role. If Diane resembles a sculptured radish, Daisy is like a sweet and sticky mouthful of pink cotton candy.

Joey himself is characterized by other methods than those used for Diane and Daisy. Much less physical detail is furnished about him than about the two women—we rarely "see" Joey, except in the passage where he's wearing red pants and punching holes in boxes to impress Daisy. When he does make a physical appearance ("with bags under his eyes and his tendons standing out in funny ways," for instance), it's surprising because it's unusual. The pattern of the story places the reader behind Joey's eyes for the most part; he's the only character whose thoughts we may read directly. He is after all the main character of the story, the protagonist, though it might be difficult to describe him as a hero.

Our sense of Joey's character comes from our evolving understanding of the way his mind works; these machinations are portrayed with comprehensive fidelity but not, in the end, with terrific sympathy. His response, in the story's first paragraph, to the prospect of harming others and himself, is revealing: "It had been a long time since he'd felt his life was in danger of further ruin, and it was fun to think it was still possible." This is a quintessentially perverse reaction, and by the end of the story Joey has thoroughly lived up to all its implications. Getting to know Joey (not altogether a pleasant experience) is the key to *why* the events of the story happen (and thus a partial replacement for the conventional interest in *what* happens—the plot proper). Gradually we come to understand that Joey really meets the definition of pervert, not because of his drug habits or his (virtually unknown) sexual predilections, but because he takes a perverse pleasure in wrecking his own life and the lives of others around him.

All the bit players and bystanders in the drama, meanwhile, are given the most thorough attention. For example:

> Evelyn was the only other girl there. She was an energetic, square-jawed woman who could type eighty words a minute. She wore tight jeans and cowboy shirts and thick black eyeliner that gathered in blobs in the corners of her eyes. Her streaked blond hair hung in her face and made her look masked and brutal. She had a collection of books about various mass murderers on her desk, and she could tell you all their personal histories.

The physical impression is extraordinarily thorough and includes both appearance (the clothes, face and makeup) and a suggestion of action (the typing). The characterization is completed by the vaguely unpleasant suggestion about her inner life in the last sentence (and notice how the word "brutal" in the physical description subliminally foreshadows her interest in murderers).

It's interesting to compare this spot characterization with the handling of one of Peter Taylor's bit players: Cousin Mamie in "A Wife of Nashville." Taylor first concentrates on the character's social position, in contrast to Gaitskill's focus on Evelyn's appearance and personal taste, but the net result is the same—to convince us of this minor character's "real" existence. Evelyn is a much less significant player in Gaitskill's story than Cousin Mamie is in Taylor's—in effect Evelyn is a fixture of the background, like a tree. If we are brought to believe that even the minor players in a story really exist, then we are all the more likely to believe in the main characters and the action—the verisimilitude of the whole becomes much more successful.

Tone

The tone of this story is cool, crisp, and a little bitter—like the flavor of one of Diane's radishes. The coolness of the tone is what makes us feel that the characters in the story are being *looked at*—examined, almost clinically, by a distant intelligence which chooses to share its information with us . . . as if space aliens had descended on these people to pick them apart without their knowing anything about it. The cool tone creates a feeling of ironic distance that inhibits the reader from responding to the story as she might to a conventional romance novel, say. Our interest in the story has little to do with anticipation of the romantic clinch. This slight but always noticeable frostiness of tone is typical of Gaitskill, and because of it her fiction, though often much more explicit about sexual behavior than "Daisy's Valentine," is never titillating in a pornographic way.

The coolness of the tone lets us know that the voice telling the story, though it has full access to the contents of Joey's consciousness, isn't really Joey's voice. As in the Taylor story, there's the implication of a narrative presence apart from any character, though it's a less amiably avuncular presence than Taylor's implied narrator. Indeed, by the end of the story, Gaitskill's implied narrator seems to have flayed Joey and pinned him onto the dissecting table for our (appalled?) examination.

Point of View

Mechanically speaking, the story is told from Joey's point of view—all the reader's information is filtered through him, we witness no scenes unless he is present, and no other character's thoughts are directly reported to us except Joey's. But although the story feeds us all Joey's information, it doesn't expect us to share Joey's opinions. By means of its cool tone, the story distances itself from Joey's interpretation of events and doubles the reader's perspective on everything that happens. We're told how Joey sees things, but the distancing effect invites us to look at things for ourselves too, and perhaps to form different conclusions.

The situation is complicated by the fact that Joey is, in his modest way, an unreliable narrator. (The unreliable narrator is another device of fiction closely associated with Henry James and especially with his short novel *The Turn of the Screw*.) When Joey tells his own story in the first person to Daisy, he lies quite a bit. More importantly for the story as a whole, the impression of Daisy he conveys to the reader via third-person narration is wholly unreliable and inaccurate. If the story was told in Joey's tone of voice (most likely to happen if it was written in first person), it would seem to be a warm and sticky love story and we would have much less of an opportunity to realize it is delusional.

Tone is used as a wedge to divide the point of view in this story (and in this sense, tone becomes a structural device). Tone splits our perspective on Daisy and allows us to compare Joey's idealized image of her with a not-so-pretty picture we can form for ourselves.

Time Management

The real-time line in this story is somewhat indefinite, but evidently a matter of a few weeks or months. Thus, while it doesn't present the huge difficulties of the twenty-year time period of "A Wife of Nashville," it also can't run as close to real time as "Depth Charge" does.

It may be surprising to realize that the first several pages of the story all consist of generalized summary—there is no full scene taking place in real time until Joey has made the valentine and given it to Daisy. It's appropriate, both structurally and thematically, that this should be so, because only when Daisy has accepted the valentine does the whole thing "get real."

Because of the extreme differences in subject, background, social situation, and so on, this story has absolutely no surface resemblance to Peter Taylor's story, yet Gaitskill uses many of the same devices as Taylor for making her extremely long summary introduction vivid and interesting. Using flashes of dialogue and bits of detail that appeal to the senses, she contructs a chain of half-scenes that leads us to the center of the action. Enough physical detail is furnished that we seem to see and hear the characters at the same time we are being told about them, and two key settings (the bookstore basement and the Diane/Joey living quarters) are established so thoroughly that we are scarcely aware of the rapid rate at which we are rushing through them. The whole opening phase of the story is a summary account of what "usually happened," but because of the half-scenes' smooth oscillation between the general and the particular, we seem to witness it all instead of just hearing about it.

The story gradually slows down to a minute-by-minute correspondence with real time when Joey begins making the valentine, then cuts into the first fully dramatized scene: Joey's first "romantic" lunch with Daisy. Thereafter the proportion of full scenes to summary passages shifts in favor of the former, but there is still a lot of real time to be covered somehow, because the Joey/Daisy romance dithers on for quite a lengthy period. Gaitskill has a number of different devices for covering this distance. Sometimes she jump-cuts directly from one full scene to another, but she also sometimes uses the half-scene summary techniques of the story's first phase to connect episodes in the story's second half. Once these different strategies have been established, the reader accepts them as they come, probably without consciously noticing them.

Dialogue

Gaitskill is especially deft at tossing snippets of dialogue into half-scenes. This technique gives us an especially vivid impression of minor characters who never appear in full scenes at all—the bookstore bit players, for instance: Tommy and Ariel.

The dialogues which occur in the full scenes usually have a typical quality to them (surrounded as they are by half-scene summary presentations). Only Diane's conclusive quarrel with Joey sounds like a unique, one-time-only event. Even the late-breaking dialogue among Joey, Eliot, and Rita seems like a typical conversation for these characters, although it startles us with its rather repugnant candor, since we didn't previously know much about what went on between these people. Whenever we listen to Daisy and Joey talk, we sense that they are endlessly repeating themselves, as lovers (alas) often do.

Gaitskill is expert in conveying the flavor of the Joey/Daisy dialogues without dragging us all the way through them from start to finish. Consider Joey's second full scene with Daisy, which takes place in the "small dark bar." Clearly we have been dropped into the middle of this conversation, and clearly it is one of a series of quite similar conversations. (Skipping ahead to this one is an efficient time-management device which shows how far the relationship has "progressed.") The tactic is similar to what Bernardini does with the opening dialogue of "Depth Charge," although in this case we never find out every last detail of what Joey and Daisy are talking about because we don't really need to know. Joey's back-story isn't *that* important. What matters is that we get a sense of the essentially false way in which the two lovers are unfolding themselves to each other.

Suspense

Glance back at the opening paragraph of the story, then take another look at the conclusion. It seems as if that first paragraph would throw away all possibility of suspense in the story by predicting quite accurately what's going to happen. And indeed that opening paragraph is a somewhat risky gambit, but the first thing it does is replace one suspense question with another.

If Joey knows that pursuing Daisy will "ruin his life," the question becomes, will he restrain himself or will he do it anyway? This question does create a certain level of suspense until the moment when Joey, after a significant hesitation, decides to go through with giving Daisy the valentine he has made.

Thereafter a certain sense of fatality takes over the story, because once Joey has committed himself, we know the probable outcome. Once we know what will happen, our interest is displaced to *how* it will happen. The how question is also capable of sustaining a measure of suspense, and it is the center of Joey's interest also—a perverse interest in savoring the nuances of his own self-destructive behavior: *Voici le temps des assassins*, etc.

Imagery and Description

The significant central image of the story is the valentine itself—pinpointed by the title as of key importance. (The title also works as a nice little functional pun, since, via the familiar phrase "Be my valentine," we eventually recognize that "Daisy's Valentine" is Joey himself.) The valentine gathers up all Joey's impressions of Daisy and concentrates them into a single image—really a perfect image of the delusional idea of Daisy that Joey enjoys so much. All the qualities he observes in her are reflected in the valentine: childishness (it begins as a children's book illustration), fuzziness (the tissue cover), unreality (the "distorted, feverish" quality of the art).

But the caption "Behold the time of the assassins" is the killer. At first the caption seems a purely irrelevant piece of affectation, but as the image pattern evolves across the story, it becomes a link between the valentine card and the explicit sado-masochistic images that occur in the penultimate scene. In his fantasies, Joey enjoys the thought of Daisy as the victim he somehow rescues, but the image pattern, by the end, helps let us know that these fantasies are a mask for his idea of Daisy as *his own* victim: "Sometimes I just want to tear you apart." Neither the valentine nor Joey's attraction to his notion of Daisy's help-lessness is as innocently sentimental as it first appears. The image cluster surrounding the valentine underlines what happens in the story in a way similar to (though less dramatic than) the use of the "depth charge" imagery in Bernardini's story.

Less centrally symbolic but still structurally important are the two stoop-sitting episodes which bracket the Daisy/Joey romance. These scenes are tableaus, which show the characters against very similar backgrounds but in very different moods and situations. In the first episode, which follows their first restaurant "date," the time they spend sitting on the steps feels reasonably pleas-ant. Daisy's childishly rebellious wish for the disapproval of the bystanding woman who's probably paying no attention to them seems merely silly. In the second tableau, in the final scene, the fact that they are still sitting on steps somewhere underlines the point that their relationship has gone nowhere and that they literally have nowhere to go. Now the social disapproval that Daisy idly wished for in the first scene comes in reality, and when it comes it makes her cry.

A less important but elegantly executed image pattern revolves around Diane's salad. The precise composition of the salad, especially the slivered radish, comes to symbolize the eccentric order and harmony of the Diane/Joey relationship. Once Joey has entered into infidelity he finds himself "accused" by radishes in other salads he orders when he's with Daisy. And when he refus-es to eat Diane's salad it amounts to a renunciation of his whole relationship with her.

Design

In a sense, this story is about the disruption of design—the intentional wreck-ing of the weird but harmonious arrangements Joey and Diane have evolved together. There is a formal rigidity to their behavior, as there is a Japanese for-mality to Diane's salad. Their high times on speed are precisely balanced with their scheduled down times, and so on. Their quasi-artistic pastimes, though purposeless and unproductive, are also very structured.

At the end of the story, all this peculiar harmony has been splintered. We don't quite know where Diane is in the end, but Joey has displaced himself into a state of chaos, imagistically suggested by the wreckage of Eliot and Rita's apartment during the search for the (probably nonexistent) bug, and by the anarchy of the street life where Joey finds himself, marooned on the stoop with Daisy in the closing scene.

Is it possible to locate a conventional climax in this story? Because the first paragraph gives up the outcome, the whole narrative has a rather anticlimactic feeling to it. Still, a couple of episodes contend for the position of structural climax; perhaps it's possible for there to be more than one of these.

So far as the dramatic action is concerned, the climax pretty well has to be the decisive fight with Diane, when she throws Joey out of the house. Many vectors build toward a crisis in this episode. For one thing it is Diane's first and only fully dramatized scene, which the reader has been subliminally expecting—Diane in action, at last. Also, if Joey ruins his life as the first paragraph predicts, he does it by breaking up with Diane. Daisy has little to do with causing Joey's problems; she is merely his pretext. The real Daisy doesn't even exist for Joey; he is only aware of the fantasy image of her he's formed in his mind (and he's even, perversely, aware of that fact). Thus the final quarrel with Diane is the most decisive plot point and so serves as the structural climax of the action proper: everything that follows it is denouement.

However, if we think of the story less in terms of what happens in the action and more in terms of what happens in Joey's mental life, we would be inclined to locate the climax elsewhere. There is some justification for reading the story this way, since it is very much about Joey's delusions and tends to be positioned quite far inside his head. From this standpoint, the climax is Joey's decision to give the valentine to Daisy. He hesitates, significantly, before doing so. Making the valentine (not giving it) may be the most satisfactory climax his attraction to Daisy ever has (far more pleasing to Joey than any sexual encounter they may or may not have later on). So long as Joey keeps the valentine to himself his infatuation with Daisy is stupid but harmless. Once he gives it to her, the fantasy is released into the outside world, and all the damage it causes there can be understood as a denouement, since after all it has been predicted by the opening paragraph.

But if we think of the story strictly in terms of its imagery, a third location for a climax becomes possible. The full implications of the Valentine image are not worked out until the penultimate scene in the Eliot-Rita apartment, when the valentine's similarities to the pornographic magazine image are revealed. This completion of the image pattern also completes the meaning of the story by disclosing the perverse nastiness that underlies Joey's whole attraction to Daisy. And of course the title reinforces the importance of this third and final climax. (Note how the structure of imagery, rather than the structure of plot, becomes a crucial design element in this case.)

Thus it appears that "Daisy's Valentine" is structured (like "Depth Charge," though rather less obviously) around three subclimaxes in a triangular pattern: first Joey's climax of decision; then the climax of the action between

Diane and Joey (at the apex of the triangle); and finally the climax of the imagery, which feeds into the denouement of the closing scene.

NOTES

1. The first sentence of this paragraph is a strikingly bald piece of exposition—even a direct statement of theme. The following two sentences keep it from protruding too much by shifting the focus to Joey's reaction to the first sentence, which seems to become more his idea than the author's. That he would enjoy playing with such a notion is the first stroke in his characterization.

2. Strict logic tells you that a bookcase can't really be "morose," but this quirky bit of personification brings the whole description to life.

3. This detail is well-positioned between the general and the specific—the old man is a type, but the specificity of the description makes you see him as an individual as well.

4. Narrative in the imperfect tense (would do this, would always do that) bogs down easily, but this passage is energized by the close specificity of the descriptions. Joey's epilepsy is never again mentioned, but the rattle of his i.d. plates makes him physically present to the reader.

5. The combination of Daisy's "soft, dopey" smile with her "slow, long-fingered movements" helps us see what about her is attractive to Joey, while at the same time suggesting (subliminally) that perhaps it *shouldn't* be attractive.

6. The order of presentation is important to Joey's characterization. Self-interest comes both first and last. His love for Diane is inserted parenthetically. But his interest in protecting the stability of his situation is at odds with his interest in ruining his life—a source of conflict for the story.

7. We're seeing Diane at a distance, filtered through Joey's summary impressions of her, but the details (particularly her isometric tension problem) are so arresting that she comes through very vividly.

8. One of the glancing advantages of this description is that it conveys a quite definite picture of their living space, thus making it easier for us to see them in it. All their behavior, notably, is superbly unproductive—vaguely "artistic" but utterly purposeless—no more than highly evolved ways of killing time. The references to their drug habit are tossed off non-judgmentally, but one might suspect that one would require drugs to remain so fascinated with these activities. And yet the use of the word "religiously" is important . . .

9. ... because the conclusion of their weekly Dexedrine cycle has the status of religious ritual. The beautifully described salad is wonderfully reassuring—you feel a sense of inner peace just thinking about it. It's a fact that rituals can stabilize a life no matter what their content. And in this paragraph we see that the pattern of Diane and Joey's whole week has a ritual order to it—the chaos of their drug-taking and bohemian dithering is contained within a highly structured frame. This is the "system" Joey refers to earlier, and this is what he has to lose.

10. Not exactly a romantic relationship. Though the author doesn't particularly stress the point, the apathy toward sex is most likely a consequence of all the speed they take.

11. Trouble in paradise ... and caused by nothing but guilty thoughts, because Joey hasn't exactly done anything yet. So far, we see Diane only through the imperfect tense, but though she has not yet had a real-time scene to play, details like her pecan-roll behavior make her presence very powerful.

12. This seems to be a description of an irritating flake. Aside from the suggestion of availability, the reader looking over Joey's shoulder may have trouble understanding Daisy's appeal ...

13. ... which, however, begins to connect with her pathetic quality. It's his sense of Daisy's helplessness that appeals to Tommy.

14. Evelyn makes no further appearance in the story, but the vividness of her description (a combination of crisp physical details and the characterizing line about the mass murderers) makes the whole situation seem more real. This attention to figures in the background, typical of all Gaitskill's work, is something that sets her apart from most of her contemporaries.

15. Again, we don't exactly "need to know" all this information about the gay men in the typing pool—they have no important role to play in the Diane-Joey-Daisy triangle. But the distinctness of the description makes the context of the story more convincing. It's important that bystanders be as credible as the main actors in this drama.

    Also, the point that all these people want to "get out" of the bookstore but none of them do it suggests an atmosphere of futility parallel to the dead-end quality of Joey's habits with Diane.

16. The decrease of inappropriateness has to do with Joey's beginning to perceive that Daisy is a loser ...

17. ... but at the same time, as her physical presence is enhanced, his attraction to her grows.

18. There's a mascot quality to Daisy—she's everybody's pet ...

19. ... and this image, so suggestive of a child in the embrace of an adult, shows that infantilism is a big part of Daisy's appeal.

20. This paragraph, rounding out the first description of Daisy, shows her as Diane's opposite in almost every way: small, soft, weak, vague, and almost cloyingly sweet-natured.

21. Thus Joey doesn't want Daisy the way you want a lover—he wants her the way you want a kitten.

22. The "answer man" episode underlines a directionless quality in Daisy which is of course compatible with a similar quality in Joey.

23. These images are innocent or fantastic or both—but once Joey brings them home they begin to cause trouble. If he could keep his crush in the bookstore, it wouldn't jeopardize his stability.

24. The salad, which is virtually a symbol of Diane and Joey's domestic harmony, is shown to be endangered in this line.

25. Their lives seem to be nothing but a cluster of inane preoccupations, but until now they have meshed in a harmonious way.

26. By breaking his routine, Joey is damaging the ritual that sustains him—the cats' irritation underlines the point.

27. Is it dumber to make these displays or to be impressed by them? But the silliness is probably typical of many courtships.

28. Announcing an important theme for the remainder of the story: does Joey want the "real" Daisy or his fantasy of what she is?

29. This single-sentence paragraph accentuates the connection to the title, stressing the point that this decision is a critical turning point in the whole episode.

30. Unreality may be the most salient quality of this piece of art. The goofiness of that grasshopper recalls Daisy's goofiness, and the general saccharine flavor is something she also shares, at least in Joey's view of her. A dedicated symbol-hunter might notice that poppies can produce opium, which in turn can produce stuporous dreams and delusions.

31. But the tissue cover is really the master touch, simultaneously suggesting Daisy's overall fuzziness (in contrast to Diane's hard edges) and the agreeably soft focus of Joey's vision of her. That the hearts are "senseless" is also highly appropriate. In its limited way, this valentine is a very expressive work of art.

   The caption, loosely translatable as "Behold the time of assassins," seems random and meaninglessly cryptic. But watch to see what gets assassinated as the story develops.

32. This might indeed be the better choice.

33. Soft or not, those "claws" add a touch of menace to Daisy's babyish greed.

34. This flat little description is a sort of anticlimax—making the valentine is a better consummation than giving it to Daisy. "Shadow captive" recalls "winglike shadow" above, reminding us that Joey's fantasy of an affair with Daisy may be preferable to what happens in "real life."

35. The unfortunate radish . . . Refusing the salad is equivalent to refusing a sacrament.

36. Odd that Joey seems fully conscious of the idiocy of his behavior. Self-knowledge is generally assumed to be a valuable character trait.

37. The radish, personified now, delivers its sting. This image has a rather complex evolution from its first appearance in the story.

38. Odd, again, how Joey seems to be aware that his whole idea of Daisy is delusional.

39. Quite a definite remark from fuzzy little Daisy, who seems to have a lucid sense that an affair with Joey has no future.

40. Diane would know what he means by this, but to Daisy the remark is completely mysterious. In any case, it's another salad rejected. The author presents Joey's drug use noncommittally, as if it were an ordinary habit like a taste for jelly beans or whatever, but we begin to see (partly through Daisy's reaction) that the drugs have a huge effect on everything that he does.

41. With this fanciful language, Joey begins to invite her into the fantasies he's formed about her "shadow" self.

42. A lazier writer wouldn't have made sure we noticed the doorman. This stoop-sitting episode will be balanced by another at the story's conclusion.

43. Reasonable question. Daisy may not be a rocket scientist, but she seems to have a fund of common sense that Joey perhaps lacks.

44. Meanwhile, Joey is prepared to explain to her that his attraction is all in his mind and it's pretty much okay with him if it stays there.

45. As romantic impulses go, this is a strange one.

46. Again, the surprisingly vivid presentation of a mere bystander.

47. This whole anecdote sounds very unconvincing, including its implications of masochism. It's not that Daisy has a taste for destructive relationships but that for some reason she thinks it might be interesting to appear as if she did.

48. From the description, it doesn't seem likely that the old lady is paying any attention to Daisy and Joey at all. Daisy is projecting disapproval onto the bystander—from her desire, already established by the bookstore descriptions, to be the center of everyone's attention. But this moment will also find its reflection in the concluding scene.

49. Does this sound like fun? It's almost a parody of star-crossed love—the Romeo-and-Juliet scenario, or pick your own—love in which there's some insurmountable obstacle. There will be a question as to whether Daisy and Joey really want to surmount the obstacle anyway.

50. Futility sets in almost from the beginning of this "affair," and the paper-shredding scene, which echoes the pointless projects Diane and Joey undertake in their apartment, is an image for that futility.

51. There's something infantile in this action—preferring the bag of jelly beans to a person.

52. These fantasies are ten-year-old level—utterly sentimental and silly . . .

53. . . . and of course propped up by the amphetamines. Watch for further imagistic connections of pills to jelly beans as the story continues.

54. Getting to know each other. All lovers have to do it, but notice that Daisy provides very little historical information about herself. Joey does practically all the talking.

55. Another writer might not have bothered with this description, so well-observed that it makes the background fully as present as the figures in the foreground of the action.

56. One of the pleasures of a new love affair is that it gives you a reason to reinterpret the events of your personal history, to recreate your idea of yourself, for the new audience, the new lover . . .

57. . . . and in Joey's case, it's a false presentation, since some of the information is false: a fantasy of himself to match his fantasy of Daisy.

58. Notice the efficiency of this scene in conveying the progress of the relationship. Although it's a real-time scene, it does some of the work of summary, making it apparent that this is one of a series of similar conversations. Because Joey has evidently told Daisy most of this stuff before, the writer doesn't have to give a *full* account of these episodes of his history—his fragmentary allusions create a sufficient impression.

59. Presented with no particular tilt from the author, this little diatribe really sounds like a pathetic self-justification from a talentless failure.

60. Debatable point. Diane is an ex-artist, at best, and we never see Daisy actually making any art, although there are some references to her artistic ambitions, as in the "answer man" episode.

61. Recall the previous uses of the word "shadow." Whether or not Daisy really meets this description, it's certainly the idea of her that Joey likes.

62. And the more they talk the *less* we feel they are actually coming to know one another. An excellent example of people talking past each other.

63. Well, isn't he supposed to want this? What's his problem?

64. For better or worse, Diane is a fully formed personality, and now Joey becomes more aware of the differences between her and Daisy which have been suggested to the reader earlier.

65. The orderly, reassuring structure of the Diane-Joey week has now been completely shattered.

66. Diane's first full real-time scene has been very well prepared for by all the information about her previously furnished.

67. Classic copout line.

68. Yes, definitely.

69. No sense of responsibility.

70. Diane is certainly capable of calling a spade a spade.

71. What makes the person more attractive than the jelly beans, all of a sudden?

72. This toss-off exchange lets us know, somewhat surprisingly, that these affairs are apparently an established habit with Joey.

    He's expecting a little much of Diane, no? Most adulterers accept the notion that if you want to go back to the person you've been unfaithful to, you have to end the other affair or at least pretend to. Not Joey. And his passivity in the face of his own choices is downright bizarre.

73. The delicate swirl of sadism in this description connects (subliminally) to Joey's attraction to Daisy's general helplessness.

74. Well-directed kick—she really knows how to hurt a guy.

75. Why this specific color selection? His concentration on the jelly beans is awfully good for someone who's just been through a wrenching emotional scene.

76. Self-knowledge is supposed to be a virtue for most people—but not for Joey. Recognizing that he's a slime-bag doesn't make him want to stop being one ...

77. ... instead, he forges ahead with his self-indulgences.

78. As inane responses go, this is championship material.

79. For all her fuzziness and babyishness, Daisy is a bit swifter than Joey to recognize that some events are likely to have consequences.

80. A fundamental incompatibility rears its head.

81. This exchange shows that the Daisy-Joey honeymoon, such as it ever was, is coming to an end. Daisy is a frivolous airhead while Joey is a pseudo-intellectual, pseudo-artistic poseur. You can't say that one is really "better" than the other, but Joey's pretensions mesh much better with Diane's quirks than with Daisy's. Basically Daisy just doesn't belong at the opera.

82. An operatic fantasy—what could be more appropriate? But because of Daisy's odd reserve of practicality it's incomprehensible to her. Joey can't get her to participate in his fantasy life.

83. A genuinely perceptive comment here ...

84. ... and Joey's reaction is a bit peculiar, isn't it? What does he do to people that love him? *Voici le temps des assassins* ...

85. Daisy's efforts to pull Joey in her direction are as futile as his efforts to suck her into his fantasies—it's supremely pointless to try to make a speed freak eat.

86. A reprise of that sense of star-crossed futility established in the earlier, fuller descriptions of similar parting scenes.

87. Now here is a *serious* problem.

88. Diane is right to interpret this as a major betrayal. The opera is a Diane-Joey ritual, and to substitute Daisy violates all the harmonies of the Diane-Joey relationship, like slashing a painting or taking a sledgehammer to a sculpture. Diane might not be a productive artist, but her aesthetic sense of balance and proportion is structurally similar to a morality.

89. What's really important to Joey: earrings, jelly beans.

90. We begin to sense a real nastiness in him—feeding on other people's pain.

91. Along with its air of menacing anarchy (this is the world inhabited by the homeless, whom Joey may perhaps be joining), this description connects the pills to the jelly beans by listing the colors.

92. It's very late in the story for the introduction of new characters. These may be some of the "people" mentioned in the first description of Diane and Joey's routine, but we haven't seen them specifically before. The shift of scene and personnel pulls the story to a different slant—Joey may appear differently against this unfamiliar background.

93. The author doesn't need to explain but simply lets us see the frenetic, paranoid urgency of an amphetamine overuser.

94. Again, the extremely thorough description we've now learned to expect from this story. We already know from Diane who Rita is to Joey, and the last line of the paragraph shows her interest.

95. Well, I bet Rita has heard Joey's line before, when she was in Daisy's present position. The author doesn't identify any tone to her reply, so you can hear it any way you want to—it *might* be wistful and longing (her eyes lit up for him, after all), but I hear it as sarcastically judgmental.

96. We don't exactly know the relationship between Rita and Eliot, but if, as seems possible, Rita's affair with Joey was an infidelity to Eliot, Eliot's attitude here is peculiar to say the least. The oddball behavior of Joey and Diane was first presented as more or less harmless or even appealing eccentricity, but now the activities of their circle begin to seem more and more perverse and degenerate.

97. Been there, done that. The shift from the light in Rita's eyes to the lines surrounding her eyes points up the evaporation of her interest in Joey—except as a drug connection, of course.

98. The innocence of "colorful tumble" reminds us of the jelly beans again.

99. For the purposes of the story's main points we have no more "need to know" about Alexander Bartolov than about Joey's epilepsy, above, but that Eliot collects Bartolov helps make him real for us.

100. What the—? This is a very long way from Joey's sentimental affection for Daisy—or is it? Rita has just been compared to the valentine grasshopper, above.

101. Reminded of Daisy's valentine by the description a few lines above, we are set up to compare that icon with this explicitly pornographic image—the title of course reinforces the importance of the moment, and the explicit comparison in the last sentence nails it down (perhaps a little too tightly). The two images seem to be in shocking contrast—the first sentimental and stickily sweet, the second raw and violent—until you think about it. In fact, both images share an essential phoniness. The fear in the porn

shot is "coy"—faked, like most responses in ritualized S&M sex games. And spanking, mentioned by Eliot above, infantilizes the person spanked. Joey's attraction to Daisy's nucleus of childlike qualities suddenly seems a lot more sinister ...

102. ... but nothing ever seems to come of it. The climax of this story doesn't stick out obviously, but we must have passed it back there somewhere, because this passage is clearly denouement, and what it shows in the first paragraph is that the affair is going nowhere. Apparently it has never gone anywhere. We don't know with absolute certainty whether the affair ever had a sexual consummation, but if it did it apparently wasn't worth talking about—the definition of an anticlimax.

Now the sad lovers have nowhere to be alone (this wrinkle is a sort of New York City real estate gag). If you're really concentrating at this point, you may suspect that the writer has left a thread dangling from the fabric. Where's Joey supposed to be living now? Presumably Diane did throw him out; she doesn't seem like the type to go back on that intention. If he has his own place, he'd have somewhere to go with Daisy, right? If he was actually homeless on the street, this whole concluding scene would probably have a more strained and desperate atmosphere. Best guess is he's staying with friends like Eliot and Rita—he did seem to be (somewhat desultorily) seeking shelter when he visited their place in the previous scene.

103. Another of Daisy's surprisingly astute insights. With Joey, there's nobody home in there.

104. And even Joey knows this ... odd how it doesn't seem to bother him.

105. The stoop, echoing the first stoop-sitting episode above.

106. Daisy's lines here are extremely fatuous on one level (given that she has significantly messed up her life for this person she can't talk to and can't get to know) but also perfectly accurate—Joey talks "at" Daisy because he's really talking to himself when he appears to be talking to her—describing the fantasized "shadow" of her he holds in his head.

107. Right again. Airheaded as she may be, Daisy really can cut through the fog sometimes.

108. During their first "dates" the fact that they can't really communicate and have nothing in common seemed at least potentially cute and sweet, but now it just produces a mutual crabbiness.

109. This "flicker" recognizes an implicit contrast between this couple and Daisy and Joey.

110. In the first stoop scene, Daisy projected a sense of disapproval onto an old lady who probably was paying no attention to her whatsoever—it gave her a sense of self-importance to do so. In this stoop scene, the disapproval is real and comes from the outside, but Daisy doesn't find it an enjoyable experience.

In one sense, this is the story's most authentic moment. Daisy and Joey are being despised by a couple who has everything they don't—starting with a place inside the building where they can be privately together. But Daisy and Joey are stuck on the stoop outside—permanently. Their relationship will never develop beyond this point. Thus the two stoop episodes place an imagistic bracket around their whole affair.

111. Daisy understands the significance of this moment, above—it's what she has to cry about. Joey, perhaps predictably, doesn't seem to get it. Daisy may not be a very "deep" person but she's suffering in a way that neither jelly beans nor amphetamines will alleviate.

112. Remember the first line of the story, when Joey anticipated ruining his life? It seems that the promise has been fulfilled, though he doesn't really seem to be aware of it. But this concluding image shows someone who has thrown away everything he had and (since Daisy has stopped responding to him) got nothing in return. He's alone at last, on the street with his jelly beans—and perhaps it doesn't really matter to him.

HEAR THAT LONG TRAIN MOAN

P E R C I V A L   E V E R E T T

"The world perhaps was laid out initially with some sort of temporal consistency, but that was soon gone. Out the window. Maybe there never was any kind of consistency. One can certainly imagine creation coming to certain parts of the globe before others, like the telephone or cable. Look around. Jets stretch their exhaust plumes across the skies over thatch huts, people whose main staple is rice watch napalm disintegrate their jungles, some people beat out conversations on hollow logs while the strata above them is filled with microwave signals."[1] Virgil Boyd re-lit his pipe and sank into his chair. "That's why," he told his friend, "I've no problem with the period inconsistency within my model."[2]

Morrison Long sipped his gimlet.[3] "I wasn't finding fault, but making an observation. Let me ask you something, Virgil: Are you all right?"[4]

"All right? Of course. Never better. Now that I'm retired I have time for my work."[5] He puffed at his pipe, but drew nothing. "Damn thing won't stay lit." Finding the box of matches on the table beside him empty, he patted his pockets and asked if Morrison had any.[6] He did not and so Virgil called out, "Williston!"

An eight-year-old boy with a large head appeared at the study door.[7] He stood erect and attended to his grandfather. "Williston, be a good boy[8] and find granddad some matches."

The boy nodded and went away. Virgil Boyd watched him trot across the living room toward the kitchen, skipping over tracks in the foyer and before the hallway.[9]

"The boy is a menace to my work," Virgil Boyd said. "Doesn't understand the seriousness of it all."[10]

"He's a boy," Morrison Long said.[11]

"Nor do *you* appreciate what's going on in this house."[12]

"Of course I do, Virgil. By the way, where is Frannie this evening?"

"I don't know. And I care only to the extent that her absence has caused me to be left alone with that boy of hers."[13] Virgil Boyd went back to the door and looked. "He's out there in the model now. Heaven knows what destruction he's causing." He looked at his cold pipe. "He's not a bad boy. But he's curious."[14]

"Not a bad thing for a boy to be."

"Ha!"

"It's an innocent fault."

"Innocence will be the downfall of us all.[15] Here he comes." Virgil Boyd took the matches from Williston and sent him on. "I appreciate his curiosity, but there's such a thing as discipline."

Morrison Long stood and went to the empty fireplace to lean on the mantel and look at the moose's head above. "Did your father really kill this animal?"

"So I was told. A crying shame, if you ask me." Virgil Boyd got his pipe going, puffing clouds of blue smoke. "I'm sure he didn't eat any of the beast. Killed for so-called sport. I keep it around as a reminder of crying shames."[16]

"Imagine the body that went with that head," Morrison Long said.

"Do you really have to go back to Chicago so soon?"

"I'm afraid so. Unlike you, I still have work. Tell me, do you miss your practice?"

Virgil Boyd chewed the end of his pipe and considered the question. "No. I don't miss the patients. They never wanted to be there anyway and saw clear of their own negligence to blame me for their pain and expense. I don't miss being on my feet all day. I'm thankful, however. Dentistry was a good profession and it gave me the skills and patience I need for my detailed work now."[17]

"Well, it really is something," Morrison Long's eye followed the tracks which ran by his feet, across the hearth.[18]

Virgil Boyd walked to the corner of the room where sprawled a replica of a small town with a central square, storefronts and houses with shrubs, trees and lawns.[19]

"What town is that?" asked Morrison Long.[20]

"Ashland, Kentucky." Virgil Boyd walked to the town. "See, the oil refinery."[21] Flames sat atop stacks and little lights glowed on the rigging. "Some of the houses on this hill are my finest work. Such detail inside."[22]

"Let's see."

Virgil Boyd shook his head. "We mustn't disturb the model."[23]

"Don't you like to admire your work?"

"I do, but I can't go around taking the roofs off of people's houses."[24]

Morrison Long smiled. "Of course."[25]

Virgil went back to his chair and sat, took a deep draw on his pipe.

"Are you quite all right?" Morrison Long asked.[26]

"I'm fine."

"You were joking, weren't you?"[27]

Virgil Boyd just looked at his friend. "What do you mean?"

"I want to see in one of the houses."

"No, I said."

"Why not?"

"Would you want somebody taking the roof off your house and looking in?"[28]

"I suppose not."

"No, of course you wouldn't. The model is very delicate. Everything is just so."[29]

Morrison Long looked at the sculpted hillsides in the corner beyond Ashland, at the tiny trees, at the gardens of the big house whose roof would not be removed.[30]

"What are you thinking?" Virgil Boyd asked.

Morrison Long sat down. "Have you ever been to Ashland, Kentucky?"

"Yes."

"The real one."

"Yes."

"I mean the one in Kentucky. The one the freeway goes through."

"There's no freeway through Ashland."[31]

Morrison Long's left hand held his right in his lap. His fingers moved to his wrist and he toyed with his watchband.[32] "Virgil," he said, "do you know who lives in that big house?"[33]

"Yes, of course I do." Virgil Boyd adjusted himself in his chair and looked his friend in the eye. "Why do you ask?"[34]

"Stop pulling my chain," Morrison Long said.

"What do you mean?"

"Just stop it. This isn't funny. Well, maybe it's funny, but it's gone too far. So, cut the act."[35]

"I don't know what you're talking about," Virgil Boyd said. "Perhaps you haven't paid close enough attention to the model. Come back down into the basement with me."[36] He led the way from the study and down the stairs. "I realize that there is an awful lot to take in, but you really must try."

Morrison Long followed, saying nothing, looking again at the massive network of HO scale world around him. He looked at a town from America's old West, a hog farm on its outskirts. He looked at glittering lights of modern Detroit in the far corner of the basement. "It's more impressive each time I look at it."[37]

"I feel the same way." Virgil Boyd took his seat behind the screen of the control terminal. "All the commands come from here."

"The scheduling and all that."

Virgil Boyd smiled. "Yes."

"Perhaps you've spent too much time on your trains lately," said Morrison Long.[38]

"I wish it were only trains."[39]

"What do you mean?"

Virgil Boyd didn't answer. He tapped away at the keyboard of his terminal. "I make it a habit to review the *scheduling* pretty frequently." He leaned back and studied the screen. The smile faded.

"What is it?" Morrison Long asked.

"There's something wrong. There is something very much wrong." Virgil Boyd typed furiously, then put his hands together in his lap as he studied the screen. "That boy."[40]

"What has he done?" Morrison Long asked.

"He's evil."[41]

"He's a boy, Virgil. What has he done?"[42]

Virgil Boyd worked again on the computer. "I can't undo it. He screwed up the routing. I can't stop it."[43]

"He's just a boy. I mean, look at all of this stuff. Remember your youth. You'd die to play with this set-up."

"Play?" Virgil Boyd shook his head. "This is not a toy. It's not a game." He turned away from the screen. "He's evil."[44]

A train went smoking by.

"Just what is going to happen?" Morrison Long asked.

"Two trains are going to collide and it's too late to stop them."

"Too late?"

"They've passed the last switching stations."

Morrison Long sighed. "Just shut the power off."[45]

"For everything?"

"If you have to."

"Are you crazy?" Virgil Boyd stood and looked at Detroit. "Do you understand the ramifications of such an action?"[46]

"Come on, Virgil, why don't you come upstairs and have a drink? Relax."

Virgil Boyd did not reply. He was to the stairs and moving up them to the first floor. Morrison Long followed. The pace was quickened through the foyer, hall, and kitchen, the leader muttering to himself.

"I'm really getting scared, Virgil," Morrison Long said at the back door.[47] He leaned against the jamb.

Virgil Boyd turned back to him. "Of course you're scared. You should be scared. A terrible thing is going to happen."[48] With that he was off again, trotting through the garden. The yard was lighted by several lamps shining upward at the bases of trees.

Morrison Long ran after him. "Virgil," he called, "this is crazy."[49] He stepped over tracks in the walk. He nearly ran into the back of his friend, who had come to a stop. "Virgil!" He grabbed the man and shook him.

"It's going to happen there," Virgil Boyd said, pointing to a trestle which crossed the goldfish pond. Colored lights shone under the water. "We're going to watch it happen, and there's nothing we can do."[50]

A train's whistle sounded.

"Let's just pick up one of the trains," Morrison Long said.[51]

"I can't interfere like that. And besides, which one do I pick up? What are the criteria for such a decision?"[52]

The second train cried.

Morrison Long said nothing, just watched the bridge.[53]

"There is only so much I can do," Virgil Boyd said. "It's hard enough just to make this shit. You know what I mean, don't you, Morrison?"[54]

ANALYSIS

Plot

The plot of this story can be stated in one simple sentence: Two aging men sit around and have a conversation about a model railway system one of them has built. Nothing else really *happens* in the story. Virgil *believes* that a train wreck is going to happen, but we don't actually see it occur. Virgil believes that Williston has messed up the routing in a way that will cause accidents, but the most dramatic thing we actually see the boy do is fetch matches to light Virgil's pipe. It's implied that Virgil *might* believe that there are little living people who inhabit the miniature world he has built for the trains to turn through, but we certainly never see these little folks. (And yet, the mind plays tricks on you. Some months after reading this story for the first time, I *remembered* an episode where a roof was removed to reveal little elves inside one of the model houses. There's no such episode in the story, but the implication is strong enough to make me think there was.)*

---

* It's interesting to compare this story to *The Mysterious Stranger*, a late and especially bitter work by Mark Twain. In Twain's story, a wonderfully beautiful youth appears in a small town and ingratiates himself with the local children by magically creating a tiny world full of animated miniature beings—who quickly begin murdering and raping each other, starting wars and so forth. Seeing the children are upset by the violence, the mysterious stranger crushes the little people like a bunch of bugs (which upsets the children even more). His subsequent activities in the town all have equally disastrous outcomes. But the mysterious stranger means no harm—he does enormous amounts of harm, but he never means to do it. Twain's radical disapproval of "innocence" is thus quite similar to Virgil Boyd's. The mysterious stranger's name, incidentally, is Satan.

Thus most of the more interesting elements of the story line are expressed as implications, rather than events. The elements of the story that create suspense, especially, are expressed as things that might have happened or might be going to happen, or that one of the characters might believe to be happening. Conventional plot interest, our interest in what takes place, is displaced to implications about what *may* take place, and so on.

As for backstory, there really isn't any of any importance. The story runs in real time or very close to it, and we pick up the small amount of necessary exposition as we go. The only piece of antecedent information that matters at all is the fact that Virgil Boyd used to be a dentist.

Character

Virgil Boyd seems to be the most important character, and he's the one we learn the most about. He's a retired dentist eccentric enough to have built a model railway system that seems to fill his whole property. Perhaps he's even more eccentric than that—for he may believe that the miniature world he has made is full of miniature but animate human beings. From the first "Are you all right?" Morrison Long's questions and reactions convey to the reader the possibility that Virgil Boyd may be insane.

Setting aside the question of Virgil's sanity, we see in him a rather odd, tough-minded cynicism about such subjects as the innocence of children or the qualities of his dental patients. His reluctance to remove the moose head, even though he regards it as a "crying shame," implies a character trait which foreshadows his later refusal to interfere with the model to stop the collision of the trains he anticipates. Virgil is someone who won't or perhaps can't interfere with the initial conditions of any situation.

The boy, Williston, is the next most important character in terms of the dramatic action (even though he doesn't do anything much and we know next to nothing about him, beyond Virgil's odd opinions). The only facts we know about Williston is that he's eight years old and has "a large head." Not once in the story does he open his mouth. He's off-stage for most of the story, although his absence is given a sinister twist by Virgil: "He's out there in the model now. Heaven knows what destruction he's causing." This shortage of information makes the boy seem rather mysterious. The mystery of his unseen movements around the model may recall this dialogue from the Book of Job:

> The LORD: From whence comest thou?
> SATAN: From going to and fro in the earth, and walking up and down in it.

Morrison Long plays a lesser role in the action proper than Williston even; the only thing Morrison actually *does* is try, unsuccessfully, to persuade Virgil to pick up one of the trains. But because he is more present in the foreground of the story, he may seem to be a more important character than Williston. What do we learn about Morrison Long? He has a job in Chicago. That's it for the facts. Otherwise we know nothing about him, except that he seems to be a rational, "normal" man, especially by contrast to Virgil Boyd, whose eccentricities seem to intensify as the conversation between these two goes on.

Morrison is a "straight man" in this situation, performing a function similar to that of a straight man in a comedy routine, which is to feed questions to the comedian that allow for gag replies. Morrison's questions and reactions unfold the peculiarity of Virgil's idea of things and hold that peculiarity up to a normative inspection. If Morrison seems almost characterless it's because he's meant to be a virtually transparent window into the story (Watson to Virgil's Holmes, etc.); his questions are intended to be those that the reader would most likely ask, in Morrison's place. Since the eighteenth century (*Gulliver's Travels* being an excellent example), it has been a common narrative device to use a character so ordinary as to be indistinguishable from the reader to pilot the reader around a strange or fantastic situation; this character tries to do what you would do, if you were in his situation.

Tone

Outside of the dialogue, the narration is almost toneless. There's a bare-bones efficiency to the descriptions, which are themselves as minimized and utilitarian as directions for a stage play (except for the descriptions of the model itself, which sometimes seem to rise toward Virgil's own sense of wonder). And the lines of Morrison Long are usually matter-of-fact and toneless too, though occasionally they express a tense feeling of alarm.

Listening for tone in this story, the reader is likely to bypass the not very noticeable overarching narration and instead hear Virgil Boyd's voice, which has stronger tonal qualities than any other aspect of the story. Virgil's tone is quirky, rather irritable, incisive and *convinced* (though perhaps delusionally convinced). But his voice certainly gains a strengthening sense of conviction as the story goes on.

Point of View

Where's the camera? A casual reader might think that the story is told from Morrison Long's point of view, because Morrison's reactions to what goes on are closer to what the average reader's responses probably would be—few readers would prefer to identify with Virgil Boyd. But, in fact, the camera's on the ceiling. Bird's-eye view, external omniscience. No one's mind is entered in this story. We know Morrison's reactions only from what he says in dialogue; we never have the chance to read his thoughts. It is as if we were watching the action and hearing the dialogue on stage, and indeed the story could be converted into a stage play with small revision.

Dialogue

This story *is* a dialogue, basically; nothing really happens other than the conversation (except for sipping of drinks, lighting of pipes, shuffling around the house, etc.). In both form and subject, it suggests a philosophical dialogue, and can even be compared to Socratic dialogues. The arguments of Socrates are frequently set up so that Socrates confronts and outwits a straight man whose general comportment is similar to that of Morrison Long. That resemblance accounts for the rather abstract feeling of the conversation here. This story too is really an argument, though not openly couched as such. The contended question of the Virgil/Morrison dialogue is, what has Virgil really made here: a toy train set or an animate microcosmos? The two characters represent opposing points of view, and the dialogue will determine which prevails.

Generally speaking, the straight man's role in a dialogue that requires a straight man tends to be a dull one. That's not a major problem here because the intentions of the story are so abstract and because the story is so short that we hardly have time to get bored with Morrison's nondescript lines (our attention is always deflected by Virgil's comebacks anyway). But in a story which is less of a parable, more of a realistic representation, straight-man dialogue can be problematic. Conversations where a straight man is used to elicit expository information from a more important character can very quickly become awkward and obvious. If it's strictly necessary to write dialogues of that kind, it's best to give the straight man his own fish to fry—some separate agenda that may expand the character beyond the limitations of the straight man's role.

Symbolism

"Hear That Long Train Moan" is the only story in this collection that really requires the use of the term "symbolism." For most contemporary, indeed for most modern works of fiction, the term "imagery" seems preferable. The two are related but not really the same.

Imagery tends to evolve organically from the total context of all the meanings a story generates. What an image may suggest, represent or "mean" tends to be organically rooted in the world that the story creates. Symbols, by contrast, have a more fixed definition, which may be recognized outside the narratives in which they occur (while images are likely to be more wholly dependent on the stories which give birth to them). A cross is universally recognized to represent Christianity, while a somewhat smaller set of observers is likely to know that an inverted pentangle represents Satanism—regardless of context. The meaning of this sort of symbol is as definite as the value of a coin. Fixed symbols of this kind often occur in narratives. (Beginning writers are sometimes overly attracted to fixed symbols, using them too obviously and reductively.)

Valentines in general are fixed symbols—everyone in our culture understands that a card with a red heart shape on it stands for gooey, sentimentalized, romantic love. The particular card that Joey makes in Gaitskill's "Daisy's Valentine" is an image which *implies* and *suggests* the fuzzy, delusional quality of Joey's feeling for Daisy—rather than being *equated* with that quality, as a fixed symbol would be.

The unconscious mind is very fond of symbolism, as Freud, Jung and their successors in psychoanalysis have demonstrated. The unconscious uses symbolism (especially the weird symbolic imagery of dreams) to send coded messages which the conscious intelligence may or may not be able to unravel (at 100+ dollars an hour—but that's another problem). In the composition of fiction, the unconscious mind may use symbolic imagery in a similar way—and sometimes the writer will not be consciously aware of this process even after the text is completed.

For example, I once wrote a novel about nuclear apocalypse that had a fairly complex religious subtext and put a number of different belief systems into conflict with each other. In one episode, a Satanist carves an inverted pentangle on a slum apartment door, inscribing a goat's head in the star. In a later scene, two of the good guys (who happen, oddly enough, to be Russian Orthodox Christians) roast and eat a whole sheep at the same location.

I didn't consciously intend any meaningful connection between these two events. After the book was finished, though, an artist I knew did a sketch for a possible cover design. His drawing showed a sheep's head levitating from the Satanic inverted pentangle. As soon as I saw it, I recognized (see "thrill of recognition," above) a symbolic pattern that had been latent in my text all along. In the iconography of Renaissance painting, lambs and sheep are often used to symbolize aspects of Christianity; a bleeding lamb may serve as an image of Christ crucified. What my artist had done was connect two images from my narrative I had not consciously known to be involved with each other and shown them in a symbolic relationship which quite nicely illustrated what *happened* in the book thematically: a positive and essentially Christian transcendence of a situation that could fairly be described as evil.

The point is that this symbolic pattern was there in the book all along, though I was unaware of its presence until the artist showed it to me. I wrote it without knowing I was writing it; my unconscious mind, in effect, wrote it for me. When you're writing really well, when you're inspired, or "hot," your unconscious mind will move in counterpoint to your conscious craftsmanship, creating effects which will be registered subliminally by the casual reader. I can think of numerous examples of this phenomenon in my own work—i.e., patterns of symbolism I was unaware of but which seemed perfectly legitimate to me once pointed out by someone writing a paper. For a better-known example, read "Flowering Judas" by Katherine Anne Porter. This story combines Christian iconographic symbolism with imagery personal to the author and characters, in such a bewildering way that Miss Porter confessed that she herself couldn't understand it.

In twentieth-century fiction, systems of imagery that evolve in this unconscious or semiconscious way seem more natural and better-integrated with the finished work than systems of symbolism which are deliberately arranged. A consciously contrived system of symbolism in a modern story usually looks too stiff, too rigid—too contrived, in short. Static symbolism is too much at odds with the realistic representation of everyday life, a task which *most* contemporary fiction undertakes to some extent.

Not that it was always like that. Many of the great narratives of the past (*Paradise Lost, The Canterbury Tales, The Faerie Queene*, and numerous plays by Shakespeare, to name a few) rely very heavily on fixed sets of symbolism, known as allegories. In an allegory, two completely articulated planes of experience are connected (frequently by numerous individual symbols) into a one-to-one correspondence. The well-known biblical parable of the buried talent is a simple example of an allegory. But times have changed, the culture has changed, and today's readers of fiction are likely to reject allegorical symbolism as being too didactic.

"Hear That Long Train Moan" breaks most of the general rules stated above. In fact, it is structured in very much the same way as a medieval or biblical allegory. By the end of the story, we should recognize that almost everything in it stands for, symbolizes, something else. Virgil Boyd represents God the Creator, the model railway represents the whole of Creation, and the boy Williston represents a satanic figure resembling the Satan of the Book of Job. (Morrison Long, the straight man, is there to represent ourselves—the audience.) Of course the story is still credible on the literal, realistic level, the plane of ordinary daily experience it seems to portray—it remains so because we never actually see the little folks that Virgil thinks live in the miniature world he has built for them. We can read this story as a realistic narrative about a nutty old man in the grip of crazed ideas, but in the end, the opportunity to read it as an allegory is more tempting.

Which just goes to show that some rules were made to be broken, indeed. It takes skill to break them and get away with it, lots of skill sometimes. But if no rules were ever broken, no new discoveries would be made.

Design

In a story in which so little happens, structure and form are unlikely to be defined by the plot. The dramatic pattern which plot would ordinarily provide is created here by other elements.

The conflict of the story is very abstract; as in Socratic dialogues, it is based on a difference of opinion about the way the world is. In Morrison's version of reality, Virgil is crazy if he really believes there are little people inhabiting his model railway; in Virgil's version of reality, Morrison is obtuse if he *doesn't* believe that. The question the reader expects to have answered is, Which character's version will prevail?

Thus the climax, the dramatic center of the story, should occur when this question is answered. One might argue that it isn't answered at all: Virgil's concluding question, "You do know what I mean, don't you, Morrison?" gets no decisive reply. But the whole of Virgil's last speech changes the terms of our reading. It's when we read the line "It's hard enough just to make this shit" (the expletive serving as a light slap to focus our attention) that we completely realize what we may have previously begun to suspect—that all along we have been reading an allegory. Thus the structural climax of the story becomes a moment of recognition on the part of the *reader.* Perhaps even more strangely, that recognition is not an insight into what happens in the story, but rather an insight into what *kind* of story it has been all along—not a realistic rendition of everyday life, but an allegory (or maybe it's both).

The design of the story ambushes us at the end, requiring us to question many of our assumptions. Most of the way toward the conclusion we are probably inclined to side with Morrison in the belief that Virgil has gone screwy. But once we recognize the story to be an allegory, then Virgil's version seems to be correct.

If the universe was created by a God, most rationalists (the Morrison Longs among us) would agree that He doesn't directly interfere, nowadays, with the world He has made. We certainly don't see huge hands coming down from the heavens to prevent our vehicles from colliding.

But if there is a benevolent Creator, why doesn't He stop bad things from happening? Perhaps He can't. Possibly His own rules prevent Him from interfering with the processes of Creation once they have been set in motion. (That's how it is for Virgil Boyd.) And if we have an anthropomorphic Creator, how would He *feel* about His inability to prevent catastrophes by direct intervention? Frustrated and irritable (like Virgil Boyd)? As for the presence of evil in the universe, the story's allegorical level suggests that it may be more a matter of childish caprice than intentional malevolence. The allegorical transformation also introduces some more recondite philosophical speculations which probably would appeal to Percival Everett, a black writer from South Carolina who holds an advanced degree in philosophy.

There is also a second way of reading the story symbolically, not as a speculation about the nature and personality of God but as a statement about the nature and limitations of the writer. The creator of the model railway who symbolizes the Creator of the universe may also represent the maker of the narrative. The limitations and difficulties are similar in many ways. To make a plausible world in a work of fiction is indeed a difficult task ("It's hard enough just to make this shit"). And once you have made it, the fictional world becomes, to some degree, deterministic. Every decision a writer makes forecloses other possibilities for plot and especially for character. Many writers are known to say that the characters they invent take on lives of their own and so cannot be made to do things in the story that they *wouldn't* "really" do—is this any less nutty than Virgil's belief that teeny people lead autonomous lives in his toy houses? As a writer, you may influence what happens in the imaginary world you make, but if you interfere capriciously the reader won't believe in you anymore.

NOTES

1. A rather large chunk of abstract discourse to start off a short story. Sounds like some sort of philosophy, and for the moment, we have no context for it.
2. Model? What model? What kind of model? The gesture toward something we can't yet see introduces a small element of suspense.
3. In a story so heavily tilted toward dialogue (and one where the main characters are scarcely described), the pipe and the cocktail give the characters some physical presence, and also serve as bits of "stage business" to fill pauses in the conversation.
4. Why is this question on his mind? As in "Depth Charge," something has already started between these two before the opening of the story, though we don't know what it is. Another sort of gesture toward something we can't yet see.
5. This apparent paradox lets us know that Virgil Boyd finds whatever he's doing now much more important than whatever it is he did for a living.
6. Stage business. Compare Everett's crisp efficiency with Gaitskill's dense rendition of background detail—Everett does no more than the absolute minimum required to move the characters around on the set.
7. All the description of Williston we'll ever get. The effect is to make him seem shadowy and a little mysterious.
8. This almost invisibly familiar phrase will find ironic echoes later in the story.
9. Tracks are sort of an unusual fixture for this location. Maybe the model is a train model, but does it run all over the house or what?
10. A very strange remark if Virgil is serious, although at the moment we may be inclined to assume that he's kidding.
11. A statement which pulls a train of connotations: "Boys will be boys," etc.

In the philosophical abstract, the inevitable essence of boyhood might include a dash of original sin.

12. Now what can it be, exactly, that Virgil thinks his friend doesn't understand? All these minor mysteries contribute to the suspense factor.

13. Frannie, we may deduce, is Williston's mother, Virgil's daughter, but she's not really a player in the drama, just a reason for Williston to be there.

14. Curiosity is indeed a normal boyish quality, so why should Virgil find it so sinister?

15. This line has quasi-theological overtones. Here innocence connotes not guiltlessness but an ignorance of one's own nature and the nature of the world. In this interpretation, Eve was "innocent" when accepting the apple from the serpent; she was ignorant about snakes and though she'd been told to stay away from the apple she had no experience to teach her the consequences of disobedience. The expulsion from Eden, often equated with the loss of innocence, is a primary educational experience.

16. For a story that stays so singlemindedly on point, the moose business is quite a noticeable digression (whereas in a Gaitskill story it would blend into a generally elaborated background). Virgil's reply is a characterizing detail, continuing to establish him (as the previous dialogue tends to do) as a man of strong and perhaps eccentric opinions, almost a curmudgeon in fact. And if he finds the moose head offensive, why does he keep it hanging above the fireplace?

17. Not just a curmudgeon but almost a misanthrope. Virgil's rather low opinion of human nature is consistent with his cynicism about curiosity and innocence. Again, the emphasis on the idea that his whole career as a dentist was simply a phase of training for the "work" he does now.

18. By having us follow the tracks, instead of looking directly at the model town, the writer creates a modest buildup of expectation.

19. Generally speaking, the model is more thoroughly described than the "real" house and the "real" people in it.

20. Interesting that even Morrison knows the model town has to have a name. In the average train set, the "towns" are nondescript background elements and the trains themselves are the focus of interest.

21. It's *the* oil refinery, not *an* oil refinery, implying that Virgil's Ashland has an autonomous existence, at least in his mind.

22. We begin to see how the skills of a dentist would apply to constructing such elaborate miniatures.

23. Seems a strangely fussy attitude.

24. What people? Now this is really strange. Virgil's eccentricity has been established previously, but this looks like real nuttiness.

25. Oddly, Morrison seems prepared for Virgil's response . . .

26. . . . prepared to interpret it as a sign of insanity, maybe.

27. He'd like to think that Virgil is kidding ...
28. ... but Virgil sure doesn't seem to be kidding. Is it possible that he believes tiny people really live in the model houses?
29. The reference to the delicacy of the model is a backtrack in the direction of rationality, or appears to be; at least Virgil is talking about it more as if it were a model and less as if it were an animated microcosmos.
30. Again, the detail of the description of the model is superior to the detail of the description of the "real" setting.
31. The steps of this exchange make it apparent that Virgil believes that the version of Ashland he has built is more "real" than the town of Morrison's experience. (Perhaps it's even superior, with trains instead of highways.) Morrison is sneaking up on the subject, but as his questions become more pointed, the answers become spookier ...
32. ... which would account for his nervous fidget here.
33. This is next door to asking straight out whether Virgil believes that there are actually little people living in the houses ...
34. ... and the answer isn't terrifically reassuring. Of course, Virgil may only mean that he's fantasized identities for the inhabitants of his model, that his imagination (like a novelist's perhaps) has proceeded to that extreme level of detail.
35. Spooked, Morrison wants to back away from the craziest implications of Virgil's answers ...
36. ... and this time Virgil's response is more comforting: he seems to be talking about the model as a model again, though still with a queer intensity.
37. Both the scope and the detail of the model really are striking. In "reality," Detroit is quite a long way from Ashland, Kentucky. Has Virgil reconstructed everything in between?
38. Morrison's attempt to minimize the implications: Virgil may be too obsessed with his hobby, but it's just a hobby after all. Isn't it?
39. From Virgil's point of view, it's emphatically not just a hobby.
40. Trouble in the microcosmos ... a snake in the garden?
41. This seems a wildly disproportionate response to the situation—even if Williston has been goofing around with the train sets, wouldn't that make him naughty or troublesome, rather than *evil*?
42. Boys will be boys, etc.
43. Why can't the problem be remedied? Most things that can be done in such a context can also be undone ... right?
44. Virgil's version of events becomes louder and more insistent.
45. Morrison's solution is perfectly pragmatic—if you're sharing his plane of reality ...
46. ... but Virgil's version of reality seems to be very different from the one Morrison would prefer. In Morrison's frame of reference (which is close

enough to ours), shutting off a toy train set just doesn't have any major "ramifications."

47. A signal to the reader to begin taking the situation more seriously.

48. And with these lines Virgil pulls the whole story further into his version of reality.

49. Morrison finally says it plainly.

50. Why can't they do anything?

51. In ordinary reality, this is a perfectly workable solution—what's so hard about picking up a toy train?

52. But Virgil just can't even conceive of interfering with the system he has set up.

53. Morrison's not going to interfere either; he now seems to be carried along by Virgil's sense of fatality.

54. This line is the snapper—the key which unlocks the system of allegorical correspondences controlling the whole story. At this conclusive moment, we should recognize (ideally with a thrilling shock of recognition) that we have been reading a parable about the nature of God, the created universe, and even the Devil.

OH, MAN ALIVE

HOLDEN BROOKS

His vision, from the constantly passing bars, has grown so weary
that it cannot hold anything else. It seems to him there are a thousand bars; and behind the bars, no world.

—from *The Panther, In the Jardin des Plaines, Paris*
by RAINER MARIA RILKE[1]

Richard takes a carrot from his bathrobe pocket, quarters it, and slides the
orange thumbs[2] down through the top side of the chicken wire cage.
"Morning, Rabbit." His own forefinger dips down slightly through the grate,[3]
and Rabbit, of a sudden, pounds her back legs in the cedar chips, lets out a
raspy, tissue-paper bark and bites.[4] Richard shakes this left hand in the air and
says to her, "What's your problem, animal?" She leaps around the bottom of her
cage, then stops to raise her body up against the criss-cross wire. "Oh, Rabbit."
Richard sees the sets of meaty teats swollen red up through the laundry-whiteness of her belly fur. Behind her in the corner of the cage he sees a pie-plate
worth of fur, pure white, shit-brindle, from her belly and her neck. She's pulled
out this feathery nest of mother-warmth[5] the night before in a false-pregnant
frenzy[6] and is guarding it. "Rabbit, I've got news for you." Richard stoops his
paisleyed, silken frame[7] and looks into her eyes, which do not seem to know
him. Richard sighs. "Not without a papa rabbit, Rabbit."[8] She stares, ears back

against her neck, nose pulsing angrily, eyes wet, wide and black, smooth and moving on an axis, like jet beads on a rosary.[9]

Richard stands and puts his hands upon his bony hips and Rabbit drops and huddles.[10] He frowns down from six feet over her, this tiny fur-lined shudder. She is a simple, fragile pumping;[11] one small heart and brain convinced, sustaining desperately the dream-litter of a tiny, dormant womb.[12] He drags her cage in from the drafty mud room to the kitchen and pours himself some coffee from the shallow brown pool in the pot.[13] "One piss worth,"[14] Richard calls it, what a single person needs to make. But for Rabbit, he's alone here.[15] He lifts his grapefruit half from inside the fridge, left from yesterday's whole, turned up skin-side on a saucer, glowing on the top shelf like a plastic breast.[16] He shakes one blue round from a vial of Prozac,[17] which hits the table with a teeter.[18] He chops off a hunk of cool sympathy cabbage[19] for Rabbit and drops the shreds onto the roof to watch her unfurl its pale greenness from below. For once they eat together.

Sitting politely and alone at the breakfast table, Richard Amurian is a tall and tweedy forty.[20] His head rises like an inverted, tilted pear, from the point of his airy beard to the bald rise of his head, skirted with a ring of hair like carded, deep gray wool. His crossed leg kicks stiffly underneath his robe, sinewy, barely haired, with bulbs for knees and ankles like his elbows, wrists, and knuckles.[21] He slides his wire glasses down his long and bending nose and watches Rabbit over his coffee cup as if she were a laboratory animal.[22] Automatically, he saves the last sip of his coffee for the pill. He places it on his tongue, still watching Rabbit flatly, and it disappears down into him.[23] She eats the cabbage up in ribbons quietly, eyes riveted forward, watching a small round and plain refrigerator magnet, waiting for it to emerge from some imagined horizon as a big, black, wing-flapping, baby-eating buzzard.[24]

"Rabbit, how am I going to explain this to Solomon?" Solomon is Richard's son, eleven now, and the reason Rabbit lives with Richard. Solomon has not lived here for seven years, since Richard's ex-wife, Naomi, moved to Chicago after they divorced. After four years of marriage. He still wets the bed and is a generally nervous child. He comes up on the train to Milwaukee by himself, which he hates, every third Friday. Today is one. Solomon is paranoid that he will fall asleep and miss his stop or that someone will kidnap him along the way or that Richard will forget, despite at least a dozen safe trips and all the rational assurance they can give him. Last night on the telephone Solomon asked what Richard knew about how trains derail.[25]

Richard keeps Rabbit for when the two of them run out of things to do. Solomon is tired of going to Richard's laboratory to watch percolating test tubes and to look at, but not touch, the big gold electron microscope. Naomi is a microbiologist, too. The two of them work on Lake Michigan, at different points.[26] It's nothing new for Sol.[27] And furthermore, he's growing into the sense that it is odd his father cannot converse freely about much beyond strains of viruses snaking in jellied petrie dishes. Mostly Richard spirals into language way beyond an eleven-year-old and Solomon drifts off into thoughts about the Coke machine down the hall. Or about somehow breathing in those viruses and dying in his sleep.[28]

Solomon's been wetting the bed since the divorce.[29] Both Richard and Naomi know it's the reason he is such a wreck.[30] They met at the lab and sort of fell into being married, then Solomon, in turn, sort of fell into the marriage. From the moment little Sol was handed to him, Richard wanted to give him back.[31] "Look, I'm sure I'm not holding him right. He won't stop crying." With his arms trembling beneath that small, red, shrieking body, it seemed to Richard that babies were always on the brink of death, literally. From falling on their heads, from snapping their tiny necks, from the flu, from forgetting how to breathe.[32] And Richard panicked. He panicked in the way most mild-mannered men do, avoidance.[33] He avoided Naomi, who seemed just an appendage to the child. He avoided the child except when it was sleeping to check its breathing. It seemed to Richard that the baby and Naomi were one highstrung mess; Naomi trying to scream Richard out of his detachment, the baby screaming endlessly for no apparent yet for every fatal reason Richard could imagine.[34]

Richard began to spend nights at the lab. He could not sleep, yet when he was home he spent hours on the couch in his study, on his back, behind closed doors, afraid of what was prowling through his house. Naomi could get nothing from him. She told Richard if millions of men around the world could handle this, he should, too. Where was his paternal instinct?[35] "It's nothing you would understand. If I could tell you what it was I would, Naomi. But I can't. That's the problem."

After a month of strained counseling, of Richard stoically paralyzed, they were divorced. In preparation for the aftershock, the loneliness, the doctor put Richard on an anti-depressant. They concluded his depression was a matter of chemicals, of neurotransmitters and so forth, which suited Richard fine and rounded out an explanation for divorce quite neatly.[36] With the blue capsules, one every morning, the darkness which subsumed him faded to a numb and opaque gray and Richard grew magnificently into loneliness.[37] Richard takes a last bite of his grapefruit and puts the Prozac vial back between the salt and pepper on the table. Tomorrow Solomon would be at breakfast, too.

Perhaps it will not be such a very hard thing to explain Rabbit's condition to Sol, thinks Richard. It could be more a lesson of psychiatry rather than sex. Yes. Rabbit has certain chemicals running through her right now which make her brain think she is going to have babies. Rabbit will prepare for these babies and get set to protect them, but they will not come. And afterwards, she will not be sad about it because she will not remember them, like sometimes we do not remember dreams.[38] She will pass through it like a flu and be a happy rabbit all over again.[39]

Richard picks his dishes up and walks to the sink to wash them. It takes ten seconds; one cup, one saucer, one plate. Under the hot rush of water, the plate splits down the middle spontaneously and slashes Richard's right thumb knuckle to the bone. He flinches, drops the other half. There is an awful crash against the basin, the water roars, and Rabbit leaps electrified around her cage. She hears the buzzards and the babies coming. Richard winces slightly, looks down curiously at the storm of fur, cedar, and dread she is creating.[40] "Rabbit, if you would, please be quiet."[41] He puts his hand beneath the stream, and calmly, silently, he bleeds.[42]

Richard arrives at the clinic at five to eleven exactly. He pulls his wool crusher down around his face and keeps his eyes down from the moment he takes off his seat belt to the moment he hits the doctor's couch. He walks the sidewalks and the hallways like a maze he's memorized.[43] First, there is the fear that someone will see him going into the shrink clinic and think that he's a crazy person. Then inside there are the crazy people.[44] As he walks past office doors he hears murmurs of their conversations coming out from underneath the thresholds. Sometimes he hears couples arguing or men crying. The worst is meeting someone in the hallway. One time he met a post-doc fellow from the lab at the front door, coming out as he was coming in. He had to look up. He expected to be met with some great surprise like "Dr. Amurian! What are you doing here?" Instead the woman looked at him with empathetic eyes and a trickle of a smile, sharing something not quite a secret or a shock. He was glad when this woman moved on to someplace else at the end of the year.[45]

The third-floor receptionist informs Richard that the doctor has been called out and the appointment will start twenty minutes late. Solomon's train comes in at eleven fifty, but he's halfway to the station downtown, anyway. He should make it just in time to meet the train when it pulls in.[46] He has these appointments once a month to renew his Prozac prescription and they are fairly painless and routine,[47] a list of questions: sleeping, eating, mood patterns. Always the same, down to half an hour. It is the coming and the going which is nervewracking, and now that he is here, it is not worth rescheduling. The receptionist sees that the waiting room is making Richard nervous and asks if he would like to sit in the doctor's office.

Richard turns the corner, goes into the office, but does not close the door entirely so he can listen for the doctor. The clinic is an old Milwaukee bungalow, like Richard's house and every other on the East Side. They have sealed up the archways, dropped the ceilings, and carpeted the place in an attempt to section it off into various soundproof offices. Richard's doctor's office was the part of the maid's quarters with pitched ceilings and deep dormers on the windows. It is set up like a parlor, with a leather couch, a hassock, an easy chair, family portraits and soothing watercolor seascapes. It is adjacent to another office, a door across the hall, and connected to it on the far wall by a shared bathroom. Richard guesses that the doctor really had rushed out because he left the bathroom door open and it is always, always, closed.[48] The ancient toilet inside is running madly, loudly, screaming almost.[49]

Richard has barely settled in the corner of the couch when he hears footsteps on the stairs and the receptionist direct someone just around the corner to the left, conceivably the other third-floor doctor's patient. Richard is watching the corner of that door, which he can see from the couch, when suddenly a hand appears around his own door, followed by a large, blonde woman. She cocks her ratty, frosted head and enters cautiously.

"Dr. . . . Silverberg? I'm Brandy Brown." Richard grips more tightly the arm of the couch which he is holding. The woman is approaching with her hand extended, inch long, pearly magenta claws lined up and pointed toward Richard. She is wearing a hooded lavender sweatsuit and her round, fleecy thighs criss-cross and rub around each other as she walks.[50] She smiles unevenly and her big white leather purse rings with a dozen key chains linked around its straps. Richard is a still, tentatively rooted reed; she is a fluorescent hot air balloon, coming closer.[51] How odd, thinks Richard. So irregular,[52] there's simply not one thing to do but watch as space comes in around him.

A small, tight woman in a red suit comes through the door just then and touches Brandy Brown on the shoulder. She speaks in that steady therapist voice, diffusing the tension, professionally.[53]

"Mrs. . . . Brown, I'm Dr. Silverberg. My office is right across here." She steers Brandy Brown, a good head taller than herself, around to the door quickly without looking at Richard. Richard watches Brandy Brown's massive purple globe of an ass move away from him. She laughs too loudly.

"I'm so embarrassed. Sorry about that." She turns her doughy, crayoned face back to Richard. "I never been here." She laughs again and Dr. Silverberg shuts them in her office.

Richard relaxes his grip and reaches for a newspaper section on the hassock. But for the toilet and the receptionist's typing and whispering radio, he reads in peace for several minutes. As the toilet noises decrescendo almost imperceptibly, the exchange in the adjoining office seeps into Richard's head.[54] He hears the Doctor's low roll, the patient's haphazard sing-song. Good thing, he thinks, he cannot hear what they are saying. Brandy Brown. Or perhaps—gads—it is Brandi Braun. Even worse, thinks Richard. Awful name. What were her parents thinking, saddling a girl with such a tacky, classless pun of a name? He wonders if her name had been Elizabeth or Mary if she would have ended up so garish. Or if her name was Anne and she had changed it herself. It sounds like a stripper's name, he thinks.[55] Before he arrived, Richard and Naomi had named Solomon carefully. Solomon was a wise, brave, and noble king. A leader and a prophet. It was a name with class and history and substance.[56]

Solomon. Richard looks at his watch. It is eleven-twenty now. Richard has risen to ask the receptionist what he should do when the toilet running ends abruptly. The conversation from the next room floods into the office, echoing through the tiled walls of the bathroom like an amplifier. The floorboards whine loudly beneath his steps, as loud as their voices, and he stops in his tracks. He wonders if the sound carries as strongly the other way.[57]

"Do you and Sam have intercourse regularly?"

"Depends on what you mean by regular." Richard hears her laugh. He curves his neck toward the open bathroom door and sees that the door to Dr. Silverberg's office is ajar in its frame, as well. If he closes it on his side, if he moves, they might see him, hear him, assume he had been listening all along. Or, God forbid, they might invite him in.[58] He stands in the middle of the room, light and frozen like a stick person.

"When you do have intercourse, are you both able to reach climax?"

"What do you mean?"

"I mean, are you both able to have an orgasm during sex?" Richard's stomach lurches. He feels like both the intruder and the intruded upon. His manners, his instincts, fail him.[59] He needs his pills, he wants to leave, he hates being put on display in the waiting room.

"Oh, Sam does, yeah. I never do. I never have, I mean."

"Really. Even before you were depressed?" Suspended, Richard looks to the outer door and prays one last time for the doctor to arrive and decide what to do.[60]

"Uh-uh. Well, I have them when I'm sleeping sometimes." Brandy snorts. "Weird, yeah?"

"During sexual dreams?"

"I dunno. Not really."[61]

Richard twists his face up and his beard moves with his chin. It is eleven twenty-two. In strange and unhuman baby steps, he shuffles his feet over the rug to the outer door and tells the receptionist he's leaving.

"I'll have to have the pills refilled over the phone. I'm just about out of them."

She calls rather loudly after him that she's not sure they can do that. How entirely irregular. Outside on the doorstep, he feels he's forgotten his hat and the autumn air begins to numb his polished skull. A young woman in a raincoat is pushing a huge, springed baby pram past the clinic and looks up at him. He comes down the steps to cross to his car and finds himself in one corner of a sloping driveway, the woman with the pram in the other. In a few steps he could be beside her. She is watching for a break in traffic and gripping the handle of the pram tightly with her slim fingers. Against his will, because it is possible, Richard thinks of loosing that pram into the street by knocking away her hands and watching the buggy roll into a truck. The woman looks to her left, to her right, at him, and he wonders if she knows the awfulness that surrounds her everywhere.[62]

At the station Richard waits among the throng of people waiting for others getting off or to get on. There are several groups of cub scouts, one hundred of
them maybe, with their den mothers flocking them frenetically. So many people still waiting on the same platform, he must be on time. His watch says so.[63]
He leans up against a shoe-shine machine screwed in to the wall, the kind with
red and black bristle brushes. Two of the little flushed-faced blue boys come
over to investigate and push their toes under the spiny wheels. They look up at
him from the corners of their eyes as if they're doing something wrong. He tries
to fix his eyes on the Pepsi clock in the snack bar, four-fifteen, it is wrong. He
drums his fingers on the metal top of the machine and clears his throat nervously. With his other hand he jangles the change in his pocket. The little boys
erupt in laughter and move back to a mother frowning and motioning to them.
The mother smiles back at him across the little beanied heads.[64] No need for
that, thinks Richard, and looks away from her. He hopes if it were Solomon,
someone would be watching him more closely than that in a place like this.[65]

He feels the world trying to seduce him into it today and he shrinks into
himself as best he can. He feels the tender ends of his fingertips stuck in the
glue-silk of a crazy web,[66] as he shifts his feet to steady his bony frame in the
rippling sea of high-pitched boys, in Rabbit's mad and messy flurry, in the wake
of Brandy Brown's sleeping orgasms shuddering through her thighs. Against his
will, he thinks about that shiver moving her from the deepest point inside,
alone, deep asleep, as alone as any one person can be, about the fleeting, faceless lover of her brain.[67] And he wonders if it is the phantom father of Rabbit's
imaginary babies, the inexplicable death-vision-monger Richard chains up in
his veins with small blue pills, one and the same.[68]

In all of this he hears one little boy crying, wailing awfully, and the other
little boys stare with spitty fingers in their mouths or twisting their yellow ties,
looking for the cry-baby. The shrieking splits Richard's ears and he is embarrassed standing there. The little boys begin to move toward the platform and
Richard realizes that the train must have pulled up without him noticing. The
lines of navy uniforms move by him, and the cry-baby stands alone on the
cement ramp down to the trains, lit up by a mean, yellow sulfur lamp.[69] It is
Solomon, and his name is hanging off him like a coat.[70] Thrown from one city,
one parent to the next, no one is there to catch him. He has fallen and the
thinkable has happened. At the sight of him, bellowing with the power of a million nightmares, Richard stops dead at the railing.[71]

Solomon is shaking violently, his knees about to buckle, his hands flailing
from the wrists pathetically. As Richard approaches, a den mother who had
been kneeling next to him looks at Richard disapprovingly and moves on with
her pack. Solomon's face is tomato-red and lacquered with hot, glossy tears.
Commuters trailing the cub scouts look at the hysterical child, possessed, then
back at Richard, with concerned eyes. Solomon's cries choke in his spindly
throat and his body convulses with the waves of volume, echoing through the

cement chamber. His little backpack straps are down around his elbows and Richard notices his white heaving belly has untucked his undershirt.[72] His streaming eyes are raised up to the ceiling and clenched so tightly he does not see Richard coming to him. He does not respond to Richard's arm around his beating shoulders, rising with the sobs.[73]

"Sol, I'm right here. I didn't see the train come in. I'm sorry." Solomon opens his eyes and looks at Richard, his eyelashes soaked and separated into tiny triangles. He has blue eyes like his mother, and they look at Richard, like Rabbit did, as a stranger, and continue to overflow. Richard's eyes, mortified and terrorized, looking back at Solomon, have little safety to afford.[74] Solomon stands planted on that ramp like he would just as soon go back to Chicago as stay with Richard. "Sol, this is embarrassing." Richard strokes Sol's dark, thin hair, hot and soaked with sweat from the underside. "People are watching us.[75] Let's go home, all right?" Richard's voice is wavering now, with frustration. Sol lets out one tremendous rising and condemning yell. Richard grabs him under his arms and brings him to himself, chest to chest. He presses his arms around the trembling, alien body, grabbing his own elbows, and walks toward the station door. He presses harder and harder and Solomon's hot breath pulses against his neck, tears soaking Richard's collar, screams projecting into the station over his shoulder. Richard looks down at Sol's dangling tennis shoes and his splayed and shaking fingers. He tightens his grip and hisses, "Stop this right now!" He presses Solomon into him, hoping he will disappear inside somehow.[76] And Richard thinks, against his will, about the bearing of his son, the bearing of his soul, screaming for every imaginable reason.[77]

ANALYSIS

Plot

Backstory

Quite a lot of material is covered in the well-written and efficient exposition on pages 148–49: Richard's haphazard marriage, his failure as a parent, the divorce and his subsequent treatment for depression, the somewhat similar anxieties of his eleven-year-old son. All these items are laid out quickly and cleanly to set the stage for what will happen in the story's present time line.

Present Action

The present-time plot of the story is brief and, on the surface, rather trivial: an account, in real time or close to it, of a typical Friday morning in Richard's life.

The present action is neatly divided, by space breaks, into three "acts," but the events in each of the three sections are of such small magnitude that the dramatic focus cannot be solely on "what happens":

1. Richard has breakfast with his Rabbit, then cuts his hand while dishwashing.
2. Richard attends his regular appointment with his psychiatrist, who is late, so that Richard must leave without seeing him or refilling his Prozac prescription.
3. Richard picks up his son, Solomon, at the train station. Because of an imperfect connection, the child is terrified and hysterical.

Each "act" does contain a deviation from the norm, but these deviations are so minor that most people would find them scarcely noticeable—or irritating at the worst. But Richard's mental balance is so delicate that anything "irregular" fills him with uncontrollable terror.

Character

"Oh, Man Alive" is really a one-character story—only Richard is fully apparent on the present time line. The exposition in the first couple of pages of the story does a great deal to characterize him, in terms of his failed marriage and ensuing depression. Exposition lets us know that Richard is someone who absolutely cannot cope with the mess and noise of parenthood— indeed, intimacy in any form seems to frighten him. We learn that he is a scientist, but scientific detachment (when he can achieve it) is a liability in his personal life—making him treat his emotional condition as a concrete chemical process which other chemicals should be able to modulate and regularize. The exposition shows Richard to be a profoundly frightened man, desperate to distance his fears from himself with therapeutic drugs—a solution which is only partially successful, at best.

In the present action, Richard is always both polite and timorous, carrying both qualities to a ridiculous extreme. His physical description, in the story's third paragraph, is both comic and somehow pathetic. His behavior shows him as nervous, vulnerable, uncommitted, abjectly indecisive, and often more than a little silly. In short, Richard is a rabbit. The full implications of his rabbitiness are reserved for the story's climax and conclusion.

It might be argued that Rabbit herself is the next most important character in the story. Although she is presented as an aggregate of animal impulses, a result of haywire instincts she can neither understand nor control, the compassionate detailing of her descriptions humanizes her in some way. But in the final analysis, Rabbit is less of a character, more of a significant image.

As for Solomon, although the opening exposition characterizes him very thoroughly in summary form, so far as the present action goes he is nothing but a scream — one of the several screams Richard is forced to listen to and try to endure. Given the setting of the railroad platform, the reader might even picture Solomon as giving forth a Munch-like scream.

Two cameo characterizations are worth noticing for their swift and sharp detail. Brandy Brown is a comic nightmare, rendered as such by the details of her dress and appearance, while Dr. Silverberg, a more ordinary person, is characterized by one crisp physical description, "a small, tight woman in a red suit," combined with her speaking tone, "that steady therapist voice, diffusing the tension, professionally."

Tone

For the most part, this story sounds like what Richard's consciousness must feel like. Sometimes the tone echoes Richard's conscious and deliberate thoughts, which tend to be formal and scientifically mechanical: "It could be more a lesson of psychiatry than sex. Yes. Rabbit has certain chemicals running through her right now which make her brain think she is going to have babies."

At other points, the tone exhibits a kind of nervous irony: "First, there is the fear that someone will see him going into the shrink clinic and think that he's a crazy person. Then inside there are the crazy people." Because of the jitteriness of its wit, this passage might well be part of Richard's own awareness; at the same time, it partially invites the reader to examine Richard from without.

Elsewhere, the tone follows the excruciating, nails-on-a-chalkboard sensation of Richard's near-constant condition of dread: "It seemed to Richard that the baby and Naomi were one highstrung mess; Naomi trying to scream Richard out of his detachment, the baby screaming endlessly for no apparent yet for every fatal reason Richard could imagine." In the rather horrifying crescendos of the story, this tone comes to the forefront.

The considerable range of tone becomes a tool for shaping the narrative formally. The peaks and valleys of the story are largely controlled by tone. The crises and climaxes tend to be disconnected from pure plot, but attention is focused on them by intensifications of the tone.

Point of View

Richard's point of view dominates throughout, but during the expository phase of the first few pages, the writer does establish the possibility of shifting it. Adopting some of the privileges and powers of central intelligence (see the discussion of Peter Taylor, pp. 84–86), she moves the point of view from Richard through a generalized omniscient overview to Solomon's interior consciousness ("Solomon drifts off into thoughts about the Coke machine down the hall"), then back to Richard again by a similar pathway.

This shift of point of view is used for expository convenience, to make the summary characterization of Solomon more lifelike, less dry. For the remainder of the story, the point of view remains within Richard or at least very close to him. But at times there is a slight split on our perspective. This split allows us to laugh at Richard as much or more than with him, during the story's blackly humorous turns. And when the crises of the story occur, we feel ourselves to be slightly distanced from the terror of Richard's reactions, because the point of view seems to have one foot inside Richard and one foot outside; we know (from the expository passage earlier) that the point of view could move further, although it doesn't actually do that. From this split position, we can both share Richard's most horrified responses from the inside and at the same time observe them from a short distance away, which is advantageous, because to be trapped wholly within Richard's experience would not be a pleasant experience.

Dialogue

Although the story runs close enough to real time that the device is not necessary for efficiency's sake, most of the dialogue in which Richard participates is partially paraphrased and summarized, with an occasional line quoted directly to enliven it:

> In strange and inhuman baby steps, he shuffles his feet over the rug to the outer door and tells the receptionist he's leaving.
> "I'll have to have the pills refilled over the phone. I'm just about out of them."
> She calls rather loudly after him that she's not sure they can do that.

The effect of this mode of presenting conversations is to internalize the story still further within Richard's tortured consciousness—to further emphasize his isolation from the people around him.

By contrast, the dialogue which Richard overhears, between Brandy Brown and Dr. Silverberg, is quoted in full. Here Brandy Brown's voice, heard from offstage, becomes responsible for half her characterization; her tone establishes her personality. Her voice is both coarse and comfortable with itself, and it's terrifying to Richard for both those reasons.

Imagery and Description

This story is structurally designed around its most important images, but even apparently minor descriptions undergo progressive intensification of their imagery:

> She leaps around the bottom of her cage, then stops to raise her

body up against the criss-cross wire. "Oh, Rabbit." Richard sees the sets of meaty teats swollen red up through the laundry-whiteness of her belly fur. Behind her in the corner of the cage he sees a pie-plate worth of fur, pure white, shit-brindle, from her belly and her neck. She's pulled out this feathery nest of mother-warmth the night before in a false-pregnant frenzy and is guarding it.

The description first makes a powerful appeal to the senses ("sets of meaty teats swollen red"), compelling the reader to visualize the scene. The phrase "laundry-whiteness" is a subtle gesture in the direction of metaphor; there's something homey, even maternal, about the thought of clean white laundry. The contrast of the two colors of the rabbit's fur, "laundry-white" and "shit-brindle," begins to suggest the messiness of organic life that is such a problem for Richard. Finally, "feathery nest of mother-warmth" is an image married to a metaphor, "mother-warmth," being an abstraction that contributes to the explanation of *why* the rabbit is pulling her fur out. The development of the description in stages is important; if the passage began with "feathery nest of mother-warmth," it would be merely confusing. Note also the use of alliteration ("feathery . . . false . . . frenzy") to reinforce the point of this conclusive sentence.

From a longer view, the story can be read as an extended metaphor so elaborate it is almost a metaphysical conceit. An implied comparison of Richard with his rabbit is evolved throughout the story, then complicated by the appearance of Brandy Brown, who also is identified with the rabbit by a couple of descriptive details: her "claws," which suggest an animal nature, and her "round, fleecy thighs," which recall the rabbit's maternal nest of fur. Richard is rabbitlike because of his timorousness and vulnerability, his tendency to freeze under stress, like a rabbit in headlights. But in the end the rabbit and Brandy Brown are more closely identified because of their meaningless, misplaced drive toward fecundity:

> He feels the tender ends of his fingertips stuck in the glue-silk of a crazy web, as he shifts his feet to steady his bony frame in the rippling sea of high-pitched boys, in Rabbit's mad and messy flurry, in the wake of Brandy Brown's sleeping orgasms shuddering through her thighs. Against his will, he thinks about that shiver moving her from the deepest point inside, alone, deep asleep, as alone as any one person can be, about the fleeting, faceless lover of her brain. And he wonders if it is the phantom father of Rabbit's imaginary babies, the inexplicable death-vision-monger Richard chains up in his veins with small blue pills, one and the same.

The convergence of these images brings the whole extended metaphor close to its completion and lets us know what's really wrong with Richard. If

Brandy Brown can be catapulted to orgasm in the ostensible privacy of her sleep, then even Prozac will never be enough to isolate Richard from the organic messiness of sexual life which impinges on him from everywhere in the world—although that isolation is what he desires more than anything else.

Design

The images and metaphors turn out to be the most important design elements of the story as a whole. The plot is divided into three distinct units, as discussed above, but the conclusive element of each unit is an image, rather than an event. Each of the story's three demarcated sections is shaped toward an image which becomes its conclusion.

The function of the first section of the story is mostly expository, so it concludes with an image which nails down Richard's characterization: the unfortunate man who's completely identified with the role of helpless victim. When he's injured, he freezes in a rabbitlike way; apparently he can do nothing but stay there, bleeding in the water. The image of the man helplessly bleeding in this way suggests the idea of Richard's psychological wound continually bleeding into the world that surrounds him—against his will and in spite of all his ineffectual efforts to prevent it.

The second section, rather more plot-filled than the first, also drives toward an image in its concluding paragraph: Richard's queer fantasy of "loosing that pram into the street by knocking away her hands and watching the buggy roll into a truck." This fantasy image is striking because in a way it's uncharacteristic—the only time we ever see him in the role of an aggressor. On the other hand, the thought itself comes to Richard like an attack from without; he is a victim of this fantasy, which is simply one more element he can't control in a world that seems to menace him from all directions. We can't really conceive of Richard as a pram-snatching baby killer, but the image begins to seem more appropriate later on when we realize how powerfully he wishes to somehow cancel out the very existence of his son, Solomon.

In the third section of the story, all the images previously established begin to act on each other like a string of falling dominoes, driving toward the ultimate conclusion. The convergence of the Rabbit/Brandy/Richard images (discussed above) produces the final clarification of what Richard's problem really is: a revulsion from the organic sloppiness inevitably found at the root of all life. Because of this difficulty the world will always be a hostile environment for poor Richard.

But the concluding tableau carries the issue a step further. We see Solomon, still screaming his Munch-like scream, folded into Richard's utterly uncomforting embrace—"a trembling, alien body." With this image before us, we understand that Richard's imagined solution to the whole problem of his existence is for Solomon to "disappear inside somehow"—to be reabsorbed into

Richard's own body (as Rabbit's body will reabsorb the symptoms of her false pregnancy, leaving her "a happy rabbit all over again"). This is a striking insight, but not a very pleasant one. It leaves Richard echoing the screams that have pursued him throughout the story with a silent scream of his own. More than likely, you'd be screaming too . . .

NOTES

1. An epigraph (that is, a quotation from some other writer placed at the opening of your text) can be a way of shaping the context in which your narrative will be read—presenting the reader with another lens through which to view your story.
2. Those "thumbs" make an evocative metaphor, and the slightly strange intimacy of this opening makes it almost appear that Richard is dismembering himself to feed his pet . . .
3. . . . as emphasized here.
4. The caged animal recalls the epigraph: rabbit instead of panther, but apparently a quite ferocious rabbit.
5. The fur is described in several energetic ways, some of which simply make it present to the reader's senses, others of which suggest a connection to the rabbit's false pregnancy . . .
6. . . . an instinct which, removed from its appropriate context, becomes pathological.
7. There's something slightly weak and effete in this description.
8. The rabbit is (unnaturally?) solitary. Here Richard speaks, perhaps ironically as will later be seen, for the natural order of things.
9. Extreme closeup. Notice how the naturalistic accuracy of the description is twisted by the unusual simile at the end of the sentence.
10. The difference in size is stressed by their opposite postures.
11. The use of these substantives, "shudder" and "pumping," presents the rabbit as mindless biological process . . .
12. . . . but complicated by something that amounts to a wish, even though it must be expressed somewhere below the threshold of human consciousness. Notice how the inevitable urgency of the false pregnancy is supported by alliteration: "desperately . . . dream-litter . . . dormant." The writer also writes poetry, and she transfers a number of poetic devices to her prose.
13. This dismal image . . .
14. . . . is reinforced by this dismal thought.

15. Like Rabbit, Richard lacks a mate. This comparison will be extended and complicated throughout the story.

16. This vivid description radiates a near-perverse unnaturalness.

17. Written in 1991, this story may mark one of the first appearances of Prozac in fiction. Here it's a shorthand message that Richard probably suffers from depression—useful to the reader because Richard is trying not to let his condition show, even to himself.

18. Perhaps Richard's mental state is teetering also.

19. The first adjective ("cool") addresses the senses, the second ("sympathy") moves toward an abstraction. This sort of combination, frequently used in the story, make this writer's descriptions both vivid and suggestive.

20. The camera pulls back. Till now we've seen everything in extreme, perhaps nervous-making closeup. Now we have a longer view which presents the whole scene . . .

21. . . . with Richard in it. Not entirely an inspiring spectacle.

22. The clinical feel of this line is a contrast to earlier descriptions that focus on the living energy of the rabbit.

23. The slowed-down description of the pill taking has something slightly sinister about it. If we expect a change, there isn't one.

24. The whimsy of this image is comical to the reader, though one must assume that the rabbit doesn't find it so amusing.

25. Richard's thought at the top of the paragraph gives a natural pretext for this block of exposition, which also does a great deal to characterize Solomon before his appearance on the stage of the story. Notice the gesture toward half-scene in the last sentence.

26. This expository summary is made vivid by the physical detailing of the laboratory.

27. This sentence, neutral in terms of point of view, is the hinge for a shift to Sol's point of view.

28. The dominant point of view in this story will always be Richard's, but the writer knows how to execute a smooth shift to other points of view—a curve that passes through central intelligence overview (as in Taylor's "A Wife of Nashville").

29. This point-of-view neutral sentence . . .

30. . . . prepares for a shift to the joint overview of Naomi and Richard together (what they both know) . . .

31. . . . and finally grounds us in Richard's point of view again. As with the earlier line about the putative buzzard, this line may be funny to us, but probably isn't to Richard. The phrase "Give him back" will turn out to have implications beyond this particular scene.

32. This exaggerated fearfulness tells us something about Richard's mental condition—morbid depression entwined with acute anxiety.

33. Rather rabbity behavior.

34. The switchback in the syntax of this concluding sentence brings out the contradictions between the reality of external conditions and Richard's inner state.

35. A reversal on the situation of the rabbit, whose maternal instinct functions all too well, exactly when it *isn't* needed.

36. The mechanical quality of Richard's analysis of his own problem seems to comfort him, but it must be rather cold comfort.

37. The nicely modulated color imagery suggests that Prozac may not be so wonderful as it's cracked up to be ... for Richard, anyway. The supposed magnificence of his loneliness is ironic, given the scene.

38. Who really knows anything about the emotional life of rabbits? This is like a fisherman saying that 'fish don't feel' as he rips out the hook.

39. But Richard wants to believe it, of course. What he wants to believe about the rabbit's emotional life is a mirror image of what he'd like to believe about his own.

40. The implied symbiosis between the rabbit and Richard turns very unpleasant here as they both begin vibrating with terror and pain.

41. There's something awful about Richard's constant politeness, which is unnecessary in his solitude.

42. This sentence clinches the first scene's image of Richard: a helpless, hopeless victim available to any predator that might be attracted by his blood spreading in the water.

43. I.e., he behaves very much like the laboratory animal he prefers to understand himself to be.

44. Funny to us but not to Richard.

45. Richard seems to be different from his fellow sufferers in that he can't seem to enjoy any sympathetic feeling with them. Where others might feel a sense of support with a common problem, he only feels more isolated and ashamed ... a reaction similar to the self-isolating response that ended his marriage.

46. A small problem but significant in the story's limited terms; this is the first practical conflict, however minor.

47. I.e., mechanical and laboratory-like.

48. It's important that we understand this floorplan precisely because of the action that follows.

49. So many things in Richard's surroundings seem to scream at him.

50. This extremely vivid description is double-edged—we see a somewhat oddly dressed woman but Richard sees a clawed threat. That fleeciness recalls the intense descriptions of the rabbit fur, earlier.

51. The extravagance of this image recalls the contrast between Richard and the rabbit earlier (see note 10). We see them not as a man and a woman who might in *some* sense be complementary to each other, but as beings from two different universes.

52. Richard is pathetically helpless before any deviation from the norm.

53. Only a therapist has the authority to rescue him.

54. The floorplan and sound effects become important here, allowing the session in the next office gradually to infiltrate Richard's awareness.

55. Any connotation of sexuality sends Richard reeling.

56 Perhaps, but does the previous characterization of the child live up to these descriptions?

57. Richard is so hideously vulnerable that he freezes like a rabbit caught in headlights, unable to move in any direction.

58. Like any little furry defenseless thing, Richard fears exposure most of all.

59. Either nature has failed Richard or he has failed nature; his instincts refuse to function as they should.

60. He's pathetically unable to make the most minor decision on his own, which is characteristic of some forms of clinical depression. Among laboratory animals, such a state of paralytic indecision can be induced by operant conditioning and is known to behavioral psychology as "learned helplessness."

61. For Richard, who can't stand to think about discussing the sexual behavior of his rabbit with his eleven-year-old son, any discussion of *human* sexuality must be an indescribable torture.

62. A young woman with a baby carriage might be a pleasant or at least an innocuous sight, but Richard's mental state turns everything he sees into a horror movie. Notice how he sees himself as both victim and victimizer in this reverie. In his imagination, no human transaction can do anything *but* harm.

63. In his mental life too, Richard is constantly groping for mechanical signals that things are "regular," the way they're supposed to be.

64. The least gesture of contact from the opposite sex is terrifying to Richard . . .

65. . . . and it instantly twirls toward his generalized sense of menace everywhere in the outside world.

66. Someone in better mental health would be more likely to respond to the world's embrace as it's suggested here. But the network of relatedness, which would be a web of support to many people, is everything that horrifies Richard: it's messy, organic, and by implication sexual.

67. This convergence of images is a sort of epiphany, which brings together many of the meanings of the story. If the rabbit is a "shudder," Brandy Brown becomes a "shiver"; both are reduced to pure process by their involuntary sexual responses (which are, in fact, "irregular"). The image is especially threatening to Richard because it suggests that one can be somehow reached and touched even when one is most thoroughly alone.

68. Rabbit, Brandy and Richard are all unable in different ways to sustain normal sexual connections. Brandy and the rabbit remain sexually respon-

sive, which is exactly what terrifies Richard so. Because of his terror, he
uses Prozac to try to bomb his own responses out of existence.

69. Everything always seems to be screaming at Richard—who is certainly not
the sort of parent who would recognize his own child's cry in any crowd.

70. A nice follow-up on Solomon's failure, earlier implied, to fulfill the
grandiose implications of his name.

71. Almost any parent would hasten toward a child in distress, but Richard
freezes "dead" into his helpless state.

72. Everything about this closely detailed description suggests an animal vulnerability, the exposed underbelly of prey.

73. Apparently the horror of Solomon's inner condition has shut down any
awareness of the outside world. Like father, like son . . .

74. . . . and their similarity alienates them rather than connecting them.

75. The ultimate terror for Richard.

76. What Richard wants is to reabsorb his son into his own body, thus revers-
ing the reproductive process that has already taken place, as the rabbit's
false pregnancy will be reversed. Here the full implication of the phrase
"give him back" (see note 31) is realized.

77. The loose reference of the phrase "screaming for every imaginable reason" (echoed from a previous passage, see note 33), is actually an advantage here: the son is literally screaming, and Richard, and Richard's soul,
are figuratively screaming too. Everything in the story screams, but without catharsis.

    The word "bearing" is used in a three-layered poetic pun, which com-
pletes the meanings of the story. Both his son and his sick soul are burdens which Richard can scarcely bear up. "Bearing" also refers to childbirth, something which Richard finds completely insupportable, both as a
process and in terms of its result. Finally, the phrase "bearing of his soul"
suggests the more conventional *baring of the soul*—the same sort of exposure that Richard has found so fearful throughout the story. What's torn
into the light in this final passage is Richard's uncontrollable, unnatural
wish to undo the very existence of his son—and indeed it *is* a hideous
exposure.

THE SKY IS GRAY

E R N E S T   J .   G A I N E S

1 Go'n be coming in a few minutes. Coming round that bend down there full speed. And I'm go'n get out my handkerchief and wave it down, and we go'n get on it and go.[1]

I keep on looking for it, but Mama don't look that way no more. She's looking down the road where we just come from. It's a long old road, and far's you can see you don't see nothing but gravel. You got dry weeds on both sides, and you got trees on both sides, and fences on both sides, too. And you got cows in the pastures and they standing close together. And when we was coming out here to catch the bus I seen the smoke coming out of the cows's noses.[2]

I look at my mama and I know what she's thinking. I been with Mama so much, just me and her, I know what she's thinking all the time. Right now it's home—Auntie and them. She's thinking if they got enough wood—if she left enough there to keep them warm till we get back. She's thinking if it go'n rain and if any of them go'n have to go out in the rain. She's thinking 'bout the hog—if he go'n get out, and if Ty and Val be able to get him back in. She always worry like that when she leaves the house.[3] She don't worry too much if she leave me there with the smaller ones 'cause she know I'm go'n look after them and look after Auntie and everything else. I'm the oldest and she say I'm the man.[4]

I look at my mama and I love my mama. She's wearing that black coat and that black hat and she's looking sad. I love my mama and I want put my arm round her and tell her. But I'm not supposed to do that. She say that's weakness and that's crybaby stuff, and she don't want no crybaby round her. She don't want you to be scared, either. 'Cause Ty's scared of ghosts and she's always whipping him. I'm scared of the dark, too, but I make 'tend I ain't. I make 'tend I ain't 'cause I'm the oldest, and I got to set a good sample for the rest. I can't ever be scared and I can't ever cry.[5] And that's why I never said nothing 'bout my teeth. It's been hurting me and hurting me close to a month now, but I never said it. I didn't say it 'cause I didn't want act like a crybaby, and 'cause I know we didn't have enough money to go have it pulled. But, Lord, it been hurting me. And look like it wouldn't start till at night when you was trying to get yourself a little sleep. Then soon 's you shut your eyes—ummmm-ummmm, Lord, look like it go right down to your heartstring.[6]

"Hurting, hanh?" Ty'd say.

I'd shake my head, but I wouldn't open my mouth for nothing. You open your mouth and let that wind in, and it almost kill you.[7]

I'd just lay there and listen to them snore. Ty there, right 'side me, and Auntie and Val over by the fireplace. Val younger than me and Ty, and he sleeps with Auntie. Mama sleeps round the other side with Louis and Walker.[8]

I'd just lay there and listen to them, and listen to that wind out there, and listen to that fire in the fireplace. Sometimes it'd stop long enough to let me get little rest. Sometimes it just hurt, hurt, hurt. Lord, have mercy.[9]

2 Auntie knowed it was hurting me. I didn't tell nobody but Ty, 'cause we buddies and he ain't go'n tell nobody. But some kind of way Auntie found out. When she asked me, I told her no, nothing was wrong. But she knowed it all the time. She told me to mash up a piece of aspirin and wrap it in some cotton and jugg it down in that hole. I did it, but it didn't do no good. It stopped for a little while, and started right back again. Auntie wanted to tell Mama, but I told her, "Uh-uh." 'Cause I knowed we didn't have any money, and it just was go'n make her mad again. So Auntie told Monsieur Bayonne, and Monsieur Bayonne came over to the house and told me to kneel down 'side him on the fireplace. He put his finger in his mouth and made the Sign of the Cross on my jaw. The tip of Monsieur Bayonne's finger is some hard, 'cause he's always playing on that guitar. If we sit outside at night we can always hear Monsieur Bayonne playing on his guitar. Sometimes we leave him out there playing on the guitar.[10]

Monsieur Bayonne made the Sign of the Cross over and over on my jaw, but that didn't do no good. Even when he prayed and told me to pray some, too, that tooth still hurt me.

"How you feeling?" he say.

"Same," I say.

He kept on praying and making the Sign of the Cross and I kept on praying, too.[11]

"Still hurting?" he say.

"Yes, sir."

Monsieur Bayonne mashed harder and harder on my jaw. He mashed so hard he almost pushed me over on Ty. But then he stopped.

"What kind of prayers you praying, boy?" he say.

"Baptist," I say.

"Well, I'll be—no wonder that tooth still killing him. I'm going one way and he pulling the other. Boy, don't you know any Catholic prayers?"

"I know 'Hail Mary,'" I say.

"Then you better start saying it."[12]

"Yes, sir."

He started mashing on my jaw again, and I could hear him praying at the same time. And, sure enough, after while it stopped hurting me.[13]

Me and Ty went outside where Monsieur Bayonne's two hounds was and we started playing with them. "Let's go hunting," Ty say. "All right," I say; and we went on back in the pasture. Soon the hounds got on a trail, and me and Ty followed them all 'cross the pasture and then back in the woods, too. And then they cornered this little old rabbit and killed him, and me and Ty made them get back, and we picked up the rabbit and started on back home. But my tooth had started hurting me again. It was hurting me plenty now, but I wouldn't tell Monsieur Bayonne.[14] That night I didn't sleep a bit, and first thing in the morning Auntie told me to go back and let Monsieur Bayonne pray over me some more. Monsieur Bayonne was in his kitchen making coffee when I got there. Soon 's he seen me he knowed what was wrong.

"All right, kneel down there 'side that stove," he say. "And this time make sure you pray Catholic. I don't know nothing 'bout that Baptist, and I don't want know nothing 'bout him."[15]

3 Last night Mama say, "Tomorrow we going to town."[16]

"It ain't hurting me no more," I say. "I can eat anything on it."[17]

"Tomorrow we going to town," she say.

And after she finished eating, she got up and went to bed.

She always go to bed early now. 'Fore Daddy went in the Army, she used to stay up late. All of us sitting out on the gallery or round the fire. But now, look like soon 's she finish eating she go to bed.[18]

This morning when I woke up, her and Auntie was standing 'fore the fireplace. She say: "Enough to get there and get back. Dollar and a half to have it pulled. Twenty-five for me to go, twenty-five for him. Twenty-five for me to come back, twenty-five for him. Fifty cents left. Guess I get little piece of salt meat with that."[19]

"Sure can use it," Auntie say. "White beans and no salt meat ain't white beans."

"I do the best I can," Mama say.[20]

They was quiet after that, and I made 'tend I was still asleep.

"James, hit the floor," Auntie say.

I still made 'tend I was asleep. I didn't want them to know I was listening.[21]

"All right," Auntie say, shaking me by the shoulder. "Come on. Today's the day."

I pushed the cover down to get out, and Ty grabbed it and pulled it back.

"You, too, Ty," Auntie say.

"I ain't getting no teef pulled," Ty say.

"Don't mean it ain't time to get up," Auntie say. "Hit it, Ty."[22]

Ty got up grumbling.

"James, you hurry up and get in your clothes and eat your food," Auntie say. "What time y'all coming back?" she say to Mama.

"That 'leven o'clock bus," Mama say. "Got to get back in that field this evening."[23]

"Get a move on you, James," Auntie say.

I went in the kitchen and washed my face, then I ate my breakfast. I was having bread and syrup. The bread was warm and hard and tasted good. And I tried to make it last a long time.[24]

Ty came back there grumbling and mad at me.

"Got to get up," he say. "I ain't having no teefes pulled. What I got to be getting up for?"

Ty poured some syrup in his pan and got a piece of bread. He didn't wash his hands, neither his face, and I could see that white stuff in his eyes.

"You the one getting your teef pulled," he say. "What I got to get up for. I bet if I was getting a teef pulled, you wouldn't be getting up. Shucks; syrup again. I'm getting tired of this old syrup. Syrup, syrup, syrup. I'm go'n take with the sugar diabetes. I want me some bacon sometime."[25]

"Go out in the field and work and you can have your bacon," Auntie say. She stood in the middle door looking at Ty. "You better be glad you got syrup. Some people ain't got that—hard 's time is."[26]

"Shucks," Ty say. "How can I be strong."

"I don't know too much 'bout your strength," Auntie say; "but I know where you go'n be hot at, you keep that grumbling up. James, get a move on you; your mama waiting."

I ate my last piece of bread and went in the front room. Mama was standing 'fore the fireplace warming her hands. I put on my coat and my cap, and we left the house.

4   I look down there again, but it still ain't coming.[27] I almost say, "It ain't coming yet," but I keep my mouth shut. 'Cause that's something else she don't like. She don't like for you to say something just for nothing. She can see it ain't coming, I can see it ain't coming, so why say it ain't coming.[28] I don't say it, I turn and look at the river that's back of us. It's so cold the smoke's just raising up from the water. I see a bunch of pool-doos* not too far out—just on the other side the lilies. I'm wondering if you can eat pool-doos. I ain't too sure, 'cause I ain't never ate none. But I done ate owls and blackbirds, and I done ate redbirds, too. I didn't want kill the redbirds, but she made me kill them.[29] They had two of them back there. One in my trap, one in Ty's trap. Me and Ty was go'n play with them and let them go, but she made me kill them 'cause we needed the food.[30]

"I can't," I say. "I can't."

"Here," she say. "Take it."

"I can't," I say. "I can't. I can't kill him, Mama, please."

"Here," she say. "Take this fork, James."

"Please, Mama, I can't kill him," I say.

I could tell she was go'n hit me. I jerked back, but I didn't jerk back soon enough.[31]

"Take it," she say.

I took it and reached in for him, but he kept on hopping to the back.

"I can't, Mama," I say. The water just kept on running down my face.[32] "I can't," I say.

"Get him out of there," she say.

I reached in for him and he kept on hopping to the back. Then I reached in farther, and he pecked me on the hand.

"I can't, Mama," I say.

She slapped me again.

I reached in again, but he kept on hopping out my way. Then he hopped to one side and I reached there. The fork got him on the leg and I heard his leg pop. I pulled my hand out 'cause I had hurt him.

"Give it here," she say, and jerked the fork out my hand.

She reached in and got the little bird right in the neck. I heard the fork go in his neck, and I heard it go in the ground. She brought him out and helt him right in front of me.[33]

"That's one," she say. She shook him off and gived me the fork. "Get the other one."

"I can't, Mama," I say. "I'll do anything, but don't make me do that."

She went to the corner of the fence and broke the biggest switch over there she could find. I knelt 'side the trap, crying.

---

* A name for water bird, derived from the French *poulet d'eau*.

"Get him out of there," she say.

"I can't, Mama."

She started hitting me 'cross the back. I went down on the ground, crying.

"Get him," she say.

"Octavia?" Auntie say.

'Cause she had come out of the house and she was standing by the tree looking at us.

"Get him out of there," Mama say.

"Octavia," Auntie say, "explain to him. Explain to him. Just don't beat him. Explain to him."[34]

But she hit me and hit me and hit me.

I'm still young—I ain't no more than eight; but I know now; I know why I had to do it. (They was so little, though. They was so little. I 'member how I picked the feathers off them and cleaned them and helt them over the fire. Then we all ate them. Ain't had but a little bitty piece each, but we all had a little bitty piece, and everybody just looked at me 'cause they was so proud.)[35] Suppose she had to go away? That's why I had to do it. Suppose she had to go away like Daddy went away? Then who was go'n look after us? They had to be somebody left to carry on. I didn't know it then, but I know it now. Auntie and Monsieur Bayonne talked to me and made me see.[36]

5 Time I see it I get out my handkerchief and start waving. It's still 'way down there, but I keep waving anyhow. Then it come up and stop and me and Mama get on. Mama tell me go sit in the back while she pay.[37] I do like she say, and the people look at me. When I pass the little sign that say "White" and "Colored," I start looking for a seat. I just see one of them back there, but I don't take it, 'cause I want my mama to sit down herself. She comes in the back and sit down, and I lean on the seat. They got seats in the front, but I know I can't sit there, 'cause I have to sit back of the sign. Anyhow, I don't want sit there if my mama go'n sit back here.[38]

They got a lady sitting 'side my mama and she looks at me and smiles little bit. I smile back, but I don't open my mouth, 'cause the wind'll get in and make that tooth ache. The lady take out a pack of gum and reach me a slice, but I shake my head. The lady just can't understand why a little boy'll turn down gum, and she reach me a slice again. This time I point to my jaw. The lady understands and smiles little bit, and I smile little bit, but I don't open my mouth, though.[39]

They got a girl sitting 'cross from me. She got on a red overcoat and her hair's plaited in one big plait. First, I make 'tend I don't see her over there, but then I start looking at her little bit. She make 'tend she don't see me, either, but I catch her looking that way. She got a cold, and every now and then she h'ist that little handkerchief to her nose. She ought to blow it, but she don't. Must think she's too much a lady or something.

Every time she h'ist that little handkerchief, the lady 'side her say something in her ear. She shakes her head and lays her hands in her lap again. Then I catch her kind of looking where I'm at. I smile at her little bit.[40] But think she'll smile back? Uh-uh. She just turn up her little old nose and turn her head. Well, I show her both of us can turn us head. I turn mine too and look out at the river.[41]

The river is gray. The sky is gray.[42] They have pool-doos on the water. The water is wavy, and the pool-doos go up and down. The bus go round a turn, and you got plenty trees hiding the river. Then the bus go round another turn, and I can see the river again.

I look toward the front where all the white people sitting. Then I look at that little old gal again. I don't look right at her, 'cause I don't want all them people to know I love her.[43] I just look at her little bit, like I'm looking out that window over there. But she knows I'm looking that way, and she kind of look at me, too. The lady sitting 'side her catch her this time, and she leans over and says something in her ear.

"I don't love him nothing," that little old gal says out loud.

Everybody back there hear her mouth, and all of them look at us and laugh.

"I don't love you, either," I say. "So you don't have to turn up your nose, Miss."

"You the one looking," she say.

"I wasn't looking at you," I say. "I was looking out that window, there."

"Out that window, my foot," she say. "I seen you. Every time I turned round you was looking at me."

"You must of been looking yourself if you seen me all them times," I say.

"Shucks," she say, "I got me all kind of boyfriends."

"I got girlfriends, too," I say.

"Well, I just don't want you getting your hopes up," she say.

I don't say no more to that little old gal 'cause I don't want have to bust her in the mouth. I lean on the seat where Mama sitting, and I don't even look that way no more. When we get to Bayonne, she jugg her little old tongue out at me. I make 'tend I'm go'n hit her, and she duck down 'side her mama. And all the people laugh at us again.[44]

6 Me and Mama get off and start walking in town. Bayonne is a little bitty town. Baton Rouge is a hundred times bigger than Bayonne. I went to Baton Rouge once—me, Ty, Mama, and Daddy. But that was 'way back yonder, 'fore Daddy went in the Army. I wonder when we go'n see him again. I wonder when. Look like he ain't ever coming back home. . . .[45] Even the pavement all cracked in Bayonne. Got grass shooting right out the sidewalk. Got weeds in the ditch, too; just like they got at home.

It's some cold in Bayonne. Look like it's colder than it is home. The wind blows in my face, and I feel that stuff running down my nose. I sniff. Mama says use that handkerchief. I blow my nose and put it back.[46]

We pass a school and I see them white children playing in the yard. Big old red school, and them children just running and playing. Then we pass a café, and I see a bunch of people in there eating. I wish I was in there 'cause I'm cold. Mama tells me keep my eyes in front where they belong.[47]

We pass stores that's got dummies, and we pass another café, and then we pass a shoe shop, and that bald-head man in there fixing on a shoe. I look at him and I butt into that white lady, and Mama jerks me in front and tells me stay there.[48]

We come up to the courthouse, and I see the flag waving there. This flag ain't like the one we got at school. This one here ain't got but a handful of stars. One at school got a big pile of stars—one for every state. We pass it and we turn and there it is—the dentist office. Me and Mama go in, and they got people sitting everywhere you look. They even got a little boy in there younger than me.

Me and Mama sit on that bench, and a white lady come in there and ask me what my name is. Mama tells her and the white lady goes on back. Then I hear somebody hollering in there. Soon 's that little boy hear him hollering, he starts hollering, too. His mama pats him and pats him, trying to make him hush up, but he ain't thinking 'bout his mama.[49]

The man that was hollering in there comes out holding his jaw. He is a big old man and he's wearing overalls and a jumper.

"Got it, hanh?" another man asks him.

The man shakes his head—don't want open his mouth.

"Man, I thought they was killing you in there," the other man says. "Hollering like a pig under a gate."[50]

The man don't say nothing. He just heads for the door, and the other man follows him.

"John Lee," the white lady says. "John Lee Williams."

The little boy juggs his head down in his mama's lap and holler more now. His mama tells him go with the nurse, but he ain't thinking 'bout his mama. His mama tells him again, but he don't even hear her. His mama picks him up and takes him in there, and even when the white lady shuts the door I can still hear little old John Lee.[51]

"I often wonder why the Lord let a child like that suffer," a lady says to my mama.[52] The lady's sitting right in front of us on another bench. She's got on a white dress and a black sweater. She must be a nurse or something herself, I reckon.

"Not us to question," a man says.

"Sometimes I don't know if we shouldn't," the lady says.[53]

"I know definitely we shouldn't," the man says. The man looks like a preacher. He's big and fat and he's got on a black suit.[54] He's got a gold chain, too.

"Why?" the lady says.

"Why anything?" the preacher says.

"Yes," the lady says. "Why anything?"

"Not us to question," the preacher says.[55]

The lady looks at the preacher a little while and looks at Mama again.

"And look like it's the poor who suffers the most," she says. "I don't understand it."

"Best not to even try," the preacher says. "He works in mysterious ways — wonders to perform."[56]

Right then little John Lee bust out hollering, and everybody turn they head to listen.

"He's not a good dentist," the lady says. "Dr. Robillard is much better. But more expensive. That's why most of the colored people come here. The white people go to Dr. Robillard. Y'all from Bayonne?"[57]

"Down the river," my mama says. And that's all she go'n say, 'cause she don't talk much.[58] But the lady keeps on looking at her, and so she says, "Near Morgan."

"I see," the lady says.

7 "That's the trouble with the black people in this country today," somebody else says. This one here's sitting on the same side me and Mama's sitting, and he is kind of sitting in front of that preacher.[59] He looks like a teacher or somebody that goes to college. He's got on a suit, and he's got a book that he's been reading.[60] "We don't question is exactly our problem," he says. "We should question and question and question — question everything."

The preacher just looks at him a long time. He done put a toothpick or something in his mouth, and he just keeps on turning it and turning it. You can see he don't like that boy with that book.[61]

"Maybe you can explain what you mean," he says.

"I said what I meant," the boy says. "Question everything. Every stripe, every star, every word spoken. Everything."[62]

"It 'pears to me that this young lady and I was talking 'bout God, young man," the preacher says.[63]

"Question Him, too," the boy says.

"Wait," the preacher says. "Wait now."

"You heard me right," the boy says. "His existence as well as everything else. Everything."[64]

The preacher just looks across the room at the boy. You can see he's getting madder and madder. But mad or no mad, the boy ain't thinking 'bout him. He looks at that preacher just 's hard 's the preacher looks at him.

"Is this what they coming to?" the preacher says. "Is this what we educating them for?"[65]

"You're not educating me," the boy says. "I wash dishes at night so that I can go to school in the day. So even the words you spoke need questioning."[66]

The preacher just looks at him and shakes his head.

"When I come in this room and seen you there with your book, I said to myself, 'There's an intelligent man.' How wrong a person can be."

"Show me one reason to believe in the existence of a God," the boy says.[67]

"My heart tells me," the preacher says.[68]

"'My heart tells me,'" the boy says. "'My heart tells me.' Sure, 'My heart tells me.' And as long as you listen to what your heart tells you, you will have only what the white man gives you and nothing more.[69] Me, I don't listen to my heart. The purpose of the heart is to pump blood throughout the body, and nothing else."[70]

"Who's your paw, boy?" the preacher says.

"Why?"

"Who is he?"

"He's dead."

"And your mon?"

"She's in Charity Hospital with pneumonia. Half killed herself, working for nothing."[71]

"And 'cause he's dead and she's sick, you mad at the world?"[72]

"I'm not mad at the world. I'm questioning the world. I'm questioning it with cold logic, sir. What do words like Freedom, Liberty, God, White, Colored mean? I want to know. That's why *you* are sending us to school, to read and to ask questions. And because we ask these questions, you call us mad. No sir, it is not us who are mad."[73]

"You keep saying 'us'?"

"'Us.' Yes—us. I'm not alone."[74]

The preacher just shakes his head. Then he looks at everybody in the room—everybody. Some of the people look down at the floor, keep from looking at him. I kind of look 'way myself, but soon 's I know he done turn his head, I look that way again.[75]

"I'm sorry for you," he says to the boy.[76]

"Why?" the boy says. "Why not be sorry for yourself? Why are you so much better off than I am? Why aren't you sorry for these other people in here? Why not be sorry for the lady who had to drag her child into the dentist office? Why not be sorry for the lady sitting on that bench over there? Be sorry for them. Not for me. Some way or the other I'm going to make it."[77]

"No, I'm sorry for you," the preacher says.

"Of course, of course," the boy says, nodding his head. "You're sorry for me because I rock that pillar you're leaning on."[78]

"You can't ever rock the pillar I'm leaning on, young man. It's stronger than anything man can ever do."[79]

"You believe in God because a man told you to believe in God," the boy says. "A white man told you to believe in God. And why? To keep you ignorant so he can keep his feet on your neck."[80]

"So now we the ignorant?" the preacher says.[81]

"Yes," the boy says. "Yes." And he opens his book again.

The preacher just looks at him sitting there. The boy done forgot all about him.[82] Everybody else make 'tend they done forgot the squabble, too.[83]

Then I see that preacher getting up real slow. Preacher's a great big old man and he got to brace himself to get up. He comes over where the boy is sitting. He just stands there a little while looking down at him, but the boy don't raise his head.

"Get up, boy," preacher says.

The boy looks up at him, then he shuts his book real slow and stands up. Preacher just hauls back and hit him in the face.[84] The boy falls back 'gainst the wall, but he straightens himself up and looks right back at that preacher.

"You forgot the other cheek," he says.[85]

The preacher hauls back and hit him again on the other side. But this time the boy braces himself and don't fall.[86]

"That hasn't changed a thing," he says.[87]

The preacher just looks at the boy. The preacher's breathing real hard like he just run up a big hill. The boy sits down and opens his book again.[88]

"I feel sorry for you," the preacher says. "I never felt so sorry for a man before."

The boy makes 'tend he don't even hear that preacher. He keeps on reading his book. The preacher goes back and gets his hat off the chair.

"Excuse me," he says to us. "I'll come back some other time. Y'all, please excuse me."[89]

And he looks at the boy and goes out the room. The boy h'ist his hand up to his mouth one time to wipe 'way some blood. All the rest of the time he keeps on reading.[90] And nobody else in there say a word.[91]

8 Little John Lee and his mama come out the dentist office, and the nurse calls somebody else in. Then little bit later they come out, and the nurse calls another name. But fast 's she calls somebody in there, somebody else comes in the place where we sitting, and the room stays full.

The people coming in now, all of them wearing big coats. One of them says something 'bout sleeting, another one says he hope not. Another one says he think it ain't nothing but rain. 'Cause, he says, rain can get awful cold this time of year.[92]

All round the room they talking. Some of them talking to people right by them, some of them talking to people clear 'cross the room, some of them talking to anybody'll listen. It's a little bitty room, no bigger than us kitchen, and I can see everybody in there. The little old room's full of smoke, 'cause you got two old men smoking pipes over by that side door. I think I feel my tooth thumping me some, and I hold my breath and wait. I wait and wait, but it don't thump me no more. Thank God for that.[93]

I feel like going to sleep, and I lean back 'gainst the wall. But I'm scared to go to sleep. Scared 'cause the nurse might call my name and I won't hear her. And Mama might go to sleep, too, and she'll be mad if neither one of us heard the nurse.[94]

I look up at Mama. I love my mama. I love my mama.[95] And when cotton come I'm go'n get her a new coat. And I ain't go'n get a black one, either. I think I'm go'n get her a red one.[96]

"They got some books over there," I say. "Want read one of them?"[97]

Mama looks at the books, but she don't answer me.

"You got yourself a little man there," the lady says.[98]

Mama don't say nothing to the lady, but she must've smiled, 'cause I seen the lady smiling back.[99] The lady looks at me a little while, like she's feeling sorry for me.[100]

"You sure got that preacher out of here in a hurry," she says to that boy.

The boy looks up at her and looks in his book again. When I grow up I want be just like him. I want clothes like that and I want keep a book with me, too.[101]

"You really don't believe in God?" the lady says.[102]

"No," he says.

"But why?" the lady says.

"Because the wind is pink," he says.[103]

"What?" the lady says.

The boy don't answer her no more. He just reads in his book.

"Talking 'bout the wind is pink," that old lady says. She's sitting on the same bench with the boy and she's trying to look in his face. The boy makes 'tend the old lady ain't even there. He just keeps on reading. "Wind is pink," she says again. "Eh, Lord, what children go'n be saying next?"

The lady 'cross from us bust out laughing.

"That's a good one," she says. "The wind is pink. Yes sir, that's a good one."

"Don't you believe the wind is pink?" the boy says. He keeps his head down in the book.

"Course I believe it, honey," the lady says. "Course I do." She looks at us and winks her eye. "And what color is grass, honey?"

"Grass? Grass is black."

She bust out laughing again. The boy looks at her.

"Don't you believe grass is black?" he says.

The lady quits her laughing and looks at him. Everybody else looking at him, too. The place quiet, quiet.[104]

"Grass is green, honey," the lady says. "It was green yesterday, it's green today, and it's go'n be green tomorrow."

"How do you know it's green?"

"I know because I know."

"You don't know it's green," the boy says. "You believe it's green because someone told you it was green. If someone had told you it was black you'd believe it was black."[105]

"It's green," the lady says. "I know green when I see green."

"Prove it's green," the boy says.

"Sure, now," the lady says. "Don't tell me it's coming to that."

"It's coming to just that," the boy says. "Words mean nothing. One means no more than the other."[106]

"That's what it all coming to?" that old lady says. That old lady got on a turban and she got on two sweaters. She got a green sweater under a black sweater. I can see the green sweater 'cause some of the buttons on the other sweater's missing.[107]

"Yes ma'am," the boy says. "Words mean nothing. Action is the only thing. Doing. That's the only thing."[108]

"Other words, you want the Lord to come down here and show Hisself to you?" she says.[109]

"Exactly, ma'am," he says.

"You don't mean that, I'm sure?" she says.

"I do, ma'am," he says.

"Done, Jesus," the old lady says, shaking her head.

"I didn't go 'long with that preacher at first," the other lady says; "but now—I don't know. When a person say the grass is black, he's either a lunatic or something's wrong."

"Prove to me that it's green," the boy says.

"It's green because the people say it's green."[110]

"Those same people say we're citizens of these United States," the boy says.[111]

"I think I'm a citizen," the lady says.

"Citizens have certain rights," the boy says. "Name me one right that you have. One right, granted by the Constitution, that you can exercise in Bayonne."[112]

The lady don't answer him. She just looks at him like she don't know what he's talking 'bout. I know I don't.

"Things changing," she says.

"Things are changing because some black men have begun to think with their brains and not their hearts," the boy says.[113]

"You trying to say these people don't believe in God?"

"I'm sure some of them do. Maybe most of them do. But they don't believe that God is going to touch these white people's hearts and change things tomorrow. Things change through action. By no other way."[114]

Everybody sit quiet and look at the boy. Nobody says a thing. Then the lady 'cross the room from me and Mama just shakes her head.

"Let's hope that not all your generation feel the same way you do," she says.

"Think what you please, it doesn't matter," the boy says. "But it will be men who listen to their heads and not their hearts who will see that your children have a better chance than you had."

"Let's hope they ain't all like you, though," the old lady says. "Done forgot the heart absolutely."[115]

"Yes ma'am, I hope they aren't all like me," the boy says. "Unfortunately, I was born too late to believe in your God. Let's hope that the ones who come after will have your faith if not in your God, then in something else, something definite that they can lean on. I haven't anything. For me, the wind is pink, the grass is black."[116]

9   The nurse comes in the room where we all sitting and waiting and says the doctor won't take no more patients till one o'clock this evening. My mama jumps up off the bench and goes up to the white lady.[117]

"Nurse, I have to go back in the field this evening," she says.[118]

"The doctor is treating his last patient now," the nurse says. "One o'clock this evening."

"Can I at least speak to the doctor?" my mama asks.

"I'm his nurse," the lady says.[119]

"My little boy's sick," my mama says. "Right now his tooth almost killing him."[120]

The nurse looks at me. She's trying to make up her mind if to let me come in. I look at her real pitiful. The tooth ain't hurting me at all, but Mama say it is, so I make 'tend for her sake.[121]

"This evening," the nurse says, and goes on back in the office.[122]

"Don't feel 'jected, honey," the lady says to Mama. "I been round them a long time—they take you when they want to. If you was white, that's something else; but we the wrong color."[123]

Mama don't say nothing to the lady, and me and her go outside and stand 'gainst the wall. It's cold out there. I can feel that wind going through my coat. Some of the other people come out of the room and go up the street. Me and

Mama stand there a little while and we start walking. I don't know where we going. When we come to the other street we just stand there.[124]

"You don't have to make water, do you?" Mama says.[125]

"No, ma'am," I say.

We go on up the street. Walking real slow. I can tell Mama don't know where she's going. When we come to a store we stand there and look at the dummies. I look at a little boy wearing a brown overcoat. He's got on brown shoes, too. I look at my old shoes and look at his'n again. You wait till summer, I say.

Me and Mama walk away. We come up to another store and we stop and look at them dummies, too. Then we go on again. We pass a café where the white people in there eating.[126]

Mama tells me keep my eyes in front where they belong, but I can't help from seeing them people eat. My stomach starts to growling 'cause I'm hungry. When I see people eating, I get hungry; when I see a coat, I get cold.

A man whistles at my mama when we go by a filling station. She makes 'tend she don't even see him. I look back and I feel like hitting him in the mouth. If I was bigger, I say; if I was bigger, you'd see.

We keep on going. I'm getting colder and colder, but I don't say nothing. I feel that stuff running down my nose and I sniff.

"That rag," Mama says.

I get it out and wipe my nose. I'm getting cold all over now—my face, my hands, my feet, everything. We pass another little café, but this'n for white people, too, and we can't go in there, either.[127] So we just walk. I'm so cold now I'm 'bout ready to say it. If I knowed where we was going I wouldn't be so cold, but I don't know where we going. We go, we go, we go. We walk clean out of Bayonne. Then we cross the street and we come back. Same thing I seen when I got off the bus this morning. Same old trees, same old walk, same old weeds, same old cracked pave—same old everything.

I sniff again.

"That rag," Mama says.[128]

I wipe my nose real fast and jugg that handkerchief back in my pocket 'fore my hand gets too cold. I raise my head and I can see David's hardware store. When we come up to it, we go in. I don't know why, but I'm glad.

It's warm in there. It's so warm in there you don't ever want to leave. I look for the heater, and I see it over by them barrels. Three white men standing round the heater talking in Creole. One of them comes over to see what my mama want.[129]

"Got any axe handles?" she says.

Me, Mama and the white man start to the back, but Mama stops me when we come up to the heater. She and the white man go on. I hold my hands over the heater and look at them. They go all the way to the back, and I see the white man pointing to the axe handles 'gainst the wall. Mama takes one of them and shakes it like she's trying to figure how much it weighs. Then she rubs her hand over it from one end to the other end. She turns it over and looks at the other side, then she shakes it again, and shakes her head and puts it back. She gets another one and she does it just like she did the first one, then she shakes her head. Then she gets a brown one and do it that, too. But she don't like this one, either. Then she gets another one, but 'fore she shakes it or anything, she looks at me. Look like she's trying to say something to me, but I don't know what it is. All I know is I done got warm now and I'm feeling right smart better. Mama shakes this axe handle just like she did the others, and shakes her head and says something to the white man. The white man just looks at his pile of axe handles, and when Mama pass him to come to the front, the white man just scratch his head and follows her. She tells me come on and we go on out and start walking again.[130]

We walk and walk, and no time at all I'm cold again. Look like I'm colder now 'cause I can still remember how good it was back there. My stomach growls and I suck it in to keep Mama from hearing it. She's walking right 'side me, and it growls so loud you can hear it a mile. But Mama don't say a word.[131]

10 When we come up to the courthouse, I look at the clock. It's got quarter to twelve. Mean we got another hour and a quarter to be out here in the cold.[132] We go and stand 'side a building. Something hits my cap and I look up at the sky. Sleet's falling.[133]

I look at Mama standing there. I want stand close 'side her, but she don't like that. She say that's crybaby stuff. She say you got to stand for yourself, by yourself.[134]

"Let's go back to that office," she says.

We cross the street. When we get to the dentist office I try to open the door, but I can't. I twist and twist, but I can't. Mama pushes me to the side and she twist the knob, but she can't open the door, either. She turns 'way from the door. I look at her, but I don't move and I don't say nothing. I done seen her like this before and I'm scared of her.[135]

"You hungry?" she says. She says it like she's mad at me, like I'm the cause of everything.[136]

"No, ma'am," I say.

"You want eat and walk back, or you rather don't eat and ride?"

"I ain't hungry," I say.

I ain't just hungry, but I'm cold, too. I'm so hungry and cold I want to cry. And look like I'm getting colder and colder. My feet done got numb. I try to work my toes, but I don't even feel them. Look like I'm go'n die. Look like I'm go'n stand right here and freeze to death. I think 'bout home. I think 'bout Val and Auntie and Ty and Louis and Walker. It's 'bout twelve o'clock and I know they eating dinner now. I can hear Ty making jokes. He done forgot 'bout getting up early this morning and right now he's probably making jokes. Always trying to make somebody laugh. I wish I was right there listening to him. Give anything in the world if I was home round the fire.[137]

"Come on," Mama says.

We start walking again. My feet so numb I can't hardly feel them. We turn the corner and go on back up the street. The clock on the courthouse starts hitting for twelve.[138]

The sleet's coming down plenty now. They hit the pave and bounce like rice. Oh, Lord; oh, Lord, I pray. Don't let me die, don't let me die, don't let me die, Lord.[139]

11   Now I know where we going. We going back of town where the colored people eat.[140] I don't care if I don't eat. I been hungry before. I can stand it. But I can't stand the cold.

I can see we go'n have a long walk. It's 'bout a mile down there. But I don't mind. I know when I get there I'm go'n warm myself. I think I can hold out. My hands numb in my pockets and my feet numb, too, but if I keep moving I can hold out. Just don't stop no more, that's all.[141]

The sky's gray.[142] The sleet keeps on falling. Falling like rain now—plenty, plenty. You can hear it hitting the pave. You can see it bouncing. Sometimes it bounces two times 'fore it settles.

We keep on going. We don't say nothing. We just keep on going, keep on going.[143]

I wonder what Mama's thinking. I hope she ain't mad at me. When summer come I'm go'n pick plenty cotton and get her a coat. I'm go'n get her a red one.[144]

I hope they'd make it summer all the time. I'd be glad if it was summer all the time—but it ain't. We got to have winter, too. Lord, I hate the winter. I guess everybody hate the winter.[145]

I don't sniff this time. I get out my handkerchief and wipe my nose. My hands's so cold I can hardly hold the handkerchief.[146]

I think we getting close, but we ain't there yet. I wonder where everybody is. Can't see a soul but us. Look like we the only two people moving round today. Must be too cold for the rest of the people to move round in.

I can hear my teeth. I hope they don't knock together too hard and make that bad one hurt. Lord, that's all I need, for that bad one to start off.[147]

I hear a church bell somewhere. But today ain't Sunday. They must be ringing for a funeral or something.[148]

I wonder what they doing at home. They must be eating. Monsieur

Bayonne might be there with his guitar. One day Ty played with Monsieur Bayonne's guitar and broke one of the strings. Monsieur Bayonne was some mad with Ty. He say Ty wasn't go'n ever 'mount to nothing. Ty can go just like Monsieur Bayonne when he ain't there. Ty can make everybody laugh when he starts to mocking Monsieur Bayonne.

I used to like to be with Mama and Daddy. We used to be happy. But they took him in the Army. Now, nobody happy no more. . . . I be glad when Daddy comes home.

Monsieur Bayonne say it wasn't fair for them to take Daddy and give Mama nothing and give us nothing. Auntie say, "Shhh, Etienne. Don't let them hear you talk like that." Monsieur Bayonne say, "It's God truth. What they giving his children? They have to walk three and a half miles to school hot or cold. That's anything to give for a paw? She's got to work in the field rain or shine just to make ends meet. That's anything to give for a husband?" Auntie say, "Shhh, Etienne, shhh." "Yes, you right," Monsieur Bayonne say. "Best don't say it in front of them now. But one day they go'n find out. One day."[149] "Yes, I suppose so," Auntie say. "Then what, Rose Mary?" Monsieur Bayonne say. "I don't know, Etienne," Auntie say. "All we can do is us job, and leave everything else in His hand . . ."[150]

We getting closer, now. We getting closer. I can even see the railroad tracks.

We cross the tracks, and now I see the café. Just to get in there, I say. Just to get in there. Already I'm starting to feel little better.

12 We go in. Ahh, it's good. I look for the heater; there 'gainst the wall. One of them little brown ones. I just stand there and hold my hands over it. I can't open my hands too wide 'cause they almost froze.[151]

Mama's standing right 'side me. She done unbuttoned her coat. Smoke rises out of the coat, and the coat smells like a wet dog.[152]

I move to the side so Mama can have more room. She opens out her hands and rubs them together. I rub mine together, too, 'cause this keep them from hurting. If you let them warm too fast, they hurt you sure. But if you let them warm just little bit at a time, and you keep rubbing them, they be all right every time.[153]

They got just two more people in the café. A lady back of the counter, and a man on this side the counter. They been watching us ever since we come in.[154]

Mama gets out the handkerchief and count up the money. Both of us know how much money she's got there. Three dollars. No, she ain't got three dollars, 'cause she had to pay us way up here. She ain't got but two dollars and a half left. Dollar and a half to get my tooth pulled, and fifty cents for us to go back on, and fifty cents worth of salt meat.

She stirs the money round with her finger. Most of the money is change 'cause I can hear it rubbing together. She stirs it and stirs it. Then she looks at the door. It's still sleeting. I can hear it hitting 'gainst the wall like rice.

"I ain't hungry, Mama," I say.[155]

"Got to pay them something for they heat," she says.

She takes a quarter out the handkerchief and ties the handkerchief up again. She looks over her shoulder at the people, but she still don't move. I hope she don't spend the money. I don't want her spending it on me. I'm hungry, I'm almost starving I'm so hungry, but I don't want her spending the money on me.[156]

She flips the quarter over like she's thinking. She's must be thinking 'bout us walking back home. Lord, I sure don't want walk home.[157] If I thought it'd do any good to say something, I'd say it. But Mama makes up her own mind 'bout things.

She turns 'way from the heater right fast, like she better hurry up and spend the quarter 'fore she change her mind. I watch her go toward the counter. The man and the lady look at her, too. She tells the lady something and the lady walks away. The man keeps on looking at her. Her back's turned to the man, and she don't even know he's standing there.

The lady puts some cakes and a glass of milk on the counter. Then she pours up a cup of coffee and sets it 'side the other stuff. Mama pays her for the things and comes on back where I'm standing. She tells me sit down at the table 'gainst the wall.

The milk and the cakes's for me; the coffee's for Mama. I eat slow and I look at her. She's looking outside at the sleet. She's looking real sad. I say to myself, I'm go'n make all this up one day. You see, one day, I'm go'n make all this up. I want say it now; I want tell her how I feel right now; but Mama don't like for us to talk like that.[158]

"I can't eat all this," I say.[159]

They ain't got but just three little old cakes there. I'm so hungry right now, the Lord knows I can eat a hundred times three, but I want my mama to have one.

Mama don't even look my way. She knows I'm hungry, she knows I want it.[160] I let it stay there a little while, then I get it and eat it. I eat just on my front teeth, though, 'cause if cake touch that back tooth I know what'll happen.[161] Thank God it ain't hurt me at all today.

After I finish eating I see the man go to the juke box. He drops a nickel in it, then he just stand there a little while looking at the record. Mama tells me keep my eyes in front where they belong. I turn my head like she say, but then I hear the man coming toward us.

"Dance, pretty?" he says.[162]

Mama gets up to dance with him. But 'fore you know it, she done grabbed the little man in the collar and done heaved him 'side the wall. He hit the wall so hard he stop the juke box from playing.[163]

"Some pimp," the lady back of the counter says. "Some pimp."[164]

The little man jumps up off the floor and starts toward my mama. 'Fore you know it, Mama done sprung open her knife and she's waiting for him.

"Come on," she says. "Come on. I'll gut you from your neighbo to your throat. Come on."[165]

I go up to the little man to hit him, but Mama makes me come and stand 'side her.[166] The little man looks at me and Mama and goes on back to the counter.

"Some pimp," the lady back of the counter says. "Some pimp." She starts laughing and pointing at the little man. "Yes sir, you a pimp, all right. Yes sir-ree."

13 "Fasten that coat, let's go," Mama says.[167]

"You don't have to leave," the lady says.

Mama don't answer the lady, and we right out in the cold again. I'm warm right now—my hands, my ears, my feet—but I know this ain't go'n last too long. It done sleet so much now you got ice everywhere you look.[168]

We cross the railroad tracks, and soon's we do, I get cold. That wind goes through this little old coat like it ain't even there. I got on a shirt and a sweater under the coat, but that wind don't pay them no mind. I look up and I can see we got a long way to go. I wonder if we go'n make it 'fore I get too cold.

We cross over to walk on the sidewalk. They got just one sidewalk back here, and it's over there.[169]

After we go just a little piece, I smell bread cooking. I look, then I see a baker shop. When we get closer, I can smell it more better. I shut my eyes and make 'tend I'm eating.[170] But I keep them shut too long and I butt up 'gainst a telephone post. Mama grabs me and see if I'm hurt. I ain't bleeding or nothing and she turns me loose.

I can feel I'm getting colder and colder, and I look up to see how far we still got to go. Uptown is 'way up yonder. A half mile more, I reckon. I try to think of something. They say think and you won't get cold. I think of that poem, "Annabel Lee."[171] I ain't been to school in so long—this bad weather—I reckon they done passed "Annabel Lee" by now. But passed it or not, I'm sure Miss Walker go'n make me recite it when I get there. That woman don't never forget nothing. I ain't never seen nobody like that in my life.[172]

I'm still getting cold. "Annabel Lee" or no "Annabel Lee," I'm still getting cold. But I can see we getting closer. We getting there gradually.

Soon 's we turn the corner, I see a little old white lady up in front of us. She's the only lady on the street. She's all in black and she's got a long black rag over her head.

"Stop," she says.

Me and Mama stop and look at her. She must be crazy to be out in all this bad weather. Ain't got but a few other people out there, and all of them's men.[173]

"Y'all done ate?" she says.

"Just finish," Mama says.

"Y'all must be cold then?" she says.[174]

"We headed for the dentist," Mama says. "We'll warm up when we get there."[175]

"What dentist?" the old lady says. "Mr. Bassett?"

"Yes, ma'am," Mama says.

"Come on in," the old lady says. "I'll telephone him and tell him y'all coming."[176]

Me and Mama follow the old lady in the store. It's a little bitty store, and it don't have much in there.[177] The old lady takes off her head rag and folds it up.

"Helena?" somebody calls from the back.

"Yes, Alnest?" the old lady says.

"Did you see them?"

"They're here. Standing beside me."

"Good. Now you can stay inside."[178]

The old lady looks at Mama. Mama's waiting to hear what she brought us in here for. I'm waiting for that, too.

"I saw y'all each time you went by," she says. "I came out to catch you, but you were gone."[179]

"We went back of town," Mama says.

"Did you eat?"

"Yes, ma'am."

The old lady looks at Mama a long time, like she's thinking Mama might be just saying that. Mama looks right back at her. The old lady looks at me to see what I have to say. I don't say nothing. I sure ain't going 'gainst my mama.

"There's food in the kitchen," she says to Mama. "I've been keeping it warm."[180]

Mama turns right around and starts for the door.[181]

"Just a minute," the old lady says. Mama stops. "The boy'll have to work for it. It isn't free."[182]

"We don't take no handout," Mama says.

"I'm not handing out anything," the old lady says. "I need my garbage moved to the front. Ernest has a bad cold and can't go out there."

"James'll move it for you," Mama says.

"Not unless you eat," the old lady says. "I'm old, but I have my pride, too, you know."[183]

Mama can see she ain't go'n beat this old lady down, so she just shakes her head.[184]

"All right," the old lady says. "Come into the kitchen."

She leads the way with that rag in her hand. The kitchen is a little bitty little old thing, too. The table and the stove just 'bout fill it up.[185] They got a little room to the side. Somebody in there laying 'cross the bed—'cause I can see one of his feet. Must be the person she was talking to: Ernest or Alnest—something like that.[186]

"Sit down," the old lady says to Mama. "Not you," she says to me. "You have to move the cans."[187]

"Helena?" the man says in the other room.

"Yes, Alnest?" the old lady says.

"Are you going out there again?"

"I must show the boy where the garbage is, Alnest," the old lady says.

"Keep that shawl over your head," the old man says.[188]

"You don't have to remind me, Alnest. Come, boy," the old lady says.

We go out in the yard. Little old back yard ain't no bigger than the store or the kitchen. But it can sleet here just like it can sleet in any big back yard. And 'fore you know it, I'm trembling.

"There," the old lady says, pointing to the cans. I pick up one of the cans and set it right back down. The can's so light, I'm go'n see what's inside of it.

"Here," the old lady says. "Leave that can alone."

I look back at her standing there in the door. She's got that black rag wrapped round her shoulders, and she's pointing one of her little old fingers at me.

"Pick it up and carry it to the front," she says. I go by her with the can, and she's looking at me all the time. I'm sure the can's empty. I'm sure she could've carried it herself—maybe both of them at the same time.[189] "Set it on the sidewalk by the door and come back for the other one," she says.

I go and come back, and Mama looks at me when I pass her. I get the other can and take it to the front. It don't feel a bit heavier than that first one. I tell myself I ain't go'n be nobody's fool, and I'm go'n look inside this can to see just what I been hauling. First, I look up the street, then down the street. Nobody coming. Then I look over my shoulder toward the door. That little old lady done slipped up there quiet 's mouse, watching me again. Look like she knowed what I was go'n do.[190]

"Ehh, Lord," she says. "Children, children. Come in here, boy, and go wash your hands."

I follow her in the kitchen. She points toward the bathroom, and I go in there and wash up. Little bitty old bathroom, but it's clean, clean.[191] I don't use any of her towels; I wipe my hands on my pants legs.

When I come back in the kitchen, the old lady done dished up the food. Rice, gravy, meat—she even got some lettuce and tomato in a saucer. She even got a glass of milk and a piece of cake there, too. It looks so good, I almost start eating 'fore I say my blessing.[192]

"Helena?" the old man says.

"Yes, Alnest?"

"Are they eating?"

"Yes," she says.

"Good," he says. "Now you'll stay inside."

The old lady goes in there where he is and I can hear them talking. I look at Mama. She's eating slow like she's thinking. I wonder what's the matter now. I reckon she's thinking 'bout home.[193]

The old lady comes back in the kitchen.

"I talked to Dr. Bassett's nurse," she says. "Dr. Bassett will take you as soon as you get there."[194]

"Thank you, ma'am," Mama says.

"Perfectly all right," the old lady says. "Which one is it?"

Mama nods toward me. The old lady looks at me real sad. I look sad, too.

"You're not afraid, are you?" she says.

"No, ma'am," I say.

"That's a good boy," the old lady says. "Nothing to be afraid of. Dr. Bassett will not hurt you."

When me and Mama get through eating, we thank the old lady again.

"Helena, are they leaving?" the old man says.

"Yes, Alnest."

"Tell them I say good-bye."

"They can hear you, Alnest."

"Good-bye both mother and son," the old man says. "And may God be with you."[195]

Me and Mama tell the old man good-bye, and we follow the old lady in the front room. Mama opens the door to go out, but she stops and comes back in the store.

"You sell salt meat?" she says.

"Yes."

"Give me two bits worth."

"That isn't very much salt meat," the old lady says.[196]

"That's all I have," Mama says.

The old lady goes back of the counter and cuts a big piece off the chunk. Then she wraps it up and puts it in a paper bag.

"Two bits," she says.

"That looks like awful lot of meat for a quarter," Mama says.

"Two bits," the old lady says. "I've been selling salt meat behind this counter twenty-five years. I think I know what I'm doing."[197]

"You got a scale there," Mama says.

"What?" the old lady says.

"Weigh it," Mama says.

"What?" the old lady says. "Are you telling me how to run my business?"

"Thanks very much for the food," Mama says.[198]

"Just a minute," the old lady says.

"James," Mama says to me. I move toward the door.

"Just one minute, I said," the old lady says.

Me and Mama stop again and look at her. The old lady takes the meat out of the bag and unwraps it and cuts 'bout half of it off. Then she wraps it up again and juggs it back in the bag and gives the bag to Mama. Mama lays the quarter on the counter.[199]

"Your kindness will never be forgotten," she says.[200] "James," she says to me.

We go out, and the old lady comes to the door to look at us. After we go a little piece I look back, and she's still there watching us.

The sleet's coming down heavy, heavy now, and I turn up my coat collar to keep my neck warm. My mama tells me turn it right back down.[201]

"You not a bum," she says. "You a man."[202]

ANALYSIS

Plot

Backstory

This black Louisiana family is accustomed to hardship, but since the husband and father was drafted and taken off the scene, conditions have become almost intolerably difficult. Everyone in the family is hungry, exhausted, and overburdened with responsibility—down to the eight-year-old son, who, by default, has become "the man of the house." At home, the family suffers the most acute stresses of poverty. In the outside world, they must also bear the stress of a racist society which discriminates against them in every imaginable way.

Present Action

James, our narrator, has a terrible toothache. Different solutions to this problem have been tried (hiding and ignoring the pain, faith-healing and prayer), but none have been successful. Finally there's no option left but to take the boy to the dentist in the nearby town of Bayonne.

A trip to the dentist, which would be a routine matter to the average reader, is immensely costly to this family, stretching their resources to the limit. Not only the cost of the journey and treatment must be calculated, but also the cost of time lost from work. Mother and son reach the dentist's office on schedule, but though they wait patiently all morning, the dentist (a white man) will not see them until the afternoon. What might seem a minor delay is very serious in this case, for it means that the mother will lose more time from her work in the fields. Worse, they must spend the hours of the dentist's midday break on the freezing winter streets of Bayonne, because they lack the means to obtain either food or shelter. They wander, cold and hungry and increasingly hopeless; their stratagems for getting off the street bring little relief, while seriously worsening their financial situation. Finally, through the kindness of a couple of white storekeepers who've observed their plight, they are able to get warm, to get something to eat, and (though only through the intercession of the sympathetic white couple) to get a promise of being treated promptly at the dentist's. When the story concludes, however, they are on the freezing street once more . . . still on the way to the dentist's office.

Up to a point, the story follows the pattern of any quest narrative. The magnitude of the goal doesn't matter—if it was your toothache, it would seem like a big enough deal to you. To the narrator and his mother it is as important to reach the dentist's chair and the relief of treatment as it is to Jason and the Argonauts to retrieve the Golden Fleece, or to King Arthur's knights to discover the Holy Grail. And, like many heroes of fairy tales, the mother and son find obstacles in their path so impregnable that it seems it will require magic to get past them.

The average quest narrative, however, eventually reaches the goal of the quest in some way or other. In "The Sky Is Gray," the goal is not exactly reached. At the end of the story, the narrator has not reached the dentist's chair, and the problem of the toothache, which motivates all the present action, has not yet been solved, though the odds that it will be solved have improved. Why should the writer have chosen to break the usual pattern of the quest narrative by leaving it incomplete in this way? The reader may recall the myth of Sisyphus, who could never *quite* manage to roll his boulder all the way to the top of the hill.

Of course, the foregoing plot summary fails to mention something which is obviously of central importance to the story as a whole: the argument that takes place in the dentist's waiting room between the preacher and the studious young man. Although the thematic importance of this episode is apparent, it has nothing directly to do with the movement of the quest plot. It has no effect on whether or not James will finally reach the dentist's chair. In this sense it stands apart from the action proper. It's something witnessed while waiting, during down time—an interruption in the forward flow of present action.

Character

Like "Daisy's Valentine," this is very much a character-driven story. Perhaps the most important revelation is our discovery of what these people are like, essentially—who they really are.

Who is the most important figure in the story? Who is the protagonist? It's a general rule of thumb that any first-person narrator will also be, inevitably, the main character. Even when positioned as a bystander or witness to the principal action, the first-person narrator tends to become the most important figure in the story simply because he or she is the medium for everything that we are told. And in this case, narrator James is central to the action as well. The important problem of the present action—the toothache—belongs to him.

In another sense, however, James also functions as an observer-narrator— someone who's chiefly telling us about the actions of somebody else on the scene, somebody more important to the plot. The person to whom James is paying the most attention is his mother. From his point of view, it's her behavior that's important (and sometimes mysterious). His own behavior matters less to him—James just does what he has to, in effect. In this way, Mama comes to share the role of protagonist—all the more so because James's idea of himself almost always comes to him as a reflection from his mother.

What do we know about Mama? She's hard-working, tough and determined. James tells us that she wastes no words, and later we see that for ourselves. She's violently faithful to her absent husband; the episode with the would-be pimp shows us that. She is utterly unsentimental and almost completely unaffectionate—by no means a cuddly Mom. Her harshly high standards for raising her children approach the boundary of cruelty, and in the redbird episode perhaps that boundary is crossed. But despite all her tight restraint there are some ways that she shows love. At the dentist's office, she breaks her intransigent silence to plead (uselessly) for her son. At the restaurant in the black section of Bayonne, she goes hungry so that James can eat, and James knows that it's useless to argue the point with her, though he very much wants her to share his small ration of food. Indeed the strong love for her which James so touchingly expresses is revealing—you don't feel that way about somebody who doesn't give you anything back.

Over the course of the story, we learn that all Mama's characteristics have motives of the most vital importance. Sheer survival is one, as the redbird episode shows. But that is not the most important motive. Almost everything Mama does in the whole story is intended to maintain self-respect—her own and her son's. Her harshness and rigidity are means of enforcing this self-respect . . . in circumstances which almost overwhelmingly would tend to break it down. As the "old lady" storekeeper observes and remarks, Mama's dominant characteristic is pride. How could a destitute woman, despised and discriminated against for her race, manage to be so proud? Perhaps because she can't afford not to be. Pride (the first of the seven deadly sins, recall) is the ultimate defense for a person in such a situation. What Mama knows is that if you permit yourself to be pitied you become abject, and once you have become abject you can easily be crushed out of existence.

This message is sent to the reader by way of lessons Mama means for James; but by the beginning of the present action, James has already learned most of her lessons very well. James is only eight, after all (as we learn with some degree of shock), and he has some appealingly childish qualities—his response to the little girl on the bus, for instance, and especially his fierce, inexpressible love for his mother, his desire to feed her, protect her, to buy her a red coat. But his childlike qualities are overlaid with other characteristics that would more likely be expected of an adult. Before the beginning of the trip to Bayonne, he is already well-schooled in stoicism. He has an astonishing capacity (for someone his age) to endure hardship without complaint and has learned to deny his hunger and pain for the common good of his family. In Bayonne, he claims he's not hungry not so much so his mother might eat, but so that the budget won't collapse on his account. It's of paramount importance to James not to be a weak link in the chain his mother has forged to defend the family, and this too is a form of pride. No matter what happens, he never complains of unfairness, or even seems to think about it. He doesn't resent even the awful redbird episode, but instead interprets it as having been necessary: "Auntie and Monsieur Bayonne talked to me and made me see."

The essential quality of James's character is that (eight years old or not) he is a man. The whole story is constructed as a proof of this point—a point which is slammed home by his mother's remark at the very end: "You not a bum. . . . You a man." James's manhood is hard-earned, perhaps premature. It's been forced on him by circumstances, but it's also something he's learned to desire for its own sake. At the end, the self-respect he has learned from his mother commands the respect of the reader too.

The word "man" itself has a significance beyond the question of James's individual character; it connects to the civil rights issue that's ever-present in the background. The story is set at a time when blacks were commonly denied the full rights of manhood. But the manhood James has earned, at his very young age, commands recognition and cannot be denied.

There's also the point that eight-year-old children really aren't supposed to have to be like this, live like this, think and behave in the ways James has to. What sort of society forces such hardships on its children? Through the straightforward description of James's situation, the story enters a mute plea for social justice, social reform.

The next most important characters in the story are the preacher and the young man with the book at the dentist's office. Mostly through the sound of their voices, they convince us as human individuals, but both also stand as representatives of something larger—the complexes of ideas and intentions that oppose each other in the background of the story about Mama and James.

These two characters have not quite hardened into symbols, but they do have a symbolic role to play.

The preacher stands for a system of belief and values which is essentially unexamined and therefore cannot bear questioning. In this capacity, he runs through most of the excuses and pretexts that have ever been deployed for the maintenance of a racist society in this country. When his set of false rationalizations collapses under the young man's questions, the preacher's reaction shows that when the rhetoric of such an authoritarian system has failed, that system must inevitably resort to violence to maintain its power. But in attacking the youth, the preacher defeats the ostensibly Christian foundation of his rhetoric even further. We may feel some sympathy for him at the end of the scene—as a human being whose belief system has failed him. But we will also feel contempt and repugnance for the power system he stands for.

The young man with the book is a more sympathetic and perhaps also a more complex character. As virtual symbol, he stands for all blacks who would use the force of their intelligence to rise up and claim their civil rights completely. Indeed, the power of his "cold logic" slices up the preacher's arguments like a laser beam. And in offering his other cheek to the preacher's blows, he shows that even though he denies religion, he can play the Christian role better than the preacher is ultimately able to do.

In all these ways, the young man is an admirable figure, but in some ways he's a little frightening as well. The nurse who talks to him in the second segment of the office episode is a little frightened as well as somewhat admiring. The problem with "cold logic" is its extreme frigidity. The success with which the young man seems to have extirpated all of his emotional responses is really rather alarming. To willingly adopt complete heartlessness for its strategic advantages is a terrible sacrifice to be made in a human life. (The high cost of this sort of transformation also appears in James's mother's occasional losses of control—the beating during the redbird episode, for example.)

But James, who reacts with both head and heart, admires the young man without reservation: "When I grow up I want be just like him. I want clothes like that and I want keep a book with me, too." By the end of the story, if not before, we'll recognize that James *already is* a lot like him. James is someone else who simply can't afford emotions (or, at any rate, can't afford to express them). He can't afford sentimentality about redbirds; he can't even afford to demonstrate his great love for his mother. The comparison of the two characters will move the reader to wonder again: what kind of society does this sort of thing to its people?

Meanwhile, the slightly less prominent characterizations of the kindhearted "old lady" and her husband "Alnest" also play a somewhat symbolic role. They are the only white people to fully "appear" in the story. Other whites portrayed are distant and indistinct—part of a remote power structure that uses men like the preacher as its tools. But the "old lady" enters the stage altogether and shows herself to be as fully human as James and his mother. Even the offstage voice of "Alnest" conveys more human warmth than the demeanor of the "white lady" who refuses them admission to the dentist.

The old lady and Alnest are there to prove that not all white people are the enemy—that some whites may be both friends and allies to black people. (This is an important theme in much of Gaines's work, and one which sets him apart from many black "protest" writers.) As symbols they also provide a counterexample to the preacher, showing that Christianity can cut both ways—can be used as an instrument of relief and reform as well as an instrument of oppression.

Characterizations of the bit players in this story are also worth noticing. Consider the extremely vivid description of the little girl on the bus (so lovingly given through James's point of view). It's her speech, so accurately rendered and so perfectly timed, that brings her completely to life. Other cameo characters are made fully present through their speech alone, such as Monsieur Bayonne or the unnamed man at the dentist's office who tosses off the unforgettable "Hollering like a pig under a gate."

Tone

With first-person narration, tone is identical to the sound of the narrator's voice. James's tone, notable first for an appropriately childlike simplicity, is also capable of some rather subtle modulations. First of all, he probably sounds somewhat foreign to the average reader, because of his regional dialect, which the writer indicates with a few efficient changes of spelling and syntax and especially with a well-tuned ear for local idiom. This slightly foreign quality of the tone is appropriate since James's experience is also likely to be quite alien to the majority of people who read literary fiction for amusement.

The next most apparent quality of James's voice is its stoicism. Almost always, the tone of his speech expresses the tough determination of the attitude he has learned from this mother—that determination to *be a man* at any cost. But also from time to time (when James speaks about his love for his mother or about the redbirds) the tone shifts and becomes less mature, more childishly wistful, more expressive of pathos. The transitions from one tone to another are modulated with enormous skill. James's response to the redbirds is more emotionally resonant than almost any other passage, but a few lines later, when he has become the direct victim himself, the tone flattens out and becomes numb: "But she hit me and hit me and hit me." Throughout the story, this friction between the legitimately childlike tone James only rarely allows himself to adopt and the tough adult tone he usually employs is designed to evoke an emotional response in the reader to the pathos of the whole situation.

Point of View

As is often the case with first-person narration, point of view and tone are closely related here. This story could be told from the point of view of the mother
with zero change in the plot—but there would be a very drastic change of
mood. From the mother's point of view, the story's tone would oscillate between
despair and suppressed rage. And important as the mother's character is, it's
more advantageous to this narrative that we see it from the outside. From
James's point of view we come to understand that Mama, despite her extreme
harshness and occasional violence, is always and absolutely the heroine of his
life. Mama herself has no such figure to look up to and depend on.

(In principle, this is a useful idea for writers at all stages: if a good story plot
somehow won't work out right, it may be that the point of view is in the wrong
place.)

There are some other advantages to James's point of view. The scenes of
comic relief, involving Monsieur Bayonne's faith healing and the little girl on
the bus, certainly play better from his standpoint. At more critical junctures of
the story, James's point of view and the reader's may separate slightly. James,
after all, is only eight years old, so we may understand some of what he sees better than he does (as in the pimp episode, for example). In the dentist's waiting
room, we look over James's shoulder, as it were, to follow the debate between
the young man and the preacher. James probably cannot follow all the intellectual intricacies of this argument, though he is able to report them.
Meanwhile, because he responds to the preacher and the young man as human
individuals rather than as representatives of ideas, his point of view helps keep
them from hardening into symbols.

Dialogue

Two different kinds of dialogue are found in the story. All the speech that
occurs in the main plot (the story of the quest to relieve James's toothache) is
most accurately rendered in the local idiom so as to contribute to the story's
general sense of verisimilitude, as well as to the building of character. Close-
mouthed as Mama may be, her dialogue eventually reveals a great deal about
her—and she has a number of different manners of speech, ranging from "I'll
gut you from your neighbo to your throat" to "Your kindness will never be forgotten." The presence of most of the other characters is primarily established
by the sound of their voices, voices which provide the story with much of its texture.

The dialogues in which the young man with the book participates, first
with the preacher and later with the nurse, have a very different flavor. They are
philosophical and abstract, rather like the dialogue in Percival Everett's "Hear
That Long Train Moan." It's noticeable too that the preacher speaks in the local

dialect, while the young man speaks in perfect standard English. The preacher is humanized by his idiomatic speech—and of course it would make perfect political sense for him to use the living language of his congregation. But the striking formality of the young man's speech is also a realistic detail, and one that helps identify the character socially. At the time when the story takes place, it was a political gesture for black intellectuals to speak with an almost tonelessly correct formality, a gesture sometimes (less formally) called "out-whiting whitey." And of course the crisp formality of the young man's diction is the ideal medium for his "cold logic."

Imagery and Description

Description here is somewhat limited by the choice of point of view. It would be out of character for James to break into long rhapsodies about the landscape. In fact, James seems to hear more than he sees, and many of the characters appear more vividly to our ears than to our eyes. Full visual descriptions of characters occur only when James focuses on them closely for some reason, as he does with the little girl on the bus.

After the sense of hearing, the sense of touch, of feeling, may be the most important to the story. James's sensations are very vivid: pain of the toothache, of the beatings he suffers, cold, hunger, wet and cold again, repeatedly. This priority of address to the senses is somewhat unusual, since most narratives depend first and most critically on the sense of sight.

It's probably intentional that the visual impression made by the story is rather dull, monochromatic, gray. There's the constant gray bleakness of the weather, the concrete gray inhospitality of the cold streets of Bayonne. The most extensive and noticeable visual descriptions involve some relationship to the title phrase, "The sky is gray." The first of these comes at a moment on the bus (section 5) when James is idle and has nothing to do but look out the window:

> The river is gray. The sky is gray. They have pool-doos on the water.
> The water is wavy, and the pool-doos go up and down. The bus go round
> a turn, and you got plenty trees hiding the river. Then the bus go round
> another turn, and I can see the river again.

This passage is deliberately unremarkable, so flat that even though the appearance of the title phrase anywhere in the body of any story usually lights up like a flare, it hardly calls much attention to itself here. Later on in section 11, the title phrase is repeated one more time:

> The sky's gray. The sleet keeps on falling. Falling like rain now—
> plenty, plenty. You can hear it hitting the pave. You can see it bouncing.
> Sometimes it bounces two times 'fore it settles.

The quality of this description is much the same as in the earlier passage, as studiedly flat and neutral, but now, because so much more has *happened* in the story, the context has changed. In light of the events we have witnessed, the grayness of the sky becomes associated with the uniform hostility of everything surrounding the mother and child—that indifferent gray cold shoulder turned to everything they suffer. There are several other passages in the story that suggest the grayness of the sky without exactly stating it, especially the concluding passage when James tries to turn up his coat collar.

Intervening between the two direct statements of the title phrase is the scene in the dentist's office where the young man, having routed the preacher, tells his odd little parable about colors. The point of this discussion is that the names of colors make a perfect example of an unexamined assumption. The names of colors are utterly arbitrary, and there is no way to prove them true. So the parable of the colors becomes a way for the young man to challenge unexamined assumptions about politics and religion which are not borne out by the evidence of experience.

Departing from this episode, we have been compelled to recognize that there is no good reason to believe that "the grass is green" is a statement more true than "the grass is black." And as the story continues, the discussion of colors acquires an interesting resonance with the title. The statement "the sky is gray" is *not* an unexamined idea. By the end of the story, we have looked at the sky very carefully, and we know from experience that the sky *is* gray. Along with the characters, we have earned the right to say it. "The sky is gray" becomes a truth earned by experience, much like the truth Mama knows about James: "You not a bum. . . . You a man."

Time Management

There's nothing too complicated about the time lines in this story. The present action is manageably brief—lasting from dawn to about one o'clock in the afternoon—and the antecedent action that requires exposition is not so very extensive. This exposition is all completed in the first four numbered sections of the story.

Because the *now* time frame of the story is expressed in the present tense, the writer can signal shifts to anterior time frames by shifting either to the past definite or to the imperfect tense, which he does mid paragraph in section 1: "I can't ever be scared and I can't ever cry. And that's why I never said nothing 'bout my teeth." The remainder of section 1 runs in the imperfect tense, the tense for what happened habitually, what used to happen—establishing the general background for the toothache. Section 2, however, quickly shifts to the past definite, the tense denoting things that happened once—unique events such as Auntie's home remedy and Monsieur Bayonne's faith-healing attempt. Generally speaking, imperfect tense is most suitable for summary and sometimes half-scene, while past definite is better for the fully dramatized scene, such as the episode concluding section 2.

Between section 2 and section 3 is a jump cut forward in the past time line, from the faith-healing episode to the night and morning immediately before the present-tense *now* of the story begins. Between section 3 and section 4 another shorter jump cut takes us back to the beginning of the present time line, where the characters are still waiting for the bus to arrive at the crossroads, but soon circles back to the past-definite episode of the redbirds—certainly the most important flashback in the story. Like Gaitskill and Bernardini, Gaines here is able to comfortably mix and match jump cuts with written-through transitions.

At the top of section 5, the story resumes the present time line only slightly later than where it first begins at the end of section 1, with the arrival of the bus. The rest of the story runs in present tense and present time, with no more recursions or flashbacks to previous events—holding so close to real time that time management ceases to present any problems at all.

But why write the story in present tense? What differences would there be if it were told in past tense, with events in anterior time lines framed in the pluperfect tense (as is the case in "Daisy's Valentine," for example)? Some writers seem to make this tense choice more or less at random, with no particular purpose in mind—maybe just by executing some computerized substitution of verbs. An apparently pointless present-tense narration became a somewhat irritating mannerism of much of the American short fiction published in the nineteen eighties; when there is no special reason in the story to justify its use, what present-tense narration mainly communicates is a sense of eternal ennui.

What present-tense narration can do if properly deployed is give the reader the sense that the story has not finished yet. The final scene will seem to be happening *right now*, instead of at some point in the past, and this effect of immediacy can add energy to a conclusion—particularly if it's a highly dramatic scene. The conclusion of "The Sky Is Gray," however, is not tremendously dramatic. The most extreme peaks and valleys of the action have already been passed, and at the end the characters are still doing what they spend so much time doing already: walking doggedly through the freezing rain toward some as-yet-unachieved goal. The effect of present-tense narration in this context is not of immediacy but of eternity. Like a kind of Purgatory, their exposure under the gray sky is still going on and feels as if it may go on forever. Again, the reader may recall the myth of Sisyphus.

Design

"The Sky Is Gray" is very much a character-driven story, so the intention of revealing character controls the decisions made about the structure, which in some ways is a little unusual. If we look at the story as a conflict-resolution pattern centered on James's toothache, it might appear something like this:

1. James has an awful toothache.
2. Home remedies prove useless.
3. At some significant sacrifice, he and his mother set out for the dentist to relieve the problem of his tooth.
4. But at the story's conclusion, the problem of the tooth remains unsolved.

In this pattern, there's no resolution of the conflict originally proposed. The story lays out the trajectory of a quest, but this trajectory remains incomplete because the goal of the quest is never quite reached; at the end of the story, the characters are still, eternally, on their way toward it. But the story does not *feel* incomplete at the end because somewhere along the way our attention has been redirected. Resolution of the plot problem should center on the solution to the toothache—that such a plot climax never occurs suggests that the story is designed around something other than the plot.

A nice symmetrical Freitag triangle (somewhat rare in contemporary short stories, as we have seen) would put the climax close to the middle of the story. Since this story is divided into thirteen sections, it's easy to put your finger on the center: section 7. But from the standpoint of the quest for dental treatment, section 7 is a long way from being climactic. It's dead time in the context of the quest narrative; James and his mother are just parked in the dentist's waiting room. Even the fact that they must wait is not particularly suspenseful in terms of the toothache plot (though it could easily have been made so), because James's tooth is not bothering him at this point; he is not even thinking about the tooth.

This is the moment where the reader's attention is redirected. Here, where the numerical measurements of the story might locate a climax to the toothache plot, something else has been substituted. The scene placed dead center by the section numbers is the debate between the preacher and the youth with the book. And this debate certainly is a good contender for the thematic climax of the story, though its dramatic role in the tale of James's toothache is negligible. By way of this scene, Gaines finds a way to introduce all the political issues in the background of the story in a state of almost pure abstraction, yet still in a manner that retains a considerable dramatic effectiveness and doesn't bog down the exposition.

Sections 6, 7, and 8 can in fact be arranged on a smaller Freitag triangle all their own. Section 6 sets the scene for the preacher/youth drama, establishes an audience for the debate, and introduces the preacher, who'll emerge as the antagonist in the coming conflict. Section 7 introduces the youth with the book—uttering the phrase that initiates the argument—and the section break here, positioned in the midst of a scene that is strictly continuous in real time, is designed to call attention to his appearance on the stage. Section 7 climaxes with the defeat and departure of the preacher, and the break to section 8 puts a period on that event. Section 8 itself constitutes a sort of denouement to this three-piece subdrama of the story: in which the youth with the book gives a fuller explanation of the thinking that supported him in his struggle with the preacher, by way of his parable of the colors.

When the story of James's and Mama's journey resumes, the philosophical drama at the dentist's office shifts position and becomes part of the background against which they move. The dentist's office episode changes, or clarifies, the general context in which their story is played out. In this changed context, we can see that the experience of the mother and son is in one sense a specific example of the kind of struggle which the preacher and the youth have enacted in a much more general way. Also, in sections 9 through 13, the implied comparison between the young man with the book and James himself is gradually heightened. In sections 7 and 8 we've seen the determination (and its cost) with which the youth sustains his ideas against the preacher. Only at the last line of the story in section 13 do we fully understand the depths of the determination with which both Mama and James sustain the idea of his manhood. The revelation of character involved in our recognition of Mama's final statement as an earned truth thus emerges as the chief climax of the entire story: the conclusive point toward which everything has been designed to lead.

Understanding the structural design of the story as laid out above may help to explain the writer's use of the numbered subsections, which otherwise might seem slightly odd. At first the section breaks seem intended to signal changes of scene, or to demarcate self-enclosed episodes (the faith-healing routine in section 2, the bus ride in section 5), or sometimes both. But between sections 6, 7, and 8, there's no change of scene and the episode is continuous. This middle set of section breaks seems designed to call special attention to the tripartite dramatic structure of the conflict between the preacher and the youth with the book, and, because any break in a regular pattern is always highly noticeable, they do so very well. Thereafter, the section breaks function in the same way as in the first few sections of the story, controlling changes of scene or changes of episode.

"The Sky Is Gray" is a linear story, which might have been successfully told without such sharply delineated section breaks. The story is enhanced by its division into numbered sections, but it doesn't really *require* them. Still, the writer's decision to subdivide the story into formally independent units is a step in the direction of modular design. In *this* book's next section, we'll see how many different formal arrangements are possible when the narrative is conceived in a modular way.

NOTES

1. This opening doesn't actually define the "it," but suggests it in a way that makes you picture an isolated crossroads stop for bus or train.
2. It's a bleak place to have come from, evidently. Bleak and cold enough to see cows' breath.
3. This passage does some exposition on the situation of the family by way of letting us know that Mama has got a lot on her mind. Everything has to be tightly controlled—there's no slack for anything to go wrong.
4. What's your guess as to the age of the narrator? Does his voice suggest that he's a small child? Whatever his age, he seems to carry a great deal of responsibility. The burden of being "the man" will come up again and again in the story.
5. The mute simplicity of his expression of love is childish in a touching way. It's also overlaid with powerful restraint. Why would a child hold back his feelings this way? Why would his mother require it?
6. Whatever the reason, it must be pretty serious if it's enough to make him try to hide a bad toothache . . . for a *month*.
7. The story is written in Louisiana dialect—dialect in general is problematic for writers to render. A good writer has an ear for speech and needs to present it so the reader will seem to hear it, rather than merely see it on the page. But if you go for complete phonetic accuracy, your text will become a forest of apostrophes and alternate spellings, and in becoming more difficult to read will have the opposite of the intended effect.

    So Gaines creates and follows a few simple rules for a dialect grammar, to convey the impression of the sound of this speech—he drops most of the auxiliary verbs and uses a few odd idiomatic words or phrases and a few dropped syllables (but not too many).
8. Seven people in this house, five of them small children . . . and only three beds (if we're even talking about actual beds). The narrator doesn't make much of this situation because it's natural to him, his status quo.
9. With the shift of tense, from present to imperfect, we've looped to the backstory. By now this is a familiar pattern: first the present scene is set, then the story backtracks to tell us about the antecedent action. It's important for beginning writers not to get tangled up in the tenses when executing maneuvers of this kind.
10. The numbers that divide the sections of the story may call attention to themselves. We've seen space breaks in several stories before marking changes of scene or time frame, but numbering the sections is more prominent. It's also noticeable that in this story Gaines will sometimes break and start a new numbered section when the scene and time frame have *not* changed.

In this case, though, the tense has changed from imperfect to simple past—thus we move from a summary of how it generally was during the month of toothache to a specific scene that transpired once Auntie found out about it.

11. This episode of attempted faith healing is the first introduction of religion into the story ... there will be others of greater importance.

12. Meanwhile, the episode is almost a comic routine ... inserted for comic relief.

13. A miracle? Maybe, maybe not.

14. If it was a miracle it must have worn off. We find out later in the story that the tooth pain seems to come and go at random.

15. This line is the punch-line of the comic routine. The whole subsection 2 is constructed like a joke ... although the background situation is serious. Notice that these people will try all sorts of alternatives before they take the boy to the dentist.

16. In the new numbered section, the mood has changed—a trip to the dentist has become inevitable. Notice too that we're circling back toward the present time of the story.

17. Why would he say this? For a middle-class kid it might be that fear of the dentist outweighs the pain of the toothache, but this is a very bad toothache and I don't think it's a middle-class kid.

18. Picking up some more exposition—explanation of the father's absence. You get the idea that life was easier and happier before he left.

19. The tightness of this budget will become very important later on.

20. This exchange sounds so casual; at the same time it might be read as a complaint and a defensive response.

21. The situation is simple, almost primitive ... but it seems to require a lot of careful diplomacy just to get along.

22. Seems to be a lot of discipline in this family. Is it an arbitrary discipline? Ty certainly seems to think so.

23. The mother can't afford to lose a full day's pay.

24. These people don't have much to eat, and so the narrator, James (this scene has let us know his name), has learned to savor what there is.

25. Ty's complaints have a comic tone, but as in the scene with Monsieur Bayonne, the comic quality is complicated by the real hardship in the background.

26. Feeling sorry for yourself is not encouraged in this family—that much is for sure.

27. The fourth numbered section brings us back into present action and present tense.

28. Another tough attitude from the mother—perhaps she has no energy to waste.

29. By following the narrator's thoughts into memory, the story makes a transition into a flashback—the same maneuver might be executed with a jump cut.
30. Literally? How much eating could there be on a redbird?
31. Do we call this child abuse? The mother beats Ty for fearing ghosts as well.
32. Interesting that he doesn't present this as crying; it's almost as if emotion is disconnected from the tears.
33. The exact detailing makes the episode seem more excruciating—as if the writer were holding the reader's nose to the scene in the same way that the mother is forcing the boy to complete the task.
34. Auntie seems to have a good point here. This is a cruel scene ...
35. ... but the boy learned what he was supposed to anyway. From his point of view, it's a hard lesson but a useful one—not just meaningless cruelty. The mother's methods are extremely harsh, but they seem to work. Why should such harshness be necessary?

    The discovery of the narrator's age here is timed for shock effect—that a child of six or seven would be put through such an experience.
36. It's not the bite of meat that matters, but the attitude: feed the family at whatever cost.
37. Section 5 resurfaces into present tense, present action. The flashbacks make the wait for the bus, on the present time line, seem much longer. Waiting is the chief activity in the story's present-time plot.
38. We might have guessed from the dialect that these characters are black, but this is the first passage to confirm it. Boarding the bus, they enter the world of a larger society than their household—a racist society, to be sure. This larger context may help explain the mother's attitude and actions.
39. The slight feeling of stoicism in the narrator's attitude here will be developed considerably later on.
40. The clear description of both appearance and action conveys the essence of this little flirtation.
41. A minor setback makes him turn away ...
42. ... toward the river and the outside world, where the title phrase makes a very unobtrusive first appearance. Often a title will point to something in the center of the story. Here it seems to point toward the general background—the overall surroundings.
43. Love comes suddenly! This is a comic moment between two cute children, but there's something touching about it too. In noticing the narrator's restraint we may (subliminally) recall that he doesn't let himself show obvious affection to his mother either.
44. Still, the scene ends on a comic note—parallel to section 2, about Monsieur Bayonne's faith healing.
45. Section 6 opens a new scene. The world of Bayonne is larger than the

world of the bus, but still it's a very small place. And the father is lost somewhere in a world which is so much larger than either Bayonne or Baton Rouge.

46. Mama has a strict standard for blowing your nose . . .
47. . . . and not staring at people . . .
48. . . . and generally walking a straight and narrow line.
49. Here's a different picture of a mother-son relationship; is it necessarily a prettier one?
50. Idiomatic expressions like these can bring a speaker fully alive in a single phrase.
51. Can you imagine what would happen if our narrator behaved the way John Lee is behaving? You can't even imagine him doing it.
52. Given the suffering of the narrator, this is a pertinent question for the story as a whole.
53. This dialogue is a rumination on the way the world is—and for these two speakers that's the same as a rumination on the nature of God.
54. The image of the preacher is the image of comparative prosperity and power . . .
55. . . . and also of a very rigid authoritarianism.
56. An old and from some points of view unpersuasive explanation for social (and racial) injustice.
57. In most stories by white writers, black people are identified as such and everyone else is assumed to be white. This story takes the opposite approach. For the narrator, black people are what's normal and white people are more noticeably different.
58. Underlining the mother's reticence, again.
59. Up until now, the section breaks have signaled shifts into a new scene or time frame or episode, but section 7 seems to be the same episode as section 6—there is not even a pause in the conversation. Why break here? The eccentricity calls attention to itself—making the new character introduced in this paragraph seem especially important.
60. These details will gain significance later on.
61. It may be that the preacher (and all he comes to represent) can't really withstand much questioning.
62. This allusion to the flag suggests that the "boy" means to challenge the U.S. government . . .
63. . . . a prospect which makes the preacher more uneasy and defensive.
64. The preacher is accustomed to use religion as an impregnable retreat, but for the boy religion is not unquestionable.
65. An attempt to assert the sort of authority a parent might have over a child . . .
66. . . . but it doesn't work. We begin to see the instrumental usefulness of the boy's tactic of questioning everything.

67. The existence of God has never been susceptible to *logical* proof . . .
68. . . . emotional conviction comes easier.
69. Is there a logical connection between the two parts of this sentence? If so it may require a larger context to make it obvious.
70. An absolute repudiation of emotion here, which may recall how disapproving the narrator's mother is of any emotional display.
71. Some similarities appear between the "boy" and our narrator: absent father, overworked mother.
72. Since his other strategies have not worked, the preacher now tries this psychological undermining—a variation on the *ad hominem* attack. He's trying to suggest that the boy's abstract ideas are a delusional result of his personal experience.
73. But the boy can't be lured into an emotional reaction. "Cold logic" serves him well, at least up to this point.
74. The notion of an organized movement of people like this is much more threatening to the preacher and what he represents than a single isolated lunatic could ever be.
75. It seems, indeed, that the preacher is losing the support of the temporary community of people clustered in the waiting room.
76. New gambit. Pity, in this case, is a form of contempt.
77. This intransigent optimism may be somewhat surprising; it shows that the boy's attitude, sometimes cynical, is not a cynicism of despair.
78. The boy recognizes the preacher's strategy and refutes it.
79. The preacher tried this gambit before, and it didn't work very well then either.
80. This line fills in the logical blank in his earlier remark about "what your heart tells you." The boy is summarizing a rather complicated line of reasoning which goes back to slavery times—when slave owners were careful to teach their slaves only the meek and submissive qualities of Christianity, leaving the more militant aspects of the religion secret. This limited Christian teaching encouraged first slaves, and later free blacks also, to accept whatever injustices were dealt them in this world on the theory that these would be rectified in the next. This way of thinking (or feeling), deeply rooted in the black community and supported by genuine and powerful religious faith, is something which black political pragmatists have often had to struggle with.
81. Verifying the insult.
82. The argument is now over because the boy has won it . . .
83. . . . and the other people in the room seem to recognize this too.
84. Why does the preacher do this? It seems a rather an un-Christian thing to do. But he has been publicly humiliated in the argument, and it seems he can't sit still for that. Again, the episode shows that the power structure the preacher speaks for will resort to violence if its rhetoric fails.

85. Quite a comeback! Who better represents the pacific Christian virtues now?
86. At this point, the preacher is committed to his course of action no matter how futile it is.
87. The whole passive resistance strategy of the civil rights movement is predicted here (in a story that takes place during World War II).
88. When passive resistance is successful, the aggressor defeats himself. The intended victim, meanwhile, appears to be utterly unaffected.
89. Total defeat of the preacher.
90. It's the "boy" whose belief system has proved to be unshakeable. (And why does the narrator call him a "boy"? The description at the top of the section is of an adult. Surely the narrator isn't echoing the white man's denigrating term for the black adult.)
91. At the close of the section, it's more obvious why it should have been formally divided from the rest—though it's part of the flow of a single scene, its particular conflict is so clearly stated and firmly resolved that it belongs in its own separate "chapter."
92. The first two paragraphs of section 8 relax a little, after the crisis and resolution of section 7. Although the scene has not changed, it has in some sense started over—building up a new movement of the narrative.
93. Re-establishing the basic conditions of the narrator's situation and the pain he always has to avoid or suppress.
94. The narrator is always hemmed in by such responsibilities, which limit everything he does.
95. The touching repetition is very much a child's response . . .
96. . . . but his sense that he must be the provider shows that he thinks of himself as an adult.
97. Role reversal: this is something the parent would be more likely to say to the child in this context.
98. The onlooker recognizes the role reversal.
99. Mama's possible smile is much more significant than it might be in a more demonstrative character.
100. Pity is a form of contempt.
101. This sudden response may be surprising—because the narrator reported the scene with the preacher transparently, with no comment that would suggest this sort of allegiance. It's a little bit like the sudden rush of love for the little girl on the bus, though here the motivation is more complex and perhaps more serious. Maybe the narrator wants to think of the young man with the book as a "boy" in some way like himself.
102. The lady seems basically in sympathy with the boy—but the atheism worries her.
103. Another queer leap—as with the earlier remark about the heart, there seems to be no logical connection between these ideas.

104. The very strangeness of the dialogue helps get people's attention.
105. And now we begin to see the point. This whole business of the colors is a way of showing how received ideas, in general, go unquestioned. From the standpoint of "cold logic," the words for colors are indeed completely arbitrary.
106. Attacking the foundation of language is more radical than attacking the foundation of religion. He's living up to his promise to question everything.
107. This passage is rather thin on sensory detail—its subject is abstract and philosophical—but the details when furnished are very telling.
108. Now we begin to see that he's challenging language in order to contrast talk and action.
109. See how religion works in the context of political repression? A demand for action in this religious context connotes a dangerously sinful arrogance.
110. A good demonstration of a received idea—the assumption that goes unquestioned.
111. Of course it's unexamined political assumptions that really need to be challenged, rather than assumptions about colors. The "boy" knows that; his remarks about colors are symbolic, part of an ongoing parable he's telling.
112. Another victory for cold logic as the parable begins to make its points. Before the civil rights movement, blacks could excercise very few of their "paper" rights anywhere in the Deep South.
113. Now we see why he feels it necessary to repudiate all emotional responses—a quality in which he resembles the narrator's mother.
114. The relationship between the young man's politics and Christianity is not a simple one. An atheistic movement would alienate too many of its most likely supporters (and could also, at this time, have been denounced as Communist). And by "turning the other cheek," the young man has already shown that he can follow Christian doctrine better than the preacher.
115. She's got a point here. Cold logic is very frosty stuff, and you can't help but feel that the boy may have sacrificed a part of his humanity . . .
116. . . . perhaps because he has no choice.
117. The abstract, philosophical part of the story is now concluded, and with section 9 (though the scene itself has still not changed) the action proper of the story resumes.
118. This is serious—we know how tightly both time and money have been budgeted for this excursion.
119. This answer is both absolute and arbitrary (like the preacher's belief system, maybe).
120. By now we know Mama well enough to imagine what this must cost

her—though her lines are couched as simple statements of fact, they almost amount to begging.

121. Again, it's so out of character for her to encourage the narrator to look pitiful that it shows the situation is severe.

122. The nurse could be nice if she chose to be—but why make that choice? She has a small scrap of absolute power and uses it arbitrarily.

123. Like the sign on the bus ... they are always sent to the rear, served last.

124. An indeterminate amount of time to be killed, and nowhere to go.

125. It would be too bad if he did, most likely.

126. The white people can get out of the weather.

127. It seems that *only* white people can get out of the weather. The black people are forever on the outside looking in.

128. The repetition of "that rag" emphasizes the repetitiveness of their movements—they're walking in circles.

129. If you're white, you can stand around the stove for no reason, but if you're black you'll be required to state your business quickly.

130. This subterfuge must be painful to a woman as proud as Mama, but she draws it out long enough for the narrator to get warm.

131. We begin to see why Mama wastes no words—a bad situation that can't be helped is only made worse by talking about it.

132. Here the section break indicates passage of time, but not nearly enough time has passed. The amount of time that has to be spent somehow becomes another problematic "budget."

133. By implication, the sky is gray. Grayness seems to permeate the whole background—sleet, concrete walls and sidewalk, the cold itself. Gray is the color of the situation's overall inhospitality.

134. Her harshness is closely connected to instruction in self-respect.

135. Some people might despair under intolerable conditions; Mama gets angry.

136. Her frustrated anger, with nowhere to go, becomes dangerous. We begin to see how the beating in the redbird episode might have gotten out of control.

137. Circumstances practically require him to deny what he really feels. What good would it do to tell the truth?

138. Not enough time has been spent yet.

139. The prayer shows desperation, but we also have been reminded by the scene in the dentist's office that practically speaking you can't pray yourself out of this kind of trouble.

140. This time the section breaks predicts a change of scene.

141. Change of attitude. He's no longer praying that the Lord won't let him die. Now he's not going to let himself die.

142. Increasingly, the title phrase associates itself with the battering these characters receive from a uniformly hostile world.

143. These repetitions draw out the scene, help make it seem interminable. The frequent paragraph breaks in this section convey the sense of time dragging.
144. It's a cycle of repetition, both thought and action. He repeatedly wishes he could buy his mother a coat . . .
145. . . . repeatedly wishes for summer and warmth . . .
146. . . . must repeatedly freeze his hand to wipe his nose. Around and around in the squirrel cage.
147. Still, things could always get worse.
148. This idea adds one more small and dismal touch to the scene.
149. Here the situation of the father and the family is spelled out more clearly than before. Like the dentist's nurse, the military bureaucracy that took away the father is an aspect of a faceless, authoritarian, repressive power (which that preacher somehow felt obligated to defend).
150. The context of this good Christian resignation to fate has been changed by the debate in the dentist's office.
151. The section break, this time, marks a change of scene. The warming of his hands repeats the situation at the hardware store—always a gray weary round of suffering and inadequate relief.
152. Contrast to the red coat the narrator imagines buying.
153. He's an expert in small sufferings and how to deal with them.
154. As in the hardware store, shelter is unlikely to be free.
155. If he tries to hide his hunger, it's for a reason . . .
156. . . . partly from a pride instilled in him; he doesn't want to be the cause of an unplanned expenditure . . .
157. . . . partly because he knows the budget; if they spend more than they planned in town, they can't afford the bus home.
158. There's a lot passing unspoken in this moment; the narrator knows that what gets his mother down is not being able to provide more for him. What's the use of talking about it?
159. He can offer a reciprocal sacrifice . . .
160. . . . but the mother won't accept it.
161. Always such a complicated balance of suffering—easing one pain may start off another.
162. This invitation might seem innocuous to us . . .
163. . . . but not to Mama.
164. Seems that Mama read the situation right.
165. She sounds pretty convincing, doesn't she? With her husband absent, she has to be expert at protecting herself.
166. Her son is eager to protect her but he doesn't have the power.
167. As in the dentist office scene, the section break is a little oddly placed, controlled not by the change of location, but by the end of the exchange between Mama and the would-be pimp.

168. It's a hollow victory after all. Mama has defeated the pimp, but it's no longer worth staying in the shelter of the restaurant, so the trial of endurance begins all over again. Solve one problem and land yourself in another. It's a very narrow line these people have to walk, no matter where they go.

169. This is just a minor extra effort, but they all do begin to add up.

170. Throughout the story, his hunger builds, and nothing seems to satisfy it. Remember, these are people who go hungry all the time.

171. This strange dreamlike poem by Edgar Allen Poe would seem very far removed from the narrator's present situation (or anything else in his life), but its wistfulness for impossibly different conditions makes it peculiarly appropriate.

172. Isn't Mama somebody "like that" herself? Someone who'd insist you know your lesson no matter what.

173. So why *is* she out there?

174. This is the first gesture of sympathy they've received on their whole journey.

175. But Mama is pretty stiff about accepting it. She will not allow herself or her child to be pitied. Pity is a form of contempt.

176. What could really be the point of such a telephone call?

177. These people are white but not well-to-do.

178. Whatever is going on has been planned between them . . .

179. . . . and now the old lady is more or less forced to admit that to Mama.

180. The plan is to offer them charity . . .

181. . . . but Mama doesn't take charity.

182. The old lady and Mama are getting to know each other during this brief exchange, and now the old lady has devised a pretext that might allow Mama to accept the food.

183. This line shows insight—so proud herself, Mama is more or less compelled to respect pride in others.

184. And Mama knows when she's been outmaneuvered.

185. These people may have troubles of their own—their own poverty, less severe than what the narrator's family endures, but still acute.

186. Why keep this character off-stage?

187. The show of toughness is calculated to appeal to Mama—no work, no eat.

188. For whatever reason, maybe the cold mentioned above, he's not able to do these things himself, but he's very concerned about her having to do it.

189. This piece of "work" seems to be completely contrived.

190. The old lady has to control everything very carefully—if Mama figures out the cans are empty, then the whole scheme collapses.

191. The pride of poverty means that the less you have, the better you take care of it. This attitude would be very familiar to the narrator.

192. The narrator's consuming hunger has been so thoroughly established that

the reader may feel as eager as he does when the food finally hits the table
... but there's always some duty which must be addressed first.

193. I bet she's thinking about how those cans seemed to handle too light.

194. Here's the point of the phone call: if a white person asks on their behalf,
they will be served sooner.

195. The odd formality of this blessing makes it stand out, showing us clearly
that what "Alnest" and the old lady are up to is an exercise of Christian
charity. As a representative of Christianity, "Alnest" is a counterexample
to the preacher at the dentist's office—so far from imposing himself, he
doesn't even appear on stage, but tries to do some unobtrusive good
from behind the scenes.

196. This is a little slip on the old lady's part ...

197. ... and she can't really recover.

198. It's too obvious that the salt meat is a gift in disguise, so Mama won't take
it. Her toughness literally never lets up.

199. Remember the budget? A reader who is paying as much attention as James
(you better believe he's paying attention) will realize that now they *will* be
able to take the bus home. Mama has saved back the quarter she spent at
the restaurant; she originally planned to spend a whole fifty cents on salt
meat. Which means among other things that the old lady has been able,
against all obstacles, to make her generosity really count for something...

200. ... and Mama is able to acknowledge it. The formality of this statement is
parallel to the formality of the blessing from "Alnest" earlier. And of
course Mama is also letting the old lady know that she understands what
the old lady has been up to all along—trying to *give* something freely in
spite of all Mama's efforts to turn it into a fair *exchange*.

201. At the beginning of the story, this insistence might have seemed cruel and
irrational, but at the end we know very well what it means ...

202. ... every pain they endure and every barrier they surmount is contributed
to this absolute affirmation.

PART
III

MODULAR

DESIGN

I SEE TWO DIFFERENT WAYS, quite distinct if not opposed, of thinking about the raw material of which narratives are made—two ways of contemplating the original experience, whether real, imagined, or some blend of the two, to which the work will give form. You may think of this primary experience as a single amorphous mass of information. Or you may conceive of it as a grab-bag of unassembled components—something like a jumble of unsnapped Legos, say.

In the first case, the task of the writer is to shape the material. The writer models a unitary mass of information in the same way that a sculptor models a blob of clay or carves a block of stone. Perhaps there is something in the mass to begin with that suggests the form the artist will give it. In that case, form is indwelling, inherent in experience, in the block. Michelangelo, at any rate, seemed to believe something of the sort when he spoke of his *discovery* of figures within masses of marble. For the writer, the discovery of innate forms underlying the superficially amorphous flux of experience is closely related to the discovery of meanings inherent in experience—if the writer is inclined to believe that the meaning of experience is intrinsic instead of being arbitrarily superimposed.

An artist with this attitude toward the raw material sees the artifact singly, as an integrated whole. Most often the work will be shaped by subtraction: only those elements which properly express the essential form are allowed to remain. That, quite literally, is the method of the woodcarver or stonecarver. Writers are less likely to think of their craft as subtractive, since in the beginning the words must always be piled up, not carved away. Still, the decisions about what to say and what not to say accomplish many exclusions, so that the mass of primary experiential material is in fact shaped by being reduced.

In narrative art, linear design provides the closest analogy to this kind of sculptural model (despite the fact that in plastic art, you really can't say that sculpture is linear). Both the carver and the writer of linear narratives are first concerned with the form of the work in its entirety. The carver thinks of the seamless smooth movement of the shape to be chiseled out. The writer thinks of the overall movement of the principal narrative vector from its start to its finish, all other issues being subordinated to this overarching concern.

In the second case, the task of the artist is not to discover the essential form of the work by whittling away the dross, but to assemble the work out of small component parts. This breed of artist is not so much a sculptor as mosaicist, assembling fragments of glass and tile to form what can be understood, at a greater distance, as a coherent, shapely image. In narrative art, this mosaic method is the basis for modular design.

If linear design can be understood as somehow subtractive, a process of removing the less essential material so as to reveal the movement of narrative vectors more cleanly and clearly, then modular design is additive. The writer adds and arranges more and more modular units which may be attractive in themselves for all sorts of different reasons, but which also must serve the purpose of clarifying the overall design of the text as a whole. In linear design, the integrity of the finished work is obviously the first concern, since the writer is thinking of the work holistically to begin with. In the case of modular design, the writer will, at the outset, approach the raw material in a more fragmentary way. A sense of integrity in the work as a whole must be achieved by symmetrical arrangement of the modular parts. In a modular narrative design, narrative elements are balanced in symmetry as shapes are balanced in a symmetrical geometric figure, or as weights are balanced on a scale.

Of course, this symmetry need not be perfectly exact. Different kinds of symmetry are found in nature, and only the lowest organisms are radially symmetrical, so that any dividing line that passes through the center will produce two halves which reflect one another perfectly. Higher organisms, from flatworms to human beings, are *bilaterally* symmetrical, meaning that only one bisecting line will produce two precisely reflecting halves. In the case of an isosceles triangle, such as the Freitag triangle of a linear design, the symmetry will be exact. In living organisms, this bilateral symmetry will be rather more rough and approximate (as evidenced by the indubitable fact that one of my ears is even larger than the other one).

Manmade objects tend to follow similar rules. An architecture based on perfect circles or perfect squares may strangle on the constraints of its own symmetry. So the symmetry of most buildings is bilateral, not radial. This principle also extends itself to modular design. By following organic rules of order, modular design makes for a more lifelike narrative.

The units, modules, of modular design may be defined for narratives in all sorts of different ways, depending partially upon scale. At the page-by-page level, the modular unit will most probably look like a text block, separated from its fellows by space breaks. We have already seen how in linear narratives these insignificant-looking space breaks can be used to signal jump cuts from one point in a narrative forward to another, to indicate other shifts in chronology, to shift scenes or to accomplish other sorts of transitions, in a style which has been very much influenced by the movies. In modular design, this semicinematic mode of transition can be used to accomplish more complicated changes. From text block to text block, a modular design may change storyline, switch from character to character, switch between first-, second- or third-person narration in the treatment of the *same* character, make radical divergences in tone and voice, and in fact do almost anything you can imagine. All these shifts and rearrangements are held back from the brink of total anarchy by observing certain basic principles of order, symmetry, and balance.

Complex modular designs are more frequent in long fiction than short fiction. The use of modular design at the level of the short story is almost exclusively a late-twentieth-century phenomenon (with *Maldoror*, the work of the earlier French writer Lautréamont, providing at least one interesting exception to this rule). The influence of film narratives on prose narratives looks to be a likely explanation for that situation.

But at longer lengths, the modular concept may be as old as storytelling itself. Within cycles of mythology, whether Greek, Roman, or Stone Age primitive, individual tales can be and often are rearranged and reordered with respect to one another, in ways that may alter the total effect of the whole body of the narrative to which they belong. Single-author story cycles also have an ancient lineage, going back at least as far as Chaucer's *Canterbury Tales*, where the overarching conceit—twelve people telling tales to one another as they proceed on their pilgrimage—allows for considerable internal flexibility and the possibility of more than one arrangement. The case is much the same with *The Arabian Nights* and with another masterpiece of the Islamic tradition, Farid ud-din Attar's *The Conference of the Birds*.

In twentieth-century American literature, the first really powerful example of a story cycle is Sherwood Anderson's *Winesburg, Ohio*. Though Anderson wrote other novels, this modular work is his best known and best appreciated and the only book-length work of his still widely read outside of scholarly circles. The linear form of the novel was not well-suited to his gifts; modular design provided him with a better solution. Anderson's one-time apprentice Ernest Hemingway published a story cycle of sorts (*In Our Time*) as his first book; this group is not so coherently worked out as *Winesburg*, but the influence of the modular conception is quite clear. No one could claim that Faulkner was incapable of writing a linear novel, but three of his books—*Go Down, Moses*; *The Unvanquished*; and *As I Lay Dying*—are excellent (and quite different) examples of modular design.

More recently (from the 1970s on up) the story cycle, or episodic novel, has been a popular resort both for nonnovelists—story writers working at book length—and for novelists interested in trying a new form. Generally popular examples of this modular design–based genre include Louise Erdrich's first book, *Love Medicine*; Harriet Doerr's *Stones for Ibarra* (a winner of the National Book Award); and Carolyn Chute's *The Beans of Egypt, Maine*. Less well-known but equally admirable are Russell Banks's *Trailerpark*, Fred Chappell's *I Am One of You Forever*, and William Vollmann's *The Rainbow Stories*.

What modular design can do is liberate the writer from linear logic, those chains of cause and effect, strings of dominoes always falling forward. Modular design replaces the domino theory of narrative with other principles which have less to do with motion (the story as a process) and more to do with overall shapeliness (the story as a fixed geometric form). The geometry of a modular design, especially one that has been well worked out in advance of composition, will be defining and confining to some degree. But the gain can be more than worth the sacrifice. The very fixity of the substructure can give the writer more latitude to improvise freely around the hidden armature with plot, character, and voice.

Of course a linear design may also show great internal diversity—in plot complication; character; shifts of point of view; shifts from one mode of narration to another; changes in voicing, tone and style. But all this diversity must be incorporated into the forward linear movement of the whole, as if the writer had taken a number of strands to make a braid. In modular design, all these ingredients can be treated less like strands and more like bricks. They can be managed as if they were discrete, particulate—capable of being assembled in more than a single way.

Time is a tyrant over all narratives: some events must always precede and others always follow. Modular design allows the writer to throw off the burden of chronology as much as is possible. It is always there, somewhere, but you may be able to proceed as if it didn't affect you. Modular design is an attractive way to show relationships between events or people or motifs or themes which are not generated by sequences of cause and effect and so are somehow atemporal, perhaps even timeless.

The sorts of problems which a modular design can solve are more likely to crop up at book length than at story length. That's partly because most writers can grasp the whole length of a story intuitively, without really thinking about it very explicitly, so that there is no real need to break it down into its components. But for most writers, a book-length work surpasses intuitive structural capacity. To try to intuit your way through a whole novel as if it were just a big story (which perhaps it is) will most likely be too overwhelming a prospect. There's a great incentive to organize it formally in advance to some degree, whether by preparing an abstract of its singular linear movement or by disassembling it into elementary component parts. And for many writers, often for the strongest and most intuitive story writers, the second, modular option will be the most appealing.

Because the composition of short stories usually doesn't require a great deal of formal advance planning, not too many writers resort to full-fledged modular designs at the length of the short story. But this rule is exceedingly well-distinguished with exceptions. The writers of the stories that follow have often adopted modular designs less for convenience than out of inevitable necessity. The modular form of such a story becomes quite inseparable from its meaning.

SIGNS OF LIFE

M I R I A M   K U Z N E T S

Same old story, he says.

    Seems like there aren't any new ones, she says.

    War, he says.

    Peace, she says.

    Good, he says.[1]

    After the movie, in the popcorn-strewn lobby, crimson with gold flecks, each is waiting for a friend to finish in the bathroom. They used to wait for each other.[2]

Nadine and Michael live in a town famous for rain—drizzling, spitting, pissing like regret. Nadine never carries an umbrella.[3]

    When she was fifteen, in her hometown on the other side of the country, she'd been struck by lightning. Her hand was on an iron fence, a teenage hand feeling romantic in a thunderstorm, no one around to see her face uplifted, eyes shut, mouth open. The shock was just that, yet she couldn't get her fingers to loosen their grip on the post until she fainted. Thereafter her classmates treated her as a daredevil. A month after Nadine was hit, her mother found a white streak in her hair, near the nape. Nadine could never see it though she tried tricks with mirrors.[4]

    Now she's twice as old.[5]

    Are you waiting for life to begin? Do you feel like just another face in the crowd? Are you ready for a change? If so, the Tyler School of—[6]

In the morning, Nadine lowered the radio so she could decipher the racket in the hall of her apartment building. She gargled coffee and flipped through the newspaper, looking for a movie to see that night. Her eyebrows rose at the revival house bill.[7]

Still listening, she picked up the exams. What is the capital of Alaska? Jupiter, her favorite student had written. Nadine didn't correct her. Mind over matter.[8]

Evil, she says.[9]

Since she last saw him, about a year ago, his skin has drooped, his slick hair has become waxy, and his eyes look as if they need a washing. He's starting to lose what he should gain and gain what he should lose.[10] He doesn't believe it so he isn't ugly yet.[11]

She's pleasantly surprised by the change, as if he were a doll that has acquired laugh lines after being played with and forgotten.[12]

Michael, across the hall at a college in this damp town Nadine chose sight unseen.[13] He gave her a bath or a backrub any time she asked. They wrestled and he tickled her until she thought she would burst. They winked at each other as they danced to slow numbers, her chin resting on someone else's shoulder, one of his shoulderblades covered by someone else's hand.

He said, I don't love you.

She said, You don't have a choice. She said, You're the back of my hand and I'm yours and all I have is time on my hands. Nadine had no idea what she was talking about; it sounded good.[14]

Get out of here, you bum.

Someone was shouting in the hall. Nadine stared at the bottom of her coffee mug. Her suspicion that Mr. Tree Ear had returned was confirmed.[15] During the night, she'd smelled him in between the drops of rain. He was a gray-bearded man with a garbage bag folded, tucked, and tied around his head, lending it the appearance of a tree ear mushroom and serving as a shower cap. He had no home and sneaked into her apartment building to rest on the balding green carpet in the hallway.

Nadine doodled on a napkin: Tree ears hear a tree fall in the forest when there's no one around.

Death, he says.[16]

She licks her lips a few times, watching his as he speaks. His is the mouth she kisses when she kisses her friend, the one in the bathroom.[17]

They are breaking a rule by not pretending they've never seen each other naked.

Michael, after college, was the *Wunderkind* at the *Daily Sun*. He was going to do it for just a year. For a year, Nadine proofread at night for the same newspaper.[18]

She corrected typos in the police ledger, obituaries, and forecasts of inclement weather. Then she opened a smudged window and hung her head out to get it wet. The only thing moving on the street was a garbage bag—Mr. Tree Ear on the curb, nodding. The other proofers left her to lock up and she made an expensive phone call to a friend in an earlier time zone. She skimmed the papers on Michael's desk, in his drawers, waiting for some sign that she had been a part of his life. They didn't see each other in person any more.[19]

Get a job. You're not crippled.[20]

She leaned against the doorway. A sweatshirt with a hole over the breast and underwear with broken elastic were not proper gear in which to save Mr. Tree Ear.

She dialed 911.

Where's the emergency?

She stuttered the answer.

What do you want from us, lady?[21]

Life, she says.[22]

Standing next to him is like standing next to her perpetually unmade bed. She would have no trouble falling asleep on him.

If she were to see him for the first time now, she wouldn't see him. He looks a bit sleazy. He could be anybody. But he runs his hands up and down the sides of his thighs, leaving his fingerprints.

George M. Clark, age thirty-one, of Young County, is suspected of murdering six young women in that area over the past two years. Late yesterday afternoon, police found in Clark's home a coffee table made of human bones and a pillow case fashioned from human skin. Police suspect George Clark's victims became his furniture.[23]

Nadine made pillowcase one word. She decided to find another profession.[24]

Bang.

The door slammed. After hastily covering herself, Nadine roamed the street, eyes peeled. Mr. Tree Ear's head was in a puddle. She crouched, cleared her throat. Can I help you?

What do you want from me, sweetheart? Yet he smiled.

What? When? Where? Who? Why? She wanted to know and hoped he could tell her.[25] She rubbed dry the back of her hand and their eyes met.

Love, he says.
He brushes a piece of hair away from her face.
It's her turn but she doesn't take it.[26]

Tell us a story.
Twenty-three little faces, all shapes and colors, waited.[27]
Your teacher is a fraud. She thinks lightning can strike twice in the same place. She believes coffee will some day taste as good as it smells. She dreams of things she can't put her finger on.
She didn't tell them this tale. Instead, she grinned and began, It was a dark and stormy afternoon and the pupils said to their teacher, Tell us a story, so she began, It was a dark and stormy afternoon and the pupils said to their teacher, Tell us a story—[28]
Get to the point.
None of them had heard the story before.

The room was dark except for a dot of red.
She hadn't turned the radio off completely earlier.[29] She had drifted to sleep in the arms of her friend and awoke to thunderclaps and grayed white walls.
Movie time soon, she said.
Why do you want to see this so badly? he asked.
She hugged him.
She stood naked before the bathroom mirror and combed her moist hair. In a summer camp, many years before, a fellow camper wore a braid, day in and out, never allowing her hair to dry. When she finally unravelled the braid, clumps fell to the floor. Nadine examined several white hairs in her comb.[30]

Yeah, same old story, he says.[31]
I suppose it's all in the telling, she says. We saw this one once together, remember? she asks.
I thought it was familiar, he says. You know, I'd ask you to come home with me, but, he says.[32]
I'm happy with the way things are now, it's better, she says.
The delicate ankles of a woman who won't be walking in the rain tonight come closer.
There's your friend, she says.
And there's yours, he says.
I hope—I feel—she says, I never was any good at endings.[33]

ANALYSIS

Plot

Lots of stories could potentially be structured in more than one way, but this one really requires a modular design. To understand why, let's try summarizing its linear plot:

A girl, Nadine, is struck by lightning in high school. In college, she meets Michael, and they become lovers, exchanging snappy, avant-garde dialogue. After college, Michael becomes a star at a newspaper where Nadine is an inkstained wretch of a proofreader; as his career surpasses hers, he dumps her. She can't get over her obsession with him, though. Finally she quits the paper and becomes an elementary school teacher. She gets another boyfriend, but she's still thinking about Michael. One morning, as she's grading papers, she finds herself disturbed by the plight of a vagrant who's seeking shelter in her building; she tries to help him but her efforts are ineffectual. That afternoon her new lover comes over, they make out and sleep. Upon waking, they decide to go see an old movie, and at the theater, Nadine coincidentally runs into Michael, who's with a new woman. After two and half minutes of conversation between these two people, it's all over.

See any *short story* in this material? I sure don't. For one thing, there is a very intractable amount of real time to deal with. Say Nadine was fifteen when lightning struck her; since we know she's "twice as old" by the time she reaches the theater, there's fifteen years to be covered somehow. Approach this in a linear fashion and you'd find yourself writing a novel. Nadine's adventures in college and afterward would balloon into hundreds of pages; you'd be forced to delve much more deeply into the stages of her relationship with Michael, and so on and so on and so on . . .

What if you preserved the economy of presentation, but straightened out the chronology of the text blocks? Theoretically, this is doable. To rearrange all the text blocks in real-time chronological order would be the work of a moment, and you might even write transitions between them so as to eliminate the space breaks. See above for a plot summary of the story that would result. It's idiotic: a relentless progression from the portentous to the trivial.

In terms of plot, the story gives you either too much to work with or too little. The present action is a 2.5 minute conversation between the principals in a theater lobby. There are plenty of events in the background, but try to talk more about them and you'll discover that you've strolled into a glue trap. When you get right down to it, it just isn't a plot-driven story.

Character

Well, then, is character the central concern?

The answer, typically enough, is yes and no. The present action scene in the theater lobby doesn't want to tell you much at all about the characters—that scene won't even supply their names. They could be anybody; their voices are like voices on the moon. But the backstory elements do finally reveal quite a lot about Nadine and a thing or two about Michael, thus adding substance to the weirdly disembodied conversation which constitutes the story's present action.

Of Michael we ultimately know this little: that he's capable of a symbiotic click with Nadine (which makes the vector 1 conversation possible). That he is losing his looks. That he cared less for Nadine than she for him and has been in the habit of treating her badly. This last and most significant point is found more between the lines than in them.

Nadine's character is a more central issue and we learn more about it. After all, it can be argued that the story is taking place inside her head. We find out more hard information about her background and career than we do about Michael's. We know that she is oppressed by the horrors of the world (George M. Clark, serial killer) and that she has quixotic impulses to rectify them. But her belief that she can significantly help Mr. Tree Ear is as problematic as her belief that coffee will one day taste as good as it smells.

So much of what we know about Nadine's character verges on the intangible. Her streak of whimsy, which leads her not to correct the student's assertion that Jupiter is the capital of Alaska. Her willingness to speak without knowing what she means, because it sounds good. This quality of Nadine's character has a lot to do with the story's tone.

Tone

Much of the story's language comes out of Nadine's consciousness; she has a flair for striking images, odd conceits and nice turns of phrase: ". . . a teenage hand feeling romantic in a thunderstorm . . ." "He's starting to lose what he should gain and gain what he should lose." ". . . as if he were a doll that has acquired laugh lines after being played with and forgotten." "Tree ears hear a tree fall in the forest when there's no one around." There are plenty of other engaging phrases like these emerging from Nadine's consciousness. That quality of Nadine's voice sets the tone for the story, which is witty, ironic, and finally a little wistful too. The same could be said of Nadine herself, for in this story the tone is really an expression of her character; the two elements can scarcely be unwound from one another.

Point of View

In this story, point of view is a rather slippery subject. In the opening text block, and in the other blocks that return to Nadine and Michael's conversation in the theater lobby, point of view is unassigned to either character, but comes from an authorial presence hovering nearby. This presence is not fully omniscient (it doesn't read the characters' minds for us), but it does present some bits of functional information, such as "They used to wait for each other."

In the other parts of the story, which deal with the history of Nadine and Michael's relationship and with how Nadine has spent the earlier part of this particular day, the point of view seems to be controlled by Nadine. The report on the romance and its failure is filtered through her sensibility and tonally colored by the language games the author has made her like to play. And when she is alone, grading papers and fretting over Mr. Tree Ear, the story is situated entirely within her consciousness. By the end, the story's point of view has tilted so far in her direction that it seems to have been her story all along.

Dialogue

Boil it down and there's not that much. What does it look like if we string it all together—restoring the theater lobby conversation to real time?

M: Same old story.
N: Seems like there aren't any new ones.
M: War.
N: Peace.
M: Good.
N: Evil.
M: Death.
N: Life.
M: Love.
N: (no comment: "It's her turn but she doesn't take it.")
M: Yeah, same old story.
N: I suppose it's all in the telling. We saw this one once together, remember?
M: I thought it was familiar. You know I'd ask you to come home with me, but . . .
N: I'm happy with the way things are now, it's better. There's your friend.
M: And there's yours.
N: I hope—I feel—I never was any good at endings.

This dialogue is extremely suggestive without ever being exactly informative. In part, its understatement is a matter of verisimilitude. The two parties in the conversation are both alluding to something (the course of their prior relationship) that both of them already know about. In reality, two people who are talking about a subject well-known to both are not going to recite exposition to each other (although it is a common mistake of beginning writers to make characters recite exposition in such a fashion).

Nadine and Michael's dialogue certainly doesn't have that flaw — it's about as stripped-down as it could possibly get. Still, we could make certain inferences about them and what they're discussing even if we had *nothing* to go on but what they say. They're both a little jaded, not only with the movies but with such chance meetings in lobbies. They know each other well enough to fall naturally into a zippy exchange of thematic abstractions — but "love" is a conversation stopper. Her memory of what they used to do together is more complete than his, but he's still willing to proposition her even though they're both with other people now. She won't take him up on the proposition — now or ever — and with her last line she can definitely say it's over between them.

All that can be inferred just by reading the dialogue alone, but other parts of the story fill in the background. By the end, the context is complete, and within that context Nadine's closing remark acquires its maximum force.

Imagery

It's not plot or character that make this story work so much as imagery. That idea is reinforced by the brevity of each text block, each small vignette. Many of the images are auditory — Nadine's clever lines. Others are visual: Michael sleazily stroking his thighs, the radio's red dot in the dark bedroom. Some images motivate action — it's the picture of "a coffee table made of human bones and a pillow case fashioned from human skin" that moves Nadine to quit her job as a proofreader. Images transform, to suggest the themes; thus Nadine's romantically lightning-struck lock of hair evolves, toward the end, into the ordinary white hairs of aging. But we don't confront Symbolism with a capital S — not allegorical symbolism. The images are natural, organic; there is no key which would decode them perfectly. It's their arrangement which lends them meaning. In the final analysis, this story is about its own form.

Design

Miriam Kuznets wrote "Signs of Life" as a student in a fiction workshop I was teaching at the 92nd Street Y in New York City. She started the class with a quite beautiful prose style, and her writing was full of striking and memorable imagery. She had a real skill in using light gestures to evoke a mood.

On the down side, her stories tended to seem (and in fact be) unfinished.

It was hard to tell what they were about; it was often hard to tell for sure what was actually happening in them. Each of the first few was lovely line by line, but incomprehensible as a whole. No one in the group could discern the intended total effect, and the stories seemed to end without concluding. Obviously there were some organizational problems to be dealt with.

Under cross-examination, Miriam revealed that one of the reasons the stories were so hard to follow is that each of her then rather long paragraphs pulled in, or alluded to, episodes from all over the chronology of her plot. Being primarily an image-driven writer, she resented the constraints of real time and wanted to break them. She wanted the freedom to deploy snippets of scenes from all over the timeline whenever and wherever she needed them to make her image work. Unfortunately, the net effect of her strategy was an impression of incoherence.

Still, I felt like she ought to keep trying to do it her own way. I didn't see much use in trying to make her write like Hemingway—or even Flannery O'Connor. If she tried to force her writing to follow a strict linear chronology, the ingredients of her images would be diffused and lose their power. The virtues of her writing, and its personality, would be dissipated. There had to be some way for her to conserve her strengths, to follow her natural instincts about how to write a story, and still come up with a final product that other people could understand. While I was worrying over this problem, Miriam took a long step toward solving it by herself with the first draft of "Signs of Life."

The first version of this story had all the virtues of her previous work— good sentence-making and strong imagery—and also suffered from the defect of chaotic disorganization. The big difference, discernible at a glance, was that where in earlier work Miriam had worked in longish, apparently sequential paragraphs that created the impression that her stories were *supposed* to have a linear forward flow, this story was presented in crisp, quite short little blocks of text, each separated from the others by space breaks. This one was *obviously* modular.

It still was hard to follow, still didn't clearly make sense. But once we had noticed that it was constructed in modular blocks, all the readers in the group recognized that these units could be rearranged. Maybe it was the task of the reader to mentally assemble them in some way that made more sense. Proceeding in this direction, we were able to figure out (without having to ask Miriam any questions) that there were three different narrative threads running through the text, all involving the same character. Two of them involved specific time-limited scenes, and the third was a current of expository background. Also, each little text block confined itself to discussing only *one* of these three narrative vectors. This development was already a significant step in the direction of clarity.

But this was as far as we could get. The arrangement of the text blocks was apparently random, the chronological order was not readily apparent, and it was still impossible to synthesize the whole thing into a coherent unified whole when you were done reading it. I felt that it was important to introduce elements of symmetry and regularity into the situation. And something had to be done to make the transitions from block to block easier to follow.

In reading the first draft, I had numbered each block either 1, 2, or 3, according to which narrative thread it seemed to belong to. Once I had done that, I could quickly check to see if there was any pattern to the arrangement of the blocks (there wasn't). Now I suggested to Miriam that she consider actually numbering the sections in this way in the finished story. Doing that would make it easier for the reader to figure out what was what. You'd have the formal curiosity of a story with numbered sections that instead of going 1, 2, 3, 4, 5, would go 1, 2, 3; 1, 2, 3, or perhaps, 1, 2, 3, 2, 1 . . . , or something even more complicated. But Miriam really didn't want to have to rely on numbering the sections. And she was right. If a story has to depend on such crude typographical signposts to conduct the reader through it, it suggests that the writing itself has failed somewhere.

I suspect it was useful for her to *think* about those numbers while she was rewriting the story, but that's another matter. Anyway, she took it back to the woodshed, where she found her own solutions. She made sure that there was an equal number of text blocks for all three narrative vectors, and arranged them in a regular repeating pattern: 1, 2, 3; 1, 2, 3 . . . So long as the numbers weren't going to actually appear as heads in the text, any fancier pattern probably would have been ungraspable. Also, to make things still easier for the reader to follow, she devised dovetails between the end of each section and the beginning of the next section that belonged to the same narrative vector, so that the *end* of each number 1 text block dovetailed with the *beginning* of the next number 1 text block—and so on all down the line.

That tactic is most obvious in narrative vector 1: the conversation in the movie lobby. The continuity of the dialogue—those one-word exchanges— makes obvious connections between the end of one vector 1 block and the beginning of the next. The presence of those connections suggests that the reader should look for similar clues to link up the blocks of vector 2 and vector 3. Vector 2 is reasonably easy to track because it is obviously expository, concerned with detailing the deep backstory of Nadine and Michael's affair. Vector 3 is another scene, and the links between the vector 3 blocks are reinforced by details like the coffee Nadine is drinking and the presence of Mr. Tree Ear. By the end of the story, we've also been given enough clues that we can assemble the three vectors themselves in the correct chronological order, so that we grasp (for instance) that Nadine's adventures with Mr. Tree Ear happen earlier on the same day she runs into Michael at the movies. We can comprehend the linear order of events in the story although we have not experienced those events in a linear fashion.

Miriam's system for this story is much easier to experience than to describe; you want to feel it more than you want to figure it out. The story is simpler and more lucid than its structural analysis—which is much as it should be. All in all, it's quite an elegant piece of work. Its form follows and expresses its function almost perfectly. Both the form of the story and its subject are patternistically repetitive. So far as Nadine and her life are concerned, the repeating pattern verges on pathology. But finally, change does occur. At the beginning of the story, she's fantasizing about her old lover, Michael, while carrying on with the new. At the end, she's able to say, truthfully I think, "I'm happy with the way things are now, it's better."

It's a tiny moment. Remember, the present scene of this story is perhaps two and a half *minutes* long, at the maximum. Everything else, technically speaking, is exposition and background. We're standing inside an extremely small circle here, and there's a lot it has to contain. Miriam had always been a specialist in tiny moments. In this story, she found a way to take such a moment and focus it so as to expand its meaning and make it fully comprehensible to readers.

For writer and reader alike, the hard geometry of the story's 1,2,3 repeating pattern functions as the armature, underpainting, chord progression—or pick your own analogy. That substructure is a stabilizing influence. Nadine's (or Miriam's) flights of fancy can whirl around it as freely as they please, but the stability of the substructure ensures that they won't whirl away into confusion.

NOTES

1. Narrative vector number 1: a classic *in medias res* opening. Who are these people? Where are they? What's their relationship and what are they talking about right now? You don't know, but the mystery is intriguing, and the exchange of one-worders has a catchy little rhythm to it, even though you have little idea, at first, what it might mean.

2. Quite a lot of questions are answered by this pair of terse and enigmatic sentences. They're at the movies; it seems they met by chance. Could be that their conversation is about the movie they've seen, though you can't know for certain if that's all there is to it. The last line lets you know that they're a pair of ex-lovers and also establishes the mood of vague wistfulness.

3. Vector 2. So far, the moves of this story would fit a conventionally linear design. A paragraph or two to set the present scene, then a switchback into a clump of background exposition.

4. What's *chosen* for the exposition is a little unusual: the eccentric detail about the umbrella, the weird episode of the lightning and the mark it may

have left on Nadine. Still, we've learned the names of our principals and feel better oriented in the story now, perhaps.

5. And with the last line, it looks like the story is going to resurface into the present scene (vector 1), which would be a totally conventional linear move.

6. But instead, we're now in vector 3. Still, the author isn't lying to us or cheating. Nadine is still twice as old in vector 3 as she was when the lightning struck her. Vector 3 is prior in real time to vector 1 (the use of past tense in vector 3 is a helpful clue to this point) but not all that *much* prior. It's earlier the same day.

7. If you're paying attention, you may catch on to that already, because here she's noticing the movie they'll see that night . . .

8. . . . and on the way out we pick up another useful snippet of expository information: in vector 3 she's a schoolteacher (thus also in vector 1).

Notice too the odd decision against using quotation marks. No typography distinguishes the voices on the radio, the student's answer on the paper, the Nadine-Michael dialogue or anything else. Later on, this device will blur the distinction between inner monologue and what's spoken aloud—what Nadine actually says and what she merely considers saying. And it produces an overall impression of interiority, as if the whole story were taking place deep within Nadine's sensibility, instead of being a series of transactions between herself and other people.

9. First repetition. We return to vector 1. The first two vector-1 text blocks are dovetailed together by the continuation of the snappy one-worder dialogue, an unmistakable signpost, and secondarily by the present tense, which is common to vector 1 text blocks and helps distinguish them from the others.

10. Our boy is not such a looker any more, we see through Nadine's eyes . . .

11. . . . and yet we also sense that she still participates to some extent in his positive opinion of himself.

12. This writer has a flair for this sort of arresting simile. Now, as the context becomes clearer, the striking images gain significance.

13. Vector 2. We begin to feel a pattern of repetition among the text blocks and the narrative vectors they each belong to. Note that all the vector 2 sections proceed in chronological order. Nadine was in high school in the previous vector 2 block, and now she's in college. The function of vector 2, across the whole story, is to furnish general background and summary information . . .

14. . . . enlivened by some closely observed detail and by half-scenes, like this one. Here it's discovered that intriguingly inscrutable conversations, like the one they're having in vector 1, have always been a feature of their relationship.

15. Because it opens with a line of dialogue from a voice that hasn't been

heard before, this text block might really throw us off the track. Then there's a completely new character introduced—Mr. Tree Ear—and that too is potentially confusing. However, since our brains are arranged to automatically anticipate regular patterns, instinct leads us to assume that we're back in vector 3. It doesn't hurt that she was drinking coffee in the previous vector 3 block, while here she's staring into the bottom of her mug: a dovetail.

    The sorting out of the story's organizational principles should be taking place automatically, somewhere shallowly below the reader's level of consciousness. The experience of reading the story is not like solving a mathematical puzzle. But the complexity of the story's structure is a large part of the pleasure of reading it.

16.   Vector 1. The exchange of one-worders is the clearest signal possible. And after two complete cycles, we feel very secure with pattern of 1, 2, 3 repeating. If she deviates now, we're going to be shocked. The safe play would be not to deviate—but she might actually *use* a deviation from the pattern for its shock effect.

17.   Is Nadine still in love with this unattractively aging guy? Certainly she seems to feel a longing . . .

18.   Vector 2 is climbing a regularly graduated ladder: high school, college, first real-world job.

19.   How they broke up, we don't know. Status quo. But what's suggested here is that at this point in real time, he's a lot more "over it" than she is. In fact, she's hurting. A thought which leads to . . .

20.   . . . this line of dialogue, which might well apply to Nadine's emotional state, though it's actually addressed to Mr. Tree Ear by some irritable tenant in her building. From here on out, there'll be an increasing resonance among text blocks that belong to different narrative vectors, according to the linear transitions from one block to the next.

    Compare this sequence across the previous vector 2–vector 3 transition:

        "I don't love you."
        "You don't have a choice . . ."
        "Get out of here, you bum."

The exchange subliminally prepares us for the idea that he rejected her—confirmed by later hints. Was the author consciously aware of this interpretation? When you are working properly, the unconscious will often give you things like this for free.

21.   This question from the 911 operator in vector 3 . . .

22.   . . . gets an answer of sorts from Nadine back in vector 1. We begin to sense a convergence effect, thematically, among the vectors.

23.   If the patterns of the story's arrangement were not already so well established, this transition would really drive us nuts. Not only is it a completely

new character, but also there's no typographical clue that this is a quote from a newspaper.

24. But we know how the story is handling quotes of any and all kinds. We know that Nadine was once a proofreader for a newspaper. And from the rhythm of repetition, we know we must be in vector 3. So we're okay.

   The odd transition does have some of the zap effect of a deviation from the pattern—though it isn't one. In fact there are no deviations from the strict 1, 2, 3 rhythm.

25. Does she actually ask this batch of existential questions of Mr. Tree Ear? I doubt it. Her first question and his reply are probably spoken aloud, but probably not this one.

   The device of dropped quotation marks is finding its justification. It also encourages the reader to make connections between scraps of dialogue that belong to different narrative vectors—as might well happen in the consciousness of the character, after she's experienced all these events.

26. By not taking her turn, *Nadine* has interrupted the rhythm, and we have become so habituated to the regular beat that this moment draws a lot of attention to itself.

27. While our attention is focused by Nadine's interruption of the dialogue pattern, the plots of the narrative vectors begin to converge. Nadine has found another profession, so we must be coming closer to the present day, where she's grading papers as a schoolteacher.

28. The tightly looped nonstory she tells her class becomes a sort of image for the story we're reading, where vector 2 and vector 3 are finally nested within vector 1, which, in real time, is the shortest of all three. It also evokes the sense of doomed and futile repetition of the bad love affair, the relationship that refuses to progress. (This must have been quite an awkward moment in the classroom.)

   The line about the lightning, in particular, lets us know that Nadine is still full of false optimism, still entertains idiotic hopes. What may that mean for the present scene—vector 1?

29. Back to vector 3—further convergence. We're on our way home. The references to rain and the movie they'll see dovetail this section to vector 1. Probably it's somewhere around here that the reader becomes *consciously* aware of the relationship between the timelines of the story—thus experiences a pleasant little *frisson* of recognition and discovery.

30. What do those white hairs stand for now? Her sense of being specially marked, by the lightning, for romance and adventure? Her sense that she is aging? Both?

31. The whole story closes on a vector 1 episode and on this recursion; like the story Nadine told her unfortunate pupils, it comes straight back to its own opening line.

32. Well now, *she* rushed out to see this movie because it reminded her of

him, but *he* doesn't even remember seeing it with *her.* This scrap of information may be a motive for her rejecting his proposition. We get the feeling that on earlier occasions, she probably has accepted.

33. And *bang,* you're out. There was just one mistake in Miriam's penultimate
draft of this story. She had appended this final two-word paragraph:
She is.

But we really don't need to be told that. The reader has to work a little to get the goodies out of this story, and so has earned the right to
draw the final conclusion on his own. For the character, it's a success.
Something has changed—the pattern *has* been broken. Nadine designed
the story for her students so that it could never come to a conclusion.
Now she's ended the story we're reading. She couldn't finish her bad love
affair—now she's brought it to a close, in the same breath.

LIZZIE, ANNIE, AND ROSIE'S RESCUE OF ME WITH BLUE CAKE

CAROLYN CHUTE

We've got a ranch house. Daddy built it. Daddy says it's called RANCH 'cause it's like houses out West which cowboys sleep in. There's a picture window in all ranch houses and if you're in one of 'em out West, you can look out and see the cattle eatin' grass on the plains and the cowboys ridin' around with lassos and tall hats. But we ain't got nuthin' like that here in Egypt, Maine. All Daddy and I got to look out at is the Beans. Daddy says the Beans are uncivilized animals. PREDATORS, he calls 'em.[1]

"If it runs, a Bean will shoot it! If it falls, a Bean will eat it," Daddy says, and his lip curls. A million times Daddy says, "Earlene, don't go over on the Beans' side of the right-of-way. Not ever!"[2]

Daddy's bedroom is pine-paneled . . . the real kind. Daddy done it all. He filled the nail holes with MIRACLE WOOD. One weekend after we was all settled in, Daddy gets up on a chair and opens a can of MIRACLE WOOD. He works it into the nail holes with a putty knife. He needs the chair 'cause he's probably the littlest man in Egypt, Maine.[3]

Daddy gets a pain in his back after dinnah so we take a nap. We get under the covers and I scratch his back. Daddy says to take off my socks and shoes and overalls to keep the bed from gettin' full of dirt.[4]

After I'm asleep the bed starts to tremble. I clutch the side of the bed and look around. Then I realize it's only Rubie Bean comin' in his loggin' truck to eat his dinnah with other Beans. Daddy's bare back is khaki-color like his carpenter's shirts. I give his shoulder blades a couple more rakes, then dribble off to sleep once more.[5]

2 Gram pushes open the bedroom door. "What's goin' on?" Her voice is a bellow, low as a man's.[6]

Daddy sits up quick. He rubs his face and the back of his neck. Beside the bed is a chair Daddy made. It is khaki-color like the walls and khaki-color like Daddy. And over this chair is them khaki-color carpenter's clothes, the shirt and pants, laid flat like they just been ironed. Gram's eyes look at the pants.[7]

Gram plays the organ at church. Her fingers in her pocketbook now are able to move in many directions at once, over the readin' glasses, tappin' the comb, pressin' the change purse and plastic rain hat, as if from these objects musical refrains of WE ABIDE will come. One finger jabs at a violet hankie. Then she draws the hankie out and holds it over her nose.[8]

I sniff at the room. I don't smell nuthin'.[9]

"LEE!!!" Gram gasps through her hankie. "What is going on here? Can't you *tell* me?" It is warm. But Gram always wears her sweater. You never see her arms.[10]

Gramp comes into the bedroom doorway and holds a match over his pipe. Whenever Gramp visits, he wears a white shirt. He also wears his dress-up hat. Even in church. He never takes it off in front of people . . . 'cause underneath he's PURE BALD. Daddy says he's seen it years ago . . . the head. He says it's got freckles.[11]

Gram puts her hankie back in her purse, straightens her posture.

On Daddy's cheeks have come brick-color dots and he gives hisself a sideways look in the vanity-mirror.[12]

"LEE! I'm talkin' to you!" Gram's deep voice rises.

Daddy says, "I'm sorry, Mumma."

Gram sniffles, wrings her hands.

I says, "Hi Gram!"

She ignores me.

"HI GRAM!!!" I say it louder.[13]

Through the open window I hear the door of the Beans' mobile home peel open like it's a can of tuna fish. I see a BIG BEAN WOMAN come out and set a BIG BEAN BABY down to play among boxes of truck parts and a skidder wheel. The woman Bean wears black stretch pants and a long white blouse with no sleeves. Her arms are bare. The baby Bean pulls off one of its rubber boots.[14]

Somethin' else catches my eye. It's the sun on the fender of Daddy's little khaki-color car. Inside the trunk is some of Daddy's carpenter tools and some of the birdhouses and colonial bread boxes he made for the church fair. On the bumper is Daddy's bumper sticker. It says JESUS SAVES. The sun shifts on the fender, almost blinds me, like it's God sayin' in his secret way that he approves.[15]

But in here in Daddy's bedroom it's different. The light is queer, slantin' through Gramp's smoke. Gram covers her face with her hands now, so all I can see is her smoky blue hair wagglin'. She says through her fingers in her deep voice, "Earlene, you don't sleep here at *night*, do you?"[16]

I says, "Yep."[17]

The dots on Daddy's cheeks get bigger. Gramp looks across the hall at the thermostat to the oil furnace which all ranch houses got.[18]

Daddy swings his legs out from the covers, hangs on the edge of the high bed in his underwear, with his little legs hangin' down. He says, "Mumma . . . I'm sorry. I didn't think."[19]

Gram moans.

Daddy has said a million times that this house is a real peach . . . good leach bed . . . artesian well . . . dry cellar . . . the foundation was poured . . . lots of closet space. He went by blueprints. He says all carpenters can't read blueprints.[20]

"Praise the Lord!" shouts Gram. She holds her clasped hands to her heart, a half-smile, a look of love. "Praise God!!" Her pocketbook is hooked over her elbow. Her arms go up and she waves them and the fingers march, stirrin' up the queer smoke overhead.[21]

Daddy's eyes go wild. "But Mumma! It don't mean nuthin'. She's just a baby!"

"I ain't a BABY!" I scream. I drop to the floor from this high bed Daddy made, made with his lathe, hand-carved acorns on the posts, stained khaki like everything else. I don't remember him makin' the bed. Daddy says he made it before my mother went to the hospital to live. He says he and my mother used to sleep in it and she had the side he's got now.[22]

I like my side of the bed best. I can, without takin' my head up off the pillow, look out across at the Beans' if I want. As I look out now I see a pickup truck backin' up to the Beans' barn. A BIG BEAN MAN gets out and lifts a spotted tarpaulin. It's two dead bears. I look back at Gram.[23]

I pull Gram's sleeve. "Oh Gram . . . What's the matter?"

"Where's your *jeans*!!?" she says. "Your *jeans*!!?"

"Under the bed," I says.

"Well, get 'em," she says.

Daddy's cryin', workin' his shoulders. The shoulder blades open and close. I pick up a sock.[24]

Gram's cool bony fingers close up around my wrist. She yanks me off my feet.

Daddy stands up in his underwear and folds his arms across his chest like he's cold. But it ain't cold. He looks the littlest I've ever seen him look.[25] Gram pushes past Gramp and hauls me to my room. My bed is covered with cardboard boxes and coat hangers. She says deeply, "Start pickin' this stuff up!"

I says, "But Gram. Our nap is over. It's time to get up. Ask Daddy!"

"I ain't askin' that sick man nuthin'!" She hurls a pile of dresses I've out-grown upon the wall. I watch 'em slide down. Gram roars, "You stay in this bed for the rest of the day, maybe *two* days. And *no suppah*!"

"Gram!"

She is panting.

"GRAM . . . I'll be HUNGRY!"

"Don't sass!" She narrows her eyes. "The Lord's good meat and tatahs ain't for no dirty little girls."[26] As she hauls the covers back, she's whimperin'. And I hear Daddy out there in the hall cryin'. He's pullin' on his pants out there . . . right in the hall. Gramp just stands there, lookin' lost under the brim of his lit-tle brown hat.

Gram takes up both my wrists and shakes them in my face. She says into my eyes, "Of course nuthin's happened!! *Of course.* I ain't sayin' somethin's *happened!*"[27]

Daddy's in the kitchen slammin' chairs around. He made all them chairs hisself. With his lathe in the cellar.[28]

Gram fits me into my bed, then kisses my cheek. She smells like rubber. Like rubber when it's hot. I see the lions and tigers of my bedspread reflectin' in her eyes. She says, "Are you Gram's little pixie?"

I says, "Yes."[29]

She pulls the door shut.

3 Daddy stays out there in the kitchen a long time cryin' . . . a way long time after Gram and Gramp are gone. The water runs in the kitchen. Prob'ly Daddy's got his favorite jelly glass out of the dirty dishes and is rinsing it out. Our well, Daddy says, will never go dry. "It's a thousand feet!" he always says. Then Daddy likes to say how the Beans got the worse side of the right-of-way for water. "All ledge and clay!" In summer time you see 'em back one of them old grunty trucks to the door and they go in and out with plastic milk jugs by the dozens.[30]

As I lay here I can still smell Gramp's pipe tobacco. It's the sweetest kind. Where Gram and Gramp live up in the village, Gram's doilies have gotten yel-low from Gramp. So Gramp stopped smokin' in the house. He gets in his car with the plaid blanket on the seat and has a smoke out in the dooryard. Or he scuffs over to Beans' Variety to sit with his friends near the radiator. Gramp's got a trillion friends . . . even Beans.[31] When he goes over to the store, he puts on his white dress-up shirt and, of course, his hat.

In the middle of the night Daddy finally comes in my room. When he puts the hall light on, my heart hits the sheet. He stands in the doorway with the hall light on his back, his hands in the pockets of his khaki pants. He stretches across my bed. He is so little his body across my ankles and feet is not much heavier than one of Gram's cotton comforters.[32]

We sleep.[33]

4 It's Saturday morning. All clouds. Very cold.

When Daddy's downcellah busy with his lathe, I go to the edge of our grass to get a look at the Beans. The Beans' mobile home is one of them old ones, looks like a turquoise-blue submarine. It's got blackberry bushes growin' over the windows.[34]

I scream, "HELLO BEANS!"

About four huge heads come out of the hole. It's a hole the Bean kids and Bean babies have been workin' on for almost a year. Every day they go down the hole and they use coffee cans and a spade to make the hole bigger. The babies use spoons. Beside the hole is a pile of gingerbread-color dirt as tall as a house.[35]

I say, "Need any help with the hole!!?"

They don't answer. One of 'em wipes its nose on its sleeve. They blink their fox-color eyes.

I mutter, "Must be the STUPIDEST hole."

The heads draw back into the hole.

A white car with one Bondo-color fender is turnin' off the paved road onto the right-of-way. It musta lost its muffler. It rumbles along, and the exhaust exploding from all sides is doughy and enormous from the cold.

The blackberry bushes quiver, scrape at the tin walls of the mobile home like claws.

The white car slowly backs into Daddy's crushed-rock driveway and a guy with yellow hair and a short cigarette looks out at me and winks. His window's rolled down and he's got his arm hangin' out in the cold air.

I scream, "NO TURNIN' IN DADDY'S DRIVEWAY!"

There's another guy in there with him. He has a sweatshirt with a pointed hood so all that shows is his huge pink cheeks and a smile. The car pulls ahead onto the right-of-way and the two guys get out.

I scream, "Daddy says KEEP OUT! You ain't ALLOWED!"[36]

The men look at each other and chuckle. The yellow-hair guy is still smokin' his cigarette even though it's only a tiny stump.[37]

My eyes water from the cold. My hair, very white, blows into my mouth.

The sweatshirt guy opens the back door and I see there's feet in there on the seat. The sweatshirt guy pulls on the feet.[38]

The other guy helps. They both tug on the feet.

Out comes a big Bean, loose, very loose, like a dead cat.[39] His arms and legs just go all over the ground. His green felt hat plops out in the dirt. About five beer bottles skid out, too, roll and clink together. The guy with the yellow hair snatches a whiskey bottle off the seat and puts it in the Bean's hand, curls his fingers around it. They both laugh. "There's your baby!" one says.

They get in the car and drive away.

My heart feels like runnin'-hard shoes. I look around. No Beans come out of the mobile home. No Beans come out of the hole.

I take a step. I'm wicked glad Daddy's in the cellah with his lathe. I can picture him down there in the bluish light in his little boy-sized clothes, pickin' over his big tools with his boy-sized hand.[40]

I take another step.

Now I'm standin' right over the Bean. He looks to me like prob'ly the biggest Bean of all. He's got one puckered-up eye, bright purple . . . a mustache big as a black hen. I cover my nose. I think he musta messed hisself. His green workshirt has yellow stitching on one pocket. I read out loud, "R-E-U-B-E-N." I squint, trying to sound out the letters.[41]

The whiskey bottle rolls off his hand.

I says, "Wake up, Bean!"

Then some heads come out of the hole.

A noise comes from the big Bean on the ground: GLOINK! And I say, "Wowzer!" It's blood spreadin' big as a hand in the dirt.[42]

The kid Beans are comin' fast as they can. They bring their spade and spoons, cans and a pail.

I look into the Bean man's face. I say, "YOU! Hey you! Wake up!" I scooch down and inspect the pores of his skin. His wide-open mouth. Big Bean nose. My quick hand goes out . . . touches the nose.[43] I say, "Stop bleedin', Bean."

His good eye opens.

I jump away.

Fox-color eye.[44]

Out of the open mouth comes a hiss. The chest heaves up. Somethin' horrible leaks out the corner of his mouth, catches in the hairs of the big mustache.

The kid Beans stand around starin' down at the green workshirt with the blood movin' out around their shoes.

I says, "Some guys brought him." I point up the road. I look among their faces for signs of panic. I say, "R-E-U-B-E-N. What's that spell?"

They look at me, breathin' through their mouths. One of 'em giggles and says, "That spells coo coo."[45]

Another one pokes at the big Bean's shoulder with its green rubber boot. The big Bean goes "AAAAARRRRR!" And his lips peel back over clenched yellow teeth.

A kid Bean with a spade says to a kid Bean with a pail, "Go get Ma off the bed. Rubie's been stabbed again."

"Go tell 'er yourself," says the kid Bean with the pail.

"No . . . *you!*" says the one with the spade.

"No-suh. I ain't gonna miss gettin' to see Rubie die."[46]

I look down at the big Bean and his hand slowly drags across the dirt to his side to the torn fabric, a black place in the body, like an open mouth. And blood fills the cup of his hand.[47]

Daddy opens the front door and hollers, "EARLENE!"

The big Bean's eye is lookin' right at me.

I says to the eye, "In heaven they got streets of gold."

Daddy screams my name again.

The big fox-color eye closes.

I say, "Oh no! He's dead!"

The kid with the spade says, "Nah! He's still breathin'."

Daddy comes off the step. "Earlene! Get away! NOW!!"

I says, "Bean wake up! Don't die!"[48]

Rubie Bean don't move. His mouth is wide open like he's died right in the middle of a big laugh. I see the blood has surrounded my left sneaker, has splashed on my white sock. I can hear the Bean kids shift in their rubber boots.[49]

I drop down on all fours and put my right ear right there on the shirt pocket where it says R-E-U-B-E-N.[50]

"Get away from there!" Daddy almost whimpers. He's comin' fast across the grass.

The heart. A huge BOOM-BANG! almost punches at my temple through the Bean's shirt.[51]

"Hear anything?" a Bean with a coffee can asks.

The fox-color big Bean eye opens, the teeth come together, make a deep rude raspy grunt. He says, "You kids . . . get the hell away from me, you goddam cocksuckin' little sons-a- whores!!"[52]

'Bout then Daddy's boy-sized hands close around me.[53]

5 I stand by the stove and Daddy gets out a new bar of LAVA soap, unwraps it. I says, "Daddy! I didn't say no swear words."[54]

He gets one of the chairs from the suppah table and faces it in the corner where he keeps his boots. "Okay, Earlene," he says. "We're all set."

I says, "But, Daddy, soap's for swear words!"[55] I fidget with the hem of my sweater.

His face is red. He pats the chair. I get on the chair facing the corner. I open my mouth. He sticks in the soap—hard, gritty. My mouth is almost not big enough.

He says at my back, "How many times have I told you to stay on your own side of the right-of-way?"

I take the soap out. "Daddy! I was in the middle!"[56] I wipe my mouth with my sleeve. I sputter.

"What those Beans would do to a small girl like you would make a grown man cry," he says.[57]

I sputter some more.

Daddy says, "Earlene, put the soap back in."

"But Daddy!"

"When I used to do what Gram told me not to do, *I got the strap*," Daddy says.

I narrow my eyes. I says, "But those was the olden days, Daddy."

"Spare the rod, spoil the child," Daddy says.[58]

We hear the siren. I start to get off the chair. Daddy puts his hand on my shoulder. "Earlene, I'm serious. Listen to me."

Them rescue guys outdoor are makin' a racket, radios and everything, havin' a time gettin' Rubie Bean off the ground. He makes the wickedest snarlin' noises.[59] But Daddy don't seem to notice. He puts his face close to mine. "If I ever . . ." he says slowly, "ever . . . *ever* . . . see you near them Beans again, you are gettin' the horrible-est lickin' the Lord has ever witnessed."

I says, smiling, "Daddy . . . you wouldn't really do that."[60]

He folds his arms over his chest. "Then I'll get Gram to do it."[61]

6 It's Thanksgiving and I help Gram set out the matchin' dishes. Every Thanksgiving is the same. Auntie Paula comes with her kids and Uncle Loren comes in his pig truck alone. You can see snow between the tree trunks goin' up the mountain overway and the gray air cracks with guns.[62]

I says, "Gram, did you used to hit Daddy with a strap?"[63]

Gram's sharp little fingers move over the potatoes, feelin' for bad spots. She says, "Spare the rod, spoil the child.[64] Praise God!"

Loren keeps going out on the back steps to get some air.

Gram says, "Darn fool dresses too warm. He's got at least ten shirts on, you know."

I look out through the kitchen glass. It's raining on Uncle Loren. His arms dangle down through his legs. He smokes hard and slow.

I hum one of the songs Gram plays on the organ at church . . . the one to give thanks after they pass the plate. Uncle Loren don't go to church. Gram says Uncle Loren ain't accepted Jesus Christ as his Savior. Uncle Loren lives alone. We never visit him. We've seen the *outside* of his place about a million times. When we drive by, only his kitchen light is on. Daddy says Loren sleeps in the kitchen. Daddy says Loren's big house is cold as a barn. Uncle Loren comes back indoor and trudges into the living room where Jerry and Dennis and I are playin' the Cootie Game which Gram keeps for us kids. Uncle Loren sits on Gram's flower-print divan and he looks me in the eye.[65]

Gram hollers from the kitchen, "Loren . . . don't go layin' your head on that lace scarf!"[66]

Uncle Loren wears striped overalls. When I look in his eyes, I get a shiver.

Gram comes to the living room door and says that Auntie Paula made that divan scarf and that the oils off Loren's head would make it black . . . eventually.

Uncle Loren says, "Earlene . . . did you know I got ghosts in my house?"

Gram says, "He's just tryin' to scare you, Earlene. Don't listen to him."

He looks big and solid and square settin' there on the divan . . . but he's really as short as Daddy. He says, "Ghosts bust up my house all the time. They don't hurt me . . . but they keep me awake rollin' them big Blue Hubbards around and smashin' up glass. They get right under the sheets with me and run around in there under the sheets."

Jerry and Dennis watch Uncle Loren with open mouths.

Gram snorts. "He just says stuff like that so no one will visit him and discover his squalor.[67] He *hates* people visitin' him. People, good Christian ones, upset him. He don't know Christ as his *Savior.*"

Then he moves his deep pale scary eyes on me.

I look away fast.

7 After dinner, I go out to where Uncle Loren is settin' on the back step and watch him strike a match on the buckle of his overalls. It's almost dark, but there's still some shots up on the mountain.[68]

Uncle Loren don't say nuthin', just squints his eyes as the smoke sifts up over his face.

I twirl a piece of my white hair and put it in the corner of my mouth.

Loren shifts his boots on the step.

"How's the hogs?" I ask.

"Good," he says.

He smokes.

I twirl my hair.

"Uncle Loren," I says, almost in a whisper, "you ever heard this word? . . . Goddamcocksuckinlittlesonsahoowahs?"[69]

Uncle Loren chuckles, sends his cigarette butt spinning through the rain. It hisses in the grass. "Why don't you ask your Daddy, Earlene?"

I trace one of my dress-up shoes with my pointing finger. I narrow my eyes. "'Cause . . . I got a feelin'."[70]

Uncle Loren puts them pale scary eyes on me. And I shiver.

8 Across the right-of-way the Beans' black dog stands by an old rug, looking at me. "Yoo hoo!" I call through cupped hands.[71]

Daddy's gone to Oxford to work on a bank . . . He's late gettin' home. They say the roads are greasy.[72]

I take a step onto the Beans' side of the right-of-way. The black dog watches me, the hair on its back raised. But it don't bark.[73]

I step over a spinach can with water froze in it, a clothespin, an Easter basket, the steerin' wheel of a car.

Out of the dog's nose its frozen breath pumps. I draw nearer to the hole with the spoons and coffee cans ringed around it. The dog charges. It gallops sideways with stiff rocking-horse legs.

I says, "You bite me and you'll regret it!!"

I look up at the closed metal door. No Beans.

The dog's eyes glow a bluish white. Its bluish tongue flutters. I say, "Beat it!" and kick a beer bottle at it.

It noses the beer bottle, picks it up in its teeth, and drops it at my feet.

"Go away! I ain't playin'." I look at the Bean windows. No faces. The dog smells my small moving feet. "You ugly grimy Bean dog. You're gointa BURN IN HELL!"[74]

There's a scalloped serving spoon at the edge of the hole. "So this is the hole," I says to myself. The dog watches me pick up a trowel. I point it at the dog. "ZEEP!" I scream. "You are instantly DEAD!" The dog blinks.

The corridor of the hole is curved. I slide down on my bottom, workin' my legs, the entrance behind me dwindling to a wooly little far-off cloud in the distance. I feel soda bottles along the way. A measuring cup. A rock drops from the ceiling, and thwonks my shoulder. A spray of dirt lets go and fills my hair. I enter a big warm room. In apple crates are what feels like Barbie clothes and Barbie accessories. There's a full-sized easy chair.[75]

"Jeezum!" I gasp. I sit in the chair. "This is real cozy."[76]

I lean forward and feel of the dirt walls, dirt floor. My hand closes around a naked Barbie.

All of a sudden there's a thunder up there.

The warm earth lets go, feels like hundreds of butterflies on my face.

"It's GOD," I says in a choking whisper. My heart flutters.

It's Rubie Bean. The tires of his old logging rig hiss over Daddy's crushed rock driveway. There's the ernk! of the gears.[77]

"Uh oh!" I says to myself. "I'm trapped in this hole. I can't go up there now."[78]

A rock from the ceiling punches my outstretched legs.

More Beans come. Three or four carloads. The mobile home door opens, closes, opens, closes. Out in their yard Bean kids big as men run over the earth's crust above me. THUMP THUMP THUMP THUMP. The soft slap of sand is on my neck. The Bean kids throw something for the black dog to catch. It sounds like a piece of tail pipe.

I hear Daddy's car.

After a while there's Daddy's voice: "Earlene! Supper!"

It's very very dark. The Beans have gone indoor.

The dog is up there at the top of the hole, sniffin' for me.

Hours and hours and hours pass. Hours of pitch black.[79]

I says to myself in a squeak, "I am goin' ta get the strap." I turn naked Barbie over and over in my nervous fingers. I mutter, "Well . . . I just ain't ever gonna leave THIS HOLE."[80]

9 There is a light again at the top. The light flutters. Boots tromp. They come down waving a flashlight—Annie Bean, Lizzie Bean, Rosie Bean. They put the light in my face. "What're *you* doin' in here?" one of 'em asks.[81]

"Nuthin'," I says. My stomach growls.

They make wet thick sniffin' sounds. Their open mouths are echoey. They fill this dirt room with their broad shoulders, broad heads. Dirt sifts down from the ceiling through the enormous light.

"You runnin' from the law?" one of 'em asks.

"NO WAY!" I scream. My scream makes more of the ceiling fall. I think I'm gonna gag from this light in my face. Now and then I can make out a Bean nose, a sharp tooth. Then it fades into the glare.

"You're runnin' away from home?" asks one of them.

I bristle. "No! I ain't!"

"Well, how come your father's up there cryin'?"

One of 'em pushes a saucer with cake on it into the light. There is only the cake, the saucer, the hand. The cake is sky-blue. "Here!" a voice says.

Their clothes rustle.

"What's *that*?" I scrunch up my nose.

"We was goin' ta eat it, but you can have it. Ain't you starved?"

I look at the cake, squinting up one eye.

"I didn't run away," I says softly.

"You prob'ly fell in here," one says.

"No-suh!" I holler.[82]

I make out a fox-color eye which is round and hard and caked with sleepin' sand.

I take the saucer and arrange it on my knee next to Barbie. I says, "I ain't never leavin' this hole. I'm stayin' here for ever . . . as long as I live."[83]

"You like it here pretty well, huh?" one of 'em says.

I am alone. Between me and them is this wall of light. I hold the saucer with both hands, careful not to touch the cake. A bit of sand spills from the ceiling onto the cake.[84]

The three of them giggle.

The cake is the blue of a birdless airplaneless sunless cloudless leafless sky . . . warm steaming blue. "Prob'ly POISON!" I gasp.

"No way!" one of 'em says. "It ain't. It's Betty Crocker."[85]

ANALYSIS

Plot

Let's see what a simplistic summary will do. First of all, consider the background information which is infiltrated into the story as it progresses.

Backstory

There's a relationship of contempt between Earlene's family and their neighbors the Beans, though it stops short of being an actual feud. Earlene's father thinks that the Beans are filthy inferior beings who permanently contaminate anything or anyone they touch. Meanwhile, his mother, Earlene's grandmother, is something of a religious martinet who feels about anyone who doesn't share her faith and morals much the same as Daddy feels about the Beans. These two set the tone for Earlene's family background; her grandfather is a cipher and her mother is permanently offstage—having been hospitalized for a long time for unknown causes.

Present Action

For convenience, we can use the writer's numbered blocks as subdivisions.

1. Earlene and her father take a nap together, as it is apparently their habit to do.
2. Earlene's grandparents arrive and are appalled to find father and daughter in bed together. The grandmother suspects incest and metes out punishments and prohibitions. Earlene doesn't really understand what's going on but is still made to feel guilty and confused.
3. After the grandparents leave, Earlene and Daddy try again to find a kind of

innocent creature comfort in each other, but it can't be the same as it was
before Gram's intrusion.

4. Earlene breaks another rule by crossing to the Bean side of the road to look
at Reuben Bean, who's just been stabbed.

5. Daddy washes Earlene's mouth out with soap as punishment for crossing the
road—and for hearing Reuben curse.

6. Earlene watches her Uncle Loren at Thanksgiving dinner.

7. Earlene asks Uncle Loren to define Reuben's curse words; he declines.

8. For the second time, Earlene goes onto Bean land; this time she crawls into
the Beans' hole and is trapped there when Reuben and other Beans return.

9. After she's been in the hole for several hours, some little Bean girls try to lure
her out with a piece of blue cake.

Now, this plot outline doesn't make much sense when reported in this
reduced way. Many of the events don't seem to have a great deal to do with one
another; moreover, the whole thing seems to tilt toward anticlimax. What's the
most significant event in the story from the average point of view? Surely it must
be the suspicion of incest. That whole issue is thrown away in the first three
units of the story. Compared to that, all Earlene's subsequent fooling around on
the Bean borders might seem inconsequential. Also, the stabbing of Reuben
Bean looks more significant from an outside perspective than does Earlene's
final action of crawling into the Bean kids' hole.

From the angle of plot summary, this looks like a story without a center.
To understand its integrity, we have to look elsewhere.

Character

Daddy is mostly characterized through his relationship to objects, objects he
wears or objects he makes. The only direct detail of physical description is that
"he's probably the littlest man in Egypt, Maine." He's defined by his "khaki-
color" car and "khaki-color carpenter's clothes . . . laid flat like they just been
ironed." His color is uniform and his neatness is uniform. He is a fastidious
maker of well-organized objects: the house, the "birdhouses and colonial
breadboxes." But even in his delicate skills we come to feel a weakness about
him, "down there in the bluish light in his little boy-sized clothes, pickin' over
his big tools with his boy-sized hand." In action, we see he's something of a
blank—mainly he's acted *upon* by outside forces—Gram, the Beans.

Gram too is characterized by a sort of Dickensian object-association:

> Gram plays the organ at church. Her fingers in her pocketbook now
> are able to move in many directions at once, over the readin' glasses, tap-
> pin' the comb, pressin' the change purse and plastic rain hat, as if from
> these objects musical refrains of WE ABIDE will come. One finger jabs

at a violet hankie. Then she draws the hankie out and holds it over her nose.

Note how well this description engages the senses, not only sight but also touch, and the suggestions to hearing and the sense of smell. In this minute observation of behavior, we feel Gram's forcefulness and authority, which will be confirmed in everything she does afterward. We see her power and authority partly by contrast—the way Daddy cowers before her assertiveness. And because she is in part a mouthpiece for religious and moral platitudes ("Spare the rod, spoil the child. Praise God!" . . . and so on) we also see that she draws her power from something beyond herself.

The Beans are also characterized by the objects that they choose—very different objects than those selected by their neighbors across the road. The Beans' objects tend to be amorphous, without clear boundaries between them—a mass of jumbled junk very different from the clearly defined, rectilinear objects selected by Daddy. And the Beans themselves are similarly indeterminate—except for Reuben they are not individuated. They appear in clusters, or if alone, as examples of a type—examples of some other species, even, as Earlene is being taught to see them. Even the rescuers, Lizzie, Annie and Rosie, are only named once, and appear in aggregate thereafter. The most outstanding quality of the Beans is *togetherness*.

And Earlene? Just because she is the closest to us, she is perhaps the most difficult to see. Let's examine her from a couple of different angles. From the Beans' point of view she would seem to be a little priss, though she takes on more interest for them as she forges further into their territory. To her grandmother, Earlene is sometimes "Gram's little pixie," but also sometimes a mere receptacle for original sin. It's rather hard to say how Earlene appears to her father—perhaps as something very precious which he nevertheless has trouble keeping track of?

For the reader, Earlene functions as a sort of pilot fish, leading the way into Bean territory and into the story in general. She is somewhat less concretely described than the other characters . . . which makes it easier for the reader to identify with her at least a little. Probably her most salient characteristic is the stubborn curiosity which, in this case, the reader may also share.

Tone

The source of the tone of this story is Earlene's voice, simple enough to identify here since she is a first-person narrator. How to describe the quality of this voice? It's a little choppy, a little abrasive. Those capital letters seem to SCREAM at us from time to time. (Curiously, Carolyn intended her all-cap phrases to represent *italics*, but by the time her first book came to print, the device was such an indelible aspect of her style that no editor would let her change it.)

Earlene's voice has a child's close focus on detail and is of course the source of the story's marvelously original language and descriptions, e.g., Gram "smells like rubber. Like rubber when it's hot." And her voice also has the child-like quality of skipping from topic to topic, if not at random, then according to some logic alien to the logic of adults. This latter quality is something which the writer can use in composing the *structure* of the story.

Point of View

First-person narrators tend to fall into two general categories: the narrator who buttonholes the reader—talks directly and insistently to you, and the narrator who sucks you down into his or her own head—so that you experience the events of the story much as if you were the narrator yourself. Earlene belongs to the latter group; she becomes our window on the plot.

The interesting twist to point of view in this story is that because Earlene is a child-narrator of a story written for an adult audience, the reader sometimes knows more than she does. Our context is more complete than hers. We know just what Gram's driving at when Earlene doesn't. The limitations of Earlene's point of view do a lot to explain the priority events are given in the story—by her voice. To us, suspicion of incest and child abuse is far and away the most important issue, but to Earlene, her effort to make contact with the Beans is far and away more important than whatever cloudy, incomprehensible thing might be bothering Gram. From Earlene's point of view, the order of events in the story makes a lot more sense.

Dialogue

Point of view has its part to play in this category too. The conversations in this story are certainly realistic and credible—the writer points up all the charac-terizations by modulating the tone of what people actually say aloud in the story. And yet the passages of dialogue don't seem as fully staged as in, for instance, a story like "Depth Charge." The reader's experience is less like watching a scene in a movie and more like watching someone think. Consider this:

> Daddy opens the front door and hollers, "EARLENE!"
> The big Bean's eye is lookin' right at me.
> I says to the eye, "In heaven they got streets of gold."
> Daddy screams my name again.
> The big fox-color eye closes.
> I say, "Oh no! He's dead!"

> The kid with the spade says, "Nah! He's still breathin'."
> Daddy comes off the step. "Earlene! Get away! NOW!!"
> I says, "Bean wake up! Don't die!"

The action of this dialogue is constantly being interrupted by Earlene's reactions—filtered through Earlene's perception and so subjectified. The dialogue seems less to be happening out on stage than to be happening somewhere within her consciousness.

Imagery and Description

The simple descriptions in this story are often quite arrestingly original. Sometimes this originality is achieved by taking a conventional description and twisting it a notch further. It's conventional to say that people "fall" asleep; Earlene, going that one better, can "dribble off to sleep."

Then there are many unusual similes, for instance, "I hear the door of the Beans' mobile home peel open like a can of tuna fish." This description works on several different levels. First of all there is the literal screechy sound of it. Then there are further implications: the cheapness of the canned product evokes the cheap flimsiness of the Bean trailer. These are people who live in a tin can. And another more familiar expression is nudged in passing, by the allusion one can of fish might make to another: the Beans live packed together like sardines. Of course a recreational reader would be unlikely to consciously consider all these levels of implication—the sentence isn't *that* important—nor is it likely that the writer deliberately planned them all. Such choices are made by the writer's unconscious mind, and they affect the reader subliminally.

Then there are more important clusters of images that suggest significant meanings for the story. Consider the introductory description of Gram again in this light:

> Gram plays the organ at church. Her fingers in her pocketbook now are able to move in many directions at once, over the readin' glasses, tappin' the comb, pressin' the change purse and plastic rain hat, as if from these objects musical refrains of WE ABIDE will come.

The passage suggests, as will prove true, that Gram is much more active than acted-upon, compared to Daddy. She's the one who *plays* the organ—and yet she is limited by her predetermined notes. Thus the reader is led to understand her as an "organ" of conventional piety—a mechanism for voicing the structure of religious and social conventions which stands behind her.

Let's try connecting up the blood imagery from section 4:

> A noise comes from the big Bean on the ground: GLOINK! And I say, "Wowzer!" It's blood spreadin' big as a hand in the dirt. . . . The kid

Beans stand around starin' down at the green workshirt with the blood movin' out around their shoes. . . . And blood fills the cup of his hand. . . . I see the blood has surrounded my left sneaker, has splashed on my white sock.

This image pattern has a lot to convey—beyond its physical grotesquerie. Through a gradual, fluid, Beanlike process, the blood flow connects all the Bean children to each other and then connects them with Earlene. (Just what Daddy was afraid of—that Earlene would be somehow stained with Beanness!) The image plays on the conventional association of blood and relationship to show Earlene joining the Beans' bloodstream. You might even say that it's symbolic, but its symbolism doesn't clonk you over the head like a crucifix; rather it's organic symbolism, almost insidious, seeping all around you before you've really noticed it.

Design

The structure of this story has a rather desultory feel to it. Each numbered modular block looks at a glance like an independent little vignette—self-enclosed and autonomous. It seems that they could be transposed and rearranged in different orders and patterns, like cards in a game of solitaire. And perhaps, in the process of composition, some shuffling of that kind did occur. One of the appealing features of a modular design is that it does become possible to physically rearrange the modular units and experiment with what different sorts of wholes they may create in different arrangements.

But if we look at this story in its final form it turns out to be impossible to rearrange it now. There is a chronological thread of cause and effect that sews all the nine subsections together in a delicate interdependency. In its final form, the story less resembles a game of solitaire than a card castle. Pull out one card and the whole thing comes down.

When we consider the story as a whole, from the point of view of Gram, or Daddy, or an average adult reader, it's very difficult to make any dramatic sense out of it. It seems to fall away from its major climax, which is stated in the first three sections—suspicion of incest and child abuse. Where exactly does it go from there?

The nine numbered sections of the story can be grouped into four movements—each with its own exposition, climax (be it great or small), and denouement positioned in the classic triangular fashion. The pattern is most obvious in the first movement—sections 1 through 3:

exposition: The nap.
climax: Gram's implied accusation of incest, etc.—Daddy and Earlene have broken a major taboo.

denouement: Earlene and Daddy rejoin each other, sort of, at the end of section 3.

This pattern may be less obvious in the second movement of the story (sections 4–5), because the issue is less obvious to the reader, but it's there:

exposition: Earlene approaches the Bean boundary.

climax: Reuben is dumped out, stabbed. Earlene is included in the flow of his blood. She puts her ear to his heart! . . . and he makes an incomprehensible mystical statement to her. The climax here is actual physical contact and communication with a Bean.

denouement: Daddy snatches her away from the situation and punishes her for breaking the taboo against approaching the Beans.

The triangular structure is hardest of all to see in the third movement (sections 6–7), because no real action is involved, only observation and conversation:

exposition: Earlene watches Uncle Loren, noticing a certain Beanness about him.

climax: Earlene takes the risk of asking Uncle Loren to interpret what Reuben Bean said to her.

denouement: When Loren won't answer the question, Earlene is thrown back on her own resources for solving the whole problem of the Beans.

This third movement of the story might be regarded as dispensable. Sections 6 and 7 could be surgically removed without materially altering the progress of events. In terms of information processed, all this movement really does is amplify themes and motifs that are fully stated elsewhere in the text. If it were gone, the story would be neater in some ways, a tidier package of three movements instead of four. But the jump cut from section 5 to section 8 would be a little awkward, since the setting and the situation are so much the same between them. The third movement fuctions structurally to make a caesura between these two more crucial episodes, allowing for changes of scene and passage of time between them.

In the fourth and final movement, sections 8–9, the triangular structure is fairly obvious because we do have action again and because the title plugs into this area of the story.

exposition: Earlene crosses the Bean boundary again.

climax: The Bean kids find her and offer her the strange and numinous cake. Is it POISON???

denouement: The cake's not poison. It's Betty Crocker.

Through this analysis, we can see that each of the story's four movements does make dramatic sense when each is considered separately, but how do they all function together? To answer that question, we have to get away from pure plot and consider how two other ingredients of the story, imagery and point of view, are used as structural elements which determine the story's final shape.

The various image patterns of the story produce an almost imperceptibly smooth affective change from the beginning to the end. Earlene's descriptions of her father—his tools, the neatness and order of his (and her) surroundings—begins by being affectionate. But the four-square khaki-colored atmosphere that surrounds Daddy gradually comes to seem oppressive and confining—associating itself with Gram's moral rigidity and her fondness for drastic punishments. Meanwhile, the sloppy disorder of the Bean environment becomes less sinister and more attractive in Earlene's eyes. The ghastly inclusiveness of Reuben's bleeding segues smoothly into the messy dirty welcoming warmth of the Bean hole—where Earlene regains the cozy creature comfort she experienced in her naps with her father, which have now become comfortless because of Gram's prohibition. The imagistic purpose of the story is to get Earlene feeling comfortable in that hole.

These image patterns work subliminally on the mind of the reader to prove the story's points; meanwhile, somewhat more consciously, the reader is obliged to enter into Earlene's point of view so as to make dramatic sense of the order of events in the story. From Earlene's point of view, Gram's suspicion of incest is not a climax but an expository event. It sets the stage for what's to come by cutting Earlene off from the only thing in her home life that's warm and snug and comforting. Looking over her shoulder, we know two things she can't consciously know: what Gram thinks happened, and that it didn't really happen. Meanwhile Earlene intuits—correctly—that her relationship with her father isn't poisonous at all . . . it's Betty Crocker.

From Earlene's point of view, if Gram's prohibition of naps is nonsensical and wrong, it follows that Daddy's prohibition of the Beans might be equally meaningless. The second and third movements of the story show her willingness to test that possibility in the face of an intensifying atmosphere of risk and threat of dire punishment. What's most important in the story for *her* is to find out if the Beans are as bad and dangerous as they're cracked up to be. From her point of view, they're not. By the end of the story, the Beans have come to stand for all the warmth and comfort and togetherness that Earlene can no longer get from her own family—and in her eyes and in their own they are as safe as Betty Crocker.

The order and organization of the four narrative movements are the bones of this story—its substructure. But that substructure is not what the reader will most immediately perceive—and more than likely it was not consciously selected by the writer either. For Carolyn Chute is an unusually holistically minded craftsman who seldom thinks of what line she'll take from point A to point Z, and always thinks of what the integrated total effect of her text will finally be. My guess is that the substructure of this piece evolved through her manipulation of its surfaces—flesh giving birth to skeleton, as it were. But no matter how it gets there, that substructure has to be there in the end.

NOTES

1. What most loudly declares itself in this opening paragraph is tone, the *sound* of the narrator's voice—the voice of Earlene. Its staccato sentences and apparently haphazard associations of topics let us know right away that we're dealing with a child speaker. It looks formless . . . but it's not purposeless.

2. The first taboo is enunciated. The whole story will be powered by taboos and their violations. The Beans are so dreadful they might even be CANNIBALS . . . or so Daddy seems to think.

3. Daddy is characterized at the outset by two qualities, his contempt for the Beans and his carpentry skill. In the child's sensibility, the MIRACLE WOOD looms larger than her diminutive father.

4. Nothing sinister about this . . . is there?

5. But the trembling of the bed does seem like a portent of doom—still, it's a Bean effect, and has nothing directly to do with what's going on inside *this* house. Thus the first numbered modular unit ends tranquilly enough.

6. The second modular unit begins with the arrival of Gram as avenging angel . . . avenging what, though? That's Earlene's implicit question and maybe should be ours.

7. Earlene, watching Gram watch Daddy, becomes aware of more of his qualities—khaki-colored everything, his neatness.

   The odd phrasing of this sentence—Gram's eyes looking at the pants rather than Gram's integrated self doing the looking—somehow invests the pants with malevolence. Gram's eyes, the way she looks at things, will make some trouble here.

8. This description establishes Gram as a sort of "organ" of conventional pieties. Whatever she smells must be metaphysical . . .

9. . . . since literal-minded Earlene can't smell it.

10. From Earlene's point of view, nothing's going on—nothing to tell. They're taking a nap, so what?

11. . . . and her mind wanders. This paragraph might seem to have no more purpose than to make a pause in the momentum of Gram's inquisition,

but it also helps amplify the importance of being covered up—you never see Gram's arms; Gramp's head is also always hidden: a tiny taboo ...

12. Is this guilty behavior, or mere embarrassment?

13. ...And what exactly is he apologizing for?

Earlene, meanwhile, has no idea what the trouble is—as often in this story, the reader must look over her shoulder to guess what's troubling the adults. All Earlene wants is to be acknowledged as usual, but from Gram's point of view, the situation is too dire for that.

14. And, vaguely menaced by Gram's attitude, Earlene retreats into observation of the Beans across the road. In Earlene's eyes, at least, the moral value of Bean behavior is unassigned. She watches them with great curiosity and no judgment.

15. Then her eye pulls back to her own side of the road, where Daddy's car, with its khaki color and its collection of neat carpentry projects, is a personification of Daddy himself. The car is washed in a shaft of light that Earlene reads (in a mental movement which is slightly out of character for her age) as God's affirmation of their innocence.

16. But God's emissary, Gram, is uninfluenced by the sunbeam. The notion of Earlene sleeping in her father's bed at night is too gruesome for her to contemplate ...

17. ...though it doesn't bother Earlene at all. Which should tell us that indeed their sharing a bed is innocuous. Sexually abused children always know that something bad *is* wrong.

18. The very convenience of the house begins to seem somehow oppressive.

19. Daddy's smallness here becomes a childlike weakness; he's helpless before his own mother's anger—whether it's justified or not.

20. The free-associative quality of Earlene's thought becomes convenient to the writer here. Daddy has arranged the house very neatly but his other arrangements are not neat enough.

21. Several images coalesce here in Gram's vatic pose—Gramp's smoke, the "queer, slantin'" light running through the smoke, Gram's "smoky blue hair wagglin'." None of these details is gratuitous.

22. The absence of the mother is an interesting crumb of information. Would Daddy and Earlene have turned to each other for sex or for comfort and companionship? His sleeping on the mother's side of the bed subliminally argues for the latter against the former.

23. It also puts Earlene (geographically) a little closer to the Beans. Who now have come home with something so acutely interesting that, from Earlene's point of view, it should completely outweigh whatever incomprehensible transaction is going on in the bedroom.

24. The importance of the clothes is lost on Earlene. The sock is mysterious to her—she has no idea what all this means to Gram.

25. Daddy can't argue . . . he's completely diminished.

26. Pow! *This* is where Earlene might really suffer some harm . . . from the punishment, not the crime (there was no crime). But her father's crying, and she's been denounced as a dirty little girl.

27. And now we find out that even Gram doesn't think that any incest has actually *occurred*. All her *sturm und drang* has been inspired by the appearance of the thing.

28. Daddy's skills are beginning to look increasingly futile.

29. What's Earlene supposed to make of this—is she a dirty little girl or Gram's little pixie? Everyone's acting like a major taboo has been broken . . . but of course it really hasn't been. For Earlene it must be all the more confusing because she doesn't even know what the taboo is, and the second modular unit closes on that mood of confusion.

30. The beginning of the third unit is in a way parallel to the beginning of the first—Earlene echoing her father's assertions of superiority over the Beans. Now it's a way for her to restore order to her experience, for surely their life is more orderly than the lives of the neighbors across the road . . . and doesn't that make it better?

31. And yet Gramp makes a little bridge between Earlene's family and the Beans. He has a "dirty habit," and even Bean friends perhaps. It is conceivable that people in Earlene's family could be friends with Beans.

32. This is sort of an awful moment, though it's also somewhat restorative. By comparison, their afternoon nap seems an almost edenic innocence. Now that guilt has been imposed from without, they can never go back to that garden.

33. And if you're still wondering just what they do in bed together, here it is. So the first movement of the story closes.

34. The second movement begins with Earlene teasing another and presumably lesser taboo—*don't go on the Beans' side of the road*. How near can she approach that line without crossing it?

35. Bean construction is very different from Daddy's neat carpentry—it's sloppy, haphazard, uses inappropriate, makeshift tools, and involves a lot of dirt.

    The vividness of the descriptions here helps account for Earlene's fascination with the Beans. The ordinary becomes extraordinarily appealing: dirt recalls gingerbread, the exhaust is "doughy." The descriptions are unusual but feel very right.

36. Another little taboo fractured—the Beans trespass on Daddy's driveway. After the first movement of the story, Earlene is very conscious of what's allowed and what's not, so this transgression seems to mean a lot to her . . .

37. . . . though it doesn't mean anything at all to the Beans.

38. Here and hereafter, Chute uses these short, choppy paragraphs that emphasize Earlene's separateness—she stands on the far side of a typographical barrier from the Beans.
39. The looseness is ominous. Remember the two dead bears?
40. Earlene is really pushing the boundary now. And somehow she feels that she's approaching a new reality … in comparison to which her father's delicate activity seems childish.
41. She's there! And nothing terrible's happened to her. We can look over her shoulder and see that something's got to be pretty wrong with this guy on the ground, but so far she's not bothered.
42. Earlene reacts to the blood with awe, not shock. She's still extremely interested.
43. She touched him!
44. The fox-color eye, as opposed to her father's khaki-color, establishes a hold on her.
45. Now she's established a dialogue with the Bean children, who previously ignored her.
46. Yes, the Bean kids are pretty tough.
47. Still, Earlene seems to share their fascination with the spectacle.
48. This set of exchanges brings all the separate *territories* of the story into juxtaposition: Daddy calling Earlene back to the shelter of the house he built, Beanness concentrated in the fox-color eye, Gram's other-worldly religiosity invoked by Earlene's remark about heaven. And Earlene seems suspended among these three possible destinations.
49. Meanwhile, Beanness is absorbing her as she becomes part of the Bean blood-pool.
50. Has Earlene made a choice here? Now she's closer than even the Bean kids are.
51. Reuben's heart punches the way Earlene's heart "hit the sheet" earlier—they have this much in common.
52. Here's Reuben's message for Earlene—only problem is, she doesn't understand it …
53. … and has no time to figure it out before she's snatched away.
54. The next modular unit turns into the punishment phase for Earlene's transgression of the unit before.
55. The situation echoes the situation in the story's first movement. Earlene really isn't sure what she should be punished for. She didn't say any swear words …
56. … and technically she didn't cross the line. She just approached it. The more she acts the way Daddy acted when confronted with the accusing Gram …
57. … the more Dad acts like Gram did in the story's first movement—hinting pointedly at the offense, but refusing to define it plainly.

58. This proverb might come straight from Gram's mouth to Daddy's.

59. As before, Earlene's mind escapes from her own house to the Beans—even though now she can only hear, not see them.

60. Earlene knows that Daddy's not likely to make good on this threat . . .

61. . . . but she also knows that Gram's authority stands more powerfully behind him. As the second movement of the story closes, she's more tightly laced with taboos and strictures than before. To an adult, incest is a bigger taboo than crossing the road you've been told not to cross, but since the incest never really happened, Earlene must see things differently.

62. The story's third movement begins with these suggestions of the passage of time and change of seasons. However, Earlene is still trying to make sense of things that have happened before.

63. Earlene wonders if the menace of Gram's punitive power is real . . .

64. . . . and Gram confirms it is.

   The structure of authority and moral discipline in Earlene's family has a hierarchical rigidity—from God through Gram through Daddy to control Earlene. Remember that the moral principles behind this authority make no sense to Earlene because the whole incest threat went over her head and never happened anyway. Maybe Daddy's prohibition of the Beans makes no more sense than Gram's nonsensical (to Earlene) prohibition of naps. Earlene isn't thinking any of this consciously—we don't read it in a thought balloon above her head—but she is feeling it, and beginning to act accordingly.

65. And as she tries to sort things out, Uncle Loren begins to appear more interesting to her. Loren doesn't seem to have a place in the religious/authoritarian hierarchy of the family—he's not saved. He even seems to be slightly taboo himself because they only see "the *outside* of his place."

66. And he has in common with Gramp this quality of dirtying up the doilies . . . a sort of Beanlike dirtiness.

67. Uncle Loren can say whatever he pleases, apparently. Nobody washes *his* mouth out with soap.

68. So, in the second unit of the story's third movement, it occurs to Earlene that Loren might be the one who can answer her crucial question and interpret Reuben Bean's message to her.

69. For the reader, and for the writer too probably, this is a wonderfully comic moment. But for Earlene it's not funny at all. Because *she* doesn't know what that phrase means, and for her it's invested with cryptic significance which she feels compelled to decode.

70. Uncle Loren's amused himself, but all he'll do is send her back to the orthodox authorities with her question, and all Earlene's experience in the story has taught her that she'll get no satisfactory answer there.

71. So where can she look now? The fourth movement of the story finds her

approaching the Bean boundary again, calling across to try to make contact.

72. Nobody's around to stop her today.

73. The dog doesn't seem to care that she's broken the taboo.

74. The dog also doesn't care a whole lot about Earlene's family authority system. The threat of hellfire doesn't make much impression on this dog.

75. The Beans' home-made cave is the opposite of Daddy's tidy four-square house designed from blueprints. The hole is curved, not straight; it's messy, dirty, warm ...

76. ... and as Earlene declares, it's cozy.

77. This little string of happenings echoes the similar movement at the end of the story's first unit, when Reuben's thundering truck appears to presage Gram's judgmental appearance on the scene. Earlene, who in this case knows just what taboo she's broken, is expecting retribution of some kind, and sure enough, as soon as she touches that naked Barbie, there's thunder above and the roof starts to fall in. But what looks like divine vengeance is only Reuben Bean, breaking that other little taboo about turning in Daddy's driveway.

78. Still, she's trapped. She doesn't want the Beans to catch her there ... does she?

79. Now she's *not* trapped. The Beans have gone inside. Why not leave the hole? She wasn't afraid of the dog before. She has a fair chance of sneaking home without being caught by either Daddy or the Beans.

80. But she stays put, defiantly, partly because and partly in spite of the threat of punishment.

81. And then the Beans do catch her, finally. This is it, confrontation with the mystery. Earlene already has a reasonably good idea what happens when she's caught by her father or Gram or God. But what happens when she's caught by the Beans?

82. She does want to make it perfectly clear to them that she's not there by accident. She's there on purpose.

83. Well, this is childish exaggeration, certainly—but has Earlene made a serious choice?

84. Maybe she is still on the cusp of choice. Because although she is on Bean territory, she still isn't really *with* the Beans. As the earlier paragraph divisions suggest, and these plain sentences declare, there's still a barrier between her and them. To cross it, she has to accept the cake. Is it safe to eat it? The cake *looks* sinister because of its blue.

85. Earlene thinks the cake must be poisoned. The Beans are a menace—she knows that from her family—and the cake looks weird so it must be bad. But in fact the situation here in the final movement reflects the situation in the first movement: the cake is as innocuous as Earlene's nap with her father. No matter what it *appears* to be, it's *really* ... Betty Crocker.

THE CHILD DOWNSTAIRS

MARCIA GOLUB

I listen to the child cry downstairs.[1] I don't think they beat or abuse him, but he cries, "Stop it, Mommy. Stop it." I do not hear hitting.[2] He has cried like this since they moved in three years ago.[3] There are two other children and a dog. There is a live-in maid. She comes from Central America and takes care of the children during the day when the mother works. The apartment has two bedrooms, a parlor, a kitchen. One bathroom. The maid must sleep in the tub, otherwise where do they all go?[4]

The boy is now eight. I am alone.[5] I am trying to read. He cries, "Stop it, Mommy."[6] What is she doing so soundlessly that makes an eight-year-old boy cry?[7] She is a single mother, a lawyer. The family is from Central America, not just the maid. Often the boy cries in Spanish. Maybe she tells him to take a bath, do his homework, stop pulling the dog's tail. I do not know. Sometimes children cry, and no one is at fault.[8]

When the little boy cries, he gasps. I remember that catch in the throat, hiccups that come when you can't get your breath.[9] He wails in Spanish. The sound pulls my ghost awake. She cries, my cheeks grow wet.[10] What would the boy think if he knew a lady sat above him, her face squeezed tight like an unhappy raincloud?[11]

Perhaps he is bored. Perhaps he wants a new toy. Do Spanish mothers tell their children to bang their heads against walls when they are bored?[12] Now he is screaming. Is she leering like a gorgon? Staring with dead eyes? "Leave me alone," my mother told me. "You're just like the rest, using me till I have no more to give. You'll grow up too and leave me." Does the mother accuse him of plotting betrayal behind his eyes?[13] I don't have children.[14] Perhaps it is just the way of children, to carry on as if they were being tortured. Perhaps it is just the way of families, to torture their youngest child.[15]

I want to tell you about a woman.[16] She is married. She has no children.[17] She thinks, "In every marriage there comes a time when one will either have a child or an affair."[18] This woman wants the former but feels the fates conspiring to produce the latter.[19] This woman, let's call her Renie, which happens to be my name,[20] used to get up every morning at seven, even on weekends. She put a thermometer in her mouth and tried not to fall back to sleep. If she did, she feared she'd clamp her jaw shut and break the thermometer (she was a tooth grinder; her dentist said so, her husband confirmed it), or else her mouth would fall open, the thermometer slipping out.

Every morning she lay on her back for eight minutes, thinking how slowly time moved till suddenly you were too old to have a child.[21] Every morning she graphed her temperature on the blue and white grid, marked coitus and mucus and menses, made coffee and toast, washed, dressed, and went to work. She had been doing this for two years.[22]

When she first began plotting her chart, it seemed just a matter of proving her temperature rose at midcycle. "Here, Dr. List, don't you see? I ovulated on the fourteenth day of my cycle. My husband and I had intercourse on the thirteenth. So I must be pregnant." She seemed to believe that, if only she could prove ovulation and intercourse took place on schedule, Dr. List would throw his hands up and say, "Yes, Renie, you got me there. Okay then, you're pregnant."[23]

What Dr. List did say was "Keep taking your temperature. Tell your husband to see Dr. Nosringer, to test his sperm."

So Barry made an appointment with Dr. Nosringer. The nurse said he could pick up a sterilized specimen jar beforehand or come in that morning and produce a sample.[24]

"What are you going to do?" Renie asked.

"I don't know. I don't want to go all the way downtown for a jar. She also said to keep it warm. Can you just see me carrying a jar of come under my coat? What if I left it on the train?"[25]

That night Renie asked how it went.[26] "Horrible," Barry said. "I told the nurse I was there to leave a specimen and she put out her hand. I said, I don't have it yet. She said, You mean you want to do it *here?* The people in the waiting room all looked at me. I felt like a child molester. She took me to a room, gave me a jar. I said, Fill 'er up? Just to break the ice, you know?[27] She didn't smile. So there I was, in the doctor's bathroom. You know how they smell, like disinfectant? It wasn't easy. I kept expecting the nurse to come in, yell at me to hurry up."[28]

"The boy is crying again," Renie said.[29] "Every day. Why do people who don't want children get pregnant?[30] Why did Alice have to have an abortion? She was using birth control." She thought of herself and Barry making love every two days from the tenth to the twentieth day of her cycle. It didn't matter if they were tired, turned on or off. She had to keep her legs up in the air like a trussed turkey for fifteen minutes afterward.[31] Was it such a terrible thing to want a child, to want to love a child to redeem her from childhood?[32]

The child has stopped crying.[33] Is he watching tv with his brother and sister? Are they eating dinner? It must be hard, all those people in four rooms, all those people dependent on one woman. I hate them.[34] Why are they so noisy? Why do they slam doors and scream and cry? Even the dog screams. It's a small lap dog. It cries like a woman who wants her husband to know she's unhappy.[35] Why can't they be happy?[36]

Abel is happy. He works with Renie.[37] Maybe he is not so much happy as self-satisfied. When he began working with Renie she disliked him. He let everyone know he was fluent in Latin, Greek, Russian, German, and "Spanish and French, of course. Who doesn't know Spanish and French?" He was studying Italian. Renie coldly assessed him. "He's pompous," she told Barry. "A prig. I can't bear him. Of course it's useful to have someone at the encyclopedia who knows all those languages, but he thinks so damn much of himself."[38]

"Give him a chance," Barry said. "He's probably okay."

Renie noticed the gap between Abel's teeth when he smiled. He had a warm smile.[39] His hair was sparse, a color that could best be described as beige. Baby fine, it floated about his head like random thoughts.[40] He always seemed to be reading when Renie came in. His hands trembled. He walked by Renie's desk on his way to the elevator, even though that was the long way around. One day it hit Renie: Abel was in love with her.[41] "That's so cute," she thought. "Here I am, married twelve years, and Abel has a crush on me."[42]

She began to dress more seductively. She didn't mean to, but she thought about Abel when she picked out her clothes.[43] She imagined his desire. She went out of her way to be friendly. Abel remained cool. It was best, she thought. She didn't want an affair, she wanted wanting.[44] His hands still trembled when he was near her, he continued to walk by her desk. "He must be afraid of me," Renie thought. She liked that best of all.[45]

Then one afternoon as Renie sat reading a manuscript at her desk, Abel reached over to get a book above her head. She turned. Seeing Abel so hopelessly in love she smiled. "Don't worry," he said. "I'm not flirting with you. I'm just getting something." Her mouth clamped shut as if spring-loaded.[46] She made no reply. That night she dreamt she was in a classroom. She looked down and saw she had forgotten to put on clothes.[47]

Children cry in the park.[48] Laugh. Sing. Play skipping games. Children are eternal. They hold hands. They race, they tag one another. "You're It," they scream. They are the same ones—red-haired, freckled, pug-nosed—who wouldn't let me in when I was a child.[49] Hearing them, the ghost inside me pulls and whines.[50] She wants to play. She forgets she is dead, a memory of a girl.[51]

"I am too old for Hide and Seek," I tell her. I am tired. I am middle-aged.[52] The children in the park don't see me. Grownups are invisible.[53] I hurry by. My feet hurt. I take the bus.

On the bus the ignored child says, "Right, Mommy?" and gets no reply. When the child crawls on the aging woman's lap and says, "Right, Mommy? I love you, Mommy," trying to kiss the woman with gray hair and tired face; when the woman says, "Stop it, sit down, be still, you're messing my hair," and the child sits, looks up, ready to be noticed, ready for a smile,[54] it is then that the little ghost inside me stretches and yawns.[55] She looks around. Bored by my middle age, she is looking for something to do. "Behave, behave," I tell the ghostly girl. I know her well.[56] She is up to no good. Looking for eggs to drop, milk to spill, curbs to trip on, keys to lose. Something, anything to annoy us.[57] I have become my mother.[58] "Can't you sit still?" we ask. Some parents are infuriated by childhood.[59] I have three sisters. I am the last. They called me The Accident.[60] The Broken Pitcher. My parents were old when I was born. By the time I grew up they were dead.[61]

Abel had the power to make her sink.[62] The way he looked at her, looked away. She saw she was nothing in his eyes.[63] But if he had never looked, his looking away would have been nothing; as it was, it was everything.[64] When she learned she was seven years older than he, she fell hopelessly in love.[65] That's when Renie became middle-aged.[66]

"Do you mean to tell me that Abel is only twenty-eight?" she asked Marian. "When did he have the time to learn all those languages?"

Marian smiled. "Twenty-eight. You make it sound like fourteen. He's a grown man, Renie. We're just growner."[67]

"Marian, think—1963. I remember 1963. I remember writing 1963 in the heading of my homework. I can't even imagine talking to someone born then, let alone taking direction from him."[68]

"What's your story, Renie? Don't you like Abel?"

The next morning Renie discovered her first gray hair. It stuck out from the side of her head like an antenna.[69] She did not pluck it. Her mother used to have her pull out her gray hairs till she started going bald. Renie's stomach would turn as she watched the white scalp kiss the plucked hair goodbye.[70]

A week later Renie noticed wrinkles around her mouth. "I can take it," she said. Then a wart appeared in the corner of her right eye. Each day it was bigger than the day before. She knew she had inherited her mother's lid polyps and would soon be a hag.[71] "My mother had perfect teeth, a winning smile,"

Renie thought, "but I got her warts, wrinkles, and psoriasis." She resolved not to use the bright mirror light anymore.

"Do I look old?" she asked Barry.

"If I were a bartender, I'd proof you."[72]

Renie kissed him. She knew he didn't see her as she was. It wasn't fair for her to point out the wrinkles, the warts and gray hairs, to steal from him his dream of a bride.[73]

"What day is it?" he asked.

"The eleventh."

"Renie, how could you let yesterday slip by?"

"I'm sorry. I was tired."[74]

When Barry's sperm all turned out to be Olympic swimmers, Dr. List suggested they see a fertility specialist.[75] Dr. Weiz told Renie to have intercourse the night before, "then come in for the post-coital examination," which seemed perverse.

"Antibodies," Dr. Weiz said. "I'm testing for antibodies. Sometimes a woman's fluids reject a man's sperm. I'll know if that's the case after taking your sample. You had intercourse?"

Renie nodded.

Dr. Weiz prepared a slide. She let Renie look in the microscope. Renie pretended to see the sperm swim. Later she told Barry they had worn glasses; some had pink bows.[76]

"Nothing wrong there," Dr. Weiz said. "You sure you don't want to try a fertility drug? If you produce more than two fetuses we can do selective elimination."

Renie ironed her skirt over her knees. "I don't want a litter," she said, "but I can't see aborting the surplus."[77]

"Renie," Abel said.[78] "Do you want to edit 'Sacred Space' or speak to John about 'A Goddess's Descent'?"

"I don't know, Abel. What do you want me to do?" She didn't smile.[79]

"Renie," he said. "What are you thinking behind your face?"[80]

When her period was late she knew. Her breasts hurt so much she couldn't put on her bra. She called the doctor's office and asked how late her period had to be before the test. "Come in anytime," the nurse said. Renie called the office. Abel answered. He asked if anything were wrong. "I'm fine," she said. "I just have to pick something up. I'll be in soon."[81]

The nurse told her to pee in a jar. She sat twenty minutes in the waiting room, wondering if the other women had cancer. Her gynecologist no longer did obstetrics. "Maybe I have a tumor?"[82]

"Congratulations," the nurse said. She handed Renie a plastic egg with a blue dot. "Do you want to keep this? A lot of women do. It shows the test was positive."[83]

The nurse was pregnant. "Thank you," Renie said. "Oh, thank you so much."[84]

"Here is Dr. Winerose's number. He's the O.B. Dr. List recommends. Call him as soon as possible."

"Oh yes," Renie said. "I will." She felt like the newest member of a club. "Oh, I'm sorry. I'm crying because—"

The nurse laughed. "It's okay," she said. "I know."[85]

Barry cried too when she called his office. "Oh Renie. I can't believe it. Oh Renie, I wish you were here. I'm so happy."

Renie laughed and cried. "I feel blessed, Barry, I know it sounds corny but I do. I feel blessed, like this has never happened to anyone before."

She called the encyclopedia. Abel answered. "I'll be in soon," she said. She didn't tell him. She wanted to but didn't. She made an appointment with Dr. Winerose for Tuesday. She went to work carefully, walking on her toes as if balancing a bowl of water in her belly.[86]

"Marian," she said. "You don't know what it's like."

Marian smiled. "I don't know. I don't want to know. But I'm happy for you and Barry. I really am."

The child downstairs rang my doorbell on Halloween.[87] He was dressed as a ghost.[88] His sister came as a table, his brother was a ghoul. I gave them Snickers. I didn't want their mother to think I would give them poisoned apples. A week earlier, my husband had gone downstairs to complain. "It's so noisy," he said.

"You think you don't make noise?" she said. "I hear you and your wife, night after night, but I don't complain."[89]

I was meant to live in the country, in a house in the woods with a big dog. My children could play outside. I could listen to them playing. When they grew up I'd hear silence. I am afraid to be alone.[90]

On Monday the bleeding started. "It's nothing," Renie told herself. "It's common for women to bleed in the early months."[91] She called Dr. Winerose's office. She hadn't had her first appointment yet. She explained who she was, asked if she should do anything or just come in the following day as scheduled. The nurse said, "Lie in bed. Put your feet up. Don't move till Dr. Winerose calls. He's in surgery. He'll call as soon as he can."

Renie concentrated all her positive energies into her womb. "Love," she intoned. "Life. Joy." She refused to allow any bad thoughts to constrict her breathing. When Dr. Winerose called two hours later, she sounded as peaceful as a madonna.[92]

"I want you to go to Dr. Raner's office for a sonogram," Dr. Winerose said. Renie knew. "Don't be alarmed," the technician said. "It's common not to find any sign of the fetus at six weeks. It doesn't necessarily mean anything." Renie knew. "Don't be alarmed," the receptionist said. "We just wrote this for insurance purposes, okay? It doesn't mean what it says."[93] Renie nodded. "Spontaneous abortion," she read, but she already knew. "Abel," she said, calling the office. "I won't be in today." She began to cry, but he didn't notice.[94]

ANALYSIS

Plot

Backstory

The double construction of the story makes this category rather difficult to discuss. The story alternates between two narrative vectors: (1) a near-plotless rumination by a first-person narrator about the unhappiness of her neighbor's child, and (2) a very sad story about a third-person protagonist named Renie who tries desperately to get pregnant, finally succeeds, but in the end loses the child to a miscarriage. *If* we follow the story's numerous hints to assume that Renie and the vector 1 narrator are the same person, then we *might* conclude that the misery and depression of the vector 1 narrator represent Renie's state once the miscarriage has robbed her of all hope for a child of her own. . . . Thus the whole of vector 2 could be seen as the backstory of vector 1.

But this reading hardly does justice to the subtlety of the story's construction. The two plot lines are so thoroughly entwined and interpenetrated that it really makes no sense to try to relate them on a single chronological line; the whole issue of backstory is irrelevant. Each narrative vector becomes the subtext of the other.

Present Action

Vector 2, Renie's story, offers more in the way of conventional plot, a story line whose issues are plainly revealed in Renie's theory that "in every marriage there comes a time when one will either have a child or an affair." What follows is the story of how Renie ends up with neither. Her opportunity for an affair with her younger coworker, Abel, may have existed only in her imagination; certainly, whatever opportunity might have been there has been lost by the end of the story. The whole affair plot line curves toward a final anticlimax. The question of the pregnancy is shaped in a similar way: a series of disappointments finally peaks with an apparent success, but Renie's brief pregnancy also collapses into anticlimax (though that's a weak word, in the context which the story creates, for the awfulness of her miscarriage).

Narrative vector 1, the story told by the first-person narrator, is comparatively thin on conventional plot interest and plot information. While Renie's story might stand alone on the basis of its plot, vector 1 almost certainly would not. Vector 1 is a report on the interior life of the first-person narrator, and it is not in any obvious way progressive.

Very little *happens*, properly speaking, in vector 1, and yet there is a kind of movement: the narrator is provoked by the misery of "the child downstairs" to remember the rather complicated unhappiness of her own experience as a child not particularly desired by her parents. The child downstairs, heard but not seen until the concluding section of vector 1, becomes connected in the mind of narrator with the ghost of her own unhappy child-self. So it's appropriate that when the child downstairs does finally appear in the last vector 1 section, he's dressed in the Halloween costume of a ghost. That movement from something heard to something seen is a plot development, albeit a small one. Similarly, the narrator's state of mind seems to shift as vector 1 progresses— from ordinary mental discomfort to a deeper feeling of despair.

Technically speaking, it might be argued that the two narrative vectors aren't really so separate at all, since the vector 1 narrator declares in the first vector 2 section that Renie's story is a story she herself is telling. But vector 2 doesn't *sound* like a story told within a story—it is too fully dramatized for that, and its tone is quite sharply different from the tone of the vector 1 narrator, often almost at odds with it. Despite the many suggestions and hints that Renie and the vector 1 narrator are the same person (so that their apparently separate stories must be one and the same), the vector 1 and vector 2 plot lines seem to be almost violently forced apart from one another.

Character

The story's double construction also complicates the question of characterization: are Renie and the first-person narrator of vector 1 the same person or not? As with respect to plot, Renie is easier to analyze independently of the vector 1 narrator than the other way around; we see much more of her in action, and our information about her life history is much more complete.

Renie is a woman approaching middle age with a light and whimsical sense of humor, which, however, masks a deeper urgency that over the course of the story evolves into desperation and then into despair. More than anything else in the world she wants a child, and her sense that if she cannot have a child she will instead have an affair may almost amount to a fear: she longs for a child to cure the restlessness that might, she believes, otherwise lead to infidelity. She is a fundamentally harmless person, and even her impulse toward an affair seems oddly innocent, perhaps because we know all along it's not what she *really* wants. At work, at home, at her doctor's offices, Renie seems to have a kind of easy charm which is even complemented by our sense of her vulnerability. Because we see she can be hurt, we increasingly suspect she will be; as the story progresses, we become better acquainted with the profound sadness that underlies her ready wit. There is a hint ("Was it such a terrible thing to want a child, to want to love a child to redeem her from childhood?") that her own childhood was unhappy.

By comparison, almost nothing about the general present circumstances of the vector 1 narrator is revealed. We learn, glancingly, that she is married and childless, but so far as the present goes we learn more about the neighbors she's constantly overhearing—about her employment, social life, and so on we know next to nothing. We experience the vector 1 narrator less as a person acting in the world and more as a mental state. On the other hand, we do learn more about her past than we do about Renie's: the cause and quality of the unhappy childhood which "both" characters seem to share is much more fully explicated in vector 1 than in vector 2. And of course the unhappy childhood which Renie and the vector 1 narrator hold in common is one of the many clues that they are really one and the same individual.

That being the case, it probably makes most sense to regard the vector 1 narrator as an amplification of Renie's inner life. In vector 2, Renie is inclined to cover her emotional responses with jokes, or, when humor has finally failed her completely, with tight-lipped avoidance. The vector 1 narrator, however, lays the raw nerves bare; she gives us a much more complete portrayal of what must, in fact, be Renie's inner pain. Her function in the story is to suffer helplessly, and her inability to do anything to help the child downstairs is an image of her own helplessness. And yet the vector 1 narrator is in charge of the story as a whole, for we know that it is her decision to break Renie ("which happens to be my name") apart from her own personality and present her as a third-person protagonist.

As for the other characters, they are truly cameos. We see husband Barry as a nice guy, sympathetic and supportive . . . and powerless to do anything about the problem he and Renie share. Otherwise he is a player in the comic skits that are set up for him. Marian is little more than a backboard for Renie's office dialogue. The nameless downstairs family of vector 1 is left deliberately indistinct, so as to enhance the unpleasant uncertainty of the narrator's speculation about them. The only time the child downstairs appears on stage, he is masked for Halloween.

Of all the bit players in vector 2, only Abel is drawn with an interesting ambiguity, and even his importance is secondary in the end. The other members of the supporting cast are virtually stereotypical, which would be a flaw if the story relied on them more heavily. But it doesn't: the depth and texture of the story come from the much more complex and sensitive portrayal of Renie/vector 1 narrator. The function of the supporting players is to provide a context for the doubled protagonist, and they perform that function more than adequately.

Tone

Like everything else in the story, the tone is divided . . . when the story is considered as a whole. The tone of the vector 1 sections is uniform, however. Tone in vector 1 is sustained by the tone of the narrator's voice, which is uniformly downbeat, weary and sad, depressed and depressing. This is the sound of someone asking herself extremely painful questions which have absolutely no hope of a positive answer.

In vector 2, the tone shifts subtlely, back and forth between comedy and a tragic resonance:

> The next morning Renie discovered her first gray hair. It stuck out from the side of her head like an antenna. She did not pluck it. Her mother used to have her pull out her gray hairs till she started going bald. Renie's stomach would turn as she watched the white scalp kiss the plucked hair goodbye.
>
> A week later Renie noticed wrinkles around her mouth. "I can take it," she said. Then a wart appeared in the corner of her right eye. Each day it was bigger than the day before. She knew she had inherited her mother's lid polyps and would soon be a hag. "My mother had perfect teeth, a winning smile," Renie thought, "but I got her warts, wrinkles, and psoriasis." She resolved not to use the bright mirror light anymore.
>
> "Do I look old?" she asked Barry.
>
> "If I were a bartender, I'd proof you."
>
> Renie kissed him. She knew he didn't see her as she was. It wasn't fair for her to point out the wrinkles, the warts and gray hairs, to steal from him his dream of a bride.

A whole tonal spectrum is covered in this quote. When Renie discovers the first gray hair, the "antenna" and its angle make a comic image, but by the end of the paragraph a variation on this same image turns her stomach. The second paragraph has the tone of black humor—the phrasing makes these symptoms of aging sound funny, down to a dialogue line which a standup comedian might employ. The two-line exchange with Barry is lighthearted and reassuring, but the next paragraph, with its central idea of a stolen dream, ends on that oft-repeated note of sadness.

The third-person narrative of vector 2 sometimes provides comic relief from its own bitterest moments—and in general, the tone of vector 2 provides comic relief from the relentlessly despairing tone of vector 1 . . . at least in the beginning. At the outset, vector 2 has a pleasant breezy feeling, and its several comedy routines distract us from the downbeat tone of vector 1. But both vectors are converging tonally (as Renie and the vector 1 narrator converge on each other). At the end of the story, the comic tone evaporates, and when Renie weeps we see her moving entirely into the mood of the vector 1 narrator, into the dominant tone of vector 1.

Point of View

At this point it should be obvious that the ingenious handling of point of view is the key element to the structure of the story as a whole. The writer's most important decision is to present the main character in two different ways: as first-person narrator and third-person protagonist. As discussed above, the two different treatments produce two different impressions of character at the beginning of the story, though by the end these "two" characterizations have merged into one another. But what makes the division right and necessary?

Dialogue

Vector 1 and vector 2 approach the rendition of dialogue in rather different ways. In vector 1, dialogue is most often embedded in passages of summary description:

> Now he is screaming. Is she leering like a gorgon? Staring with dead eyes? "Leave me alone," my mother told me. "You're just like the rest, using me till I have no more to give. You'll grow up too and leave me." Does the mother accuse him of plotting betrayal behind his eyes? I don't have children.

As we've seen before, the interjection of dialogue into a summary passage provides a flash of half-scene vividness, but what's especially interesting here is that the dialogue lines belong to a *different* scene—not the episode where the narrator listens to the child downstairs through the floor, but an earlier episode remembered from her childhood. Embedding dialogue in summarizing paragraphs always produces a stronger effect of interiority—we are listening to the narrator think, rather than watching her behave. In this case, the device also allows the narrator to merge and combine episodes that are widely separated in time, and is used for that purpose frequently throughout the story.

   The dialogue of vector 2, by contrast, is usually broken out of the descriptive paragraphs and more fully dramatized. Often it is simply utilitarian, serving to move the plot along. There are also some fine examples of good comic dialogue:

> "Nothing wrong there," Dr. Weiz said. "You sure you don't want to try a fertility drug? If you produce more than two fetuses we can do selective elimination."
>
> Renie ironed her skirt over her knees. "I don't want a litter," she said, "but I can't see aborting the surplus."

Here Renie has a devastating reply to the "straight" line proffered by the doctor—it's knee-slappingly funny, until you really think about it. In fact, the straight line isn't really all that straight. "Selective elimination" is a grisly euphemism, and it's left to Renie to use the baldly accurate term: abortion. So this exchange (like so much else in the story) isn't all that funny underneath.

Imagery and Description

The vector 2 sections of the story rely mostly on plot; vector 2's forward momentum is considerable, and it doesn't linger much over its images. Vector 2 images are often comic: "Renie pretended to see the sperm swim. Later she told Barry they had worn glasses; some had pink bows." Sometimes they are poignant: "She went to work carefully, walking on her toes as if balancing a bowl of water in her belly."

Imagery in vector 1 is more detailed and complex; vector 1 is less plot-driven and more imagistic than vector 2. Almost all the images of the child downstairs and his family are *sound* images: the screaming dog, the sound of heads banging on the wall. "When the little boy cries, he gasps. I remember that catch in the throat, hiccups that come when you can't get your breath."

Visual images come from deep within the vector 1 narrator's inner life and superimpose themselves on what she sees in the present:

> On the bus the ignored child says, "Right, Mommy?" and gets no reply. When the child crawls on the aging woman's lap and says, "Right, Mommy? I love you, Mommy," trying to kiss the woman with gray hair and tired face; when the woman says, "Stop it, sit down, be still, you're messing my hair," and the child sits, looks up, ready to be noticed, ready for a smile, it is then that the little ghost inside me stretches and yawns. She looks around. Bored by my middle age, she is looking for something to do. "Behave, behave," I tell the ghostly girl. I know her well. She is up to no good. Looking for eggs to drop, milk to spill, curbs to trip on, keys to lose. Something, anything to annoy us. I have become my mother. "Can't you sit still?" we ask. Some parents are infuriated by childhood. I have three sisters. I am the last. They called me The Accident. The

Broken Pitcher. My parents were old when I was born. By the time I grew up they were dead.

Here the superimposition of imagery is used to make crucial connections between the children she sees in the present narrative, the ghostly children she will never bear, and the ghost of her "dead" child-self. This image pattern draws in the child downstairs when he appears on her doorstep dressed as a ghost for Halloween.

Design

As mentioned above, the decision to split a single main character into a first-person narrator and a third-person protagonist is what defines the structure of the whole story. The division of the main character creates a parallel structure: two separate narrative lines presented alternately. Or perhaps it makes more sense to visualize the narrative vectors as curves rather than as lines, which gives us a pattern something like a football:

This story clearly shows us the moment where vector 2 separates from vector 1: "I want to tell you about a woman. . . . This woman, let's call her Renie, which happens to be my name. . . ." From this moment of division, the two narrative vectors begin diverging from each other.

Vector 2

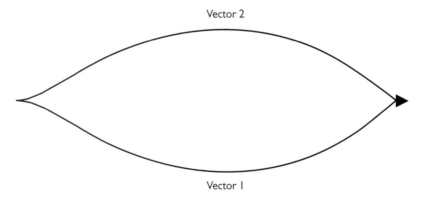

Vector 1

Vector 2, Renie's story, curves upward along a path which does after all resemble the shape of the conventional Freitag triangle. Exposition tells us that Renie believes she must have either a child or an affair; rising action develops her opportunities for both; her brief pregnancy might be positioned at the top of the curve, but soon, like the idea of an affair with Abel, it collapses into the concluding anticlimax.

The curve of vector 1 is more subterranean, less plot-driven, delves more deeply into the narrator's inner life. As it develops, many clues reinforce its rapport with the vector 2 plot line, of which it becomes a dark reflection. The "climax," here expressed as a trough rather than a peak, is the discovery of the nature of the narrator's unhappy childhood: "Some parents are infuriated by childhood. I have three sisters. I am the last. They called me The Accident. The Broken Pitcher."

Toward the end of the story, the two narrative vectors curve toward a reunion. The last vector 1 section identifies the vector 1 narrator very strongly with Renie: "'You think you don't make noise?' she said. 'I hear you and your wife night after night, but I don't complain.'" Renie's grief at the close of vector 2, when she has lost everything she wished for, flows naturally into the dark mood the vector 1 narrator has sustained throughout: "I am afraid to be alone." The statement has its corollary: *I am doomed to be alone.*

This pairing of narrative curves makes for an elegant and complex design, but was it chosen for its elegance alone? To answer this question, imagine it done differently. If told solely from Renie's point of view, it is too flat, too distant. If told solely in the voice of the first-person vector 1 narrator, it is unbearable—too awful to be spoken.

In fact, the story's split structure is a forceful way of dramatizing the psychological pain of the situation. The two vectors separate *because* the vector 1 narrator cannot bear a direct discussion of her failure to bear a child. So she distances that experience into the third-person, into Renie's story. Such distancing is a common ploy of the unconscious mind, which projects the most unbearable material into the symbolism of dreams; a psychoanalyst might define this distancing as repression.

Meanwhile, the first-person supplies both the background to her/Renie's story and its aftermath in direct discourse. The unhappiness of the childhood as disclosed in vector 1 intensifies this character's psychological need for a child of her own. And what happened to Renie in the conventionally plotted vector 2 finally explains the vector 1 narrator's morbid sensitivity to the child downstairs . . . her despairing response to the story's most painful and least answerable question: why do children come to those who don't want them and can't handle them rather than to those who do and can?

NOTES

1. This opening is both arresting and depressing.
2. There's something heartrending about the child's line . . . but the narrator (and reader) have no way of knowing the cause of his unhappiness—the situation is too opaque for that, and for the moment it is heard, not seen.
3. This long duration intensifies the seriousness of the problem (and by implication it intensifies the wearing effect on the narrator).

4. Basic exposition: the only problem in the neighbor family the narrator can accurately surmise is this overcrowding.
5. This phrase will be amplified through repetition.
6. ...and this other repetition turns up the dial on the child's perceived suffering.
7. For the narrator, there's a peculiar painfulness in being aware of the child's suffering without being able to learn the cause of it.
8. In fact, she can't know if the child is being mistreated in any way. The information that comes through the floor is not enough to explain things or assign blame ...
9. ...but what comes through the floor is heartbreakingly vivid.
10. The allusion to the "ghost" is a forward reach to a trope of the story which will be developed later.
11. The image is whimsical, almost comic, the sort of thing one might find in a children's book, but the context saddens it considerably. This style of dark whimsy will be further developed as the story goes on.
12. Presumably the narrator hears this sound of headbanging, which tends to undercut the more optimistic speculation of the first couple of sentences in the paragraph.
13. In these few, rather staccato sentences, ideas topple forward like a string of dominoes falling. The narrator's empathy for the child she hears is connected to unhappiness in her own childhood—a rejection by her own mother which may also connect to the "ghost" mentioned above.
14. Now this line may seem to be a casual aside, almost a non sequitur even, but later it will prove to be acutely relevant.
15. Resignation is generally supposed to be a wise and good thing, but taken to this extreme, resignation seems almost perverse.
16. Following the space break, a new character is introduced and a second narrative vector is established. The new character will be handled in the third person, rather than the first.
17. Here's something she has in common with the first-person narrator of narrative vector 1.
18. This interesting axiom could certainly be challenged ... but the character's belief in it is probably enough to make it true for her.
19. This sentence plainly lays out the conflict for narrative vector 2.
20. Still a more major coincidence—what's going on? Most likely the reader will already suspect that the first-person narrator of vector 1 has chosen to tell part of her own story in the third person in vector 2—but why? Is it a pointless complication?
21. The shifting of scale in this sentence—eight minutes compared with who-knows-how-many years—makes this whole description of the "biological clock" issue especially poignant.

22. Here is a portrait of extreme dutifulness, perhaps slightly comic considering what some of the duties are, but the tone is not at all comic so far.

23. This imagined exchange, delivered in the manner of standup comedy, is clearly meant to be funny, and is. But behind the humor there's an edge of frustration—Renie has done her duty, so why can't she be rewarded?

24. This passage of general summary . . .

25. . . . is enlivened by a half-scene element: this directly dramatized exchange of dialogue . . .

26. . . . but without slowing the story's rapid pace through events. This very efficient tactic will often be used in the remainder of the story.

27. Funny stuff here, good material for a standup comic once again . . .

28. . . . but the end of Barry's speech is not so funny—it imports a feeling of frustration, anxiety, and rising pressure into the situation first presented as comic.

29. This line should nail down the identification of Renie with the first-person narrator of vector 1. It also completes the shift from Barry's comic routine above to a much less jovial feeling in Renie's lines that follow.

30. This question will gather importance as the story goes on. The corollary question (why do people who *do* want children *not* get pregnant?) is not asked here.

31. Under such pressure, sex becomes work.

32. A third connection is implied here between Renie and the first-person narrator of vector 1, who seems to be haunted by a ghost of her own unhappy childhood.

33. Vector 1 resumes—the change signaled both by the space break and the repetitive reference to the child's crying first mentioned in the first sentence of the whole story.

34. The narrator's response to the noise is perhaps disproportionately strong—annoyance would certainly be understandable, but why hate?

35. Description of the downstairs family is still restricted to the sense of sound—but this personification of the dog's scream makes a very evocative image.

36. "Why do people who don't want children get pregnant?"

37. The space break and the use of Renie's name signal the return to narrative vector 2.

38. The reader who remembers Renie's axiom that all marriages lead to either childbirth or affairs may already feel a shadow of attraction in her exaggerated distaste for Abel . . .

39. . . . and sure enough, she does begin to find some attractive qualities in him.

40. What makes this simile so striking is its odd comparison of the concrete to the abstract.

41. It's not that she's attracted to him, it's the other way around . . . as she sees it, anyway.

42. Hint of an age difference here, which instead of being a disadvantage for Renie allows her to think patronizingly of Abel's crush—as an adult would patronize the whim of a child.

43. But soon enough, her notion of his attraction evolves into her attraction to him.

44. The repetition of "want" here makes Renie's desire for desire itself feel more forceful. Because of the either/or structure of her marriage axiom, the sentence also reminds us that she wants not an affair but a child.

45. She likes that because it places her in an (adult) position of power and control.

46. But if her idea of Abel's crush is delusional . . .

47. . . . then her idea of her own power and control might be delusional too. What if, as this dream image suggests, she's hopelessly out of control?

48. The word "children," like "child" in the first line of previous vector 1 sections, helps signal the return to vector 1 here.

49. Deep sadness in the narrator's report of exclusion here.

50. Is it the ghost of the child the narrator once was or the ghost of her own unborn child? Perhaps both options are possible . . .

51. . . . but in either case, to picture the ghost girl as dead seems bitterly pessimistic.

52. The narrator's fatigued lack of engagement with the ghost child will soon be echoed elsewhere in the narrative.

53. The narrator's invisibility will be echoed later on.

54. Here's a real child of a weary, aging mother . . .

55. . . . and it's her appearance that rouses the narrator's ghost child.

56. Because the ghost child is a version of the narrator herself?

57. And yet the ghost girl has also now become the narrator's adversary.

58. Now the narrator takes the position of the too-old, child-weary parent. This personality is painfully at odds with the ghost of her former child-self. The sentence carries additional irony because we know the vector 1 narrator has no children.

59. One infers that the narrator's parents had this attitude—which also seems to be shared by the mother downstairs in vector 1.

60. "Why do people who don't want children get pregnant?"

61. See note 32, above: Renie, in vector 2, also has an unhappy childhood which requires redemption—a need which connects Renie's wholehearted desire for a child with the narrator's tortured ambivalence.

62. The mention of Abel is now sufficient to signal the return to vector 2.

63. She's invisible to Abel, as the vector 1 narrator is invisible to children in the preceding passage.

64. If she had never had the idea that he was attracted to her, his indifference wouldn't matter.
65. The tables turn. It's almost as if Renie set this trap for herself.
66. . . . as if falling for a younger man sets the seal on her middle age. The thought connects subliminally to the idea of being too old to bear children.
67. Good point for Marian here.
68. An uncomfortable twist is added by the fact that middle-aged Renie is actually the subordinate of this younger man.
69. Comic image here . . .
70. . . . but it turns unhappily disturbing here.
71. The lines are witty, but we know that Renie is seriously unhappy about these signs of aging, and the contrast produces an odd doubling of tone.
72. Nice guy.
73. But his deft reassurance is not at all reassuring to Renie.
74. Behind the cosmetic consequences of Renie's aging is the much more serious issue of her declining fertility.
75. The space break here signals a jump cut in the action of vector 2, rather than a return to vector 1 as previously. Nevertheless we can follow without confusion because the cast of characters and the situation make it plain that we are still in vector 2.
76. There's forced optimism in this wit . . . the humor tends toward gallows humor.
77. Her lines are witty but also very bleak.
78. Names of the characters establish that the preceding space break marks a forward movement within vector 2.
79. She's dropped any idea of flirtation and relates to Abel in a strictly businesslike way.
80. But is Abel trying to rekindle the thought of flirtation?
81. Why bother to include Abel in these scenes? The reason will become apparent later.
82. This extremely downbeat thought comes from a character who's grown afraid to hope.
83. Expectations of an announcement of her pregnancy have been built very high, so the writer retains interest in the scene by *not* making the announcement in so many words.
84. In this euphoric moment, it seems like fertility is everywhere.
85. Her success in getting pregnant wins Renie a membership in a happily fertile community—sharp contrast to the sterility of her office life and to the alienation of the vector 1 narrator.
86. This striking image of delicate balance also serves to foreshadow danger.
87. The last several space breaks have signaled jump cuts in narrative vector 2, but the phrase "the child downstairs" in the first sentence lets us know

that we're returning now to vector I.

88. His costume reinforces his connection with the ghost child who haunts the narrator . . . a ghost who is also mysteriously wounded, cries and is perpetually unhappy.

89. This line further identifies the vector I narrator with Renie, whose sex life has evolved into a constant desperate effort to get pregnant.

90. The vector I narrator's last line is an extremely grim and pessimistic twist on her phrase "I am alone," in the first vector I section.

91. This forced optimism begins a brief and futile pattern of denial.

92. Renie's concentration here echoes all those dutiful efforts she made to get pregnant in the first place.

93. The nurse's line is somewhat in the style of the black humor passages presented earlier—like the standup comedy routines it's absurd, but because of the gravity of the situation it's no longer comic in the least.

94. The final outcome of Renie's axiom is that she will have neither a child nor an affair, which makes a doubly embittering conclusion to an elegantly constructed but very sad story.

RED HANDS

W I L L I A M   T .   V O L L M A N

1 Seamus (so he told me[1] to call him here) had rank red hair and a reddish-blond moustache. He wore a black overcoat. Purity and sincerity were in his face.[2] I suppose he felt the need to talk that any man feels when he has done something that he will be hunted for,[3] and he is by himself in some open plain of phobias and the wind of death is blowing in his face and he would like nothing better than to discover on the horizon the cabin of a wise man who will invite him in and listen to him and tell him what to do,[4] although Seamus knew that there was nothing to do.[5] It is sometimes a hard thing to be a man and stand by the thing that you have done.[6] He would have liked someone to take him out of the wind,[7] but no one is supreme[8] enough to do it; so, faced with us through some accident, Seamus looked to us for distraction, and when he was through with us and other caravans came by he told his tale again, searching each man's face to see if he was the wise man[9] that every man needs, but nobody was . . . "Well, see, that's all I did at first," he said, looking down at his burrito.[10] "I had a big back yard, and had a good-sized shed in the back. It was a good place to drop things off on the—you know, between here and there. I ran a safe house.[11] That's what you call 'em here, don't you?"

"Yeah."[12]

"Place to hide. Place to get a meal an' a shower, a bath. We didn't have a shower. We had a bathtub, though." He stopped for a minute to eat.—"I studied in Canada," Seamus said. He had a trick of hunching his shoulders.[13] "I got my degree, and went back, and the first year I was back at Ulster I was teaching at a little school. My sister was still living at home at the time. I guess she was

276

about seventeen years. She hadn't even started university yet. And she took ill. There was a curfew at the time. So the old man broke the curfew and tried to get her to a doctor, but he was caught on the streets after dark. He was detained. They held him for two weeks, and he died of a heart attack. When we picked up his body, we could see it'd been beaten. It was obvious. You know, the black and blue marks. You could see that there were fractures in his skull. You know, at that point . . ."[14]

He stopped. He looked down at his food.[15] "I mean, I grew up . . . Everybody hated something. Hatred is like—oh, fuck, how do you say it?—it's a way of life.[16] It really is. We're very much a prejudiced nation, I guess you could say. If you're Catholic, you learn to hate the Protestants because you're forced to live in the ghettos. Your opportunity for employment and any chance for a good life is limited because of your religious belief.[17] And you've got the Unionists, the Libertarians . . . Ireland's a land of factions. It's almost as bad as France, if you think about it.

"I got beaten up the first time when I was about six years old," he smiled. "There was a group of boys—must've been about fifteen of 'em. They did it 'cause I was Catholic. I didn't even know what being Catholic *meant* at the time."[18]

As he talked, he forgot to eat. His voice was always soft.[19] "After my old man died, I was pretty bitter. I watched my mam drink herself to death. Took about two years to do it. And at the same time, I travelled through India. I saw the hash runs through that part of the country. Started doing those things to raise money. When I was out of Ireland, I'd learned that the religious thing wasn't the big deal. It's not whether you're a Catholic or a Protestant that matters.[20] But I felt that the British, they didn't belong. They didn't belong there. I felt that we were a nation of men, that we could deal with our own fucking problems.[21]

"I was never involved, so to say, when I was younger. I used to go out on the streets and throw rocks and track tanks. Fuck with the soldiers, light off firecrackers. I'd do anything I could. I always tried to stay out of it, but I was always involved in it, 'cause it took my family. So I felt there was a need for involvement, for vengeance.[22] I opened up my house. I let people stay there. We even got people out of Russia. But then one day—I guess it was about the same time that Bobby Sands started the hunger strike[23]—I heard in the south there was a warrant for my arrest. I didn't go willingly. I ended up getting shot four times. I was tried without a jury, and I got a long sentence for something that was never proven, so to say.[24] Not the way the judicial system works here. At that time I guess the British were desperate. And the single written testimony of another man was enough to incriminate you. So that's how I was introduced to the Block."—Seamus's red eyelashes twitched.[25]

In the H-Block he had lived his life watching the British warders, with their scared baby faces and their truncheons.[26] Once they had tortured one of his comrades. The man wouldn't talk. So they showed him a video of his six-teen-year-old daughter being raped. He still wouldn't talk.[27]

"Most of the alleged terrorists were all kept in one area," Seamus said. "There were about eight hundred of 'em. I was with twenty-three others that got fed up. We took an opportunity, and gained our freedom. I guess I was a little more fortunate than some. Half of us were captured in the first week."

"So the escape went well?"[28]

Pride came into his face. "Did the escape go well? It went like bloody fucking *dominoes*." He looked at the tape recorder defiantly.[29] Then he said, "Like dominoes. Just like when we blew up the department store."[30]

2 "So what happened when the department store was blown up?" I said.[31]

"I wasn't there," he said.[32]

"Trust him, man," said the fellow in the back of the kitchen,[33] but Seamus was silent.[34]

"Well," I said, "if you had any advice for people who want to blow up department stores, what would it be?"[35]

"Don't do it," he said. "It's not worth it."[36]

3 "That's why I hang out in the woods so much, in the mountains," Seamus said. "Just me an' Him."[37]

4 "We had to kill a British soldier to get out," he said. "Not just anybody, but a British soldier. The largest manhunt in the history of northern Europe. Hey, they got sixteen of us, out of the twenty-four that got out! When I left that front gate, I said, 'We may be brothers, but from here we're on our own!' I was one of the selfish ones. It was the ones that stuck together and tried to help each other that got caught."[38]

5 After the escape, he had gone down into Belfast and hidden on the Catholic side. Time obscured him further from the British, who were required to cali-brate their hours according to the freshest cases.[39] Presently he began his career of false voyages. He hired onto a Swedish ship as cook and carpenter. Upon completion of the journey, he joined an Italian freighter, and then a Dutch fishing boat, each time under a different name.—Finally he signed on a ship bound for New York. I don't know what he thought during those grey days on the grey sea; quite likely he thought of his two sons.[40]—They came into New York Harbor late at night, passing through the Narrows while Seamus said his goodbyes. Everybody knew. They had a party for him, and it was a good one, since Seamus was fine to drink wine or Guinness or Jameson with; but every now and then at parties I have seen him suddenly look down at the table and fold his hard sunburned arms across his chest and fall silent; at those times I notice his sloping forehead, which seems more bare than it used to, and there are wrinkles at the corners of his pale eyes, and against his red and weather-beaten face his hair might be reddish-blond or it might be going white.[41] And that is how I imagine him[42] at that other leave-taking party when he must have been saying goodbye to Europe and Ireland, not that I *know* it because his is a story told by a man of professional reticence,[43] friendless forever, and we can grasp it only provisionally and approximately, by dreaming up our own ill-informed impressions of the scene,[44] not omitting the smell of garbage which must have blown into Seamus's nostrils from the landfill on Fresh Kills Island;[45] and Staten Island would have been very big and dark on his left,[46] while New York began to grow, revealing its vastness, cruelty and coldness in the grin of its skyscraper-teeth,[47] and lights burned dingily in Brooklyn; and ahead of him, behind the passionately upraised torch of Miss Liberty in her green old age, were the bright pyramids and dark rectangles of Manhattan, the tall buildings whose luminous dots of windows transformed them into dominoes,[48] the docks whose light cast the coast behind them into greater darkness, and of course the customs-houses.[49] The stubby skyscrapers became taller and wider now, casting their burdens of light upon the harbor; and cars whizzed steadily along the shore freeway like glittering beads,[50] and between the skyscrapers Seamus could see the dark urban canyons into which a man could go and come out another man, or not come out at all.[51] Let us suppose for artistic reasons that a great Cunard liner went by,[52] maybe even the *Queen Elizabeth II*; Seamus would have given it the finger, but out of all the tourist faces peering from every porthole not one would have seen him;[53] and then the moon went behind a cloud to have a cigarette, and everything was almost as bright as before, but harder with a beetling hardness.[54] Seagulls rose in the mist and swirled around the ship before finally returning with screams of disappointment to Miss Liberty's feet. Ahead of him, through the masts and cranes of his ship, he saw long low-roofed warehouses like barracks, and dismal grey prisms of buildings honeycombed with windows, as if they were vertebrae from which all the marrow had been pecked.[55] The American skyline was an interminable rampart which must somehow be scaled, made up of cubes and tall towers ridged and latticed like bones, all crammed together upon the land, crushingly tight, going on and on in a complexity that no one could understand; and the ship came closer until each skyscraper became itself a wall, ribbed and raised and vast, and there were millions of other walls behind it.[56] His only hope was in the narrow spaces five hundred feet high between them where he might be able to sneak through if he could pull himself out of the water, dragging his belly over slimy concrete and salt-impregnated stumps of power poles and barbed wire; then he would have to skulk past the bright-lit foyers of the office towers, dodge past pay phones (water streaming from him all the while), encouraged by the realization that interstitial life might be possible since the in-between-spaces must be getting bigger if the skyscrapers were still getting bigger and bigger and bigger . . .[57] His comrades had told him that when you jumped, it was important to get a running start to keep from getting sucked into the propeller.[58] He walked back fifteen feet and started running.[59] He cleared the railing; in that transitional moment of regret and expectation, he must have had a sense of being at a great height, for below him was a whole world of black water and yellow lights.[60] He began to fall, and continued to do so for a long time. No doubt he wondered whether or not he could save himself from the propeller.[61] When he hit the water at last, his arms and legs had already begun to swim.[62] Through that cold, dark and utterly foul water he made his laborious way.[63] Not far from his left shoulder, the ship continued on without him. His possessions were his clothes and two hundred U.S. dollars in a watertight pocket.[64]

It is literally true that he was washed up on a dead-end street. Now began his new life, which he must live without anyone, without even himself.[65]

6 "All right, one further story," he said with a smirk. "We were in London, and what I call hoity-toity, kind of like upper-class. It was a rude section near Soho Park. Me and my friends were a bit drunk. We came across this café, and there were some people sitting there eating, and they *looked* at us. And I was offended. I walked over to the railing and I pulled down my zipper, and I pissed on the food."[66]

7 "I'll tell you," said the doctoral student, Oliver (not his real name[67]), "that's why I was so queasy about doing this. I haven't worked with live animals since high school.[68] The power of it is very impressive.[69] I was very impressed[70] with how we bled the mouse the other day. We took the serum out. I usually do it by injection. Of course I won't deny that I'm getting sick of this mouse. In fact, the last three nights have been very difficult. She even keeps *struggling* when I inject her in the belly![71] I'm glad it's her big day today."[72]

"What's the best way to do it?"[73]

"To kill them, the easy way is to put them in a bag of CO_2. But it's supposedly very painful for the mouse, and it also adds another variable.[74] It may do something to the physiology. That's why it's much better just to break their necks."[75]

"So you use a cervical dislocator?"[76]

"Yes. It's called a pencil."*[77]

8 The lab had the usual formaldehyde smell. Being rich in glass bottles and plastic tubes, it was its own world, which you came to every day, not knowing

---

* We are all of us technicians and researchers in ethical laboratories. One common denominator is *procedure.* —"Clocks with alarms are grand!" I remember Seamus saying to me. "Look at this one from Radio Shack. They have others that you can set up to a year in advance. I like this one, 'cause it's got the alarm on it, right? And it's got enough of an electrical pulse to set off a detonation. You need only very low amperage to do a job."

whether or not you were going to have a good day until you shuffled over to the centrifuge for radioactive materials, flipped the switch, and listened to its good comforting hum, and suddenly it was clear after all that you *did* know which opening to dispense Parafilm through.[78] There were hundreds of drawers to play in, hundreds of shelves and cabinets, and lab benches piled with a mole of this and an aliquot of that. Every chemical was like the muscle of a giant eye which allowed the researchers to see something which they had never seen before.[79] They knew that their powerful reagents would permit them to shatter the unwanted cells, which were like boulders covering some antique tomb that the anthropologists were sure must be glutted with treasure which they could transfer from its underground grave to a public grave in some museum, where gold and bones lay in shame behind daily-cleaned glass.[80]

Through the microscope I saw, on a pinkish field, the red mouse-spleen cells, like translucent beans. They looked like meat; they looked nourishing, but there were not enough of them to eat.[81]

Just as I = AMP and II = TET (as it said on the wall), so the mouse had to die.[82] Their books said, "An upward slope at low pH is reported from frog muscle and squid giant axon."[83] They had killed a lot of things here.[84] But they *had* to kill them to understand them.[85] And this is not blameworthy, because we must each one of us feed on death, whether we maliciously inhale to trap bacteria in the fatal caverns of our lungs, where they must die so that we come to no harm,[86] or whether we wear leather shoes.[87] In those things we kill not out of sadism but tangentially, to achieve a result in some other sphere, and it is the same with the scientist and the terrorist.[88] That is why Oliver remained a little squeamish[89] while he and his companion made the final preparations, their gloved hands in the sanctuary of the BioGard™ hood ("Creating Immaculate Atmospheres"[90]). They turned on the germicidal lamp, and then the fluorescent lamp. In the hood was a double bottle of prismatic construction, each side containing its own reddish liquid. Oliver sterilized the tip of his pipette in the ever-burning Bunsen. Then he worked the red fluid, which was frothy with living cells, up and down in the pipette. He took another bottle, held its mouth briefly in the flame, and poured more red stuff from it into a flask with a stubby pointed bottom, like a pencil.[91]—How peculiarly steadfast that BioGuard hood must appear at night, with only that gas flame burning . . .[92]—He held the tip of the flask in the flame, and then sealed it and set it into a beaker. From a bottle of what appeared to be blood-red cough syrup, his companion pipetted a specified amount into a Petri dish.

It was time for Oliver's mouse to die now.[93] Somebody else had to kill another mouse, and he said, "Let's race them first!",[94] but Oliver refused.—He took her out of her cage. Of course this rodent tragedy would not be on the order of the one in the department store, when Seamus's bomb went off and people screamed and fell down clutching their stomachs and blood rained and flesh rained;[95] in fact, Oliver's mouse did not even squeak or struggle as Oliver set her on his bench and laid a pencil across her neck.[96]—"Okay," he said to her, "this is your day to *shine!*"[97]—He squeezed her neck down with the pencil, grasped her head, and jerked it up and backwards.[98] There was a quiet dismal crack. Her skinny legs twitched. Then she raised her tail, and her bowels moved.[99]

They took her to the BioGuard hood and proceeded to subsequent steps of meticulous dismemberment (now that spontaneous generation has been disproved, it seems that we must cannibalize matter in our projects, just as the revolutionary must destroy in order to establish his own order[100]). I began to wonder what would be the outcome of the magic trick.

9 I am not entirely certain of the connection between the tale of Seamus and the tale of Oliver, but they both have red hands[101] and they both acted for what one might as well call structural reasons.[102] Not being mice, we tend to think that Seamus committed the greater crime,[103] if either of them committed a crime at all[104] (in any event my interest in the dead mouse and the dead people in the department store does not partake of judgment; let us leave that to judges[105]). Seamus did what he thought was right, and so did Oliver.[106] Seamus killed some people and will be affected by it for the rest of his life. Oliver killed a mouse and was affected by it for less than five minutes.[107]

ANALYSIS

Plot

Backstory
Not exactly a relevant category here. The chronological relationship between the Seamus episode and the Oliver episode is unstated and also unimportant. The manipulative hand of the author/interviewer seems to bring all events into the same chronological frame.

Present Action
In a sense, the plot of the story is neatly summarized by the last two sentences: "Seamus killed some people and will be affected by it for the rest of his life. Oliver killed a mouse and was affected by it for less than five minutes." The two episodes are fleshed out with varying degrees of detail. The most important events of Seamus's life are recounted (somewhat circuitously) in summary form. But our information about Oliver is quite strictly limited to the scene in which he commits his act. On the one hand we have a complete capsule biog-

raphy of an IRA terrorist; on the other an account of a few relatively trivial minutes in the life of a scientific researcher.

The plot crises for both episodes are similar, in the "structural" sense. Both episodes revolve around killings, though they are killings of vastly different magnitude. The killings are presented differently in each case. In the Seamus episode, the bombing of the department store is a point which is constantly circled but never quite reached: a subject of frequent allusion but only glancing description (the most direct description of the bombing occurs in the Oliver episode, apropos of the death of the mouse). By contrast, the killing of the mouse is described in almost excruciating detail.

Information supplied and information withheld are curiously symmetrical between the two stories. We are told almost everything about Seamus's background but very little about his act of killing. We are told almost everything about Oliver's act of killing but very little about his background. The type of material studiously omitted from each episode is supplied by the other. This tactic produces a somewhat unusual effect of overall symmetry. Because the two episodes seem to be inverted reflections of each other, they can be fitted together like puzzle pieces.

It's the author/interviewer who does the fitting, of course. What is his function in the plot? He is present for Oliver's action and for Seamus's recapitulation of his career, but his presence is very shadowy. He appears only as a voice that asks questions or as a mind that reacts to the answers. It seems clear that he has no effect on the events of either episode, but without his presence there would be no connection between them.

Character

In the conventional sense, Seamus is certainly the most fully developed character. We are told a great deal of pertinent information about the character-forming sufferings of his childhood and youth. We know the essentials of what he has done with his life. We learn that he has a religious sensibility; he communes with God when alone in the wilderness. We are told that "purity and sincerity were in his face." At the same time we also know that he is capable of pissing on someone else's dinner table in a fit of drunken displeasure, and that he is capable of much graver acts of violence too: the killing of the British soldier in his prison escape, the bombing of the department store.

What characterization does this information about Seamus add up to? What conclusion does the author/interviewer, who has gone to the trouble of collecting all the information, draw about Seamus in the end? In the first paragraph of the story, the author defines Seamus's central problem: "It is sometimes a hard thing to be a man and stand by the thing that you have done." Toward the end of the episode, the author/interviewer concludes (quite touchingly) that Seamus "must live without anyone, without even himself." It's as if all the information about Seamus cannot be integrated into a whole image of a person; his worst deeds cannot be conformed to the more positive aspects of his personality. In this way, Seamus's difficulty in standing by his action comes to be shared by the writer (and reader) who observe him.

We know a great deal about Seamus's history and nothing at all about Oliver's. Any impression of Oliver's character must be derived from his behavior during the brief scene depicted in the lab. What can be said about Oliver? He is presented as an example of the scientific mind at work—presumably detached and impersonal. But his response to the mouse *is* personal. In section 7 he confesses to queasiness; he also admits that he's sick of the mouse and that he's happy the moment of her death will come soon. His squeamishness as he prepares to dispose of the mouse is given an odd twist by what he says to her at the key moment: "Okay, . . . this is your day to *shine!*" This frivolity may be a mask for Oliver's discomfort about what he has to do, but it also carries a tinge of real sadism. Did Dr. Mengele ever feel squeamish while conducting his "scientific" experiments in the Nazi death camps? There's a great difference of scale between the two cases, but both involve the justification of cruelty by scientific purposes. In the end, Oliver's character is at least as hard to read as Seamus's.

Should the author/interviewer be considered as a character in the story, properly speaking? His presence has no apparent effect on events. On the other hand, all our information is filtered through his personality before it reaches us, and in this sense, at least, he influences the conclusions we may draw from what is told. He also steps inside the story to draw his own conclusions, visibly. But because we know him exclusively through the sound of his voice, his characterization is more a matter of tone.

Who is the reader supposed to like or root for in this story? Because we are told most about Seamus's own sufferings, we might say that Seamus is the most sympathetically presented character—still, it's hard to snuggle up to him because of the enormity of his crimes. By contrast, Oliver has done nothing *enormously* awful, but the way the narrative dwells on his dispatch of the mouse may make him seem rather less appealing a character than Seamus. As for the author/interviewer, he exhibits an impressive range of tone, but without ever becoming what you would call ingratiating.

Tone

In dialogue with both Oliver and Seamus, the author/interviewer's tone is clinically neutral: "So what happened when the department store was blown up?"; "So you use a cervical dislocator?" etc. This intentionally affectless tone is sometimes (but not always) echoed in the main body of the text (when the author/interviewer speaks not to the other characters but, in effect, directly to the reader): "No doubt he wondered whether or not he could save himself from the propeller"; "Her skinny legs twitched. Then she raised her tail, and her bowels moved"; etc. Sometimes the flat tonelessness of the language rubs against the content to make certain passages seem even more horrific: "Once they had tortured one of his comrades. The man wouldn't talk. So they showed him a video of his sixteen-year-old daughter being raped. He still wouldn't talk."

But compare that disturbing description to this one: "Of course this rodent tragedy would not be on the order of the one in the department store, when Seamus's bomb went off and people screamed and fell down clutching their stomachs and blood rained and flesh rained. . . ." The more vivid description and the metaphorical use of "rain" gives the second passage a much more impassioned tone than the first. And of course the descriptions and metaphors are often much more elaborate and fanciful than that. Sometimes they are whimsical and ironic: "How peculiarly steadfast that BioGuard hood must appear at night, with only that gas flame burning . . ." Sometimes the author/interviewer sounds extraordinarily pedantic, and yet his odd combinations of abstractions also have a whimsical tone: "now that spontaneous generation has been disproved, it seems that we must cannibalize matter in our projects, just as the revolutionary must destroy in order to establish his own order."

Thus the story has not one tone but many: irony, whimsy, pedantry, passion, and a queer clinical coldness. The narrative flickers from one tone to another and also combines them in rather strange ways. To complicate things a little further, Seamus's longer speeches have a distinctive tone of their own which has little to do with any of the tones adopted by the author/interviewer.

As with the Peter Taylor story, though with a strikingly different affect, the tone (or tones) of "Red Hands" implies the presence of a peculiarly personalized narrator. Indeed, the presence of such a narrator is more openly acknowledged in "Red Hands" than in "A Wife of Nashville," by the insertion of the author/interviewer's lines of dialogue and other such gestures. When this narrator speaks, we can almost see him, and yet he always stands just barely out of our line of sight. We can perceive only whatever he is looking *at*, and, of course, the different ways he thinks about it. We experience the story by being caught up in his process of thought.

Point of View

Where's the camera? If we disregard the role of the author/interviewer in the story, what we seem to have is an externally omniscient overview. We become acquainted with Oliver and Seamus exclusively through what they do and say (and, in Seamus's case, through paraphrased summary of what he has presumably told the author/interviewer about his past career). There is no direct relation of the thoughts or feelings of either Seamus or Oliver (or the mouse for that matter).

However, the role of the author/interviewer cannot be disregarded, and when it is taken into account the story feels much more as if there is a first-person narrator on the scene. The author/narrator seldom refers to himself directly as "I" or "me," but because the tone of the story is so quirkily personalized, the reader seems to experience events *not* from a standpoint of neutral omniscience (as in Percival Everett's story, for instance), but strictly through the eyes of the author/interviewer. Therefore our sense of the point of view fluctuates along with the frequent shifts in tone.

The long description of Seamus's approach to the New York City shoreline provides a curious example of these variations in the point of view:

> The American skyline was an interminable rampart which must somehow be scaled, made up of cubes and tall towers ridged and latticed like bones, all crammed together upon the land, crushingly tight, going on and on in a complexity that no one could understand; and the ship came closer until each skyscraper became itself a wall, ribbed and raised and vast, and there were millions of other walls behind it.

This sentence is certainly entirely in the voice of the shadowy first-person narrator—it's the author/interviewer's point of view, his way of seeing. In the following sentence, however, a slight shift occurs:

> His only hope was in the narrow spaces five hundred feet high between them where he might be able to sneak through if he could pull himself out of the water, dragging his belly over slimy concrete and salt-impregnated stumps of power poles and barbed wire; then he would have to skulk past the bright-lit foyers of the office towers, dodge past pay phones (water streaming from him all the while), encouraged by the realization that interstitial life might be possible since the in-between-spaces must be getting bigger if the skyscrapers were still getting bigger and bigger and bigger . . .

The point of view in this sentence has shifted partly toward Seamus—it speaks of his "hope" and of his being "encouraged"—but the complexity of the language and the difficult abstraction, "interstitial life," still maintains the very strong presence of the author/interviewer's point of view. In the next sentences, the *tone* shift is more radical:

> His comrades had told him that when you jumped, it was important to get a running start to keep from getting sucked into the propeller. He walked back fifteen feet and started running.

These sentences are briefer, drier, shifting from the impassioned rhetoric of the sentences preceding to a comparatively cool and clinical tone. With this shift in tone the point of view becomes much less personalized to the author/interviewer and begins to feel more like neutral omniscience. The next sentence swings back in the opposite direction:

> He cleared the railing; in that transitional moment of regret and expectation, he must have had a sense of being at a great height, for below him was a whole world of black water and yellow lights.

The phrase "regret and expectation" implies a point of view internal to Seamus, but the verb phrase "must have had" lets us know that it's actually the author/interviewer's *speculation* about Seamus's inner experience. Meanwhile the intensification of the imagery makes the personal point of view of the author/interviewer felt again. The next sentence is neutral and declarative, by comparison:

> He began to fall, and continued to do so for a long time. No doubt he wondered whether or not he could save himself from the propeller.

The concluding sentence, another speculation about Seamus's thoughts and feelings, is labelled as a speculation by the phrase "no doubt." All these maneuvers suggest that the author/interviewer will never say anything definite about a character's subjective experience that he has not explicitly been told . . . which is a kind of honesty and should evoke the reader's trust.

The curious aspect of this passage is that the most vivid descriptions (and these are the most vivid descriptions in the whole Seamus episode) are given from the point of view of the author/interviewer; you don't have to be a fugitive IRA terrorist to describe the New York City shoreline by night. When he speaks of Seamus's own subjective experiences, the author/interviewer is much more conservative, limiting himself (somewhat in the scientific manner) to what he can know for certain.

Time Management

Chronology doesn't seem to be a very important issue in this story, but why not? In most stories with two distinct episodes, their relative timing should be important, but here it hardly seems to matter—the reason being that there is no cause and effect relationship between the Seamus episode and the Oliver episode whatsoever. A clear chronology is mandatory to maintain a chain of cause and effect, but because the Seamus episode and the Oliver episode are connected only at a level of abstraction, their relative timing makes no difference.

Within the Seamus episode, cause and effect does matter; his most grievous actions appear to be caused, at least in part, by the injustices he has suffered in childhood and youth. Within this episode, events are not presented in strict chronological order, but there is sufficient clarity about the order of events that the timeline can be straightened out by the reader.

Both within the Seamus episode and in the story as a whole, events are presented in an order which seems to be determined by the whim of the author/interviewer. It's his presence in the story that makes the nonsequential presentation possible. If we agree to listen to him at all, then we also accept his arrangement of events, without questioning it.

Dialogue

The handling of dialogue (like almost everything else in the story) is somewhat eccentric. The lines of the author/interviewer quoted in dialogue are always dry and neutral—typical "straight-man" material. And there isn't very much in the way of back-and-forth conversational exchange anyway, just enough to prove that the author/interviewer was there asking his questions—which is a way of legitimating his story.

Otherwise, it seems to be the intention of the author/interviewer to convert his characters' dialogue into monologue. Seamus's speeches sometimes are walled off as mini-monologues, each occupying its own numbered section. Oliver's speeches are less extensive, but still they don't require much response from the conversational partner. In both cases, the author/interviewer seems to step aside momentarily, allowing Oliver and Seamus to speak directly to the reader.

Imagery and Description

The author can, when he wishes, deliver descriptions of an extraordinarily vivid, sensory realism, but they are seldom simply that:

> They had a party for him, and it was a good one, since Seamus was fine to drink wine or Guinness or Jameson with; but every now and then at parties I have seen him suddenly look down at the table and fold his hard sunburned arms across his chest and fall silent; at those times I notice his sloping forehead, which seems more bare than it used to, and there are wrinkles at the corners of his pale eyes, and against his red and weatherbeaten face his hair might be reddish-blond or it might be going white. And that is how I imagine him at that other leave-taking party when he must have been saying goodbye to Europe and Ireland, not that I *know* it because his is a story told by a man of professional reticence, friendless forever, and we can grasp it only provisionally and approximately, by dreaming up our own ill-informed impressions of the scene, not omitting the smell of garbage which must have blown into Seamus's nostrils from the landfill on Fresh Kills Island; and Staten Island would

have been very big and dark on his left, while New York began to grow, revealing its vastness, cruelty and coldness in the grin of its skyscraper-teeth and lights burned dingily in Brooklyn; and ahead of him, behind the passionately upraised torch of Miss Liberty in her green old age, were the bright pyramids and dark rectangles of Manhattan, the tall buildings whose luminous dots of windows transformed them into dominoes, the docks whose light cast the coast behind them into greater darkness, and of course the customs-houses. The stubby skyscrapers became taller and wider now, casting their burdens of light upon the harbor; and cars whizzed steadily along the shore freeway like glittering beads, and between the skyscrapers Seamus could see the dark urban canyons into which a man could go and come out another man, or not come out at all. Let us suppose for artistic reasons that a great Cunard liner went by, maybe even the *Queen Elizabeth II*; Seamus would have given it the finger, but out of all the tourist faces peering from every porthole not one would have seen him; and then the moon went behind a cloud to have a cigarette, and everything was almost as bright as before, but harder with a beetling hardness. Seagulls rose in the mist and swirled around the ship before finally returning with screams of disappointment to Miss Liberty's feet.

The first sentence contains the most thorough and particular description of Seamus himself found in the entire story. Here for the first time we see him fully in the round; previously we have known him chiefly by his voice and by much briefer glimpses. The first sentence slows down the narrative, signaling a shift out of the summary preceding into the fully rendered scene which will follow.

The monstrously long second sentence begins by announcing the act of imagination which the writer must commit in order to deliver the description which follows; with the phrase "smell of garbage" this description begins with an address to the senses and proceeds to lay out the geography in a matter-of-fact style, but with the first reference to New York City proper ("revealing its vastness, cruelty, and coldness in the grin of its skyscraper-teeth") the description doubles: producing a strong sensory impression on the one hand and (through the metaphor) introducing a value judgment on the other. The remainder of the second sentence is less demanding; it means only to sustain our sensory impression of the scene, and the first segments of the third sentence seem to have similar intentions, but the conclusion of the third sentence, via the metaphor of "dark canyons," turns the description toward a more thematic point about the transformations which Seamus will undergo in this place.

The opening of the fourth sentence reminds us again that what we are reading is being presented as an imaginative speculation, but nevertheless the description is presented with such authority that we seem to see Seamus's action even though the sentence has shifted to the conditional (what "would have happened"); we see the tourists at their portholes with equal clarity, and when the sentence shifts back to past definite ("the moon went behind a cloud"), we have made a firm return to lapidary realism—not merely hard, but "with a beetling hardness." The description of the seagulls which ends the quoted passage is straightforwardly realistic except for a single anthropomorphic touch: it's unlikely of course that the seagulls really experience "disappointment," but the use of the word adds to the emotional coloration of the scene, which is spectacular, awe-inspiring, but also awful and menacing—a marvelously inhospitable place.

Note too how the sentences build from shorter to extremely long to short again throughout the passage, giving it a curved ogival shape. This manipulation gives the passage its structural form: with the longest sentence it builds to a crescendo of sorts, then declines to a sort of lull (from which it can begin to build again as the whole paragraph continues to roll forward).

Sometimes Vollmann's imagery is even more frankly metaphorical:

> I suppose he felt the need to talk that any man feels when he has done something that he will be hunted for, and he is by himself in some open plain of phobias and the wind of death is blowing in his face and he would like nothing better than to discover on the horizon the cabin of a wise man who will invite him in and listen to him and tell him what to do, although Seamus knew that there was nothing to do. It is sometimes a hard thing to be a man and stand by the thing that you have done. He would have liked someone to take him out of the wind, but no one is supreme enough to do it; so, faced with us through some accident, Seamus looked to us for distraction, and when he was through with us and other caravans came by he told his tale again, searching each man's face to see if he was the wise man that every man needs, but nobody was . . .

In one sense the "plain of phobias" is clearly an abstraction (we are shifting from one "plane" of reference to another), and yet the writer takes certain pains to develop it as a plausible physical location. The plain of phobias has many features in common with plains in the material world: wind, a wise man's cabin, caravans . . . Vollmann's most abstract images are interpenetrated with physical details in this way; inversely, his most vivid sensory descriptions are often interpenetrated with abstractions (as in the description of the New York City shoreline, above).

A simpler example:

> —How peculiarly steadfast that BioGuard hood must appear at night, with only that gas flame burning . . .

In almost every respect this sentence presents a straightforward sensory image—except that the whole description hinges on the unusual use of the word "steadfast," which is technically inappropriate since steadfastness is not a quality that can be possessed by a machine (is it?). With this one word the description doubles itself and becomes metaphorical, referring to a complex of associations about scientific dedication and perseverance. Vollmann makes frequent use of this device throughout the story.

Design

The structure of "Red Hands," like almost every other aspect of the story, is wholly controlled by the visible presence of the author/interviewer within the story. That presence breaks a general rule to the effect that writers of modern fiction are supposed to keep themselves out of their stories, that their manipulations of the text should be invisible, and that any appearance of the writer in the story constitutes a disruptive, distracting, "authorial intrusion." William Vollmann is not by any means the first contemporary writer to break this rule, but he has shattered it more thoroughly than anyone else (in this story and in most of the rest of his very extensive body of work*).

The author/interviewer is not an important character in the story in the sense of being an influence on what *happens*; as discussed above, he has no apparent effect on the events of either episode but merely stands by as an observer and reporter. The author/interviewer is supremely important to the reader because he is the conduit for everything that is told; everything is colored by his personality, his tone, his point of view, and often by his opinions. Most significantly of all, the voice of the author/interviewer constructs a bridge from the Seamus episode to the Oliver episode; without his presence there would be no connection between them.

The breakdown of the story into modular subsections has no repetitive formal pattern as it does in "Signs of Life" or "The Child Downstairs." There are certain rhythms in the arrangement of the text blocks (brief dialogues or monologues tend to alternate with longer, denser descriptions, for example), but one cannot detect a thoroughgoing system or completely regular pattern. This degree of disorder would not be tolerated by the reader if not for the tangible presence of the author/interviewer within the text. The story is held together, made coherent, in the mind of the author/interviewer, and the reader observes this process as it takes place. One might say that the arrangement of the text blocks is the result of the author/interviewer's whim—or that the arrangement reflects his way of thinking about the material he is presenting.

The two episodes are displayed asymmetrically in terms of their size: six sections are devoted to Seamus's episode, and only three to Oliver's. By the

---

* See, for example, his first collection of short fiction, *The Rainbow Stories*, or his second historical novel, *Fathers and Crows*.

same token, Seamus's story is "bigger" than Oliver's in almost every way: it takes longer to happen and its stakes are much higher (on the human scale, anyway). But the function of the author/interviewer's visible manipulations of the material is to eliminate these distinctions between the two episodes.

The manner in which the author/interviewer approaches his structural goal may not be altogether agreeable to the reader. The closely detailed and slow-moving description of the killing of the mouse is a nasty episode from which many readers would prefer to recoil— but the author/interviewer insists on holding your nose to it all the while. More subtlely, the reader's of experience of being forced to participate in the author/interviewer's way of thinking about the two episodes may not be very pleasant either, and in all probability it isn't supposed to be. The subject of the story is instrinsically disturbing, but the way the author/interviewer compells us to think about the subject is even more disturbing.

What the author/interviewer tries to demonstrate (the reader may or may not be entirely convinced by the demonstration) is that Seamus's act of killing unknowing innocent victims at random in a department store bombing and Oliver's act of killing a mouse as a sideline procedure in a lab experiment are intrinsically similar—if the difference in scale between them is eliminated or ignored. Thus both men are killers—"they both have red hands." (The title phrase is purely metaphorical, of course; Seamus is too remote from the scene to be stained with any actual blood, and the killing of the mouse is technically bloodless because of Oliver's choice of method.) Both killings are motivated by "structural reasons"—neither is an end in itself. Seamus has no personal vendetta against the anonymous department store shoppers; he murders them in service to a political principle. Oliver doesn't enjoy killing mice; he kills his mouse in service of a scientific principle. "Not being mice," we see a vast difference of degree between the two actions, but the author/interviewer does compellingly show that this perception is very much a matter of one's point of view—and that the comparison, once established, cuts both ways. As well as making Oliver's actions seem more severe, the comparison can make Seamus's actions seem less so, if they are regarded as strictly utilitarian means to some other end: "the revolutionary must destroy in order to establish his own order."

Some complicity with death, reasons the author/interviewer, is an inevitable consequence of the processes of life; what makes one person a "killer" and another not is a difference of degree, and perhaps of definition. This complicity cannot be avoided by anyone (not even strict vegans!) "because we must each one of us feed on death, whether we maliciously inhale to trap bacteria in the fatal caverns of our lungs, where they must die so that we come to no harm, or whether we wear leather shoes." The author/interviewer's apparently arbitrary arrangement of the events of the story makes us consider the idea that man-slaying and mouse-slaying and leather shoe–wearing all have this structural similarity among them. The differences we make among them (the author/interviewer proposes) are differences of scale, and how that scale is read depends upon where one stands in relation to it. We may not agree with this conclusion, but the design of the story forces us to think about it seriously.

NOTES

1. This parenthetical interjection establishes the presence of an author who's assuming the right to make certain intrusions.
2. This sentence marks a rapid shift from the concrete description of the first two sentences to abstractions, which are still, however, presented as an aspect of Seamus's *appearance.*
3. This portion of the sentence jacks up suspense very abruptly.
4. The expansion from the first clause of the sentence is dizzying. The image, meanwhile, is a highly evolved conceit. The metaphor, "plain of phobias," is a fusion of the abstract with the concrete, and both its abstract and concrete implications are expanded by the fact that it is a plain with a cabin on it.
5. The last clause of the sentence descends the height of the metaphor just scaled and fastens the text back to the character.
6. An overt statement of a conflict in the story. We don't feel that it's *too* obvious because we're distracted and bewildered by the complexities of the writing surrounding it.
7. Harking back to the metaphor previously established—this wind blows across the plain of phobias.
8. Use of this word suggests that Seamus's problem would require divine intervention to be solved.
9. Another allusion to the metaphor of the plain of phobias—the paragraph is constructing itself almost allegorically.
10. This first dialogue line drops us into the middle of a specific scene, and the burrito makes it firm and definite. We've come back to earth, so to speak.
11. First hint that Seamus's problem might be rooted in criminal or political activity. This *in medias res* approach heightens suspense because we don't know exactly what's under discussion.
12. This exchange establishes a sort of interview format, though so far the author/interviewer is noticeably noncommittal.
13. There's not a lot of detail on this scene—for instance, we have no idea at all of the setting—but the details about Seamus make him visible.
14. The passage is expository, part of the background of Seamus's character, but expository to what? We still don't know exactly what is the issue under discussion.
15. The pause here suggests that perhaps Seamus himself has some difficulty

connecting this background material to whatever action it is supposed to explain, "the thing that you have done" he somehow has to "stand by."

16. A bleak insight here.

17. Now the situation becomes clearer: Seamus must be some kind of IRA terrorist.

18. This episode is first in a chain of episodes of senseless suffering—suffering inflicted because of unreasonable prejudice—like Seamus's father being beaten to death.

19. These details, always focused on Seamus, keep us connected to the present scene, where Seamus is apparently being interviewed ... for reasons we don't yet know.

20. An interesting take on the troubles in Ireland, and whatever it may be worth as a generalization, it shows how Seamus's character developed ...

21. ... into angry determination.

22. His history of profoundly personal injury makes Seamus's involvement in the conflict all the more bitter and harsh.

23. Establishing the historical context.

24. Something added to the list of unfair injuries.

25. This time the descriptive detail might suggest a reaction to stress.

26. This over-the-shoulder detail is very arresting. The British appear as frightened children ... but with clubs.

27. The author chooses to paraphase this episode rather than relating it in Seamus's words—the idea is quite hideous enough, even with the additional filter factor.

28. The author/interviewer asks the straightest, most obvious, interview-style questions.

29. The attitude of defiance prepares us ...

30. ... for this: the first direct reference to the act which has underlain everything that Seamus has said so far.

31. The section break draws attention to the significance of the remark Seamus has made at the conclusion of section 1—otherwise the scene might just as well be continuous, as presumably it is in real time. Cf. similar section breaks in "The Sky Is Gray."

32. But Seamus backs off from a full description of his act and again becomes evasive.

33. Here's the only real gesture toward broadening the setting and background—and it still has an "off-camera" effect. The exclusion of background detail tightens our focus on Seamus.

34. This scene begins to take on the aspect of ritual, religious confession (Seamus is a Catholic after all) with the author/interviewer in the position of confessor. But Seamus has trouble completing his confession: "It is sometimes a hard thing to be a man and stand by the thing you have done."

35. The author/interviewer/confessor tries another tactic to draw out Seamus's confession with this apparently frivolous and ghoulish question . . .

36. . . . and Seamus's answer amounts to an expression of regret—forceful enough to conclude section 2.

37. So there is a God present in the story (at least for Seamus). We've been told earlier that "no one is supreme enough" to absolve him of his crime, but maybe that means "no other human being." This situation would explain Seamus's preference for the solitude described here, and the point is important enough to be framed in its own section.

38. Why should this statement merit a separate section? Perhaps because it's focused on a killing—a killing for a utilitarian purpose. We have earlier hints that Seamus prefers to isolate himself because of his crimes, but the end of this section shows that his isolation also has a utilitarian purpose—helping him avoid capture.

39. The extension of the image of time into the phrase "calibrate their hours" creates a sustained metaphor similar to the "plain of phobias" above.

40. The author inserts himself in the role of interviewer, reminding us of the limits of his knowledge.

41. In the middle of the sentence, the rather dry and distant, fact-focused reportage of events cuts to a microscopically detailed description of Seamus as he appears while being interviewed. Because the sentence fuses two different time frames as well as two different styles of description, it attracts considerable attention.

42. The next move is to reunite the level of vivid description of the present scene of the interview with the events which Seamus has recounted from his past. Placing himself in the foreground, the writer lets us know that what follows is his own imagining, and invites us to join him in the act of imagination.

43. The point that the following description is an invention of the author is reinforced once . . .

44. . . . and again.

45. Here the sentence, already quite long, draws a deep breath for a still longer run. The momentum produced by the length of the sentence helps carries us through the imaginative phases which permit the experience more drily related by Seamus to be described as if we and the author had in fact been present for it.

46. The geographical accuracy of this segment . . .

47. . . . is complemented by the metaphorical intensity of this one.

48. The word harks back to Seamus's pride in the exactitude of both his escape from prison and the department store bombing. Through the metaphor of the dominoes, a shadow of inevitability is cast over the whole description.

49. We've been in this sentence for a long time now. It sweeps the reader from a statement of the author's imaginative intention altogether into the result of that intention.

50. The unusual idea of light as a "burden" and the image of the cars as "glittering beads" combine to make this description distinctive.

51. At the end, the sentence veers from intensely detailed description toward a more abstract reference to the situation of the character, even to theme. This fusion of disparate elements is typical of Vollmann's style.

52. Now the writer reminds us once again of his presence, that he is imagining the scene.

53. The shift to the conditional tense emphasizes the act of imagination that powers the description . . .

54. . . . and with the return to the past definite here, the description asserts its power to say what was rather than what merely *might have been*. There's a curious doubling effect as the writer undercuts the authority of his description and then reasserts it all the more forcefully.

55. Another highly unusual comparison which really forces us to stop and pay attention to the landscape being described, which along with being striking to the senses is gaining some quite sinister implications.

56. As the image of the city develops, it seems hardly a hospitable place . . . more like some sort of surreal prison.

57. The almost mathematical abstraction of this image pulls us back for a moment toward the mind of the author.

58. Notice the shaping of the whole passage from the hugely long sentence at its inception ("And that is how I imagine . . .") through several shorter (though still quite long) sentences which allow the reader to recover— these sentences gradually become longer until we are flung into another hugely long sentence whose three-dot elliptical conclusion feeds into the brief emphatic downbeat of this declarative sentece, which makes a statement about action.

59. By contrast to what has preceded, this sentence looks acutely compressed. The sentences shorten and become much plainer as we shift from the ornate description of the shoreline to the account of Seamus's actions.

60. Two fusions in this sentence: a definite description merged with an authorial speculation, and a concrete image "black water and yellow lights" conflated with Seamus's "transitional moment of expectation and regret."

61. Again the writer separates himself and us from the character, reminding us that he's speculating about Seamus's subjective experience.

62. Three very simple and dry little sentences compared to what has come before—their brevity helps taper the whole of this long section toward conclusion.

63. This sentence is still brief, but rather more elaborately phrased—the

intensity of the writing is beginning to build again . . .

64. . . . but it tapers off once more with these short and simple concluding sentences. It's been a very long paragraph.

65. A rather direct thematic statement . . . on the part of the author. By maintaining his presence in the description, the writer licenses himself to make such statements, opening a window through which he can reach to manipulate the text before our eyes.

66. Like section 4, this section consists of nothing more than a few lines of direct dialogue from Seamus, and what he says here seems even less pertinent to the general drift of the story than the contents of section 4. It's a characterizing detail, and almost the last detail we'll hear about Seamus in the whole story. In terms of content it seems almost random, but it does express a couple of the essentials of Seamus's character as we've come to know it: anger and the willingness to act violently on that anger. Structurally, its brevity helps finalize a conclusion to the Seamus phase of the story (as the briefer sentences at the end of section 5 help taper that section to its conclusive point).

67. The use of an alias implies a connection between Oliver's episode and Seamus's.

68. Huh, what? We seem to have a radical change of subject here. But the neat modular divisions created by the numbered sections make it more convenient to introduce completely different content than it might be otherwise.

69. Without more context, this sentence is rather hard to understand. What sort of power is he talking about?

70. Impressed how? Intellectually? Emotionally?

71. How inconsiderate of her—has she no regard for science? The tone of Oliver's remarks evoke a "scientific" disregard for the subjective aspects of any experience whatsoever.

72. Overall the passage betrays a quite complicated attitude on Oliver's part. On the one hand he lays claim to a pure scientific detachment, but on the other he admits to being "queasy" and to being "sick of this mouse." The use of the coy euphemism for the mouse's impending euthanasia, "her big day," is ambiguous in the context so far created, but it may suggest a trace of sadism.

73. We recognize this tone: the clinically inquisitive voice of the author/interviewer. Notice how the central subject, the killing of the mouse, is skirted in much the same way as the bombing of the department store was skirted earlier.

74. Which factor is more important to the scientific mind?

75. The utilitarian motive is paramount.

76. The author/interviewer begins to echo Oliver's taste for elaborate scientific terminology—which in this case also serves as a euphemism.

77. A note on Vollmann's footnote: The concern for procedure identifies

Seamus with Oliver and gives us our first definite idea of what connects the two disparate episodes of the story. Seamus and Oliver may not seem very similar, but they do share this enthusiasm for technique. Notably, these lines of Seamus's are one of the most direct references to the department store bombing in the whole story.

78. ...whatever that means. The sense of scientific certainty about procedure is more important than the reader's full understanding of the procedures involved; the use of odd terms of measurement, "mole" and "aliquot," reinforce this point, along with a general atmosphere of the arcane.

   Note how the language begins to build again in this section—the brief and pointed first sentence feeding into this much longer one.

79. This extremely unusual simile is nonsensical as a *sensory* comparison but makes perfect sense at the abstract level.

80. This long, elaborately sustained simile uses the same tactics as the "plain of phobias" metaphor in section 1.

81. The idea of eating the mouse cells brings them from the sphere of scientific abstraction into the same physical space shared by writer and reader.

82. The similarity between the clauses compared here is not so self-evident as the syntax proclaims, but the writer is contending that the necessity of the mouse's death is as firm a given as any abstract scientific axiom.

83. Whatever that means ...

84. The switch from scientific mystification to the thought of killing might seem a non sequitur ...

85. ... but the connection is made here; these killings are executed for utilitarian reasons.

86. The mock-oratund presentation makes this thought almost comic. Although it's certainly true, this is something no one worries about (except of course, the Jain sect of India, whose members wear cloths over their faces so they will not murder insects by inhaling them).

87. The issue is one of scale. Wearing leather implies one level of complicity with death, killing a mouse implies another, killing human beings still another.

88. This is a quite usual way of looking at deaths that take place for the sake of science, but a somewhat unusual way of looking at deaths that take place for the sake of political causes. At any rate, the comparison of the Seamus episode and the Oliver episode seems be drawing tighter.

89. Again, this line seems a non sequitur at first, but what is probably meant is that Oliver doesn't expect to enjoy killing as an end in itself ... it is a means to some other end.

90. This slogan conveys a marvelous irony, since the atmosphere of the story is thoroughly corrupted by complicity with death.

91. The preceding passage concentrates most thoroughly on the details of the scientific procedure ...

92. ... then turns fanciful with this idealized image of unwavering dedication ... on the part of a piece of equipment, which makes it rather comic.
93. As if in consequence (indeed in consequence) of the scientific procedures enacted above.
94. This frivolity seems a little bizarre because of the sober scientific context, and certainly it also has an edge of sadism.
95. Of course not; the comparison is ridiculous ...
96. ... or is it? There's something awful about the image of the mouse pinned helplessly under the pencil. The difference is a difference of scale.
97. Is this line sadistic, or a masked expression of Oliver's squeamishness?
98. The use of the personal pronoun, "her" instead of "its," makes the mouse's death seem more poignant.
99. This paragraph contains the most direct descriptions of both the department store bombing and the death of the mouse, but the latter is given the more unflinching treatment; every detail is precisely recorded, and in much the same manner as the more neutral scientific procedures described above. After all, from the standpoint of the scientist, killing the mouse should not be qualitatively different from any other necessary procedure.
100. Again, the identity of the two propositions connected by "just as" is not exactly self-evident.
101. The moment of title justification: obviously the hands are red with blood.
102. That is, they acted to achieve some other end than the deaths their actions entailed.
103. It all depends on your point of view ...
104. Huh? Of course killing people is a crime. Isn't it? On the other hand, if the two actions are somehow equated, and killing the mouse is not considered a crime, then ... The comparison can cut both ways.
105. Whoever they may be. It may seem that the author/interviewer has set himself up as a judge (certainly he is in charge of the connection between the two episodes), but he implies here that he means to present them neutrally, as a mere reporter, not as a judge.
106. Of course this is itself a kind of judgment
107. Fair enough, no? After all, killing people is a much more serious affair than killing a mouse and so should affect the conscience of the killer much more gravely ... right?
    The concluding two sentences sound like a completely neutral presentation of data, but is there some judgment implied?

COMIC STRIP

G E O R G E   G A R R E T T

Mine heritage is unto me as a lion in the forest; it crieth out
against me; therefore have I hated it.

— JEREMIAH 12:8

1 THE WITNESS

Miss A. thought she saw a crime committed, but she couldn't be sure.[1] It happened when Miss A., who was a middle-aged trained nurse,[2] was returning
home from work in the early hours of the morning. She took the subway. The
only other people on the car were three men, two who were sitting together and
seemed to be arguing about something, and another at the other end of the car
who was reading a newspaper.[3] She didn't pay much attention to them. She
whiled away the time reading advertising placards.[4] Shortly before she got off
at 96th Street she noticed that one of the two men who had been talking
crossed over and approached the man who was reading a newspaper. He
seemed to be asking him a question.[5] The man lowered the newspaper until
just his eyes showed over the edge.[6] His eyes were dark and thoughtful, abruptly thoughtful and maybe perplexed and pained like the eyes of a man who has
been caught telling a lie or in a shameful act.[7] They were pitiable eyes, but
they did not ask for pity, she thought.[8] This may have been because all she

could see were his forehead and eyes.[9] She could not see the line of his lips, but she imagined that to fit the expression in his eyes they must be turned down and drawn in a tight line like the lips of a child not quite ready to take a dose of bad-tasting medicine.[10]

She was naturally shy of making direct encounters with strangers, especially men, and she stopped thinking about him and went back to looking at the advertisements.[11] The man who had spoken to the man with the newspaper walked back and sat down beside his companion, but he didn't say anything to him. The two men sat very still, and she saw out of the corner of her eyes that they were looking at the bright-colored placards too.[12] The other man was not reading the newspaper now, but he had slumped down in his seat with the newspaper lying across his face.[13]

When she started to get off at 96th Street, when she stood waiting at the sliding door and holding on tight to her pocketbook,[14] she knew that the man had put aside his newspaper and was looking at her.[15] She also knew without looking that the other two men were looking at him.[16] She decided to risk returning his glance,[17] and she saw that he was a round-faced, soft-jawed man with beautiful eyes like a girl's.[18] He looked at her, she thought, imploringly, with the desperate resignation of someone about to be wheeled away to an operating room.[19] He was asking for more than compassion, but he knew he would not get that much.[20] Just then the subway stopped and she stepped off quickly.[21] She didn't want to look back, but she thought she ought to.[22] She waited until she heard the door close and then she turned around to look.[23] The subway had begun to move, and in the noise it was like standing under a waterfall or within the center of a crashing wave.[24] She saw the man who had been reading the newspaper standing at the door, beating against it with his fists and with his face pressed out of shape against the glass. His face was wet with tears and his lips were moving though she could not hear him.[25] She saw as the subway flashed forward into the dark tunnel that the two men were standing beside him and looking at him.[26] She could not see their faces but she could tell by the tight rigidity of their bodies that they were about to do something sudden. They managed while they were standing straight to look as if they were crouched to jump.[27]

Afterwards she thought about it a good deal.[28] She began by reading all the newspapers carefully for several days to find out if anything terrible had happened. She found out about a number of other terrible things but there wasn't anything which could answer her special questioning. She wanted to talk to someone about it, just to tell them exactly what had happened as you would tell someone about a bad dream that you had. She hoped that if she told someone exactly and completely what she had seen, that then she would feel better, *lighter.* She felt heavy as if she were carrying around a large rock and she didn't know what to do with it.[29] Miss A. tried to tell several people. She didn't want to tell her good friends because she knew that none of those few shy people who were too much like herself[30] would really understand. She felt that she would only be adding her burden to their own.[31]

So she tried out the story on several people with whom she had managed to keep a cordial but impersonal acquaintance. She tried to tell it to the grocer and to the superintendent of the apartment house and she even tried to tell it to another nurse who was having coffee with her one night at the hospital. She couldn't make sense out of it as it was and she knew she couldn't expect anyone else to unless she told it exactly as it was and in the right order.[32] And she couldn't tell it that way because nobody had time to listen to all of it and in order to keep their interest she had to start at the end with the man crying and beating on the subway door and work backwards.[33] That part was interesting because you don't often see people doing it. But that was all they were interested in. They didn't want to know why and if they did she couldn't tell them.[34] She couldn't tell what happened afterwards either, so it didn't make much sense and it didn't seem very important.[35]

It was important to her though. She stopped riding the subway and started riding the bus so that she wouldn't be reminded of it.[36] She stopped trying to tell about it to anyone.[37]

As she thought more about it she decided that there was more to it.[38] Now that time had passed she could see it as if she had seen it all at one glance. She began to see herself as one of the actors and this led her to think she had had an active part in what happened.[39] Reviewing it, she wished to tell herself what was going to happen.[40] She began just at the point when she was about to step off the subway and meet the question in the man's eyes. She saw herself tightly holding on to her purse[41] and she saw herself refusing to be involved until after the door was closed and there was glass between her and the man's need, whatever it was.[42] She imagined many endings. At first she wanted violence. This seemed logical and was the most satisfactory because, no matter how guilty she might feel about not helping, violence put an end to it.[43] She felt relaxed imagining that the two men had participated in some unspeakable violent act against the other and she knew that if that was what happened there wasn't much she could have done anyway.[44] On the other hand she figured that maybe nothing like that had happened. And if nothing happened to stop the man from crying then it was left that way forever and she was stuck with the image of his face against the glass weeping and speaking words she could never hear.[45] Whatever happened the two men who saw the end of it were luckier than she was.[46]

Besides this, her thinking gave her a new sense of being more than the middle-aged trained nurse on the subway.[47] When she found that she could look at herself as if she were looking at another person and when she discovered that she didn't even have to have understanding or sympathy for herself,[48] she was astonished. It meant so many things at once. Most of all it meant loss.

She felt that she had been deprived of a personal possession.[49] And as Miss A. thought about it more and more she saw that she could even think about herself thinking about the scene. And she saw that even the second self, an almost pure eye, was not blameless.[50] She felt as if she had done something hectic and fierce like smashing a public mirror and now she saw herself in many ways as if her image were distributed among jagged fragments of glass.[51] She could not trust herself anymore.

Her life before had been tranquil, a calm which was intense because of her close knowledge of physical suffering. Now she could not view physical suffering in the direct uncomplicated way that her vocation required. She found that she began to feel a contempt for the suffering of other people. She did not communicate this contempt directly though. Instead she found that she increased in her efforts, began to pamper patients and be more concerned about their comfort. Their response was invariably to be grateful and when she saw this and saw that she could not make them know that she hated them for their frailty, her contempt increased. With it increased her reputation and success as a nurse and now she knew more about the world.[52] She saw that everyone lived fixed and sullen somewhere in a life like an invalid in a shabby room. She decided that everybody lived the life of a raging recluse while outside fantastic things were going on at great speed with unbelievable noise.[53]

Miss A. had stopped trying to tell people the truth.[54] Her talk was full of incidental and irrelevant slight things which made her a delight to listen to. She learned how to make a number of clever anecdotes out of nothing at all and because of this her patients were glad to have her around. She seemed to brighten everything.[55] She was pleased to think of this image of herself. It was a bitter pleasing thought to have, knowing all the time that she possessed a knowledge which could shame and confound them.[56] She felt as if she could see through people's clothes.[57]

Here she stopped, fixing her life as she had fixed her thinking. She committed herself to the day-to-day discipline of falsely rendered service while knowing, curiously, that her life was a wheel on which she was tied and tortured with herself the impersonal tormentor.[58] It was remarkable to think that as she sinned she was at the same time doing penance. The world flooded away and she was glad of it. By losing everything she found herself in control of everything again,[59] and as soon as she was sure, she could reconstruct things to suit herself.[60] Time and again she saw herself going on beyond her destination and while the other two men held down the struggling weeping man, in the midst of all that roar of forward moving she felt an exhilaration, a new and tugging lightness like a gas balloon on a string.[61] She saw herself wielding a knife she had not owned before.[62]

2 THE ACCURSED HUNTSMAN [63]

Professor B. engaged in some novel research and it changed his way of living.[64] As a fairly young man in the profession he had a good reputation as a scholar and a teacher of history. If you'd asked any of his colleagues at the university what they thought of him, they would have replied that he had a fine mind. They would be implying that he taught history like a good policeman. He could shoulder his way in a crowd of unruly details. He could restore order to the facts and give significant testimony.[65] He wrote a number of articles for learned journals and once he wrote a book which was well thought of by his fellow teachers. If you'd asked his students what they thought of him, they would have answered that he was a very good teacher. They would be paying due praise without having to say that they liked him.[66]

As a matter of fact, his colleagues and his students neither liked nor disliked him. They just didn't know him. He was pleased with himself and what he was doing, but he didn't feel a need to share this satisfaction. He didn't even need to share the moderate joy of his work with his wife. She never asked him about what he was doing and he never thought of telling her. He was all for keeping each thing in its proper place, and he was satisfied to have his work in one place and his marriage in another.[67] His wife was happy with this arrangement, too, except for the rare times when it occurred to her that perhaps he thought of his marriage as secondary to his career, like a coaling station or a dry dock.[68] (He had once vaguely compared for her the life of the mind to a sea voyage.) They didn't have any children.[69]

So, Professor B. was sure of himself and secure in the world. When he realized this he was pleased that he had been honest enough to recognize the truth.[70] His next step was to bring this idea outside of his mind and to try to make something out of it. He became fascinated with his family tree. He'd never cared much about his background before. Now he thought it would be a pleasure to find out about his ancestors.[71] Certainly he was equipped and well-trained to do this kind of work. He trusted in a rational power of divination that would tell him when imposing facts were misleading and when a shabby, nondescript piece of information might be desperately important.[72] He also had a certain gusto like a private detective.[73] He was so enthusiastic that he told his colleagues about it, and it became a joke among them. A young instructor suggested that Professor B. might be able to prove he was legitimate.[74] An older professor said that Professor B. ought to be careful about digging up graves—he might end up digging his own. Whether or not he guessed what people were saying about him, Professor B. was undaunted. He went so far as to confide in his wife about his plans. He told her that every civilized man ought to know something about his ancestors, and she agreed with him.

It took time. After the first enthusiasm had gone, he remained interested but he found a place for it in the normal scheme of his life. It became a hobby. He even reached the stage of apologizing for this hobby to his still-amused colleagues, but this was rightly understood as a kind of eccentric pride concealed in modesty. He was surprised that so much information could be turned up. After a while he had a whole filing case full of old letters, photostats and copies of documents, a few pictures and a few books with marginalia, and even a rather dreary diary. He discovered good evidence that a respectable married lady of his line had carried on a brief affair with a local blacksmith after the Civil War, but, even though there were cautious allusions to the affair as recently as the letters of his late maiden aunt, he was convinced that it had never amounted to much. He found a man who had been decorated for an extraordinarily brave act at the second battle of Bull Run, but he discovered that the moment of glory hadn't been enough to raise the man's life above a level of solid mediocrity.[75] Even so he studied what he could find and got a lot of pleasure from carefully re-creating the lives of otherwise forgotten people. It was like participating in an imaginary masquerade ball, and it helped him with his work. His students thought his lectures were better. His colleagues remarked that his recent articles showed signs of increasing subtlety. This was partly praise and partly a reserved suggestion that Professor B. might be getting a little confused.[76]

He was unperturbed. He noticed how his hobby was helping him in his work and he started to think of it as a sort of private discipline. He told his wife that it was like taking intellectual calisthenics.[77] He was inwardly zestful when he was able to track a reluctant ancestor down to the last available fact and then with logic and a little imagination to remake the person from the facts. He could watch the dead file by, naked and mediocre, with the disinterested feelings of the warden of a prison.[78] He thought there was a pleasing sadness about the truth. Faced with all these obscure people, he began to think that the world was universally tinted with a drab pathos, but it was strangely exciting to know this. He had felt secure before. Now he was beginning to feel free.[79]

Then he uncovered C., and right away he knew he was challenged. The first mention of C. was in a letter written by a distant forbear, an early nineteenth century clerk. It seemed that the clerk was happily resigned to his way of life—the family trait[80]—and was telling in a mock heroic discourse about the joys of making a virtue of necessity. Midway in the pleasant letter the clerk seemed to turn around and cringe before an assailant.[81]

> I fancy that I am not the last, as I am surely not the first, of a long and dreary line of comfortable men, blessed with only moderate talents and harassed by no more than ordinary follies, stunted it may be, yet curiously happy dwarfs. Still there is C., my maternal grandfather, for whom I confess I harbor little love and no little malice. What an intolerable burden it is to labor under the towering shadow of a dead man's example![82]

The letter at once resumed its amiable pace and without any further mention of C. Professor B. was disturbed. He was quick to guess that the key to, and maybe the cause of, the letter was in that passage.[83] Against the level background of sober words, those sentences stood out of place like a rake, a ne'er-do-well uncle in a procession of family mourners.[84] B. responded by copying down the words on an index card, and he got himself ready for the long slow search for C. His feelings worked against him. Signals warned him to be suspicious. He felt a sense of undirected threat from C. and he felt embarrassed at the frankness of the clerk. If the truth is really humiliating, he thought, then you ought to deny it again and again until you can begin to believe in the denial.[85] Thus embarrassment changed into contempt.[86]

The search for C. began idly enough but before long it was a quest. It turned out that C. had been a New England sea captain who commanded and owned a small merchantman. He sailed between Europe and the New World carrying goods and a few passengers and he became quite rich. Then, while he was still in his prime, he sold his ship and gave up the sea for the land. He was active in social and civic life and he seemed to have been a deeply religious man. After his death, prominent clergymen cited him as an almost saintly example. He had a reputation for being a wise and virtuous man. The handful of his letters that Professor B. managed to uncover showed that he was a sober man with a good mind, but they were unmarked by any wit or strong emotion.[87] He began to conceive of C. as a kind of geometric figure, bloodless but well-made. Still, he was fascinated by C. There was his reputation which grew larger as Professor B. traced the network of it. C. began to appear as a positive instrument of good. Just how this came about and how it could be explained was more than he understood. Finally, there was something very strange, he felt, about the *exact* sobriety of the man. It looked more like choice than accident and this might explain the indignation of the clerk, his grandson.

Professor B. couldn't explain how his own indignation came to be.[88] He began to dislike and distrust C. He disliked him because of his reputation. He disliked him because of the careless freedom by which the sea captain had been able to give up one way of life completely for another.[89] And out of dislike grew distrust. He decided that once and for all C. must be unmasked. He went at it methodically, but all he could find only added to the man's dull glow of virtue. He was irked to find that all he could do to the man was to restore some of his original energy. It began to take more and more of Professor B.'s time. In fact he spent a year's leave of absence from the university doing nothing else but chasing the elusive ghost. He became secretive. What had been a hobby, then a discipline, became almost a passion.[90] Professor B. felt like a blindfolded chess master who is playing a group of amateurs and who gradually discovers that one of his invisible opponents has, by a series of quite ordinary moves, laid a clever trap for him.[91]

It was desperately exciting to match wits with C. Somewhere, he was sure,

C. could be apprehended and exposed to shame. Professor B. learned to control his own shame by concentrating on the *method* of his investigation. He wasn't sure what he was looking for, but he had the idea that one small common folly or one persistent mediocre vice would cut C. down to the size of his descendants.[92] So, he worked on, writing letters, digging up obscure details, poring over the facts as he could find them. His enemy had time on his side, years in which to hide himself, while Professor B. had to struggle to find time to continue the investigation. He was bitter about C.'s advantage of time and his wealth. Only a rich man could be so successfully obscure.

Bitterness led him toward the answer. He saw that he had failed to recognize a simple pattern. How did C. really get his money? Why did he quit the sea? Professor B.'s intuitive response was to guess that the two things were related. C. must have quit the sea not because he had money enough to retire but because of something connected with the way he got the money. C.'s life ashore might be thought of as an atonement for something. Well then, now he knew what to look for.[93] He knew also that it would take almost all of his resources and energy to locate C.'s shame, and he was afraid that C.'s shame might be already assigned to a decent oblivion. Given only the slightest hints, though, he knew he could find it, and he was never as ready to do it as now. His mind had become as sensitive to subtle changes as a barometer.

He didn't find exactly what he wanted but he found more than he was looking for. Piece by piece he constructed a story. C. hadn't always been content to ply the course between Europe and the colonies. Once, twice, several times he had with great care managed a secret voyage to the African coast, a sortie for slaves, and a trip to the West Indies with his cargo. C. had shown amazing ruthlessness and a really marvelous sense of historical deception.[94] There was a curious pattern of desperation about these trips. At that time the slave trade was legal and not even morally condemned. What was important was that C. had acted to conceal what he was doing. You saw that he knew he was doing something terribly, unpardonably wrong and he acted like a man intent on his own personal damnation.[95] He had purged himself just as deliberately. The last voyage was incomplete. Halfway across C. must have given up for good and given up the sea as well. Professor B. saw what the man had done. He had decided to commit himself for all time with a final act. Almost arbitrarily he had decided against selling another cargo of slaves. The solution, then, was to dump them all overboard and immediately to turn his face toward the land not even looking back on all that thrashing agony in the waves behind him.[96]

If the truth was simple, the answer was complex; for C. was unperturbed by the truth. Nothing could add to his knowledge or to his despair. He seemed to grin across foolish years at Professor B., and the professor turned away, disgusted and ashamed of himself, feeling that he had been unmasked by the dead man.[97] He felt a new confinement. He felt that all his life he'd been in chains.

He taught history with a sense of awful resignation.[98] The study of history is a nasty occupation, he told his students, and they laughed and liked him.[99] You never even know about innocence until you've lost it, he told his colleagues. They wondered what had happened to him.[100] "I feel like a child who spies on his parents making love, ashamed of them and guilty because he shouldn't be looking," he told his wife.[101] She listened bitterly because she didn't have a child.[102]

3 HOW THE LAST WAR ENDED [103]

Captain G.,[104] U.S. Army, lay face down in a ditch by the road, the stagnant water, strangely warm for such a bitter day, soaking through his fatigues.[105] It crawled along his stomach and bathed his loins. His head, hidden from the sky by the dark bowl of his helmet, was just above the water, his lips close enough to kiss the disturbed scum. He lay there while the noise was above and elsewhere, not in the least afraid, feeling almost sleepy.[106] He was thinking of himself as a bullfrog sprawled in the mud at the edge of a hyacinth-choked lake, but this dissolved and he began to have an erotic daydream. It seemed to involve a colossal blonde, dressed only in silk stockings, broad-assed, huge breasted, before whom he was sprawled in a ditch in some kind of penance or initiation.[107] It was absurd, the things that came into his mind while the war was going on around him.[108] It was absurd, too, for the war to *be* going on. They had signed the armistice yesterday and it was all over, on paper at least.[109]

He was neither astonished nor afraid when he raised his head in the silence and saw the mud-gorged boots at the edge of the ditch, the pants ripped at the knees, the heavy belt, the downslant of the bayonetted rifle at the hips, and, gradually the whole shape of the enemy soldier like an isosceles triangle converging on a small troubled face, dirt-stained, half-bearded under the flat shadow of the steel helmet.[110] It was like being a little child again and looking up at the angular and inscrutable shape of the adult world. He laughed out loud and splashed water with his feet and hands.[111]

"I'm taking a bath," Captain G. said in the soldier's language.[112]

The soldier looked at him and laughed. The rifle drooped.

"I'm taking a bath," he repeated.

"You look like a sow in the sty," the soldier said. "Come on out. You're dirtying your uniform."

"Come on," the soldier said, good-naturedly enough, "come out of the water."[113]

The Captain got up slowly and climbed out of the ditch. He stood beside the soldier and without speaking they both looked at the road. The great truck[114] had turned over on its side, the front wheel still spinning like a roulette wheel running down.[115] The Captain's driver was a limp shape on the road beneath the shadow of the turning wheel. He'd been trying to load his carbine but the clip had dropped when he was hit and some of the penny-colored shells had rolled on the road.[116] The other two bodies were behind the truck, one in a dark splash of blood, rolled sideways as if asleep, clutching his rifle to him like a toy.[117] The other one was spreadeagled alongside the far ditch. He had no weapon and his helmet had come loose and fallen on the road. He had been keeping toilet paper in his helmet so it would stay dry and now it was festooned extravagantly on the road.[118] It looked as if an ocean breaker had crashed over them, scattering them in its flashing roll, and dashing them up drowned.[119] All around the cropless fields were bare and the sky was pale and smudged like a dirty sheet.[120]

"It is curious how awkwardly they died," Captain G. said.

The soldier grunted and then without paying any attention to the Captain he sauntered across the road to the body of the spreadeagled soldier. He had seen the glint of a wristwatch. The Captain squatted by the road and policed up the carbine shells and put them in his pocket.[121] Then he looked carefully at the fields. Three-quarters of a mile away maybe was the farm house, a poor dung-colored block of stone with a couple of wind-picked, stunted trees nearby and behind that the gray haze of woods. He saw a crow, laborious, ungainly, leathery, fly out of the woods and light on a limb of one of the trees near the farm house. He was very concerned about that. He decided to ask the soldier if he would mind shooting the crow and he turned to look for him.[122] He was coming back across the road, grinning, looking sheepish.

"Broken," the soldier exclaimed.

"It's no wonder," Captain G. said, looking sympathetically at the shattered watch.[123]

They walked over the muddy field to the farm house, taking their time, smoking. The soldier had slung his rifle on his shoulder and tipped back his helmet jauntily. He kept talking about how good the Captain's cigarette tasted to him. When they got up close Captain G. could see the machine gun, but nobody was around it. It sat in a little hole, idle and captivating on its slim tripod, surrounded by a wealth of spent cartridges. Suddenly another soldier came around the side of the house eating something out of a can with his fingers while he walked. He walked right by them without paying them any attention.[124] The first soldier pushed the door of the house open and Captain G. walked in behind him.

"Sir," he said, "here is one of them." He walked out the door again.

Getting used to the dark room, Captain G. saw a man lying on the floor, blanketed, rubbing his eyes. The man leaned on his elbows with the blanket still wrapped around his legs and looked at Captain G.[125]

"You're all wet," the officer said. "How did you get so wet?"

Captain G. remembered abruptly that he was still wearing his pistol.[126]

He pulled it out of his holster and offered it, grip first, to the officer.[127]

"I suppose you'll have to take this."[128]

The officer stood up slowly and stretched. He didn't have his pants or shoes on.

"I see you're not wearing the regulation socks," Captain G. observed.[129]

The officer fumbled in a corner of the room until he found a candle and lit it so he could look at the pistol.

"An inferior weapon," he said. "Definitely an inferior weapon."[130]

He seemed to be very cold. His thin legs were goose-pimpled and his hands were shaking. He threw the pistol across the room. It landed on the edge of a table and fell off on the floor. It could easily have gone off. Quite suddenly Captain G. was angry.[131]

"This is fantastic," he yelled. "The war is over. Don't you understand? They stopped it last night."

"Really?"

"Of course. Why would I lie to you? You should be *my* prisoner. You are all my prisoners."[132]

The officer shrugged and went back to the corner where he began to fumble on his hands and knees for something else. The Captain went to the door. It had started to rain. Three or four of the soldiers were sitting in the mud near the machine gun playing cards.

"Put up those cards," Captain G. shouted. "Put them away. You're supposed to be on duty."[133]

They looked up blankly, stared at him for a moment, and resumed their game without a word. Angry, the Captain strode towards them, but when he saw the soldier who had captured him, he took off his wrist watch and gave it to him.

"It's all right," he said. "You can have mine."[134]

When he got back inside the farm house, he found the officer squatting on the floor trying to get the cork out of a wine bottle with a bayonet. Captain G. stood over him watching with some concern until the officer gave up and just pushed the cork down into the bottle.

"One never has time enough for all the amenities," the officer explained.

"It's quite all right," Captain G. said. "I am not a connoisseur."[135]

They sat down on the cold stone floor facing each other and passed the bottle back and forth politely while they talked.[136]

"I know what it's like to be defeated," Captain G. said. "I am a Southerner."

"So?"

"I would like to tell you a story about wine, if you don't mind."

"Please," the officer said, "by all means, go ahead."

"In Georgia, you see, my great-grandfather was a very important man. He had a large house, many acres and several hundred slaves. But you mustn't think he was provincial. On the contrary, even though he was living way out in the country, he was a cultured, I might even say cosmopolitan man. He could read books in Greek and Latin and he played the violin."[137]

"Is that so?"

"Please, I'm getting to the point of the story."

"Excuse me. Go ahead."

"I'm trying to tell you about the defeat and the part about the wine."

"Go ahead, please."

"Among his other accomplishments, my great-grandfather was a connoisseur. He had a wonderful wine cellar and they bought wine from all over Europe for it. Now, it happened that he was away during the war and his wife was alone with the children and the slaves."

"Naturally," the officer said, nodding.

"And, you see, Sherman's Army came through that part of Georgia. They were terrible. They lived off the land and the truth is that wherever they went they burnt and raped and looted. Well, they hadn't arrived yet at my great-grandfather's house. And one day my great-grandmother was in her room knitting socks for my great-grandfather[138] when Lewis, that was the house servant's name, came in the room.

"'Ma'm,' he said, 'I hear there's a troop of cavalry in the neighborhood.'

"'Whose cavalry, Lewis?'

"That was just like my great-grandmother. She knew very well that there wasn't a troop of Confederate cavalry any nearer than Atlanta, but she wouldn't be made to appear irrational even in defeat."

"A remarkable woman," the officer said.

"Lewis didn't even sigh or appear exasperated. 'Shermer's cavalry, ma'm,' he said. He had form, too.[139] He wouldn't even pronounce the name right. 'In that case,' she said, 'we ought to do something. What shall we do?' 'I'm in favor of destroying the stock of wine before they get their hands on it.' 'I think you are quite right,' she said. 'It wouldn't do to have a troop of drunken soldiers in the yard.'

"So now I ask you to imagine it.[140] Late afternoon, the light and heat only just beginning to fade. The lady sitting upstairs in her quiet room. Outside they are busy. The slaves bringing up out of the dark, cool cellar all those wonderful bottles and barrels while other slaves are digging a shallow trench.[141] When the digging is finished Lewis gives the order and one after another the bottles are broken and the barrels staved in. The wine flows in the ditch. Every last bottle cracked into the trench, the red and the white mixing together indiscriminately, almost golden in the light, I imagine, a shining river of wine.

"Then, suddenly, into the yard, kicking up dust, scattering the lazy chickens in a blizzard of feathers and squawks, the cavalry troop arrives. They're wild men, dusty, bearded, thirsty. In a moment they've leapt off their horses and, lying flat on their bellies like pigs in the mud, they are lapping the wine with their tongues, cupping it with their hands, splashing it on each other and all the while laughing outrageously, deliriously!"[142]

The Captain finished and they sat for a moment in the quiet room hearing only the faint whiskbroom sound of the rain on the roof.

"What a pity," the officer finally said. "What a terrible story."[143]

He got his blanket and wrapped it around his legs. The night was coming and it was getting cold.

"You and I know about these things," the officer said, "the utter absurdity of defeat."[144]

"And the triumph," the Captain exclaimed. "Don't you see the triumph, the splendid indifference. There is the marvelous shrug of the surviving."[145]

"No," the officer said emphatically, "only the perversity of the defeated."[146]

He rolled over and wrapped the blanket more tightly around him. He groped for something to use as a pillow.

"Use my helmet," Captain G. offered.

"So what does it mean?" the officer said.

"Nothing. It doesn't mean anything," Captain G. said. "Does it have to mean something?"[147]

The officer smiled, closed his eyes gently and dozed. Captain G. again felt anger coming on him. He stood up and walked up and down the room briskly.

"There was a crow," he said. "There was a crow that lighted in one of your trees. I would like you to have that crow shot."

There was no answer, not the least stir of life.

"I insist that you have that crow destroyed," the Captain shouted. "I order you to do it!"[148]

But by this time the officer was already sound asleep and there was no one to notice Captain G. whether he wept or not.[149]

ANALYSIS

Plot

Backstory

As is often the case in stories with a modular design, the issue of backstory is more or less unimportant here. The order of presentation of the three episodes certainly counts for something, but their chronological order seems not to matter, and can't really be determined anyway, for each episode is given a sufficiently abstract treatment that it cannot be definitely placed in any particular period.

Within the episodes there is no anterior action either. Each episode begins at the beginning and moves straight ahead without any flashbacks or recapitulation of events in the past. The first two episodes are recounted entirely in summary form, while the third, although fully dramatized, creates a similar effect of open, straightforward simplicity—in terms of its presentation, if not its implications.

Present Action

The plot of each of the three episodes has an almost skeletal simplicity. The plots of the first two are almost entirely summed up by the opening line of each:

1. "Miss A. thought she saw a crime committed, but she couldn't be sure." What follows in the first episode expands on the opening sentence by tracking the progress of her reactions to the ambiguity of what she saw (from guilt to contempt to cynicism to a strange sense of identification with the attackers in the end), and by describing the effects of those reactions on her life among other people.

2. "Professor B. engaged in some novel research and it changed his way of living." What follows in the second episode merely adds detail to this opening statement, relating how the professor's discovery of someone in his past who has committed and concealed a truly monstrous act changes both his perception of himself and also the way in which others perceive him.

In the third episode, the opening sentence immediately declares a style and approach quite different from that of the first two:

3. "Captain G., U.S. Army, lay face down in a ditch by the road, the stagnant water, strangely warm for such a bitter day, soaking through his fatigues." Instead of laying out the subject to be covered in the abstract, this sentence simply introduces the main character and places him, quite viscerally, within a realistic scene . . . which is, of course, the task that a realistic short story is normally expected to accomplish as quickly and efficiently as possible.

The opening sentences of episodes 1 and 2 would probably be severely criticized in the average fiction workshop for being too dry, too abstract, too much like topic sentences in academic papers. By laying out the subject so completely, these sentences eliminate much of the reader's curiosity about what is going to happen (although replacing it, as we've seen before, with an interest in *how* it will happen). And the first two episodes then proceed much as their opening sentences would predict. In both there is a drastic imbalance of summary and scene. In the first episode, only the action on the subway is fully dramatized; in the second, there are no full scenes at all. Both episodes could be criticized for being underdramatized, oversummarized, and overanalytical. Some fundamental rules of fiction writing seem to have been broken here—neither of the first two episodes gives the reader much of the sensory texture of real life that one expects from a realistic short story.

By contrast, the third episode creates that texture immediately and sustains it throughout. The third episode is fully dramatized and therefore seems plottier than the other two. The action itself is much more dramatic: a U.S. Army officer is captured on the battlefield and taken into the custody of an enemy officer. Although the key scene between them consists of a conversation rather than action, the anecdote which the captain tells is also a highly dramatic war story.

Why such an extreme difference between the plotting of the first two episodes and the third? A possible answer is that in summarizing the third episode, one would speak about specific actions, but in summarizing the first two one must speak almost entirely about mental events. What Miss A. witnesses to begin with is an action, and yet it is incomplete, with its outcome unknown; thereafter the plot of the first episode consists entirely of inner events—the sequence of Miss A.'s reactions to what she has seen. In the second episode, all the key events are mental—even the professor's research into his family history (the "accursed hunt") is an intellectual pursuit. In the third episode the plot contains more action and so is given a more active rendition. In this sense we can say that each episode is given a treatment appropriate to the subject matter. Why such stylistically different episodes should be assembled together in this way is a question that remains to be answered—an issue of design.

Character

In this category as well, some quite obvious differences are noticeable between the first two episodes and the third. We get to know the protagonists of episode 1 and episode 2 less through observing them in action than through a series of direct statements about what they think and what they feel. Miss A.'s reaction to the scene she witnessed evolves from sympathetically horrified identification with the victim across a spectrum of intermediate phases to, at the very end, an enthusiastically sadistic identification with the attackers. Professor B. begins with a clinically academic interest in his own genealogy which gradually becomes a competitive interest: he is determined to prove that none of his forebears could possibly have surpassed him, but this ambition is defeated when he learns the truth about C. In response he becomes cynical (somewhat like Miss A.), full of "awful resignation" and a sense of his lost innocence. For both Professor B. and Miss A. these changes in character constitute the narrative— for not much else is going on in their respective episodes.

The case of Captain G. is very different: we learn about him almost entirely through his speech and actions, and in very sharp contrast to the other two episodes there is next to no direct discussion of his thoughts and feelings, his interior state. This exclusion, quite conventional for modern fiction, is sometimes perplexing—we aren't told why the Captain is so upset by the thought of the crow, but somehow have to deduce the answer for ourselves. Certain conclusions can be drawn about the Captain on the basis of his behavior. He is often concerned, in the midst of the confusion and bewilderment of the war's end, with maintaining whatever order he can: picking up those shell casings, commanding enemy soldiers to comport themselves more properly, demanding the shooting of the crow. (This orderliness is also found in Professor B., the "good policeman" of history.) But there is also a chaotic side to the Captain's personality, expressed by his nutty fantasy about the blonde and by his foolish paddling in the ditch ("I'm taking a bath") at the moment of his capture. Throughout the story these factors of the captain's character seem to be in an uneasy balance, like the uneasy balance between decorum and anarchy maintained in the story he tells about the Civil War.

In the first two episodes the reactions of others to the main characters are deployed in an ironic way. As Miss A.'s contempt for human suffering increases, she compensates by *behaving* even more compassionately with the patients she nurses, and this pretense is rewarded by even greater success in her profession. Before she became cynical she was shy and withdrawn and had few friends, but once she stops "trying to tell people the truth," she becomes socially successful and others think her charming. There is a strange dislocation between her inner life and her outer life; people around her believe that she is warm and witty and sympathetic while she secretly pictures herself "wielding a knife she had not owned before."

Outside reactions are given a slightly more detailed treatment in the second episode. The reservations of his students and colleagues described in the first chapter let us know right away that Professor B. must be a somewhat wearisome pedant; he is grudgingly respected but will never be popular. Yet in the end, after his thorough disillusionment, popularity does come: his students "laughed and liked him." Throughout the story there's an inverse relationship between others' opinion of the professor and what's really going on in his private life; at the end, when his sense of self has been completely overthrown, his students and colleagues see him as much more engaging and admirable than ever before. Only his wife (who previously parrotted all his opinions) seems to see through him at the end; her embitterment about their childlessness penetrates to the sterility which seems to have always been at the heart of his character.

Our sense of outsiders' reactions to the protagonist is much less important in the third episode. There is some divergence of interpretation of the Civil War anecdote between the captain and the enemy officer, but this seems much less significant than the perfect inversion of inner and outer lives that occurs for Miss A. and Professor B. Of course we have heard almost nothing about the Captain's inner life. Everything in the personalities of the other two characters is thoroughly dissected before our eyes, but the Captain's psyche remains so mysterious that in the last line we don't know for certain "whether he wept or not," and—pointedly—no one else in the episode is watching to see if he does either. But perhaps this final image of isolation is not so different from what has happened to Miss A. and Professor B. at the ends of their respective episodes.

Professor B. and Miss A. are given almost bodiless presentations; we experience them first and last as *minds*. Despite the very detailed description of their psychological processes, their characterizations feel abstract and rather impersonal (which itself makes for a curious contrast effect). Captain G., on the other hand, is much more strongly introduced as a physical presence, and because we follow the experience of his senses from moment to moment, we may feel more intimate with him than with the other two, despite the fact that we have much *less* access to the workings of his mind. Yet he does share (in his namelessness, for instance) a certain anonymity with the other two—an averageness. All three characters have been deliberately depersonalized to some degree, as if to suggest that anyone might react as they do if faced with the same exact circumstances.

Tone

Certainly there is a substantial shift of tone between the first two episodes and the third. In the first two episodes the effect is of listening rather than watching; we seem to be hearing a story rather than seeing a movie or a theater play (because almost everything is summarized). But the voice telling us the story doesn't have the warm conviviality of the voice telling "A Wife of Nashville" or the intrusive quirkiness of the narrative voice in "Red Hands." In "Comic Strip" the voice is intentionally toneless, clinical, icy, and almost perfectly transparent—a self-effacing voice which definitely does not want to make us aware of itself. (The quote from the clerk's letter in episode 2, which has a distinctly personal tone, makes a striking contrast to the impersonal tonelessness of the text surrounding it.) This general tonelessness of the first two episodes much enhances the overall effect of abstraction.

This situation reverses itself in episode 3, when we seem to watch the story unfold rather than hearing about it. The level of detail is much higher, we experience the action from moment to moment, and there is no sense of an intermediary presence filtering events on their way to us. Because we experience everything alongside the captain, this episode feels rather more personal than the other two, and yet at the same time the tone does remain neutral and cool, giving us a clear, untinted window on what the captain undergoes. In the third episode, tone is used as a tool to realize clear, almost photographic images of what the captain sees. That the tone of the third episode retains at least some of the impersonal quality of the tone of the first two is revealed by the contrast with the tone of the anecdote the Captain tells about the Civil War, which is much more personal and passionate.

Point of View

Where's the camera? In the first two episodes, it's clearly up above in the realm of perfect omniscience. The narrative voice has lifted off the tops of Professor B.'s and Miss A.'s heads like a pair of pot lids and allowed us a thorough, comprehensive view of the processes which have taken place inside. There is a curious paradox to the manipulation of point of view in these episodes: we know the inner lives of these characters very thoroughly, but hardly in an intimate way, because we learn what we learn from a distanced perspective, as if we were seated high up in some operating theater, observing the dissection of their psyches.

In episode 3, the point of view sits as it were on the Captain's shoulder, but only occasionally peeps all the way inside his head. The reader experiences everything through the Captain's senses, but has access to his inner reactions much less frequently (and usually in matters of relatively minor importance). The point of view is almost imperceptibly in motion, then; it never shifts entirely from one character to another, but it does change its position slightly in relation to the captain. In the closing sentence, significantly, the point of view moves entirely away from the captain for a moment, long enough to take one good look at him from the outside.

Dialogue

Dialogue is a nonissue in the first two episodes because there isn't any. But the third episode, much more thoroughly dramatized than the other two in every way, has plenty of conversation, all of which is colored by the fact that it presumably takes place in some foreign language; since we are told that the Captain first addresses his captor in his own language we assume that he continues to speak this language, whatever it is, in his subsequent conversations with the enemy soldiers and their officer. Because of this circumstance, the writer is prohibited from using any especially American idioms or figures of speech. Because of this restriction, much of the dialogue seems more formal, perhaps even more abstract, than it otherwise would: for example, the Captain's statement about his slain comrades, "It is curious how awkwardly they died," has a ring of abstract formality about it. This slight feeling of abstraction gives it something in common with the tone of the other two episodes.

Much of the dialogue seems almost nonsensical, especially considering the context. Consider this exchange when the contextual details are stripped away from it:

> "I'm taking a bath," Captain G. said. . . . "I'm taking a bath," he repeated.
> "You look like a sow in the sty," the soldier said. "Come on out.

You're dirtying your uniform. Come on," the soldier said, good-naturedly enough, "come out of the water."

This is not the sort of conversation that you'd expect to take place between
one soldier being taken prisoner by another. It more resembles a willful child
being patiently persuaded by an adult (as a preceding line of description also
suggests), or a madman being persuaded by an attendant of the madhouse. The
friction of the conversation's tone with the much more grim and serious context in which it takes place creates a sense of disorientation (which the Captain
himself might well be experiencing).

The following exchange sounds downright goofy considering the context
where it takes place:

> "Broken," the soldier exclaimed.
> "It's no wonder," Captain G. said, looking sympathetically at the
> shattered watch.

When we recall that the enemy soldier has just looted the watch from one of
the Captain's slain companions, his sympathetic reply seems weirdly inappropriate — a real non sequitur.

This slightly loony disconnectedness persists in the conversation between
Captain G. and the enemy officer.

> "I see you're not wearing the regulation socks," Captain G.
> observed. . . .
> "An inferior weapon," [the officer] said. "Definitely an inferior
> weapon."

In this exchange the two officers are talking past each other in an almost comical way, and that effect persists later on during the Captain's Civil War anecdote, for although the two seem to be talking about the same thing in this
instance, their reactions are so different that it's clear that they don't perceive it
in at all the same way. Finally, the most striking apparent non sequitur of all is
the captain's demand that the crow be shot — although this line also drives
home the point of the whole third episode.

Time Management

Here's yet another department in which the third episode differs drastically
from the first two. The third episode is told strictly in real time; there is no summarizing whatsoever and next to no recapitulation of past events. Even the
ambush, which must have occurred seconds before the story begins with the
Captain in the ditch, is not described through retroactive summary, but rather

we deduce what must have happened from what the Captain sees once he has risen from the ditch.

Episode 3 takes perhaps twenty minutes or a half-hour of real time to transpire; episodes 1 and 2, which are told almost entirely in summary form, take much longer: months in the case of Miss A., and presumably years in the case of Professor B.

Suspense

The first two episodes seem to throw away much of their suspense potential with their opening sentences, each of which makes a very accurate general statement about what is going to follow. What we want to find out, the carrot that lures us through these episodes, is just how the changes announced will take place. Our curiosity is redirected from the events of plot to the close dissection of psychological process which each episode unfolds, and this navigation of mental labyrinths does have a suspenseful quality.

In the third episode suspense comes much more directly from the plot situation: the Captain has been captured by enemies who have just killed his companions, so what will happen to him now? As the story moves into the encounter with the enemy officer, this question twists into another which is both ironic and slightly ludicrous: who is whose prisoner in this situation? But this question is never really answered; instead it is dropped. By the end of the episode it no longer seems to be an important issue, for the story's focus has shifted to something else.

Two rules for suspense might be put this way: "Don't answer suspenseful questions too soon" and "Make sure to eventually satisfy the curiosity you've aroused." The first two episodes clearly break the first rule, while the third episode, somewhat less obviously, breaks the second. In all three episodes, the mechanics of generating suspense are manipulated in unconventional ways.

Imagery and Description

Because of their high level of abstraction, the first two episodes don't contain much in the way of sensory description, though we do find some in the fully dramatized subway scene of episode 1:

> Just then the subway stopped and she stepped off quickly. She didn't want to look back, but she thought she ought to. She waited until she heard the door close and then she turned around to look. The subway had begun to move, and in the noise it was like standing under a waterfall or within the center of a crashing wave. She saw the man who had been reading the newspaper standing at the door, beating against it with his fists and with his face pressed out of shape against the glass. His face

was wet with tears and his lips were moving though she could not hear him. She saw as the subway flashed forward into the dark tunnel that the two men were standing beside him and looking at him. She could not see their faces but she could tell by the tight rigidity of their bodies that they were about to do something sudden. They managed while they were standing straight to look as if they were crouched to jump.

This description is highly detailed and very vivid — it needs to be because this is the tableau which will stay with Miss A. and influence changes in her character throughout the remainder of the story. Most of the passage involves direct literal description of the attitudes the three men have adopted. But the description of the sound of the train is a simile which uses a comparison to something from a completely different context: "like standing under a waterfall or within the center of a crashing wave."

Most of the imagery in the rest of the episode is accomplished in the style of this wave/waterfall simile. For instance:

> She hoped that if she told someone exactly and completely what she had seen, that then she would feel better, *lighter*. She felt heavy as if she were carrying around a large rock and she didn't know what to do with it.

or:

> She felt as if she had done something hectic and fierce like smashing a public mirror and now she saw herself in many ways as if her image were distributed among jagged fragments of glass.

These images, like the wave/waterfall simile, have nothing to do with the literal context of the episode's action. Miss A. doesn't have a "real" rock to carry around, nor has she smashed a "real" mirror. This disconnection from the literal action of the story makes the imagery seem more abstract and contributes to the general feeling of abstraction in the episode. From this plane of abstraction it's easy to shift to full-fledged symbolism, and the public mirror image does stand as a symbol for the shattering of self-image which both Miss A. and Professor B. experience.

At the end of episode 1, abstract and concrete imagery are reunited:

> She committed herself to the day to day discipline of falsely rendered service while knowing, curiously, that her life was a wheel on which she was tied and tortured with herself the impersonal tormentor. It was remarkable to think that as she sinned she was at the same time doing penance. The world flooded away and she was glad of it. By losing every-

thing she found herself in control of everything again, and as soon as she was sure, she could reconstruct things to suit herself. Time and again she saw herself going on beyond her destination and while the other two men held down the struggling weeping man, in the midst of all that roar of forward moving she felt an exhilaration, a new and tugging lightness like a gas balloon on a string. She saw herself wielding a knife she had not owned before.

The images of the torture wheel and the gas balloon are abstract and disconnected, but the image of the knife is almost alarmingly definite, and it signals Miss A.'s somewhat surprising re-entry into the subway scene so vividly described in the opening of the episode.

The disconnected metaphors and similes of episode 1 usually involve some sort of sensory information, while those in episode 2 are more based on situations:

> . . . he taught history like a good policeman. He could shoulder his way in a crowd of unruly details. He could restore order to the facts and give significant testimony.

or:

> Professor B. felt like a blindfolded chess master who is playing a group of amateurs and who gradually discovers that one of his invisible opponents has, by a series of quite ordinary moves, laid a clever trap for him.

or:

> "I feel like a child who spies on his parents making love, ashamed of them and guilty because he shouldn't be looking," he told his wife.

Rather than appealing to some object of the senses, as in episode 1, all three of these similes from episode 2 refer to a character and situation outside the literal context of the episode. The level of abstraction thus achieved, however, is much the same as in episode 1.

In the third episode, imagery and description are much more directly related to the immediate scenes as they take place.

> Captain G., U.S. Army, lay face down in a ditch by the road, the stagnant water, strangely warm for such a bitter day, soaking through his fatigues. It crawled along his stomach and bathed his loins. His head, hidden from the sky by the dark bowl of his helmet, was just above the

water, his lips close enough to kiss the disturbed scum. He lay there while the noise was above and elsewhere, not in the least afraid, feeling almost sleepy.

All the descriptive details here involve the character's most immediate sensory experience. But in the next line of the paragraph the pattern changes:

> He was thinking of himself as a bullfrog sprawled in the mud at the edge of a hyacinth-choked lake, but this dissolved and he began to have an erotic day dream.

The new image is still drawn from an entirely natural scene, but in midsentence it begins to shift to a more mental construct:

> It seemed to involve a colossal blonde, dressed only in silk stockings, broad-assed, huge breasted, before whom he was sprawled in a ditch in some kind of penance or initiation.

This is a concrete image, but decontextualized in the same fashion as the imagery of the first two episodes. The reference to "penance or initiation" at the end takes the image further toward abstraction. But the next description returns to the immediate realities of the scene and its action:

> He was neither astonished nor afraid when he raised his head in the silence and saw the mud-gorged boots at the edge of the ditch, the pants ripped at the knees, the heavy belt, the downslant of the bayonetted rifle at the hips, and, gradually the whole shape of the enemy soldier like an isosceles triangle converging on a small troubled face, dirt-stained, half-bearded under the flat shadow of the steel helmet. It was like being a little child again and looking up at the angular and inscrutable shape of the adult world.

Realistic and sensory as this description is, it also refers to the decontextualized image of the blonde, since the enemy soldier's position and pose is much the same as hers. The last sentence in the passage reinforces the comparison by subtly recalling the idea of "penance or initiation"—a child might expect to encounter such things when rubbing against the "inscrutable shape of the adult world."

Many other passages of the third episode combine extensive realistic and sensory descriptions with some other sort of image whose relation to the scene is more abstract:

The great truck had turned over on its side, the front wheel still spinning like a roulette wheel running down. The Captain's driver was a limp shape on the road beneath the shadow of the turning wheel. He'd been trying to load his carbine but the clip had dropped when he was hit and some of the penny-colored shells had rolled on the road. The other two bodies were behind the truck, one in a dark splash of blood, rolled sideways as if asleep, clutching his rifle to him like a toy. The other one was spreadeagled alongside the far ditch. He had no weapon and his helmet had come loose and fallen on the road. He had been keeping toilet paper in his helmet so it would stay dry and now it was festooned extravagantly on the road. It looked as if an ocean breaker had crashed over them, scattering them in its flashing roll, and dashing them up drowned.

Every detail is perfectly concrete and definite except for the simile of the last sentence, which presents a decontextualized image similar to those used in the first two episodes. The common use of this device helps give all three episodes a certain cohesion, despite the many obvious stylistic differences between episode 3 and the other two.

Finally, consider the key image of the crow:

He saw a crow, laborious, ungainly, leathery, fly out of the woods and light on a limb of one of the trees near the farm house.

This description is part of the realistic sensory context of episode 3, but one can also imagine that it might appear as an abstract, decontextualized image in either of the other two episodes.

Design

What structural analysis can be made of each episode on its own? Individually, the episodes are quite simply linear; they proceed in strict chronological order without any flashbacks or other chronological complications; and they develop conflict in fairly conventional ways.

In episode 1, the seed of conflict is Miss A.'s reaction to the scene that she witnessed on the subway. Indeed the entire plot of the episode is based on Miss A.'s constant replay of this scene in her mind. The resolution that the episode achieves comes from her changes in attitude toward the scene she keeps revisioning. Is there a climax to the processes of Miss A.'s changing character? Perhaps it comes with the very last line when Miss A. fills herself into the scene, "wielding a knife she had not owned before." This resolution also provides the subway episode itself with a climax and conclusion which it previously lacked—because Miss A. did not witness the end of it. Indeed her final image of herself as a willing and aggressive participant seems to be prompted by the very human appetite to know the outcome of any narrative, for better or worse.

Episode 1 consists of a single event, the subway scene, embedded in a narrative about psychological process. If we use this principle to diagram the episode according to the Freitag triangle, we see Miss A. ascending the left side of the figure as a shy, lonely and underconfident woman. The subway scene itself, along with the conclusion Miss A. eventually supplies for it, occupies the climax position at the apex of the triangle. Once she has passed this vertex, Miss A. descends the right side of the triangle radically changed by her experience, in two ways. Inwardly, her self-image has shattered and she has become cynical, but outwardly she has become far more confident and socially adept than ever before.

In episode 2, a story-within-a-story—the narrative of C.—also occupies the climax position in the triangular diagram of a linear design. Conflict builds around the professor's efforts to prove definitively that there has never been any member of his family less mediocre than himself. As in the first episode, this tale develops as a narrative of psychological process rather than of action, detailing the changes in the professor's personality (and in the ways he's perceived by others) as his quest unfolds. At the climax, the object of the quest turns out to prove the opposite of what was intended. Professor B. (much like Miss A.) descends from this climax as a radically changed individual: inwardly he is disillusioned and cynical, but he also seems to have won the outward appearance of a wise man (in the eyes of everyone but his long-suffering wife, of course).

Character is the most important design element in the first two episodes, each of which is a narrative of psychological process, moved forward by changes in the psyche of its protagonist. By contrast, the third episode is much more designed around plot. The character of Captain G. remains comparatively opaque and the reader's interest is directed toward two conventionally suspenseful questions: what will become of the Captain after his capture and the slaying of his companions? and, in these queer circumstances, just who has really captured whom? Both these questions are begged in the end, although we would normally expect them to be answered at the climax. Instead, the climax position, as in the first two episodes, is occupied by a story-within-a-story: the Civil War tale told by Captain G. In this anecdote, we find a distorted mirror image of the Captain's own concern for creating pockets of order within the anarchy of the war he has been fighting: the decorously considered decision of mistress and slave to dispose of the wine cellar produces the chaotic spectacle of smashed bottles and barrels and crazed enemy soldiers swilling wine from a ditch.

Captain G. descends from this curious climax toward his final demand for the shooting of the crow, which may seem the ultimate non sequitur in an episode full of non sequiturs. The significance of his desire is not analyzed for us in the manner of episodes 1 and 2, where everything is analyzed exhaustively. We are left to infer for ourselves that the Captain is distressed because he knows that the crow must be making its "laborious, ungainly, leathery" way toward a feast on the bodies of his dead companions. Captain G. does not like to think of the crow eating their eyes. We have seen the Captain to be an order-ly person, and in a properly ordered world such things would not be allowed to happen—but in a properly ordered world people would not die in the anarchy of warfare in the first place. At the end, although the Captain's army may have won the war, he has been personally defeated by the irreducible chaos of war-fare in general, and so he really does have something to cry about.

Individual analysis of each episode discovers a substantial structural similarity among all three: each substitutes a story-within-a-story in the position of con-ventional climax and uses this embedded narrative for the purposes climaxes usually serve. Nevertheless, the differences between the first two episodes and the third are more numerous and more obvious, and the three seem to be fit-ted together in a somewhat awkward and asymmetrical way. A more orderly craft consciousness might have chosen to place the unlike episode in between the two more similar ones, creating a stronger impression of symmetry in the whole of the modular design.

But perhaps the design was never intended to express orderliness at all. Garrett evolved what he calls the "comic strip" principle of narrative design as a way of arranging material that lacks conventional linear continuity, and in other stories of similar design ("What's the Purpose of the Bayonet" is a good example), he uses the principle to manage material which is inherently untidy. The formal constant in a newspaper comic strip is the sequence of a small number of panels (medieval and Renaissance altarpieces also meet this condi-tion). After that, the sky's the limit. You can put any kind of material you want into the spaces the panels define, and the ways in which the panels relate to one another are limited only by your imagination. Conventional comic strips frequently display linear continuity from panel to panel (one, two, three, joke!), but the relationships between panels can just as well be imagistic or thematic, as in Garrett's "Comic Strip" here. Furthermore, comic strips are infinitely expandable; they can go on forever, in theory anyway, and one can keep adding onto them at either end. (In fact, this particular "Comic Strip" once contained other episodes that don't appear in the final published version.) Garrett con-ceives the comic strip design as something that can keep growing, like crystals or fronds on a fern, in ways that suggest principles of organization without being strictly symmetrical.

At the heart of each of the three episodes is something inherently, irre-ducibly disorderly. The scene Miss A. witnesses on the subway is disorderly because it is incomplete at both ends. We don't know the outcome and we also don't know the motivation. Miss A. supplies a sort of outcome for her own pur-poses, but still we don't *really know* what happened. As for the story of C. unveiled in episode 2, who can explain it? What do you make of a man who can engage in the slave trade while knowing (decades ahead of his time) that it's morally atrocious—then renounce it suddenly by *drowning his cargo of slaves* and sailing on to live a live of righteousness and piety? On the basis of these actions, C.'s character really defies analysis, and the professor's responses make sense to us precisely because what he has discovered cannot be explained or reduced. Captain G. must somehow react to the absurd anarchy of warfare as it appears both in his present experience and in his family history. His reactions make a sort of sense, but war itself remains intractably absurd—one cannot tidy it up or explain it away.

The protagonists of all three episodes are compelled to swallow experiences which cannot be digested. These experiences create awkward lumps within their personalities, like bulges in the body of a snake which has swallowed stones. The efforts of Captain G. and Professor B. and Miss A. to order and organize these experiences can never be perfectly successful. And so perhaps the structural asymmetry of "Comic Strip" reflects this indigestible lumpiness that all the characters must somehow cope with. The balance between order and disorder expressed by all three episodes and by the story as a whole is an uneasy, teetering one.

I was once a student in a workshop where Garrett said that the ultimate question of *any* story must be, What is the meaning of experience? The reader expects to have this question sensibly answered by the narrative, and more often than not it is answered . . . or seems to be. But no answer to this question can be absolutely definitive or complete. There are some experiences which cannot be summed up or paraphrased or explained or understood. Like what is revealed by the voice of the whirlwind in the Book of Job, they just *are*.

NOTES

1. This opening sentence is drily declarative, almost affectless, like the topic sentence of some sort of report.
2. The presentation of the character is also dry and impersonal; she is established according to categories to which she belongs. This impersonality is reinforced by the fact that she is given an initial instead of a name. (The story was first published in 1957, when the use of the honorific "Miss" would notify the reader that the character has never been married.)
3. Again, the description is nonspecific and rather abstract, with no details given as to the men's appearance, clothing, or anything of that sort.
4. This somewhat more personal detail establishes that the men are of no importance to her so far.
5. The arid style in which this information is conveyed suggests the flavor of a police report.

6.   This detail is much more visually striking than anything preceding it; suddenly we seem to see the scene directly rather than learning about it in abstract summary.

7.   And now the description becomes not only much more particular but also much more subjective . . .

8.   . . . perhaps because it's the subjective reaction of Miss A., as suggested here. Miss A. is making an extremely precise distinction between a pitiable look and a look that *asks* for pity. It's implied that the man is not, as yet, aware of her.

9.   Here the description resumes its original abstract and distant tone.

10. But here it becomes simultaneously more subjective and more vivid, via Miss A.'s rather fanciful comparison.

11. In one sense her shyness is a personalizing detail; in another, her aloofness to whatever is happening among the three men is probably a typical reaction for most people.

12. Nothing remarkable here, except the attention drawn to the two men's stillness.

13. The third man's attitude seems quite unusual and yet the dry presentation blunts our reaction to it.

     Almost everything about the recounting so far has been completely mundane. The tension the reader may feel in reading the passage occurs because the first sentence has announced that something unpleasant is about to happen—an efficient way of coloring an otherwise unremarkable recital with suspense.

14. The instinctively defensive posture that one tends to strike on the subway and in other urban situations that place one alone among strangers.

15. This direct gaze violates the unwritten conventions of subway behavior, where eye contact is intrusive or even aggressive.

16. All this looking conveys a sense of alarm; people are not expected to look at each other with such attention on the subway.

17. Returning the look is a kind of involvement . . .

18. . . . and once she involves herself to this extent, the description becomes very much more vivid. All the details present this man as vulnerable in her eyes . . . she's seeing him as a probable victim.

     These personalizing details appear much more striking because the sentences surrounding them are so thoroughly impersonal.

19. The whole sense of menace comes from this man's attitude—no threat has so far been presented by the other two.

20. This analysis, implied by the preceding sentence to be a further reaction of Miss A., is despite its abstraction extraordinarily precise; she is drawing very large conclusions from very small nuances of the encounter.

21. Indeed, this is a less than compassionate response, though certainly a typical one.

22. The glance they've exchanged creates this sense of obligation ...
23. ... but Miss A. delays her backward look until the subway door has fore-closed any possibility of her further involvement.
24. A very vivid image in an otherwise matter-of-fact setting—it prepares us for a sort of climax to the episode.
25. It's peculiar that his effort to communicate with Miss A. becomes much more intense once the opportunity for getting any clear message through has already passed.
26. What's so terrible about this? On the bare facts, nothing ... but it feels extremely sinister.
27. She doesn't really see them do anything. She doesn't really see them pre-pare to do anything. Apparently it's only a feeling she has, but Miss A.'s conviction that something terrible is under way is communicated com-pletely to the reader.
28. Have we had a climax or an anticlimax? After all, we don't know exactly what happened once the train pulled out of the station.
29. A strikingly concrete image in an otherwise rather abstract context.
30. This aside tells us quite a lot about Miss A. and her social situation.
31. What exactly is she burdened by?
32. As with any story, arrangement is of paramount importance.
33. Here the writer is alluding to his own strategy for holding the reader's interest in the subway episode. By announcing that a crime of some sort is going to be witnessed, he focuses the reader's attention on several para-graphs of quite unextraordinary events.
34. And this may be a fairly typical audience response—attention directed to the major plot points. Miss A. can't guide her audience toward a theme in her story because she is not sure how to interpret it herself.
35. Ignorance of the outcome prevents the story of what happened on the subway from having a complete shape ... either for Miss A. or for anyone she might try to tell it to. It's a story without a conclusion. Perhaps that's why she finds it burdensome.
36. So her life has been changed in some way by what she witnessed. If you were mugged yourself on the subway, it would make sense to stop using it, but what if you only witnessed something as ambiguous as this?
37. The phrasing here suggests that her need to tell the story is as strong as ever; she stops telling it to others but keeps on retelling it to herself. In other words, it becomes her obsession.
38. A process of interpretation begins ...
39. Is this true? Did she have an effect on events? and if so, was it an "active" effect? One might certainly say she had a passive effect on whatever hap-pened—by doing nothing, she allowed the event to continue on its mys-terious course.

40. That is, she wishes to provide some sort of ending to the story.
41. This form of defensiveness . . .
42. . . . is balanced by this more serious form of defensiveness: the "refusal to get involved." Of course, "Don't get involved" has become an axiom of urban life, a pragmatic strategy of self-preservation, but some of its consequences are psychologically disagreeable.
43. Does she mean that she imagines herself acting violently to rescue the victim, or is she referring to the violence that seemed likely to happen whether she witnessed the episode or not?
44. Apparently it's the latter.
45. Here's a clearer description of Miss A.'s "burden"—the image of this man's desperate need. She can't know now if she could have helped him or not. All she can know is that she didn't try.
46. It's common enough to feel that it's better to know an outcome, however awful, rather than to remain in uncertainty, but this sentence also prepares for the somewhat more radical step Miss A. will take at the end of this first section of the story.
47. Now it's not just her behavior that's been altered by what she saw, but her whole idea of her identity.
48. That is, she can look at herself in much the same way that she looked at the men on the train.
49. She's been deprived of her sense of identity.
50. Perhaps there's no such thing as an "innocent bystander."
51. Instead of a single integrated self, she now experiences many fragmented possibilities for different potential selves. The fact that the image presents a "public" mirror prepares for changes in her relations with others.
52. There's a tremendous irony here: the fact that she once ignored the suffering of the man on the train leads to a contempt for all human suffering—yet her efforts to conceal this contempt make her *appear* to be more compassionate than ever before.
53. The extremely abstract analysis which occupies most of the paragraph is made more definite for the reader by the concluding two sentences of more vivid and concrete imagery.
54. In her new cynicism, truth has become relative.
55. Ironic that Miss A., who used to be shy and lonely, has through her new cynicism become popular and socially adept.
56. But of course the change is illusory . . . one of a number of images from the fragmented "public mirror."
57. Having seen through herself, it's easy for her to see through others.
58. Through this rather abstract metaphor, she comes to identify as much with the tormentor as with the person tormented, which prepares for the radical shift in the episode's last line.

59. The use of the words "sin" and "penance" invite a reading in a Christian context, while this phrase recalls (ironically?) the paradoxical Christian prescription that one must lose one's life to find it.

60. That is, she can reassemble the fragments of that shattered "public mirror" to form whatever self-image pleases her.

61. This strong sensory image creates a feeling of almost wicked anticipation . . .

62. . . . and what's anticipated is this 180-degree reversal. Originally, she felt most connected to the man she identified as the victim; next, she envied the two supposed attackers because of their knowledge of the outcome; and finally, she identifies with the attackers not only because of their knowledge but also because of their act. Could it be that knowledge corrupts as thoroughly as power?

63. Here we have not just a section break but what seems to be a whole new story with a title of its own.

64. The manner of introduction is very similar to that of section 1. We have a nameless, anonymous character who's identified only by his profession, in a topic sentence which states the subject very plainly and drily.

65. The concrete imagery of the preceding three sentences gives some liveliness to the abstractions being discussed.

66. The presentations of Professor B. and Miss A. are both rather dry and skeletal. However, we first learn about Miss A. through what she thinks of herself, while we first learn about Professor B. by what others seem to think of him. Both characters seem to be rather isolated, though for different reasons.

67. This compartmentalization sounds extremely tidy, but perhaps it isn't really all that healthy.

68. Presented in this way, the professor's compartmentalization of his life no longer sounds like a good thing at all.

69. This fact is presented tonelessly and without comment but in the context it may suggest a problem in the marriage—a problem in Professor B.'s commitment to his home life.

70. For Professor B., the "public mirror" is still intact: his image of himself is coherent and much resembles the image others have of him. He's conscious of the neatness of this arrangement, which pleases him.

71. . . . as a way of adding depth and detail to his neat and tidy image of himself.

72. That is, he plans to approach his own family history "like a good policeman."

73. But the task of the private detective is usually to ferret out some kind of guilt.

74. Metaphorically, this is quite true: Professor B. is out to legitimize his image of himself. But this part of the paragraph opens a small crack in the "pub-

lic mirror"; the professor's colleagues *don't* quite see him the same way he prefers to see himself.

75. What do these two episodes from his research amount to? His forebears remain perfectly ordinary despite the occasional unusual deed. Somehow they "never amounted to much." The impression of "solid mediocrity" begins to reflect on the professor's self-image in ways not entirely agreeable.

76. An experience analogous to Miss A.'s. Although the professor's family research seems disappointing in some way (and has begun to vaguely undermine his sense of self), it makes him more confident and successful in the eyes of others ... or does it? The outside perspective (less important in the case of Miss A.) doesn't perfectly agree with his impression of himself.

77. There's a solid or perhaps dreary mediocrity to this way of thinking about it.

78. This image is considerably more sinister than the image of the "good policeman."

79. If he learns that everyone in his heritage was as mediocre as himself, he can confront his sense of his own mediocrity (implied throughout by the reservations of his colleagues and students) without much discomfort.

80. This trait is thoroughly shared by Professor B. himself.

81. Typically for the story as a whole, the insertion of a suddenly vivid image stands out against the general context of abstraction.

82. The tone of the letter, so strongly suggestive of a different historical period, makes a striking contrast to the cool tonelessness of the surrounding text. But in content the letter seems to echo or predict the professor's own attitude of "curiously happy" resignation to his general lack of distinction—except in the last line. The spectacle of a normally proportioned person in one's lineage may destroy one's happiness in being a dwarf. Note that the clerk does not say whether the "towering shadow" of his grandfather is a good example or a bad one.

83. After all, he *is* a good policeman.

84. Using the image of a family black sheep to evoke a sentence in a letter about a family black sheep produces an odd hall of mirrors effect.

85. This is a very peculiar principle—it presents the most drastic self-deception as a positive good.

86. But the principle works in a way; once it has been installed in the professor's mind, it makes his feelings about the clerk's letter less uncomfortable.

87. So far, then, C. seems much the same as any other member of the family.

88. This is indeed a curious question since so far the relative seems to be quite admirable.

89. This freedom is something the other members of the family, especially the

professor himself, do not share.

90. ... or an obsession, like Miss A.'s obsession with the narrative of what she witnessed on the train. Miss A. becomes obsessed, so to speak, with plot. Professor B. has become obsessed with character.

91. The chessmaster, like the "good policeman," should have more authority than his opponents, but this change in the image destabilizes that arrangement of power.

92. Repetition of the word "mediocre" betrays the professor's motive: he can't bear for one of his ancestors to be larger than himself.

93. Indeed, the professor is a good policeman.

94. These qualities may not be admirable but they aren't mediocre either.

95. This is, after all, quite different from denying the truth till you believe the denial. C. may not be a "better" man than the professor (who after all has not done anything so awful—or significant—as engaging in the slave trade) but somehow he seems to be a larger man.

96. C.'s secret isn't mediocrity at all, it's monstrosity.

97. ... whom he had intended to unmask. As the professor's colleague whispers behind his back above, in exhuming your ancestors' graves you may dig your own.

98. From this new perspective, the more you know about the past the more it binds you. Strangely, it's as if the professor has inherited the chains from his ancestor's slave ship.

99. As with Miss A., inner disillusionment provides a curious path to greater popularity in the outside world.

100. Perhaps in some way he has become wise (instead of merely erudite) ...

101. ... but if so it's a cringing guilty wisdom that brings him no joy.

102. The wife is really a cipher in the whole story, but this final shift to her point of view illuminates an essential sterility in the professor's whole life.

103. The subtitle is careful not to specify any particular war—just the last one, whatever it might be.

104. We seem to have skipped a few letters of the alphabet here. It might conceivably be significant that George Garrett himself served in the army in Europe toward the very end of World War II.

105. Although Captain G., like Professor B. and Miss A., is introduced only by an initial and a mention of the categories into which he fits, this opening sentence is otherwise quite different from the beginnings of the preceding two sections.

106. The description is much more vivid and detailed than the abstract openings of the other two sections. It addresses several of the senses, with references to the crawl of warm water, to kissing, to noise. Because of this higher level of concrete detail, the scene is both more immediate and seems to proceed more slowly—we're in real time, rather than in accelerated summary.

107. Because he's face-down in a ditch, the captain doesn't have a lot to look at, but the description addresses the sense of sight through his imagination.

108. Absurd, certainly, yet the idea of penance and initiation will have some further relevance.

109. Now we get some exposition on the general background of the situation, but we still don't know exactly why the captain's lying in the ditch, and we may feel some suspense on that point.

110. ...in very much the same position as the captain imagined that "colossal blonde."

111. His sense of childishness perhaps permits the odd frivolity of his responses.

112. What language is not specified, and in this sense the scene remains abstract (despite its dramatization and detail); it might be any country, any war.

113. This dialogue is oddly amiable for an encounter between enemies.

114. Use of the definite article shows that the captain recognizes the truck even though we don't.

115. So the truck turned over quite recently—the captain has been in the ditch perhaps only a matter of seconds.

116. The color of the shells imparts real vividness to the scene, along with a peculiar contrast, the innocence of pennies in this context.

117. Now the immediate exposition is more or less complete: we infer that the captain's vehicle was ambushed and that all his companions have been killed.

118. There's real poignance in this detail, which personalizes the nameless corpse.

119. This image is rather impersonal—it's as if something vast, natural, and inevitable happened to the dead men, not so much as if they had been killed by their enemies (for no good reason, since the war has supposedly ended).

120. Any personal or emotional reaction on the part of the captain is noticeably absent; the scene is described vividly but with little affect, so that the background details in the last sentence seem no more or less important than the presence of the slain men by the truck.

121. This seems a rather pointless action; after all, the real sloppiness of the situation has more to do with the bodies and blood. Perhaps the captain is clinging to a military ritual.

122. Why on earth should he be concerned about the crow? This is his first personal response to the whole scene. It resonates oddly with his tidying of the cartridge cases.

123. Crows are also scavengers; the captain is upset by the crow but oddly sympathetic to the scavenging of his captor.

124. Everything about this situation is weirdly slack and casual; we don't feel any of the tension or the necessary alertness of men at war.

125. The man on the floor has power over Captain G., presumably, but nothing in their respective poses suggests that.

126. ... while his ostensible captor is unarmed—yet another absurd aspect of the situation.

127. This formal gesture of surrender ...

128. ... is slightly undercut by the diffidence of this remark.

129. A rather absurd thing to say to someone who also has on no pants. The insistence on regulated behavior recalls the captain's tidiness with the cartridge casings, and perhaps his anxiety about the crow as well.

130. In a way this is an appropriate reply to the captain's remark about the socks. The enemy officer seems to be pronouncing the official opinion of his army, not his own personal thought about the pistol.

131. Deviations from regulation procedure are upsetting to Captain G.

132. This exchange does a lot to explain the general sense of topsy-turvyness. That the captain should be the prisoner of these men is absurd because his army has won the war, but the fact that he is their prisoner makes that victory equally absurd.

133. All the appropriate military relationships have become nonsensical; now the captain is behaving as if he were the superior officer of these enemy soldiers.

134. This oddly sympathetic gesture humanizes the captain and makes it hard for us to think of him as a military martinet.

135. The issue may be larger than the wine. Those "amenities" include all the military protocols that are being flouted because the situation makes them irrelevant.

136. Once they have obliquely acknowledged that the military protocols are no longer in effect, they can stop behaving like enemy officers and begin to behave like ordinary people in the process of getting to know one another.

137. This story within a story will be complete with exposition on the general background and exposition of character.

138. This detail slows down the narrative and signals the story-within-a-story's shift from summary to full scene.

139. Southern manners can be as rigid as military protocols, and in this case they have the same purpose: to preserve a sense of order in the midst of rapidly expanding chaos.

140. This rhetorical gesture announces that the key scene of the story-within-a-story is coming up and that it's important to picture it as vividly as possible.

141. The shift to present tense makes this key scene of the story-within-a-story more immediate.

142. An odd inversion of the captain's own recent experience of lying wet in a ditch.

143. Do you agree? The scene is peculiar, even bizarre, but terrible? The officer's reaction may seem a little surprising.

144. That the scene the captain has described is absurd is certainly true. The scene which he is now experiencing is equally absurd ... for the victor as well as for the defeated (and of course it remains unclear which is which).

145. If it's a stretch for the enemy officer to describe the scene as terrible, it's also a stretch for the captain to describe it as triumphant.

146. Where the captain wants to see a sort of triumph, the enemy officer only sees a terrible waste—a waste of wine which stands for the general, wanton wastefulness of warfare. We might remember at this point that the captain's comrades in arms are lying wasted on the road beyond the farmhouse.

147. This is merely a petulant reply. The captain is quite devoted to meaning, and in this respect he is much like the rest of us. We demand that our stories should mean something ... always.

148. This is a thoroughly irrational demand—perhaps the most absurd ingredient in a story full of absurdities. The crow is innocent—it started no war, killed no one. But crows sometimes feed on carrion, like vultures do, which gives them a reason to follow battlefields. Although he has cleaned up the spent cartridge casings, the captain knows that his erstwhile companions are still lying dead in the road—food for the crows, though he never states this idea directly, perhaps not even to himself.

    The ridiculousness of the captain's "order" underlines the point that all protocols really have failed in this situation; the impulse to impose order on events is defeated by expanding disorder.

149. The long-delayed emotional response comes here (perhaps). It would be absurd to weep about a crow, less absurd to weep about the crow's implications. Of course, the phrasing of the sentence leaves it ambiguous whether the captain actually cries or not ... but I think we can be pretty sure he feels like crying, in the end.

LITTLE RED

G I L M O R E   T A M N Y

I sit, I sit, lonely, perturbed as a button cake on this Thursday in between jobs.1 My belly is swollen with too much ravioli. I am trying to tell an old story in an interesting new way:2

The little girl's eyes were as black as prune pits. Her heart was damsel-in-distress blue.3 Often—

I stop because "Little Red Riding Hood" is of little interest to anyone over six, even in a revamped form. I look to the wall for inspiration4 and am reminded—

I was eating a green pepper, sliced green pepper, on Tuesday. I was walking and eating my green pepper (sliced) and all of a sudden I thought—God!! What do I do with this knowledge? Green peppers? Why on Tuesday? Like when someone points out a house to you and says, "I almost lived in that house." Whatever am I expected to do with that knowledge? How did that information possibly go in my head? It rings and rings and I go over and over it but it cannot settle to a conclusion. Green peppers are a door slamming, an irreducible bit of truth, of naming, a green pepper—5

The ravioli is rolling over in my stomach like a tired old dog. "Little Red Riding Hood" is much simpler than grappling with a description of that ridiculousness.6 Sometimes I feel sumptuous when I'm this bloated, like a sultan, but other times I wish I had my child's body back.7

The girl's eyes were as black as burnt prune pits.[8] Her heart was damsel-in-distress blue. She wore a red, of the purest pigment, red coat with a hood that brought out the delicate ruddiness of her smooth child's cheeks. She was visiting her sick grandmother that day, and tucked a bunch of preserves and johnny-cakes and other outmoded snacks in a napkin lined basket.[9] She placed her bag of heroin and works next to that.[10]

This, of course, is evil (not to mention obviously and childishly invidious), suggesting child drug addiction.[11] But I've always resented the sort of antiseptic presentation of fairy tales. Because of no direct reference to the glories of adolescence or sex[12]—organs, bras, drugs, periods, orgasm and the like—fairy tales are considered much more salubrious reading than, for example, a Judy Blume. HA! Cannibalism, sexual repression, rape, bestiality, all team underneath the acceptable surface.[13] But Little Red on the nod would mean death to the plot so:[14]

She placed a bag of gumdrops for herself beside the bag[15] to eat on the way there. So she set out into the woods, woods that had the faintest touch of autumn splotching the tall trees. The trail she set out on was thickly pebbled. Red Riding Hood stopped for a second and looked up at the considerable distance between herself and the tips of the tall trees. "Ah," she said, "the inscrutable verdant hieroglyphics of the forest . . ."[16] She left the sentence unfinished and made a mental note to herself to write this down as soon as she got to her grandmother's.[17]

She continued on her way, skipping a little, humming to herself. Then she heard a rustling in the grass. She crept closer and noted several pairs of rabbits copulating vigorously in a scratchy yellow patch of weeds.[18] She popped a gum drop in her mouth.[19] Wondering if they would ever stop their twitching and shuddering, she stood transfixed for several minutes.[20] But what Little Red Riding Hood didn't know was that in a patch behind a thick wavy-leaved bush lay a wolf, his avaricious eyes taking her in—[21]

It seems so difficult to draw out the character of the wolf without touching on some pedophiliac tendencies.[22]

"Hello, little girl," said the Wolf, leaning against a tree, startling Little Red Riding Hood.[23]

"Well, hello there," she said, a little nonplussed by the large beast's glinting fangs.

"So," the Wolf continued, "what are you doing out on this lovely day?" She looked at him and thought it best to be civil. What hot putrid breath he had!!!

"Sir," she said with an awkward formality, "I'm going to my grandmother's house because she is feeling ill. I'll be on my way then. Good day." She gave a dismissive nod and walked off down the path. The wolf smiled, and gave a slight bow at her departure, taking off his fedora. As soon as she was out of sight he dropped to all fours and slunk out of sight.[24]

I'm beginning to feel worried for Little Red, because she is so oblivious and inno-cent and polite. The more I think . . . now I am feeling really anxious, my heart is a clenched fist, my mind dumb-struck with dull fear . . . I feel as if I'm setting up a person to be raped, I don't know, I feel like I'm abandoning her . . . best con-tinue . . .[25]

Little Red Riding Hood continued along, feeling vaguely anxious. She wished she hadn't talked to that wolf—he gave her the willies. But, she noticed the bright sunshine and the sweetness of the fall air, and began to cheer up again. A few leaves skittered across the path. "Ah leaves," she said, "leaves."

By midafternoon she had made considerable progress toward her grand-mother's house, so she felt entitled to a rest. Her burden was becoming quite heavy. She sat on a large rock and shared some johnny cake with some squir-rels. She heard a groaning from off in the distance. Some deer were rutting in between the trees.[26] She picked up another johnny cake in her hand.

She stared at it.

And stared at it. And stared at it.

What on earth is this? she thought. Why this, she wondered, why now? "Johnny cake," she said aloud, feeling a slight rush of power, "yes this is a john-ny cake. A johnny cake. Pardon me, ma'am, but this is a johnny cake," she chuckled to herself and rummaged through the basket.[27]

"Aha!" she said, "here's a PEACH. A peach. If you'll excuse me, this is a peach." She bit into the peach. A delightful sense of possessiveness washed over her—her word, her fruit, her sweetness, she was reducing her world to this peach, its flavor, its supple flesh yielding to her teeth, ah, everything was all right!! Everything!!![28]

She stood up on top of the rock, crying, "Peaches! hey Peaches!!" the weather was beginning to change. A storm began to gather in the distance as charcoal clouds twined into circles in the sky. The wind picked up, whisking leaves about in circles. The animals moved about, unsettled. Little Red Riding Hood was waving her arms in the powerful motions of a preacher sermonizing in the pulpit.[29]

"Peaches! You see, Peaches!!" She picked up the basket, "—and a wicker basket! Johnny cakes!! And, yes, yes," she fished between the red napkins, "Gumdrops! Gumdrops!" she cried out to the storm that was now flashing light-ning and trees that shivered against the bottle green and gray sky.[30] She threw the basket out into a clump of bushes. "HA! Wicker baskets!!! Peaches!!!!" she suddenly jumped up and down, her voice soaring from a shout to a shriek.

"But wait—there's more!!!! Like, uh, yeah, STAPLERS!! As well as Peaches!! Shelled peanuts!! Groceries!!! Potato peelers, yes POTATO PEEL-

ERS!!! And BUNIONS!!! EXCUSE ME!!!" she pointed to a buck that was looking warily at her, "BUT THERE ARE BUNIONS!!! and Groceries! Peritonitis!! Silver cow cream dispensers!!"[31]—she gasped for breath as her shouting competed with the storm for audibility. She opened her arms up.

"Linseed oil!!! Groceries!! Trikedepsiphobia!!! Rock lichen!!! And Yes, HAIR NETS. HAIR NETS. HAIR NETS!!!" She was panting loudly, her body shaking as the storm rattled the trees in a final mighty gust, "Arable land!!!! AND YOU SIR," she shouted, pointing to a squirrel bouncing nervously by, "ARE A SQUIRREL!!!!" Her red cloak billowed around her like a wizard's,[32] and in a final splintering scream, "GROCERIES, GROCERIES, GROCERIES!!!!!!!!!!!!" She sank to her knees.

The storm broke up quickly as it had gathered. The sun came out again. Birds fussed over their wind-ruffled feathers. Red Riding Hood sat for several minutes. Her chest rose and fell with exertion.[33]

Feeling pleased, she lifted her fine dark eyes to the afternoon sun, unaware that the wolf was not so far away.[34]

Apparently I've been shouting rather loudly—was interrupted by a loud pounding at the door.[35] Mrs. Jefferson, who lives downstairs, wanted to know if everything was all right. Mrs. Jefferson is an agoraphobic in her late fifties, who I've never seen out of her bathrobe, which I think is a bunch of fuzzy toilet seat covers sewn together—with all that time inside she does come up with some pretty weird craft projects. She once showed me some plant holder made out of macraméd coffee tops. Anyway, she wasn't convinced by my excuses so I invited her in for a cup of tea. She very reluctantly agreed.

She came in and noted my writings and hedged over for a better look. I took them from the table and placed a cup of cranberry tea in front of her.

"Are you sure you're all right, dear???" she asks, concern all over her white face.

"Yeah," I say. "Sorry if I scared you." She doesn't look convinced so I squeeze her hand. "Really, everything is fine."

"Well," she says, gulping her tea, which is much too hot to drink yet, "you never know, with all the different types of people who live here, you know,"—she rolls her eyes upwards and mouths some words at me, presumably some derogatory name to refer to our upstairs neighbors, an inter-racial couple, "—you never can be too sure."

I can tell she is dying to get back to her own home; she has that agitated look I remember from a fire alarm we had last month—I am flattered by the concern that it must have taken to get her out of her apartment.[36]

Well, lunchtime is long past, it is those pendulous sunny hours between noon and late afternoon, that seem as if they could go on forever. I wish I could put a pear between my breasts to catch the afternoon sun slanting through the windows. No pears, not enough breasts.[37]

Feeling pleased, Little Red Riding Hood lifted her fine eyes to the afternoon sun, the sun of those pendulous sunny hours between noon and late afternoon.[38] She leaned back and took a nap.

When she woke, it was getting on toward late afternoon. She gathered up what she could of the basket's contents from the grass. The cakes were a little nibbled at, but the preserves were just fine. She rearranged them as neatly as she could, brushing off some large black ants that still clung to the cakes.[39]

After straightening her red cloak around her shoulders, fussing over the basket one more time, and clearing her throat she began singing, "We're off to see the Wiz—"

Oh, just ha-ha.[40]

Straightening her red cloak around her shoulders and fussing over the basket one more time, Little Red Riding Hood went off to finish her journey in ebullient spirits.

"I'll visit Grandma, and we'll have tea and cookies and she'll have that delightful lace tablecloth on the kitchen table, and we'll talk and talk . . . now if I could just remember what I was saying earlier, herumph, let's see . . . the verdant semiotics of the forest, no, er, the indestructible semiotics of the forest's fair green tresses, no, now what was that . . . ?"[41]

So Little Red Riding Hood prattled on, having a running narration at everything she passed that interested her. And, before she knew it, she had arrived at her grandmother's house.

So here she finally is—in front of grandmother's house. Ugly sense of apprehension, I can almost hear the rumble of horror movie music in the background.[42]

Little Red Riding Hood marched up the path to her grandmother's cottage, and knocked three times. "Oh Grandmother!!!" she called out in a singsong voice, hopping from one foot to another. She really did have to pee and was getting hungry after her meager snack that afternoon.[43] She knocked one more time, loudly. Sighing, she was about to make her way to the back entrance when she decided to try the front door. It was open.

Previous to her arrival, the wolf had surprised Little Red Riding Hood's grandmother as she was crocheting leftover tea bags into an afghan.[44] He ate her, crocheting needles and all. The wolf then snuck into her room and put on one of her flowered bathrobes and got into the bed. He dozed a bit, and was awakened by Little Red's knocking at the door. He awoke and, in the highest pitched voice he could muster, said, "Come in, if that's you, dearest Little Red Riding Hood."[45] Little Red entered, saying, "Grandmother? Are you doing your Mel Tormé impression again?[46] You sound awfully funny." Little Red went into the bedroom, where she saw the wolf.

"Who are you?" she asked.

"Why, er, I'm your grandmother, Little Red Riding Hood," said the wolf.

"Bullshit."[47]

no no no, a little rough[48]

"Why, er, I'm your grandmother, Little Red Riding Hood," said the wolf.

"No you're not. My grandmother doesn't have a pelt, or glistening fangs. I'm not stupid."[49]

The wolf began to get out of bed and move toward Little Red. He threw off the robe, smiling. A flash of understanding and dawning *déja vu* hit Little Red as she looked at the wolf.[50]

"You intend to eat me?" she asked.

He looked at her. "Yes, Little Red Riding Hood."

"For heaven's sake, look at me, wolf," she said, shaking him, "in the eye. Do you actually want to do me physical harm??????"

"Yes."

"Why, you don't look hungry, look how big your belly is."

"I'm not hungry."

"Then why?" Little Red Riding Hood said plaintively. "Why?"

"No one can answer that."

"Listen, I like peach melba and want to write brilliant lyric verses when I get older. I learned to spell hippopotamus in nursery school."

"This means nothing."

"And you still want to do me actual physical harm that will cause me untold anxiety and torment for the rest of my life?"[51]

(I guess the answer is yes, but it can't be. Does this exist? Is this how it is?)[52]

So he began to move toward her to force her down his throat. Little Red Riding Hood, at first still astonished, began to fight as he attempted to gulp her down—

Oh I can't stand this. How can I stand by and let this happen to another person??????? If I was on the street, right now, and saw this happening I'd intervene, I'd try to stop—[53]

Little Red continued to struggle, squirming, wriggling like a greased pig, and felt a heavy weight put in her hand. She looked over. It was a gun.

"For heaven's sake!!" she said.[54] The wolf looked over and abruptly backed away, holding his paws up. He laughed a little, a nervous dribble of a laugh, "Easy with that thing, Little Red Riding Hood, I was just rough-housing before—"

"Where did this come from?" Little Red asked no one in particular. She pointed the gun in the general direction of the wolf. The wolf tried to grab the gun and was frozen like ice.

From me.[55]

Little Red Riding Hood said—"You mean you just invented this .38 Magnum, and placed it in my hand? And the wolf, did you freeze him?"

Yes, Yes—I can't stand to see you struggle so—how can I do this to another human, fictional or otherwise? I know you're scared, Little Red, I'm scared. I want to see you back with your picnic basket, invoking thunderstorms, and shouting, strong as air, not this horror of being assaulted by something that scares you, will scare you for the rest of your life—

"But is that realistic? I mean would this happen in real life??"[56]

No, of course not, but listen, you're in a different world than reality.[57] *You know you're a fictional character, that someone has made you up and you've become a sort of archetype??*

"Well, I don't know what an archetype is, I mean I'm only supposed to be a kid, but I had already kinda guessed at the fictional part. There are spaces in my head—you wouldn't believe how the negative space in between letters and words can add up to vast gaps of consciousness. I am made up of words. My knee is the word 'knee'—your knee is flesh, yes?[58] I'm two-dimensional, so, listen, about this gun—"

Watch the wolf—the ice is melting. He is trying to grab you again.[59]

Little Red stepped back a few steps from the wolf, saying out loud, "I'm sorry. If this was happening in the world, no .38 would drop into a pre-pubescent girl's hand to protect her. Many a person has been eaten with no champions, no protectors, no magical guns. It's silly to pretend otherwise. In respect, I must be no different."[60] Little Red dropped the gun on the ground and waited for it to disappear. It wouldn't.

In the real world no one would refuse the gun.[61]

Little Red shook her head. "Let go," she said.[62]

(Long pause)

The gun disappeared.[63]

(Long pause)

Fight. FIGHT.[64]

Little Red struggled with the wolf for several minutes, but to no avail. She was eaten, his cruel teeth grazing her face, gashing her cheek. She bled and bled and bled and she went down his rippling gullet, squeezed, bloody . . . . . .[65]

_____

_____

_____

_____

_____

_____

_____

_____

_____

_____

_____

_____

_____(*yes, this was stolen from Tristram Shandy.)*[66]

Little Red was wadded up in the belly of the wolf, hemorrhaging, with the withered limbs of her partially eaten grandmother twining around her like bloody snakes. The wolf could barely move with the weight of the two in his belly. He staggered out of the bedroom to the back yard and toppled to the ground.[67]

It was around suppertime when a Mary Kay consultant named Linda, who had graduated with honors from college but was unable to find anything else honorable to do with her hard-earned English degree, had had an appointment to see the old lady and made her way toward the little cottage. Linda knocked on the door and heard no response. She stood on the doorstep thoughtfully chewing her Bruised Sunset Pink varnished nails.[68] Linda knew how the old lady never went out of her house, not even to buy groceries. Concerned, Linda went around to the back door, carefully side-stepping a pair of praying mantises who were beginning to copulate.[69]

Linda gasped as she turned the corner of the house. There lay the biggest mangiest animal she'd ever seen. Some sort of horrible dog, she imagined.[70] She tip-toed closer. It began to snore with deep guttural snorts, disturbing the mating of the mantises. Linda began to feel nervous, and was making her way back down to her car when the wolf started to choke. It would later be revealed that Little Red Riding Hood had wedged the old lady's reading glasses toward the wolf's esophagus for just this effect, causing the wolf to choke violently. Linda had just taken a first aid course at the Y, and although a little nervous, had full faith that she could complete the task before her. She grabbed the wolf from behind, noticing how its fur was littered with ticks, and with a few good hefts, began to administer the Heimlich Maneuver.[71]

It worked. The wolf began to retch, loudly, until the grandmother came up covered in greenish stomach bile, then Little Red, who was barely alive and bleeding badly. Linda gasped, horrified at the results of her effort, and ran inside to telephone for help.

The wolf sputtered and coughed like a drowning person. As the blood and bile began to trickle down his muzzle, the spasm began to quell. He turned over and saw the black venom in Little Red's eye, just before she went into shock.

With this as a cue, The Righteous Squad descended with cattle prods and hot irons and red ants and moved toward the wolf . . . [72]

hmmm . . . vengeance vs. reform vs. veracity vs. vengeful reform vs. reformed vengeance vs. realism . . . .[73]

With this as a cue, a team of doctors, sociologists, psychologists, psychotherapists, descended on the wolf, all dressed in lab coats, rubber-gloved fingers twitching in experimental anticipation.[74]

come on . . .[75]

The wolf looked away and began to weakly push himself toward the forest, leaving a trail of gruely vomit behind. No one would ever know what happened to him.[76]

The paramedics finally arrived and just saved Little Red Riding Hood and her grandmother from the jaws of death. They both spent several months in physical recovery.

Little Red's grandmother's fears of leaving the house became so bad after she came back from the hospital that she could no longer leave the room they put her in after she left the hospital. Little Red Riding Hood agreed to move in with her, to take care of her and be taken care of by her. Little Red understood all too well the trauma her grandmother showed. Sometimes they would sit in their rooms all night, sleepless, unable to move with grief and fear.[77]

They tried to help each other, but in taking care of her grandmother, Little Red had slowly taken on many of her fears as well. She found herself unable to go outside anymore. The two had groceries delivered by friends. Little Red Riding Hood would sit by the window, in her grandmother's rocking chair made of old hairspray cans,[78] and stare out the window all day. Little Red had come back from the hospital with scars the size and shape of caterpillars, which she felt often, idly, while staring at the birds outside.[79]

Winter passed. Spring swept in, trailing the moist hot air of summer behind.

One late day in July, Little Red Riding Hood was in her usual position by the window when she noticed an exceptionally large pair of rabbits in her front yard. "Oh," she said aloud, enraptured. She had been staring out the window for a good ten months but she had not been seeing. They continued to eat. Maybe, Little Red thought, if I go outside real quiet I can watch them a little closer.[80] Outside!!! Little Red got up from her chair. Her grandmother looked up, startled, "Where are you going, dearie?"

"Outside, Grandmother, to look at those rabbits," Little Red replied, trying to be nonchalant.

Her grandmother gasped, "But No!!!! You could get hurt or trip or fall or—"

Little Red Riding Hood began to breathe harder and her eyes glowed green.

"Goddammit," she said, "we sit in this house, like two cornered animals! Well, today I'm going outside, and I'm going—"

"Little Red!!! Think of what happened—" her grandmother said, fear bringing a tremor to her voice.

Little Red Riding Hood let out a scream that could have cut cheese.

"That son of a bitch!!!" she shouted. "Look what he's done!!! We're acting as if we can't go outside!!!" She threw a houseplant against the wall. "Well listen, I'm not staying in here another minute,"—she tromped outside—"I'll take my chances!!!"

Little Red Riding Hood's face had become as red as her coat. She stormed onto the porch. She raised her fist, as the trees began to sway back and forth with a blustering wind, and clouds began to twine together in dark swirls. "YOU MOTHERFUCKER!!!!!" Little Red Riding Hood screamed. "YOU GODDAMNED COCK-SUCKING SON OF A BITCH!!!!!! YOU ASS-FUCKING FUCKHEAD!!!!! I'LL FUCKING KILL YOU IF YOU EVER COME NEAR ME OR MY GRANDMOTHER AGAIN, YOU PIECE OF SHIT, DICKHEAD, ASS-WIPE—" The scars on Little Red Riding Hood quivered and turned purple as the clouds overhead and looked as if they were about to pop off. "YEAH, FUCK YOU FUCK YOU FUCK YOU FUCK YOU, YOU STUPID BASTARD, I'LL KILL YOU IF YOU EVER COME ROUND HERE AGAIN, I'LL FUCKING RIP YOUR HEART OUT, YOU PISSANT STUPID-ASS ASSHOLE SON OF A BITCH FUCKER!!!!!!"[81] Lightning struck a nearby tree with a mighty crack and the thunder shuddered the windows of the little cottage.[82] Little Red Riding Hood's grandmother grabbed her from behind and tugged her in the house, Little Red struggling and kicking all the way, and the torrent of expletives not slowing for several minutes.

Little Red Riding Hood sobbed till she was so tired she could barely move.[83]

"OK, Grandmother, OK," she said, as her grandmother still held her closely. "It's OK, let go, let go." Her grandmother let her go reluctantly, her face pale and very frightened.

"Little Red Riding—" her grandmother began.

"Just call me 'Red' from now on, OK?"[84] She gave a deep sigh. "You can go back to your jigsaw puzzle now. I'm all right, really." She squeezed her grandmother's hand. Red moved over to the desk and pulled out a piece of paper. After an hour or so she began to write,[85]

Who knows what horror lurks within the inscrutable verdant hieroglyphics of the forest . . .[86]

ANALYSIS

Plot

Backstory

There is none, in either narrative vector. Both vectors begin at the beginning and proceed to the end with no deviations from chronological straightforwardness. Right?

On the other hand, it can be argued that the conventional Little Red Riding Hood fairy tale, presumably known to the reader, serves as a sort of backstory to vector 2. Certainly the vector 2 story plays off our knowledge of the original. As for the vector 1 narrative, the narrator doesn't ever *tell* us anything about her past, but at the end, it may be possible to make some general inferences.

Present Action

In vector 2, we have the traditional Little Red Riding story in its most familiar edition (though in the primal version of this tale, the little girl and her grandmother stay eaten). Most of the variations added here don't directly affect the plot proper, which retains the original pattern of journey, conversation with the wolf, being eaten, deliverance at last from the belly of the wolf. The vector 1 narrator/author has added only two significant plot points (which in a way reflect each other): Little Red's ecstatic outburst, early in her journey, on the "itness" of everything, and the long denouement where Little Red and her grandmother strive to cope with their posttraumatic stress disorder after being regurgitated, a problem which is finally resolved by Little Red's second, more violently cathartic outburst. Sure, the original fairy tale has been messed around with in lots of other obvious ways, but most of the other additions are peripheral to the essential story line—insertion of copulating animals and Mary Kay consultants, changes in the content of Little Red's discussions with the wolf, and various direct authorial intrusions and manipulations which come from vector 1.

In vector 1, perhaps less is happening, for the vector 1 protagonist is merely sitting alone in her room, as writers are wont to do. She has eaten too much ravioli and at the outset she must struggle with writer's block—or at least some difficulty in getting started. But presently she gets so involved in her story that she screams and shouts along with her character, so much so that her upstairs neighbor comes down to make sure she's all right. After this interruption the vector 1 narrator has some difficulty getting started again, but soon is well underway, so engaged with the story that she can have direct arguments with the character she has invented. By the last scene the vector 1 narrator has effaced herself entirely from the story, which ends with a curious suggestion that Little Red herself, the vector 2 protagonist, may somehow have written the whole thing herself.

It's worth noticing that the vector 1 plot is essentially the story of a successful writing experience (can one also call it a happy one?). Beginning the story is not all that easy—the writer is awkwardly self-conscious, unpleasantly aware of details like her bloated stomach. But she surmounts these difficulties and begins the story. Next she must deal with the intrusion of craftsman's self-consciousness, for her thoughts about how it's "so difficult to draw out the character of the wolf" and so on also interrupt the flow of the story she's trying to tell. But after she has worked a little longer, the story takes her over altogether and she identifies with her character so completely that she shouts and hollers along with Little Red without even knowing she's doing it. (*You put yourself apart from yourself and enter the imaginary world.*) That's what all writers want and need to do—to get into the story entirely, as if it were reality.

But then comes the intrusion from the outside world—something else all writers have suffered (the unwelcome phone call, cries of your child falling down the stairs, the knock at the door just as Coleridge is about to express the essence of "Kubla Khan"). After Mrs. Jefferson has left, the writer has some problems getting back into the story, is again distracted by self-consciousness (although her revery about the pear is more dreamy and fantastic than her earlier self-consciousness about the ravioli, etc.). But since the story has already been well begun, it's easier for her to get back into it on the second attempt (and she's even able to convert some of her quaint observations of Mrs. Jefferson into the characterization of Little Red's grandmother).

Thereafter the writer experiences the story less as a person who's making it up and more as a dreamer who's dreaming it—which is to say that it's controlling her as much as she's controlling it. The story has "come to life." The main character, Little Red, has come to life in a comically frustrating way—

asserting her autonomy against the wishes of the vector 1 narrator/author. Once the story has come to life in this way, its course appears to be irrevocable; there are many kinds of tampering on the part of the writer that the story just won't allow. From this point on, the story appears more or less to "write itself," and the vector 1 narrator/author seems to experience it and learn from it in almost the same way that we, the readers, do.

Character

The personality of the vector 1 narrator is given an indirect exposition. We are told next to nothing of her history, and her present moment is almost entirely occupied by the composition of the vector 2 narrative. First and foremost, she is a voice talking to us and so is primarily characterized by her tone. We learn, perhaps, that she is a classic daydreamer (which for a writer is a virtuous characteristic). Yet absorbed as she may be in the world of her imagination, she can still emerge to deal pleasantly with Mrs. Jefferson's unwelcome intrusion, making her a cup of tea and listening tolerantly to her conversation.

The vector 2 heroine, Little Red, is much more directly portrayed. She is, as she points out herself, "supposed to be a little kid," but she is a very determined and stubborn little kid. She shares with the vector 1 narrator a fascination with "irreducible bits of truth," with the essences of objects in the world around her. Perhaps this quality helps her to confront the wolf so directly and to ask him such probing questions. A bit later on she confronts the vector 1 narrator in much the same way. All along she is entirely determined, so to speak, to call a spade a spade. By the end of the story, this determination has evolved into a kind of moral courage which gives her the power to recover from terrible suffering.

As for the wolf, he is one of those essential facts of life that so fascinate both Little Red and the vector 1 narrator, but his is the essence of evil, of indifferent malice—his appetite for wanton destruction and cruelty has nothing to do with necessity. Like the vector 1 narrator, we recoil from the wolf, asking "is this how it is?" and are reluctantly forced to admit that "the answer is yes." The wolves are out there in the world and cannot be explained away.

A couple of cameo characterizations are worth noticing also. Mrs. Jefferson, who appears for barely one page, is very vividly presented: her frowzy appearance (bathrobe made of "fuzzy toilet seat covers sewn together"), her eccentric craft objects (the "plant holder made out of macraméd coffee tops"), her provincial disapproval of the interracial couple in the building, and her perpetual jitteriness about anything at all unusual. Vector 1 represents the "real world," so Mrs. Jefferson's is a basically realistic characterization with a few fanciful elements. Vector 2 represents the world of the imagination, and there Linda, the Mary Kay consultant, is given a more fantastic characterization, but with a few realistic elements thrown in: she "had graduated with honors from college but was unable to find anything else honorable to do with her hard-earned English degree." Her "Bruised Sunset Pink varnished nails," along with her habit of chewing them, make her instantly present to the reader. And of course the fact that Linda would be much more at home in a realistic narrative is what makes her appearance in vector 2 so comical.

Tone

Tone is what expresses the personality of the vector 1 narrator more than anything else, and her tone is alternately whimsical, dreamy, pensive, goofy, grim, despairing or outraged. This very broad spectrum of tonal variation makes reading the story a sort of roller-coaster ride and makes us feel that being the vector 1 narrator must be a rather up-and-down affair. And it's clear all the way through that the vector 1 narrator is also generating the tone of the narrative in vector 2.

The humor of the story depends a great deal on sudden shifts in tone, which have a comic effect in themselves. For example:

> Little Red struggled with the wolf for several minutes, but to no avail. She was eaten, his cruel teeth grazing her face, gashing her cheek. She bled and bled and bled and she went down his rippling gullet, squeezed, bloody . . . . . .
>
> ————————————————————————————
> ————————————————————————————
> ————————————————————————————
> ————————————————————————————
> ———————————————————— (*yes, this was stolen from* Tristram Shandy.)

The opening description has a quite grimly realistic tone and the long run of blanks suggests that the rest of the scene is too ghastly to bear description. But the tone of the *Tristram Shandy* allusion is flip and casual—it lifts us out of the grisly immediacy of the eating scene and reminds us that we don't have to take things too seriously because after all it's only an invention of the vector 1 narrator. The tone shift itself contributes to the moment of comic relief. The whole story is full of such hairpin turns in tone, a tone which can catapult itself from light whimsy to grim seriousness with equal suddenness.

Dialogue

Much of the vector 2 dialogue is fast-paced and witty, its humor often depending on the insertion of a line that breaks the context of the conventional fairy tale:

He awoke and, in the highest pitched voice he could muster, said, "Come in, if that's you, dearest Little Red Riding Hood." Little Red entered, saying, "Grandmother? Are you doing your Mel Tormé impression again? You sound awfully funny."

For Little Red Riding Hood to start talking about Mel Tormé is so ludicrously unexpected that it surprises a laugh from the reader.

But some of the dialogue is more serious and significant—for instance, Little Red's interrogation of the wolf:

> "You intend to eat me?" she asked.
> He looked at her. "Yes, Little Red Riding Hood."
> "For heaven's sake, look at me, wolf," she said, shaking him, "in the eye. Do you actually want to do me physical harm??????"
> "Yes."
> "Why, you don't look hungry, look how big your belly is."
> "I'm not hungry."
> "Then why?" Little Red Riding Hood said plaintively. "Why?"
> "No one can answer that."
> "Listen, I like peach melba and want to write brilliant lyric verses when I get older. I learned to spell hippopotamus in nursery school."
> "This means nothing."
> "And you still want to do me actual physical harm that will cause me untold anxiety and torment for the rest of my life?"

The situation here is comical in one sense—the whole idea of Little Red Riding Hood cross-examining the wolf in this way is funny, and the humorous aspects of the passage are stressed by fanciful references to peach melba, hippotami, and so on. But the content and significance of this interview are quite serious, and as the reader becomes aware of that seriousness, the mood of the passage changes, becomes grimmer and more portentous.

Probably the most important passage of dialogue is the argument between Little Red and the vector 1 narrator—not least because it breaks the barrier between vector 1 and vector 2:

> Little Red stepped back a few steps from the wolf, saying out loud, "I'm sorry. If this was happening in the world, no .38 would drop into a pre-pubescent girl's hand to protect her. Many a person has been eaten with no champions, no protectors, no magical guns. It's silly to pretend otherwise. In respect, I must be no different." Little Red dropped the gun on the ground and waited for it to disappear. It wouldn't.

In the real world no one would refuse the gun.

> Little Red shook her head. "Let go," she said.

(Long pause)

The gun disappeared.

(Long pause)

Fight. FIGHT.

As in the case of Little Red's discussion with the wolf, the whole idea of the character arguing with the author this way has its comic side, but the tone has shifted; the sympathy and concern of the vector 1 narrator for Little Red has become serious and poignant. But it seems that the narrator/author has no choice but to let the character win her case (which in this situation feels very much like a choice of martyrdom). It's a curious paradox, for in theory the author has all the choices all the time—yet Little Red is more convincing when she argues that once the course of the story has been set, there are limits beyond which it cannot be further manipulated or tampered with.

Almost all of the dialogue in the story has more than one dimension. The conversations are comic, more often than not, but most of them also present serious questions or odd intellectual challenges—as above.

Imagery and Description

Descriptions in this story, often very vivid, sometimes work by drawing in unexpected comparisons: eyes "black as burnt prune pits"; "a nervous dribble of a laugh"; "the ravioli is rolling over in my stomach like a tired old dog." Because the surface tone of the story is often light and comic, the reach for these similes can be somewhat exaggerated—but the same principle, more conservatively applied, works to enliven descriptions in narratives that are more uniformly serious in tone. Indeed, some of the descriptions here are thoroughly serious, like this one, which is viscerally convincing if not entirely "realistic": "Little Red was wadded up in the belly of the wolf, hemorrhaging, with the withered limbs of her partially eaten grandmother twining around her like bloody snakes."

The descriptions of the wolf are often full of realistic details: his fur is "littered with ticks"; when he regurgitates his victims, "he stuttered and coughed like a drowning person." Sometimes he is described as a natural, animal wolf, but at other times he is rendered as the fairy tale archetype of the wolf as avatar of bad human qualities and evil in general. Part of the story's wit involves moving the wolf very fluidly between these two conditions: "The wolf smiled, and gave a slight bow at her departure, taking off his fedora. As soon as she was out of sight he dropped to all fours and slunk out of sight."

The chief archetypal figure in the story is Little Red Riding Hood herself, of course, as the narrator argues during their debate. Along with being an archetype, she is also a visual icon. The story rides on the assumption that the reader will be familiar enough with the conventional image of Little Red Riding Hood to picture her clearly the moment her name is mentioned. Thus the description can slightly twist the details of the reader's assumed preconception of Little Red, sometimes in matters of visual detail—"She wore a red, of the purest pigment, red coat with a hood that brought out the delicate ruddiness of her smooth child's cheeks"—but a bit later, this coat has turned into a wizard's cloak. Little Red departs from the conventional image of herself in other ways, such as her speech:

> "Who are you?" she asked.
> "Why, er, I'm your grandmother, Little Red Riding Hood," said the
> wolf.
> "Bullshit."

no no no, a little rough.

Indeed. But that roughness serves to remind us that Little Red can be separated from the conventional fairy tale context, to become fuller, more realistic, perhaps more adult ("Just call me 'Red' from now on," as she requests toward the end). Like the image of the wolf, though more subtly, the image of Little Red is flexible, undergoing a process of change. Her most radical transformation is her identification with the vector 1 narrator/author, hinted at throughout the story and confirmed in the conclusion.

Design

To begin with, it has to be said that the most obvious design feature of this story is intentional incongruity—anachronisms, tone breaks, Little Red Riding Hood talking about Mel Tormé—you name it. By making the process of revision part of the story, the writer licenses herself to commit every excess and make all sorts of mistakes in front of the audience. She has manipulated the context so that the "mistakes" aren't mistakes—instead, they are part of a realistic rendition of the behavior of the writer as a character in the story. This sort of prestidigitation is hard to duplicate, and the story might fail if it relied on nothing else, but beneath the chaotic surface are some much more carefully calculated principles of organization.

Like "The Child Downstairs," "Little Red" begins by declaring that the narrator of one narrative vector is also telling the story in the other. In "The Child Downstairs," however, as soon as the two vectors have split, they remain strictly separate—the reader can and should infer that the two vectors are different aspects of the same story, but will not be told so outright. By contrast, we are constantly reminded that the vector 1 narrator of "Little Red" is always composing, revising, and trying to manipulate the vector 2 narrative. The two vectors are constantly interpenetrated, continually break through the barriers that would hold them apart.

Consider first the more standard structure of "Little Red" vector 2, which is based on, though it does not strictly follow, the structural design of the fairy tale's most familiar versions:

exposition: Little Red Riding Hood sets out on her journey.
rising action: She meets the wolf and carelessly reveals her destination.
climax: When she arrives she is eaten by the wolf, who is disguised as her grandmother (previously consumed).
falling action: Digestive processes are under way.
denouement: A kindly hunter (or whoever) appears to deliver Little Red Riding Hood and her granny from the belly of the wolf.

Tamny's revision of the tale uses this pattern but introduces to it some new structural elements:

exposition: Little Red sets out on her journey.
rising action: She meets the wolf and carelessly reveals her destination. After the encounter she feels a vague anxiety.
subclimax: Little Red purges her anxiety in a gestalt epiphany, an ecstatic explosion of insight into the irreducible essence of everything.
falling action: The subclimax tapers off into exhaustion and sleep.
rising action: Little Red reaches her grandmother's house, argues with the wolf about his intentions, and rejects the vector 1 narrator's efforts to reach in with magical devices which might save her.
main climax: Little Red is eaten by the wolf.
falling action: Digestive processes. Linda, Mary Kay consultant, turns up to deliver Little Red and her granny from the belly of the wolf.
rising action: Little Red and her grandmother are cooped in the house, greatly inhibited by the trauma of their ordeal. Little Red suffers increasing tension and resentment in this situation.
subclimax: Little Red declares her autonomy in another wild outburst which reflects the one in the first subclimax, but this second one is more violently cathartic. Like the first, it involves naming the things of the world in their essence, but this time Little Red concentrates on naming the wolf as evil (with graphic, though somewhat incoherent, obscenity). This act of naming seems to give her power to withstand her enemy, the wolf.
denouement: Following the second subclimax, Little Red weeps herself into exhaustion. When she recovers, she gives herself a new name too. Then she picks up pen and paper and, through an odd extradimensional twist, reveals herself to be the writer of the story we've been reading all along.

The new structural elements added by Tamny are the two subclimaxes—Little Red's parallel essentialist outbursts. And these are very appropriate additions to a version of the tale which is so conscious of itself as a construction of language, for both involve powerful acts of naming. The first is an innocent, positive affirmation; the second (after Little Red's innocence has been ravished by the wolf) is darker, more terrible. But both exhilarate the character with a new sense of power. It logically follows that acts of naming should be very powerful in a world made out of language, where Little Red's knee is the word 'knee,' and so on. But it's also implied that naming, truth-telling, confrontation of the irreducibility of truth for better or worse, can be a powerful act in the "real world" too.

In most respects, the structure of vector 1 follows the structure of vector 2. In the expository phase, the vector 1 narrator must overcome some difficulties in order to "get into" writing the story, but once she's well under way, she experiences the story much as the reader does. She is wholly absorbed into the world of her own imagining in vector 2 (as all writers need to be during the process of inventing and imagining their stories), and so she shares the peaks and valleys of the vector 2 structure with the character she's inventing, Little Red. There are some interruptions when the vector 1 narrator draws back to consider the vector 2 narrative from technical points of view, or when intrusions come from outside (Mrs. Jefferson's visit). But for the most part she is wholly within the world of vector 2 and in this world she really does have magical powers because it is a world of her own creation. When Little Red names all those commonplace items in her first ecstatic outburst, her act of naming is powerful enough to affect the weather. Meanwhile, the vector 1 narrator can create the weather outright (along with most other circumstances of the story) with strokes of her pen . . . with her choice of words. This shared power, a power of language, contributes to the identification of Little Red with the vector 1 narrator that develops throughout the course of the story.

The main climax of vector 1, however, should be located in a slightly different place than the main climax of vector 2. For the vector 1 narrator, the main climax comes when Little Red turns to face her author and finally asserts her own autonomy against the author's wishful intention to change the circumstances of the story to help her out. As Little Red successfully argues at this point, there are some kinds of interference the writer will not be permitted—interference the story just won't tolerate. The vector 1 narrator/author can make the wolf wear a fedora or inspire Little Red with the will to fight back, but she can't make weapons fall into the story out of thin air. Once the story has been sufficiently realized, it (and its author) must abide by its own laws of reality—some things can happen but others cannot.

Once this point has been settled, the devouring itself is falling action—from the vector 1 narrator's point of view. Like the reader, she already knows what is going to happen—she shares Little Red's sense of dawning *déja vu*. But the subclimax of the story's third, concluding phase still holds some surprises for the reader and the writer too.

Where is the conflict for the vector 1 narrator? What is at stake in the story for her? Most evident is her sympathy for the character (analogous to the reader's sympathy) which evolves into her fervent and futile desire to protect Little Red from the wolf. But the progressive identification of Little Red and the vector 1 narrator (a twist at the end makes them appear almost as reflections of each other) suggests a further answer. There are hints (that "*déja vu*") that Little Red and the vector 1 narrator may share similar traumatic experiences. There are very strong indications (those praying mantises) that the wolf's attack on Little Red is a symbolized sexual assault. From these clues it may be inferred that the vector 1 narrator shares with Little Red, if not the experience of an actual assault, at least an apprehension of the likelihood of such assaults (as many women do in the real world). If so, then the whole story, vector 1 and vector 2 combined, constitutes an effort to find a way to cope with the presence of malevolence in the world and to manage the radical loss of innocence that the confrontation with evil entails.

The third phase of the story differs sharply from the conclusion of the original fairy tale. In Tamny's revision, rescue does not erase the awful effects of what Little Red and her grandmother have undergone. There are no magical solutions (after all, the character herself has already rejected them), no flicks of the wand to make everything all right again as if it had never happened. Little Red has to find her own way to deal with the lingering trauma of the wolf's assault—which makes for a very realistic conclusion to what has otherwise been a fairly fantastic tale.

But the story's last line adds a different twist. Vector 1 and vector 2 are designed to be interpenetrated all the way through, and this interpenetration works in both directions. It's declared at the beginning that the vector 1 narrator is composing the vector 2 narrative, and we're reminded of this often enough by her frequent intrusions into vector 2. But Little Red is a writerly personality herself. As she moves through the story, she composes sentences about it in her head ("'Ah,' she said, 'the inscrutable verdant hieroglyphics of the forest . . .' She left the sentence unfinished and made a mental note to herself to write this down as soon as she got to her grandmother's"). In her climactic conversation with the vector 1 narrator, she's arguing about *how to write the story*. Then, at the very end, we see her picking up the pen to begin writing a version of the story we've been reading. This maneuver allows the end of the story to flow almost seamlessly into its beginning, creating a continuous, endless surface reminiscent of a mobius strip. Seen as a whole, the design of this story recalls the famous Escher print of the two interlocked hands, each drawing the other one.

The reciprocity of this image evokes the similarly reciprocal relationship between author and invented character. It evokes a reciprocal relationship between the real world inhabited by writers in general and the world of the imagination which writers must enter in order to do their work. Most of the vector 1 narrative in "Little Red" is devoted to a portrayal of creative process as such, of the devices and stratagems which the writer deploys to put herself in the right state of mind for imagining, then rendering, the story. When these devices and stratagems are successful, the story does indeed take on a life of its own, asserting its own verities in a fashion which is (however paradoxical it may seem) separate from, though generated by, the intentions of the writer. In that sense, "Little Red" is a striking demonstration of what writers are talking about when they make the claim that one of their stories has "written itself."

NOTES

1.   How perturbed can a button cake be, and by the way, what is a button cake? There's an eccentric whimsy in the tone from the word go.

2.   . . . which is what we all have to do, after all.

3.   One way of making it new is by scrambling conventional terms of description: blue heart instead of blue eyes, the noun phrase "damsel-in-distress" pressed into service as an adjective.

   Two narrative vectors have been clearly defined in these first two text blocks (and distinguished by differences of typeface and indentation). Vector 1 features a first-person narrator who's trying to write a story. Vector 2 is the story this narrator is trying to tell.

4.   Ever done this? The vector 1 narrative will be quite faithful to the tics and fidgets of a writer having problems with the story.

5.   This text block looks very much like free association, consciousness streaming absolutely at random. One solution to writer's block (which the vector 1 narrator seems to be experiencing to some degree) is to just scribble down anything, whatever you're thinking, as fast as you think it. In this way, you may find out you're thinking things you weren't aware you were thinking—the exercise is a way of allowing the unconscious mind to look for a subject. But the randomly scribbled part would be excised from most stories.

   At a glance, this passage may look like a string of pointless gobbledy-gook—but some of the notions that flash by here—"irreducible truth" and the power of "naming"—will turn up again later on in the story.

6.   Vector 1 narrator is making a decision about what to write: the archetypal story of Little Red Riding Hood will be an easier task to confront than the portrayal of essences (which is what the green pepper riff is essentially all

about). It's not that she can't describe that ravioli most vividly, but that it's too hard to give the description a point.

7.   This transitional line at the end of the vector 1 passage suggests a motive for the narrator's interest in the figure of Little Red Riding Hood.

8.   Note the slight revision of the description above; revision of both form and content will be a constant motif of the developing relationship between vector 1 and vector 2.

9.   Except for the sarcastic, context-twisting use of the word "outmoded," the description so far has a "classic" flavor that seems quite faithful to the tone of the original fairy tale . . .

10. . . . but this wildly inappropriate detail shows that the vector 1 narrator is very willing to mess around with the "old story" she's retelling—she's giving herself license to be capricious here.

11. The vector 1 narrator gives herself permission to comment openly on the narrative she's manipulating in vector 2.

12. See note 18, below . . .

13. Good point. Fairy tales are quite faithful in rendering (often in a disguised form) the horrors and hazards of both the inner life and the outer world, and "Little Red Riding Hood" is no exception.

14. This line implies that the vector 1 author isn't really omnipotent over the vector 2 text—in theory, she may be able to do whatever she wants to, but in practice, some things just won't work all that well . . .

15. The revision tones it down nicely . . . gumdrops may sound a little anachronistic in the fairy-tale context, but certainly they're a less abrasive contrast than heroin.

16. This line, rather inscrutable in its own right, is almost as inappropriate to the presumed naiveté of the traditional Little Red Riding Hood character as the bag of heroin—and thus has a comic effect. Jumbling up items from different contexts is a source of the story's humor throughout.

17. Literary ambition appears to be something the vector 2 character has in common with the vector 1 narrator—or perhaps the two are being mixed up somehow . . .

18. Here's a faithful representation of events that do take place in nature, and yet it seems hilariously inappropriate to the innocent-seeming surface of the fairy tale. But this sort of thing would be going on in the background of fairy tale settings too . . . whether or not it's mentioned in the text.

19. Still, Little Red Riding Hood's first reaction is the very picture of innocence . . .

20. . . . but her second reaction betrays a bit more sophistication, possibly.

21. The threat of the wolf is also sexual (the word "wolf" being archaic slang for "sexual predator") . . .

22. . . . and the vector 1 narrator confirms this notion, while giving it a new twist—inviting us to see the wolf as a child molester.

23. ...and the suggestion made by the vector 1 text block preceding makes this first approach seem sinister in a whole new way.

24. The dialogue of this encounter is perfectly in tone with the original fairy tale—but the details of the description ("glinting fangs," "hot putrid breath") are less stylized, more vividly particular, and somehow more "adult" than the descriptions of traditional fairy tales. The wolf's anachronistic fedora provides slightly comic reinforcement of his identificaton with sexually predatory human beings . . . but of course the story also requires him to go on all fours like a real wolf.

25. Wait a minute—isn't the vector 1 narrator in charge of this story? Why should she act like she's powerlessly afraid of the story when she's the one telling it? Why act as if she has no choice but to go on with the tale?

26. What to make of this sexual activity, comically painted into the background? On the one hand, it seems harmless enough; on the other, it's implied connection with the wolf makes it seem vaguely sinister.

27. The tone and content of this passage recall the peculiar run on green peppers and the like at the beginning of the story. The question behind it is so overwhelmingly general as to be almost ludicrous: why does information present itself to us as it does? and why after all do particular things exist?

28. The vector 1 narrator's frustration with the irreducibility of truth and of naming is given a positive twist here—as if Little Red Riding Hood is having an intoxicating, exhilarating moment of insight into the essence of peachness—an epiphany, or, as it might also be called, a gestalt experience.

29. In fact, she is giving a sermon—lecturing the surrounding world about the marvelous insight into the essence of things that she's having.

30. There's an incantatory power to this act of naming—she seems to be influencing the weather.

31. The passage gets funnier as the items on the list become increasingly incongruous. And after all, when you're exalted by the essence of absolutely everything, bunions and staplers are fully as marvelous and wonderful as . . . whatever.

32. Appropriately, since her chant gives her a magical power over her surroundings. There's a lightly implied comparison to the power of the writer, controlling and shaping reality with words.

33. A slight sexual flavor might be observed in the building to climax and collapse into exhaustion which sets the pattern of this section.

34. One of the effects of Little Red Riding Hood's incantation is to purge away the "vaguely anxious" feeling she had at the beginning of the section . . . however, the threat is still present whether she's worrying about it or not.

35. Apparently the vector 1 narrator must have been acting out the role of the vector 2 character . . . which further suggests some identification between them.

36. The structural function of this episode is to create a pause within the vec-

tor I narrative that matches the exhausted pause that follows Little Red's incantation. One might also think of it as a comic encounter between the author and an uncomprehending (and unwilling) audience.

37. The mind of the writer floats around dreamily, randomly, trying to get started on the story again.

38. As often happens, details of the writer's situation leak into the situation of the character.

39. This minor detail reminds us that not everything in nature is perfectly sweet and nice—that the background of this story is less stylized and more realistic than the natural setting of a conventional fairy tale.

40. Of course the vector I narrator is having a fine old time introducing context-inappropriate material into the story. But the flip into the Wizard of Oz story line (like the introduction of the heroin earlier) is a little too much even for her.

41. These transformations of the "inscrutable verdant hieroglyphics" of the forest can now be connected to Little Red Riding Hood's epiphany of naming earlier, and to the general irreducibility of truth.

42. On the one hand, this mood of menace is what the vector I author/narrator wants to evoke (what the story more or less requires her to evoke), but on the other hand it's threatening for her as well. Of course it's important that the story you tell should also convince you, yourself—but does that also imply a loss of control over the narrative?

43. Again, these realistic details grate a little against the less fully physical world of the conventional fairy tale.

44. This detail is drawn from the vector I narrator's observation of her upstairs neighbor (and is thus a good example of how to adapt details from real life for use in fiction). Mrs. Jefferson will be used again as a source for the grandmother's characterization in vector 2.

45. This line comes "straight" from the style of the original fairy tale and so briefly establishes a sense of the familiar . . .

46. . . . but this context-inappropriate gag is funny precisely because it breaks the tone of what precedes it. This device is familiar from *Saturday Night Live* skits, for example.

47. Same thing—the curse in the mouth of Little Red Riding Hood is shocking and comic at the same time.

48. However, the vector I narrator feels she may have gone too far . . .

49. So she edits out the "rough" word on revision.

50. The reference to *déja vu* seems odd—somehow Little Red Riding Hood has been here before, heard this same story before . . .

51. In one sense, this conversation is comic because of its incongruity—its departure from the expected and conventional line of discussion between Little Red Riding Hood and the wolf. At the same time, two quite serious points are made: that the violator totally disregards or perhaps willfully

seeks to destroy the integrity of the victim (the "peach melba" recalls her earlier epiphany involving peaches), and that the damage of the violation is permanent and somehow irrevocable.

52. The wolf's answers have been perfectly straightforward—he doesn't try to evade any of the questions, doesn't even try to pretend that his intended act is based on need (he's not hungry). But even the vector I narrator (who presumably made him up, remember) has trouble confronting the ruthlessness and wanton cruelty of the wolf's intention. Why, after all, should there be rapists and murderers and child molesters in the world? But there they are.

53. The vector I narrator author is losing control of the story she's writing— she no longer seems to have a choice about what's going to happen.

54. Her line gives a moment of comic relief in what promises to be an unpleasantly visceral scene (at the same time as the arbitrary appearance of the gun reminds us that we're in an invented story, not the "real world").

55. Now the author and the character are talking to each other directly.

56. This is hilarious in a way—the whole idea of a character debating the author about what can appropriately be done in a story and what can't. At the same time, the question of what an author can or can't do with a story is a serious one—at least for the vector I narrator.

57. Guess where this is headed: the vector I narrator is going to argue: "If it's a made-up story anyway, why can't I make anything happen in it that I want to have happen?"

58. The character's consciousness of being is played for comedy here, alongside a rather genuine effort to imagine what it might be like to be constructed of words.

59. The author (the real one, not the vector I narrator/author) is very attentive to keeping all the different aspects of the scene and situation going at once.

60. She's right. Even a made-up story has to follow some kind of self-consistent rule or it will turn into nonsense.

    Many writers talk about the moment in a narrative when their characters "come to life" and exercise their own decisions about what they'll do (it's almost a cliché of creative process), but to have a character actually turn around and talk back to you is even more radical, and comic for that reason. At the same time, the character is using this speech to define herself in a very serious way.

61. True, but not good enough for the character.

62. It's not funny anymore. The standoff between author and character becomes poignant, even tragic, because we know there'll be an awful outcome if the author isn't allowed to intervene.

63. Finally the author has to give in. Maybe having your characters start making their own decisions isn't always such a happy experience.

64. This much is allowed. Fighting back doesn't arbitrarily break the rules the story has set for itself, so the author can still furnish the character with the will to fight back . . .

65. . . . though it isn't enough to change the outcome.

66. The self-censorship of these blanks (vector 1 narrator averts her eye from her own scene) makes it all the more horrifying, given the bloodiness of the description that precedes. Sometimes horrors are worse when left to the imagination . . . Meanwhile, the allusion to *Tristram Shandy* (an 18th-century novel by Lawrence Sterne which contains a blank page with marbled decoration, along with many other anomalies) provides a moment of relief by breaking the illusion of reality, reminding us that someone is writing the story, and by injecting a brief note of comedy.

67. But when we return to realistic-sounding description at the end of the eating episode, it's still very nasty, visceral stuff.

68. The whole idea of a Mary Kay consultant strolling into the story of Little Red Riding Hood is completely ludicrous—providing further comic relief from the awfulness of the eating episode.

69. This is the third in the series of animal sex acts—because we know the female mantis will eat the male during the act, we're encouraged to think that the wolf's eating Little Red Riding Hood is also a form of sexual molestation.

70. Seen from the context of the Mary Kay consultant, the wolf doesn't seem all that impressive or menacing.

71. Introducing the Heimlich maneuver into the tale is even funnier than introducing Linda herself.

72. The Righteous Squad, like the gun earlier, comes out of absolutely nowhere (but the vector 1 narrator's wishes).

73. The vector 1 narrator has now internalized the argument she had earlier with the character over the decorum of the story—what can and can't be properly written into it.

74. Despite the deft comic treatment, these are serious alternatives. Ought we to treat victimizers as wicked and sinful criminals who deserve punishment and revenge or as victims of illness who need to be rehabilitated and somehow cured?

75. But the vector 1 narrator rejects this idea too. This pattern of putting something into the story and then openly retracting and revising has been established earlier and is now being used to manipulate the theme.

76. No consequences then. No magic solutions are furnished by any omnipotent author—all such possibilities have been rejected. The wolf walks.

77. Just as Little Red Riding Hood predicted when she interviewed the wolf

before he ate her, the psychological consequences of the attack are very far-reaching.

78. This whimsical detail is appropriated from the figure of Mrs. Jefferson in vector 1.

79. In fairy tales with happy endings, all damage is magically erased in the conclusion. Something similar occurs (rather less convincingly) in the last lines of the Book of Job. But in this story the damage does not magically disappear. The scars remain.

80. This scene evokes the mood of the earlier episode when Little Red had just set out on her journey and experienced her epiphany on staplers, etc.—but now, because the wolf has traumatized her, she's barred from entering that ecstatic state.

81. In a way, this flood of imprecations is comic because it's somewhat childishly inexpert—at first Little Red (who's "supposed to be a little kid") uses the words as if she doesn't have much experience with them—though she gets better as she goes along.

   But in another sense her outburst goes beyond the insults for which such language is commonly used nowadays and becomes a ritual Curse with a capital C. The act of naming gives the namer power over what is named; when the naming is also a curse, it can be seen as an effective act of self-defense. It makes a difference if you can call the enemy what it really is.

82. The weather phenomena recall those of the ecstatic epiphany earlier—they remind us that Little Red's incantations have real power over the world she exists in (which happens to be, as she and the vector 1 narrator have discussed, a fictional world made out of language). But it seems that Little Red can become powerful only by making herself powerful, as she does here. She can't be furnished with magical powers from outside the vector 2 narrative, but must somehow discover power within herself.

83. As with the earlier epiphany, climax is followed by exhaustion. But where the earlier episode was wholly ecstatic, this one resembles a tragic catharsis—purging the emotions through terror and pity.

84. One of the things she renames is herself: this too is an act of empowerment.

85. It doesn't always come all that quickly or easily, does it?

86. A very interesting move to end the story. Of course Little Red has been planning to write down some version of this line for some time—but this intention is something that connects her to the vector 1 narrator, and with this conclusion (through a looping, mobius turn) an identification between the two characters seems confirmed. Vector 1 and vector 2 are united in this conclusion—both can now be seen as different versions of the same story, about someone striving to control the horrors and threats of her world through the use of the power of language.

PART
IV

A PHILOSOPHY

OF COMPOSITION

WHATEVER HAPPENED TO the unconscious mind? Well may you ask, after several hundred pages of microscopic textual analysis, all much more characteristic of craftsmanship consciousness than anything that might flow from the unconscious. And any reader who has made it this far will certainly have figured out that the stories can be read much more smoothly and easily (and pleasurably) *without* paying attention to all those notes. In fact, the notes seem to stop each story in its tracks, don't they? And you may also be silently screaming, as you plow through the analyses: *surely these writers couldn't have deliberately planned all this elaborately complex interlocking of minute effects.*

Right. They didn't plan it all. Probably could not have done so. At least not deliberately — not consciously. But somehow they accomplished it anyway. All those subtleties of narrative design were somehow put in place in all those stories, and without them the stories could not stand and would not move the reader as they do.

Edgar Allan Poe once wrote a curious document entitled "The Philosophy of Composition" in which he set out, in exhaustively misleading detail, his ostensible method for writing his best-known poem, "The Raven." Nowadays Poe is probably best known for his horror stories, secondarily for a handful of his poems. We have mostly forgotten that he also invented the modern detective story. His detective, Dupin, first used the methods of reasoning later popularized by Sherlock Holmes and Poe himself used similar methods to prove that a famous "automaton" known as Maelzel's Chess Player had a man concealed inside it. In a book entitled *Eureka*, Poe even invented his very own cosmological system, which provides a thoroughly rationalist explanation of everything in the universe.

In "The Philosophy of Composition," Poe is wearing his rationalist hat. "I select 'The Raven' as the most generally known," he commences. "It is my design to render it manifest that no one point in its composition is referable either to accident or intuition — that the work proceeded, step by step, to its completion with the precision and rigid consequence of a mathematical problem."

This statement makes the project nice and clear. Poe is intent on denying the unconscious mind any role in the creation of the poem — it was all executed, he seeks to prove, by conscious craftsmanship. Of course Poe could not have thought in terms of the brain physiology discovered long since his death, but nevertheless what he asserts, in effect, is that his left brain wrote the whole poem and his right brain had nothing to do with it.

According to himself, the decisions Poe made about the poem before writing it were arranged in the following steps. First, having balanced the brevity necessary for unity of effect with the duration necessary for the delivery of a strong impression, "I reached at once what I conceived the proper *length* for my intended poem—a length of about one hundred lines. It is, in fact, a hundred and eight." Next he needed to decide what impression should be delivered by the poem—simple enough since he was already of the opinion "that Beauty is the sole legitimate province of the poem." Step 3, however, is a bit more complicated:

> Regarding, then, Beauty as my province, my next question referred to the *tone* of its highest manifestation—and all experience has shown that this tone is one of *sadness*. Beauty of whatever kind, in its supreme development, invariably excites the sensitive soul to tears. Melancholy is thus the most legitimate of all the poetical tones.

Notice that this passage, although it strives to appear to be perfectly rational, really isn't rational at all. The phrase "all experience has shown" is a magician's flourish which has no more legitimacy than the use of the word "obviously" in a geometric proof. In fact, Poe is presenting his own aesthetic opinion (a quite individual and peculiar opinion, some might say) as if it were a universal truth.

The next stage involves the problem of "obtaining some artistic piquancy which might serve me as a key-note in the construction of the poem—some pivot upon which the whole structure might turn." Poe runs through his repertory of effects and decides that the poem needs a refrain, but what should that refrain be?

> Having made up my mind as to a *refrain*, the division of the poem into stanzas was, of course, a corollary: the *refrain* forming the close to each stanza. That such a close, to have force, must be sonorous and susceptible of protracted emphasis, admitted no doubt, and these considerations inevitably led me to the long *o* as the most sonorous vowel, in connection with *r* as the most producible consonant.
>
> The sound of the *refrain* being thus determined, it became necessary to select a word embodying this sound, and at the same time in the fullest possible keeping with that melancholy which I had predetermined as the tone of the poem. In such a search it would have been impossible to overlook the word "Nevermore." In fact it was the very first word which presented itself.

I'll bet it was—and that all the ratiocination explaining the choice was concocted sometime afterward. Yes, it might be possible to reach such a conclusion by a process of pure reason, but surely intuition would get there faster.

Poe's next problem is to devise an excuse for the constant repetition of the word "Nevermore" at the end of each stanza:

> I did not fail to perceive, in short, that the difficulty lay in the rec-

onciliation of this monotony with the exercise of reason on the part of the creature repeating the word. Here, then, immediately arose the idea of a *non*-reasoning creature capable of speech; and, very naturally, a parrot, in the first instance, suggested itself, but was superseded forthwith by a Raven, as equally capable of speech, and infinitely more in keeping with the intended *tone*.

Indeed. One may say that this decision, if not precisely rational, is at least well-advised . . . although the substitution of a parrot in the poem could make a nice skit for *Saturday Night Live*.

> I had now gone so far as the conception of a Raven—the bird of ill omen—monotonously repeating the one word, "Nevermore," at the conclusion of each stanza, in a poem of melancholy tone, and in length about one hundred lines. Now, never losing sight of object *supremeness*, or perfection at all points, I asked myself—"Of all melancholy topics, what, according to the *universal* understanding of mankind, is the *most* melancholy?" Death—was the obvious reply. "And when," I said, "is this most melancholy of topics most poetical?" From what I have already explained at some length, the answer, here also, is obvious—"When it most closely allies itself to *Beauty*: the death, then, of a beautiful woman is, unquestionably, the most poetical topic in the world—and equally is it beyond doubt that the lips best suited for such topic are those of a bereaved lover."

Can we possibly call this line of discussion rational? On the contrary, it is a lyrical assertion, though camouflaged by rationalist phrases such as "obvious," "beyond doubt," "according to the universal understanding of mankind," and so on. What is truly "beyond doubt" is that Poe himself was obsessed with the Death of Beautiful Women—much of his work besides "The Raven" stands in evidence of that fact—but this obsession is not universally shared by all mankind.

It's also noteworthy how long Poe describes himself as taking in getting around to thinking about the *plot* of a poem which does, after all, have a fairly strong narrative thread. Is it really likely that he would have selected the tone, the refrain "Nevermore," and the Raven to repeat it, before giving any thought at all to the plot situation and to the first-person narrator who in fact speaks the final version of the poem? But before he could "put pen to paper" (according to him), Poe had still to choose the suitable rhythm, "trochaic," and the suitable meter: "octameter acatalectic, alternating with heptameter catalectic repeated in the *refrain* of the fifth verse, and terminating with tetrameter catalectic."

It's true of course that the meter and rhythm of "The Raven" are as Poe describes them above; it's also true that the other devices and qualities he identifies in the essay are present in the poem and important to the total effect that it produces. But for all of those devices and qualities to have been *consciously* selected in the way he asserts is so implausible as to boggle the mind.

It's conceivable that the elements of "The Raven" really did present themselves to the mind of the writer in the same rough *order* that's presented here — although this order of inspiration would be a little unusual from the narrative point of view. But many poets, and some fiction writers, may begin with some inchoate idea of the impression to be created, or just as well with some sound — in this case the sad sound of wind sighing across the neck of an empty bottle, which might resolve itself to Poe's long *o*, and thence to the word "Nevermore." From that point one can imagine oneself trying to dream up a poem which would convey that tone of sighing-wind sadness and allow for constant repetition of the word "Nevermore." But is this a strictly rational process? Hardly. Poe sets up "The Philosophy of Composition" as if to show that every choice made in the writing of the poem was as logically deterministic as the steps of a computer's solution of some complex problem — and of course the essay itself stands as evidence that Poe's mind did work that way, sometimes . . .

. . . but not all the time. What "The Philosophy of Composition" really is is a nice example of reverse engineering. Poe the critic and rational analyst turns around to study the artifact that Poe the artist and poet has previously produced — and produced with the use of the intuitive faculties which the essay tries so hard to deny. Yes, Poe could sometimes be an alarmingly stiff-necked rationalist, but had he been nothing but that, he would be remembered only as the creator of a shadowy prototype for Sherlock Holmes — if he were remembered at all.

The reason that Poe's horror stories are so vividly impressive is because they represent an assault on reason. The idea that reason will be overthrown is vital to setting the tone of all Poe's horror-tale narrators. The horror stories come smoking out of the scariest, most resonant recesses of the unconscious, from the darkest side of the human sensibility where reason loses all its powers. Even Poe's poems have irrational tendencies — they make more sense in terms of their musicality and their mood than in terms of their content (and "The Raven" is no exception). Reason and intuition, the respective faculties of the conscious and the unconscious mind, coexist most uneasily in Poe. Each constantly seeks to defeat and eradicate the other, but also they somehow cooperate — they had to cooperate, to produce the artifacts which Poe has left behind him.

What was true for Poe is also true for the rest of us, though (most usually) in less extreme ways. Within the mind of every imaginative writer, reason vies with intuition, the left brain will struggle to dominate the right (and vice versa), the faculty of conscious craftsmanship engages with the inexplicable choices and decisions of the unconscious mind. One of the writer's projects is always to try, somehow, to turn this engagement into less of a battle, more of a partnership.

The "Linear Design" and "Modular Design" sections of this book are, like

"The Philosophy of Composition," exercises in reverse engineering. In the analyses, conscious craftsmanship looks back over something which unconscious intuition surely must have had a much larger role in creating. Each analysis is a way of describing what has been done, rather than the true process by which it was done. In both the first imagining and the final realization of all the stories here, the unconscious mind will have played a much larger part than retroactive analysis can conveniently admit.

The craftsman's toolbox of analysis is most useful for dissection, for picking apart. But there is too much rigidity about it. After all, most organisms stay dead after their dissection, and a narrative is no different. Once you've got the thing picked apart, you may need to remind yourself that it would take more than reassembling the components to make it live and breathe again. Remember that both the procedures and the results of dissecting a narrative are apt to be a little arbitrary. Even the most general distinction in this book, between linear and modular narrative structures, has its arbitrary side. At the extremes, the distinction is clear, but there is a wide foggy area between the two categories, instead of a rigid boundary. Gilmore Tamny's "Little Red" is as much a braid as a mosaic, while Ernest Gaines's "The Sky Is Gray" shows how a straightforwardly linear narrative can be subdivided for a more modular appearance.

The cloudiness of the distinction between linear and modular design is just one large example of the fundamental inaccuracy of thinking, when matters of creativity are involved, in terms of rigid absolutes. The experience of imagining and composing any story is much more fluid than any reverse-engineered analysis could convey. So too is the experience of *reading* a good story. The reader is carried fluidly along in the currents of the narrative, is moved and influenced without quite knowing how it happened. What the unconscious mind of the writer has wrought, the unconscious mind of the reader will often respond to.

Excellent as "The Philosophy of Composition" is as a work of literary criticism, it is fundamentally implausible as a description of Poe's or any other writer's way of imagination. The analytic methods he relates can describe a poem but not write one. For the same reason, the analytic methods used in this text ought not be used as a cookbook for writing stories of your own. The first conception of the work needs intuition and imagination more than the craftsman's toolbox, and so does its final consummation.

In that case, why study craftsmanship at all? First of all, because it can *be* studied—while the processes of the unconscious mind are much murkier, and, for the purposes of group activity, probably best left alone anyway. Secondly, because if left to itself the unconscious mind will never stop playtime or come down from drifting in the clouds; the unconscious isn't terrifically fond of *work*, but craftsmanship can help guide it into harness. And finally, because the instruments of craftsmanship, once acquired, are something which the unconscious mind can also make use of. In this sense, the writer's study of craft is analogous to the sculptor's study of anatomy, the musician's constant practice of scales. Once fully known, these elements of craftsmanship become reflexive. They are not the property of either the conscious or unconscious mind but of both. Once the tools of craftsmanship have been mastered to that extent, you can use them *without* thinking about them, to make your imagination more mobile and ultimately more free.

There is not one philosophy of composition, but many—perhaps as many as there are writers in the world. And if you mean to be a writer, it's necessary sometimes to think, clearly and consciously, about what you are doing. But the actual process of imagining the work is more like dreaming than thinking. *You put yourself apart from yourself and enter the imaginary world.* Still, there are many passports and pathways to the world of the imagination, and all writers, in the end, are in charge of choosing their own.

Glossary of Terms

Allegory A narrative whose literal objects, characters, and/or events are systematically related to some grouping of more abstract concepts on some other plane, often philosophical or religious.

Authorial intrusion Any uninvited or unwelcome manifestation of the writer within the story. Usually treated as a flaw, the authorial intrusion can sometimes be deployed to good effect.

Backstory Antecedent action, whatever has happened before (leading up to) the present action of a narrative. Backstory is the material which exposition must somehow relate.

Cameo A small (usually singular) role in a narrative.

Catharsis Purgation of the sensibility by some powerful experience which the reader may enjoy vicariously. Catharsis produced by pity and fear is part of Aristotle's definition of tragedy.

Central intelligence This phrase, invented by Henry James, denotes a method for shifting the point of view from one character to another within a narrative . . . on a curve which usually passes through an omniscient phase at its height.

Character An actor in a fictional narrative—a personage invented by the writer.

Characterization Method of portraiture of invented personages who appear in fictional narratives.

Climax The moment (usually but not always a moment in the plot) when the forces deployed in a narrative come to a head.

Comic relief A break in a serious and/or suspenseful tone—an interruption by some sort of joke.

Conflict The opposition of forces (of character, plot, or sometimes imagery) in a narrative which leads to climax and thence to resolution.

Denouement The "wrap-up" phase at the end of a narrative, the phase where final outcomes are explained.

Design The structural, formal organization of all the elements present in a given narrative.

Dialect Idiosyncratic manner of speaking which may depend on combinations of region, class, race, nationality, and so on.

Dialogue Conversation occurring among characters in a narrative.

Epigraph A quotation from some other writer's text used to introduce your own. Epigraphs are often used to suggest the theme of a narrative.

Epiphany This term, coined by James Joyce, designates the moment in a narrative when events, images, ideas, or any combination of these have reached critical mass and produce for the reader an explosive (and usually unparaphrasable) recognition of meaning.

Exposition The relation of whatever background information is necessary for the reader to understand the present action of the story.

Falling action Sequence of events following a climax of a narrative, usually involves declining tension and suspense.

Flashback A recursion from the present action of a narrative to some full scene in that narrative's prior chronology.

Freitag triangle Graphic rendition of a narrative's movement to and from its climax.

Full scene Any episode in a narrative that is given a full dramatic rendering. A full scene makes the reader feel as if he is present for the action, or watching it in a theater or film.

Half-scene A partially dramatized scene, with some summary elements included; a hybrid of full scene and summary.

Imagery The use of descriptions in a narrative to suggest or evoke something beyond what is literally being described. Imagery may approach the quality of symbolism, but is less rigidly defined.

In medias res Literally, "in the middle of things"; describes the tactic of opening a narrative in the middle of a sequence of events rather than at the beginning, usually without much exposition offered up front.

Inscape Poet Gerard Manley Hopkins coined this term to identify the same phenomenon that Joyce called "epiphany."

Linear narrative A story organized in a linear sequence. The simplest linear narratives proceed from the beginning through the middle to the end without deviations, usually tracing relationships of cause and effect.

Metaphor An implied comparison which does *not* use words such as "like" or "as" to connect the subjects being compared.

Modular narrative A story organized according to some nonlinear principle — and usually without a strict cause-and-effect structure. Modular narratives are organized by juxtapositions rather than by linear continuity.

Narration Mode of telling a story. In first-person narration, the story is directly related to the reader by a speaker called *I*. In third-person narration, the reader experiences a story about Bob or Susan; *he* or *she*. Second-person narration, the sort of story where some kind of *you* is specified as the protagonist or as a character, usually amounts to nothing more than a programmatic substitution of this *you* for the third- or first- person pronoun; sometimes, however, one finds a second-person narration which is in fact faithful to the mode of direct address.

Narrator A character in charge of telling the story from some position within it.

Non sequitur Anything that appears not to follow in the normal course of a narrative, appears to be misplaced.

Omniscience The power of knowing everything about the actions and/or the thoughts and feelings of any and all of the characters in a narrative. Omniscience is a power of God sometimes usurped by writers. A story which reports only the actions of all the characters is said to be *externally omniscient*; a story which also reports the thoughts and feelings of the characters is *internally omniscient* as well.

Plot What happens in a narrative, the sequence of events.

Point of view Perspective on events of a narrative; the position (which may change) from which the story is told.

Present action Whatever is happening in a narrative's present time frame.

Realism A mode of story-telling which appears to present an accurate picture of the real world as we commonly know it.

Real time Time as inescapably measured by clocks and calendars: hour by hour, month by month, decade by decade. Real time, which does not skip or condense any of its moments, is something that storytellers must often distort.

Resolution The outcome, positive or negative (or inconclusive), of conflicting energies in a narrative.

Reversal An unexpected turn, usually in the plot; a reversal of the reader's expectations.

Rising action Sequence of events approaching a climax in a narrative, usually involves a build-up of tension and supense.

Setting The physical environment in which a narrative takes place.

Simile A stated comparison which makes use of words such as "like" or "as" to connect the subjects being compared.

Straight line Typical utterance of a straight man.

Straight man In comedy, a nondescript, "average" character who makes average, typical remarks which cue the comic responses of the principal character—the comedian.

Subtext Information which lies below the stated surface of the story; see **Backstory**, above.

Summary An efficient account of events in a narrative that are not given full dramatic rendering. When reading summary, the reader has the sensation of being told something, rather than witnessing it.

Surrealism A mode of story-telling which depends on fantastic alterations and distortions of the world as we commonly know it.

Suspense An urgent desire to know a piece of information or an outcome, large or small— whether you will be guillotined tomorrow, or whether you will be able to dislodge that piece of barbecued pork from between your teeth. Suspense in fiction is usually generated by withholding information.

Symbolism The systematic use of something in a narrative to represent something else— often the use of some concrete object to stand for an abstraction.

Theme A message or meaning embedded in a narrative, or (preferably) evolving naturally out of a narrative.

Time management System for organizing the events of a narrative vis à vis real time.

Tone What the story sounds like; analogous to tone of voice in ordinary conversation, which often does more to convey the mood of the speaker than does the actual content of the speech.

Unreliable narrator A character whose version of the events of the story is not to be entirely trusted.

Vector (narrative vector) A line defining the direction of movement in a story, roughly synonymous with a plot line. Such vectors may be construed as separate structural elements, especially in modular design.

Contributors

Craig Bernardini is an alumnus of Johns Hopkins University and the MFA Creative Writing Program at the University of Utah. He watches Japanese horror movies, listens to heavy metal, and has been at work for a long time on a novel called *The Voivod's Tooth.*

Holden Brooks is an alumna of Johns Hopkins University and has her MFA from the Columbia University School of the Arts. She works as a newspaper reporter in Saint Johnsbury, Vermont, and is finishing her first novel.

Carolyn Chute is the author of the best-selling novel *The Beans of Egypt, Maine,* which is part of a trilogy also including *Letourneau's Used Auto Parts* and *Merry Men.* She lives in rural Maine with her husband, dog, and geese.

Percival Everett, author of several works of fiction (most recently *God's Country* and *Watershed*) is also noted as a painter and guitarist. He teaches in the Creative Writing Program at the University of California in Riverside.

Ernest J. Gaines is the author of several well-known novels, including *A Gathering of Old Men* and *The Autobiography of Miss Jane Pitman.*

Mary Gaitskill is the author of a book of stories, *Bad Behavior* and a novel, *Two Girls: Fat and Thin.* She lives in the California Bay Area.

George Garrett is the author of more than thirty books of fiction and poetry, most recently *The King of Babylon Shall Not Come Against You.* He is a founding editor of *Poultry,* a magazine of parodies, and co-author of the filmscript of *Frankenstein Meets the Space Monster,* winner of a Golden Turkey Award as one of the worst movies of all time. He teaches in the Creative Writing Program at the University of Virginia in Charlottesville.

Marcia Golub is the author of two novels, *Wishbone* and *Secret Correspondence.* She lives in New York with her husband and son.

Miriam Kuznets is an alumna of the Iowa Writers' Workshop. She lives in Austin, Texas, where she is completing her training as a clinical psychologist.

Gilmore Tamny, an alumnus of Goucher College, was featured in *USA Today* as an original Riot Grrl. She publishes her zine, *Wiglet*, from Columbus, Ohio.

Peter Taylor, author of many collections of short stories and three novels, including the prize-winning *A Summons to Memphis*, died in the fall of 1994.

William T. Vollmann has published more than fifteen massive books of fiction since his first novel appeared in 1985. He is also a professional adventurer, who reports on his travels for *Spin* magazine.

Permissions Acknowledgments

Submit! Student Fiction

W.W. Norton & Company announces a call for submissions of short stories by creative writing students for inclusion in a second edition of *Narrative Design: A Writer's Guide to Structure,* compiled with notes and commentary by Madison Smartt Bell. Six student-authored stories will be chosen for inclusion.

Instructors in graduate or undergraduate creative writing programs are eligible to submit manuscripts; please limit your submission to one story per instructor. Stories by alumni of such creative writing programs are eligible so long as they were completed while the writer was enrolled as a student. Stories should not exceed 7500 words in length.

Instructors, please complete this form with your student and submit it with the manuscript and a cover letter on institutional letterhead. Submissions must be postmarked by December 31, 1998, and will not be returned. Stories may be concurrently submitted for (nonexclusive) publication elsewhere. Please send your submission to:

Madison Smartt Bell
English Department
Goucher College
Towson, MD 21204

Student Information

_____

Name

_____

Home Address (very important for gaining permission)

_____

City   State/Prov.   Zip/PC

_____

College/University

Instructor Information

_____

Name

_____

Address

_____

City   State/Prov.   Zip/PC

_____

College/University

_____

Semester student was enrolled in your course